Death on Base:
The Fort Hood Massacre

Anita Belles Porterfield
John Porterfield

Number 8 in the North Texas
Crime and Criminal Justice Series

University of North Texas Press
Denton, Texas

Permissions:
University of North Texas Press
1155 Union Circle #311336
Denton, TX 76203-5017

The paper used in this book meets the minimum requirements of the American
National Standard for Permanence of Paper for Printed Library Materials,
z39.48.1984. Binding materials have been chosen for durability.

Library of Congress Cataloging-in-Publication Data
Porterfield, Anita Belles- author.
Death on base : the Fort Hood massacre / Anita Belles Porterfield, John
Porterfield. -- Edition: First.
pages cm -- (Number 8 in the North Texas crime and criminal justice series)
Includes bibliographical references and index.
ISBN 978-1-57441-596-4 (cloth : alk. paper) -- ISBN 978-1-57441-605-3
(ebook)
1. Fort Hood Shooting, Fort Hood, Tex., 2009. 2. Domestic terrorism--Texas--
Fort Hood. 3. Mass murder--Texas--Fort Hood. 4. Soldiers--Crimes against--Tex-
as--Fort Hood. 5. Hasan, Nidal Malik. I.
Porterfield, John- author. II. Title. III. Series: North Texas
crime and criminal justice series ; no. 8.
HV6432.44.F67P67 2015
364.152'3409764287--dc23
2015005410

Death on Base: The Fort Hood Massacre is Number 8 in the
North Texas Crime and Criminal Justice Series

The electronic edition of this book was made possible
by the support of the Vick Family Foundation.

for *all* of the victims of the Fort Hood Massacre

Contents

Military Rank Abbreviations

Cpt.	Captain
Col.	Colonel
Cpl.	Corporal
Gen.	General
Ltc.	Lieutenant Colonel
Maj.	Major
Pfc.	Private First Class
Pvt.	Private
Sfc.	Sergeant First Class
Spc.	Specialist
Ssg.	Staff Sergeant
Cw.	Chief Warrant Officer

Preface

Fort Hood, Texas

April 9, 2014

In a painfully similar setting just a scant five years after Nidal Hasan killed twelve soldiers and one civilian, President Barack Obama stood before thousands of mourners and eulogized three soldiers gunned down by Specialist Ivan Lopez. To insure their safety, the bereaved were surrounded by walls of concrete shipping containers and guards who patrolled the perimeter of the make-shift chancel. Just below the dais was the Fallen Soldier Memorial—three pairs of empty boots with Kevlar-helmeted rifles standing behind them and photos of the victims in front. A soldier called out the names of the dead—a silent roll call that went unanswered. As a bugler played Taps an unspoken question hung thickly in the air. How could this happen again? And how could it happen on a domestic military installation, a carefully guarded enclave that one general characterized as America's most exclusive gated community? Mass shootings were certainly not new to Americans, but they were unknown on military bases in the United States until Hasan's murderous rampage on November 5, 2009.

Americans were introduced to mass shootings on a cool September morning in 1949 in Camden, New Jersey. In a carefully planned outing, Howard Unruh arose at 8:00 a.m. and dressed in his best suit and a crisp bowtie. He ate a large breakfast prepared especially for him by his mother and left his apartment openly carrying a 1947 German Luger semi-automatic pistol. As he casually strolled down his neighborhood street he calmly shot and killed thirteen people and wounded several others. After expending all thirty-three cartridges he walked back home and climbed into bed. When police surrounded his apartment building, he willingly surrendered.

Sixty years later, in an eerily similar incident, Nidal Hasan callously and deliberately murdered twelve fellow soldiers, a civilian medic and wounded forty-three others. Both men had carefully planned their shooting rampages in advance and both executed their victims without hesitation. Journalist Meyer Berger of the *New York Times* won a Pulitzer Prize for his reporting on Unruh's mass murder but the publicity surrounding the shooting died down very quickly. Today, few people are familiar with Unruh's shooting rampage largely because of difficulties in rapidly disseminating information to the public-at-large in 1949.

Television and radio "breaking news" came about with the assassination of President John F. Kennedy in 1963. By the time Charles Whitman shot and killed fourteen people from the top of the University of Texas Tower in 1966, the practice of interrupting normal programming on television and radio, while still uncommon, was successful in garnering the public's attention. The advent of satellite communications in the mid-1960s provided a mechanism for more advanced news gathering and reporting.

Within minutes after the first 9-1-1 call from the Soldier Readiness Processing Center at Fort Hood, most major broadcast media outlets interrupted normal programming to report Nidal Hasan's shooting rampage. CNN invited anyone on post to call in for a live on-the-spot interview. Social media went wild with "tweets" from the scene of the shooting and thousands of people posted on Facebook. Nidal Hasan's mass murder ushered in a new era of dynamic, interactive crowdsourcing made even easier with personal electronic devices such as smart phones. The days of passive media consumption became instantly defunct.

One of the dangers inherent in crowdsourcing is the dissemination of misinformation. During Hasan's rampage there were erroneous reports of two shooters and an announcement that Hasan was dead. Fort Hood's Darnall Medical Center asked radio and television stations to broadcast a request for health care providers to report for duty, but Fort Hood was locked down and medical personnel couldn't get back on base. After the shooting, media coverage gradually dwindled, picked back up during Hasan's court-martial, and then, for the most part, disappeared.

Yet the massacre remains firmly entrenched in the nation's collective consciousness as evidenced by public discussions following the 2014 Lopez shooting and later that year when it was disclosed that Nidal Hasan had written to the leader of the jihadist organization known as ISIS seeking membership into its ranks. He will continue to attract media attention as Congress debates the status of benefits for the survivors, as his case moves forward through a myriad of mandatory appeals, and, of course, if it ever comes to that, when he is executed.

Fort Hood Soldier Readiness Processing Center

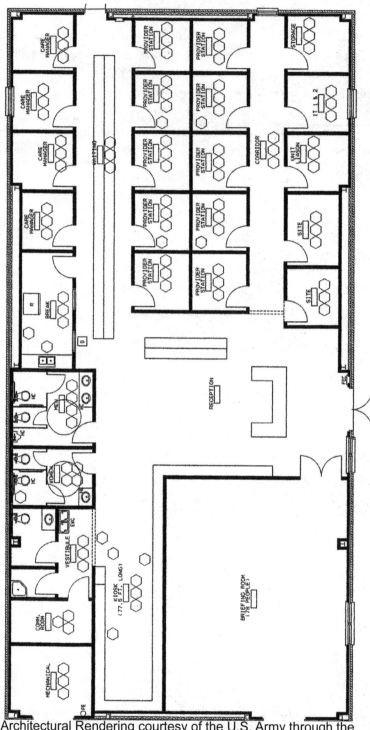

Architectural Rendering courtesy of the U.S. Army through the
Freedom of Information Act

1. Station Thirteen

05 November 2009
1320 hours
Soldier Readiness Processing Center
Fort Hood, Texas

*Men never do evil so completely and cheerfully
as when they do it for religious conviction.*
~Blaise Pascal

L atoya Williams glanced up from her desk at Station Thirteen
in the Soldier Readiness Processing (SRP) Center. Standing in
front of her was a pudgy, bald soldier in fatigues. "Ma'am," he
said, "Major Parrish has an emergency and she needs you."

Williams wondered why on earth this man, who she didn't know,
would be telling her to go find Maj. Parrish. She glanced up at the clock
on the wall. It was twenty-five minutes after one o'clock.[1]

"Ma'am, she said it was urgent."

Williams looked at the embroidered name tab on his shirt: "Hasan."
His insignia told her that he was a major.

Just as she got up and moved toward Major Parrish's office, for-
ty-four year-old petroleum supply specialist Paul Martin walked into
the crowded Fort Hood SRP Center hoping to be cleared for deployment.[2] He had completed the maze of inoculations, dental and eye
checkups, a complete physical, and most of the endless paperwork
required for clearance. Three hundred soldiers were packed into the
center and chairs were at a premium in the congested space at Station
Thirteen. Martin finally spotted a place in the fourth row where he
could sit and finish filling out the last of the required deployment
forms. Although his unit had been mobilized from New Jersey the
week before, Martin had come straight to Fort Hood from his hometown of Adel, Georgia, where he had just buried his father. A tall fit
man, a basketball star in his youth, Martin and his cousin joined the
Army right out of high school.[3] After twenty-seven years Martin still

Soldier Readiness Processing Center Complex

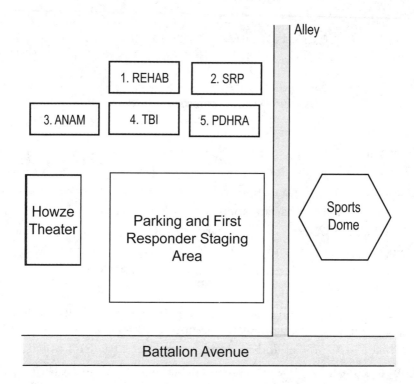

Alley

1. REHAB
2. SRP
3. ANAM
4. TBI
5. PDHRA

Howze Theater

Parking and First Responder Staging Area

Sports Dome

Battalion Avenue

Key

1. Rehabilitation Building
2. Soldier Readiness Processing Center
3. Automated Neuropsychological Assessment Metric Building
4. Traumatic Brain Injury Building
5. Post-Deployment Health Reassessment Building

loved the disciplined life of a soldier. That Army discipline kept him in shape, and it may very well be that his physical conditioning saved his life.[4]

Martin is the first to admit that he was deep in thought and not paying close attention to his surroundings when he heard a fellow soldier shout "Allahu Akbar!"— Arabic for "God is Great!"—and commence shooting. At first he thought it was a prankster with a paintball gun but when people around him began screaming and falling to the floor, Martin realized that this was no joke. The soldiers in that packed space were sitting ducks. He felt a strong blow to his arm and looked down at his hand. It was covered in blood. Martin dropped to the floor and played dead.[5]

An empty magazine from the killer's gun fell to the floor and he shoved a full one into the gun.

Clatter. Click.

One and one-half seconds to reload.[6] The red and green laser lights on his pistol cast macabre patterns and shadows on the walls and the faces of the victims as he methodically sprayed the room with bullets.

When Martin heard the shooter re-arming his pistol he watched some of his buddies jump to their feet and run. Martin did the same but the gunman shot him again, this time in the back. He crawled to a safer spot, then in a few seconds he managed to get up and run for his life.[7]

At 1:25 p.m., twenty-one-year-old Spec. Dayna Ferguson walked up to the counter at Station Thirteen, signed in, and took a seat behind a divider that separated her cubicle from the common area. As bullets pierced the divider behind her chair, people screamed and hit the floor. Ferguson heard the gunman "coming, shooting, getting closer" and in the background there were cries of "my baby, my baby, don't shoot, please don't shoot."[8]

Ferguson spotted an open door and attempted to escape but the killer saw her and fired. The high-powered bullet tore the flesh and muscle from her raised arm. With unusual calm and grace the gunman used a fan motion to spray his unwitting targets with high-velocity bullets from a handgun that could discharge twenty lethal projectiles in a span of seven seconds.[9]

Clatter. Click.

After mowing down several other soldiers nearby, the shooter turned back to Ferguson and shot her twice again, one bullet hitting her leg and the other penetrating deep into her shoulder. She managed to get a glimpse of him—he was fierce, focused, and deliberate. She watched him chase down some of his victims and brutally execute them in cold blood; others he passed over. Ferguson tried to shield herself with a chair. She screamed in terror and prayed, then lost consciousness, remembering nothing until long after the ambulance ride that whisked her away from the carnage.[10]

Josh Berry had just returned from a tour of duty in Afghanistan and needed to file some paperwork before heading home to Ohio. When the shooting began, Berry called his wife, Melissa, and told her someone was firing a weapon in the building. After telling her he loved her, he ran. He did not turn his phone off and Melissa heard the commotion in the background. During his escape, Berry dislocated his shoulder.[11]

Ssg. Michael Davis walked into the center just before the shooting started. "It sounded like M-16 fire," he remembers. At first, like many of the solders, he thought it was a training exercise. He asked someone if it was common to have a drill in the SRP Center. Then Davis got shot and hit the ground. He crawled under a desk and played dead. The shooting stopped for a moment and when he heard the gunfire resume outside, he ran all the way to Battalion Avenue into traffic and stopped a truck. The driver took him straight to Carl R. Darnall Medical Center.[12]

Maj. Laura Suttinger was in an exam cubicle with her primary care provider when the shooting started. She knew immediately that something wasn't right and quickly concluded that it was gunfire. She remembers that it lasted less than three minutes. After the shooting stopped she ran out into the open area and tried to administer first aid to several soldiers, but they were dead.[13]

After a quick lunch, civilian Physician Assistant Michael Grant Cahill had just returned to the center with a full afternoon of physical exams ahead of him. Despite a recent heart attack, and against doctors' orders, he had resumed his duties as a civilian contractor at Fort Hood five days after his coronary. He loved his work at the SRP Center so much that he commuted one-hundred-twenty-miles every day from his home in rural Cameron, Texas, a small community seventy-one miles northeast of Austin. Cahill, a former member of the National Guard and Army Reserves, was unyielding in his commitment and desire to deliver first-rate healthcare to his soldiers. No one under his aegis could go to war unless he or she was declared fit for combat. As usual, Cahill was performing a physical exam inside one of the tiny cubicles that served as an examining room. When he heard shots he grabbed a chair and charged the shooter. The gunman callously turned his semi-automatic pistol on Cahill and stopped him in his tracks.[14]

Clatter. Click.

The killer was no stranger to Sgt. Alonzo Lunsford. He had met the man a month earlier while they were working at Carl R. Darnall Army Medical Center on base. They had an argument over a patient who needed to be transferred from I.C.U. to the psych ward. Lunsford had noticed the shooter earlier that morning in the SRP Center when he caused a scene by refusing a smallpox vaccination.[15]

Lunsford watched in horror as Michael Cahill stormed out of his cubicle and attempted to take down the assassin with a chair. When the gunman abruptly turned and shot Cahill, the flustered six-foot-nine Lunsford jumped up from his seat. As he did, the shooter turned to him and they made eye contact. Lunsford froze as the laser lights on the pistol moved eerily across his line of sight. The killer shot him in the head and Lunsford fell to the floor.[16] He was hit four more times in the back, abdomen, and upper chest before he managed to get out of the building.[17]

Clatter. Click.

A few feet away Pfc. Lance Aviles and his battle buddy Pfc. Kham Xiong had been chatting while they waited at Station Thirteen. Xiong heard a shout and turned to look at its source and saw "a tanned, balding man wearing an Army combat uniform and carrying a black pistol." When Aviles saw smoke coming from the weapon he and Xiong dove out of their chairs and lay motionless on the floor. Aviles glanced over at his buddy—he was dead. Aviles grabbed his cell phone and video-recorded the mayhem. Later that afternoon his commander ordered him to delete the footage."[18]

Spec. Logan Barnett also thought the commotion was a drill. But when he saw his friend Ssg. Shawn Manning take six shots to the torso, Barnett hit the floor and started crawling toward the exam cubicles. He watched as Capt. John Gaffney grabbed a folding chair and ran towards the shooter. The killer stopped Gaffney in his tracks, killing him with a burst of bullets. When he stopped to reload, Barnett picked up a folding table, but before he could throw it, the killer shot him in the head. Using his body as a shield while two other soldiers made their getaways, Barnett managed to crawl out of the building.[19]

Clatter. Click.

Sgt. Alan Michael Carroll was sitting with his friend Pfc. Aaron Nemelka in a row of folding chairs when the shooting started. Carroll thought, at first, that someone was firing a pop gun, but when he was hit by a bullet in his shoulder he realized that it was all too real. His friends were shot, too, and he tried to help them, but they were dead. When he finally got out of the center, he had four bullets in his body.[20]

Police officer Kimberly Munley was parked at a car wash cleaning her patrol car when a call came in that shots had been fired at the SRP Center. Munley, a civilian law enforcement officer for the Department of Emergency Services at Fort Hood, immediately drove the half-mile to the SRP Center. She pulled into the parking lot next to another patrol car, got out, and drew her hand gun, a Beretta M9 pistol. A throng of screaming people pointed out the shooting site to her. In the distance Munley heard gunshots and shouts for help. She ran toward the buildings.[21]

Michelle Harper, a civilian lab technician, was sitting at her desk in the SRP Center talking to a friend on her cell phone when the shooting commenced. She believed that the pop, pop, pops she heard were firecrackers. When she realized that someone was firing a gun inside the SRP Center she dove under the desk and called 9-1-1 on her cell phone. "Oh my God, everybody's shot!" she screamed. Several soldiers piled on top of her and as she watched from a crack under the desk, she glimpsed a pair of feet striding past.[22]

Clatter. Click.

Once the gunfire ceased, Harper got up and ran out the back door. She watched in horror as a police officer rounded the corner of the building, engaged in a gunfight. Harper ran to her car, jumped in, and hit reverse. She floored the accelerator and tore through grass and a ditch and between two barracks.[23]

Non-commissioned officer-in-charge (OIC) of the SRP Center, Sfc. Maria Guerra, was sitting in her office at Station Ten when she heard a shout followed by four popping sounds and screams from the packed waiting room.[24] She ran to the doorway and yelled "get down, get down." The scene was total chaos with "soldiers and civilians … running, running and screaming."[25] She recognized the shooter, a balding man about 5' 9" tall, carrying two weapons. He had been to the Center several times in preparation for his deployment to Afghanistan. His paperwork was never correct and the clerical staff was frustrated because he couldn't, or wouldn't, do it right. To make matters worse, earlier that day he had refused his small pox vaccination.[26]

Clatter. Click.

Guerra stood frozen in horror as the shooter nimbly fired, reloaded three times, and began walking toward her. She retreated into her office where she could still hear the soldiers' screams. A female voice shouted hysterically "please, please don't, my baby, my baby." More shots, then it was quiet.[27]

Guerra cautiously opened her office door, then without hesitation, she flung herself into the maelstrom of death and blood. Fueled by adrenaline, she stumbled through the carnage to the front of the building and quickly bolted the door. Her training kicked in and she began triaging patients, marking the foreheads of the dead with a marker.[28]

The air at Station Three was so thick with smoke and heavy with the smell of gunpowder that Guerra could taste it. The room was a field of devastation. The floor was strewn with bodies and no one was moving. She shouted "is everybody okay?" In response, there were moans and cries for help.[29]

Guerra could still hear gunfire in the rear of the building and shouted for those who were mobile to get out. She placed chucks[30] over the faces of Michael Cahill and a nearby dead female staff sergeant. Guerra remained in the building and treated the injured until police officers rushed in a few minutes later.

Monique Archuleta heard the gunfire and retreated to her office until Guerra called her out. Archuleta ran from dead soldier to dead soldier before she found Lt. Col. Juanita Warman and knelt down by her side to try and help her.[31]

"I'm not going to make it, I'm not going to make it. I'm going to die," Warman whispered to Archuleta. Archuleta tried to comfort her but her injuries were so severe that she slipped away.[32]

Fort Hood police officer Mark Todd was on patrol when he received a call that shots had been fired at the SRP Center. He quickly drove to the site where onlookers pulled him in the direction of the shooter. Todd spotted the red laser at the same moment that the gunman saw him. Shots rang out and Todd ducked behind a building and radioed that "dozens of shots have been fired."[33]

Twenty-one-year-old Pfc. Justin Johnson had been chatting with his mom on his cell phone when the volley of gunfire erupted. At first his mother thought that her son was playing video games while he talked and she chastised him for it. But then she heard screams and cries of terror in the background. Johnson's mom would spend anxious hours awaiting word of her son's condition. She thought back about his desire to join the military right out of high school. After a couple of years of college she finally acquiesced and gave Justin her blessing to enlist in the Army. He adapted very quickly to military life and she had become comfortable with her son's career choice. And now this.[34]

When the bald major pulled out a pistol and started shooting into the SRP crowd, Johnson initially thought that it was a surprise training exercise. He felt a sharp blow to his back but before he could process what was happening he was shot a second time. He watched helplessly as the gunman aimed and fired at the defenseless injured soldiers who were attempting to crawl to safety.[35]

Clatter. Click.

Johnson managed to flee the building and some friends screamed for him to get in their truck. He almost made it but he couldn't run fast enough and they pulled away without him. When the killer ran out of the building and began firing at people in the parking lot, Johnson ducked behind a car. He realized that he had a buddy's keys in his pocket. He very quickly spotted his friend's truck and burned rubber out of the parking lot.[36]

Clatter. Click.

Spc. Frederick Greene watched as his buddies Pfcs. Michael

Pearson and Aaron Nemelka were brutally gunned down and he knew he had to stop the shooter. He charged him, running in a zig-zag pattern. They locked eyes and the shooter emptied his magazine in him. Greene fell to the floor with a dozen bullets lodged in his body.

Officer Munley spotted her partner, Sergeant Todd, in close proximity just to the west of her. When she saw the killer run out of the back door of the SRP building she got in position to shoot, but bystanders were in the line of fire. The gunman fired in Munley's direction and she returned the volley. He ran behind the building and Munley circled around in the opposite direction, hoping to corner him. When she spotted him, he began firing in her direction, hitting her on her hand and knee. She returned fire but her pistol malfunctioned. She went down.[37]

Maj. Steven Richter, OIC of the SRP complex, was making rounds of the buildings when he heard shots. He ran outside and took cover in the parking lot behind a white van and called his supervisor.[38]

"The shooter appeared between the buildings...firing upon a soldier tripping in the grass....A female white officer assumed a [tactical] position and she fired off a couple rounds and at that point ...he turned and began firing. It appeared to me she was defenseless ...he just stood above her, shot a couple more rounds, turned and started to walk toward my direction again."[39]

The gunman ran over to the officer's pistol and kicked it away from her.

Officer Todd spotted Munley on the ground and saw the shooter take cover behind a telephone pole. Todd shouted at him to drop his weapon. The gunman fired and Todd emptied four shots into him. He saw him wince a couple of times as he slid down the pole.[40]

Clatter. Click. Nothing.

Major Richter ran to the gunman and grabbed his weapon. It was so hot that the barrel of the gun seared his fingers. Because of the large number of bullets fired and the rapid rate of the volleys, Richter's instincts told him that there could very well be a second gunman.[41]

"My thought was that there was a second gunman out there. I needed to grab the weapon...my attempt was to engage additional shooters," says Richter.[42]

He pulled up the gunman's shirt and stuck one of his fingers into a spurting bullet hole in the gunman's chest to stop the bleeding. He almost certainly saved Nidal Hasan's life.[43]

ON THE MORNING OF NOVEMBER 5, 2009, SSG. CHELSEA GARRETT woke up happy to be alive.[44] After six long years of working toward her Bachelor's Degree in Liberal Arts, today she would finally graduate from college. Chelsea came from humble beginnings and grew up with two sisters in Louisiana. She was ecstatic that she would be the first in her immediate family to graduate from college. An Army medic,

Soldiers participating in their college graduation ceremony broke away from the celebration to treat another wounded Soldier on the steps of Fort Hood's Howze Theater in the aftermath of Nidal Hasan's attack. Photo by Jeramie Sivley, Fort Hood Visual Information, courtesy of the U.S. Army.

Chelsea had spent three years in Germany where she began working on her college degree. After Germany she had been stationed at Fort Hood for four years. With the last two assignments she was able to give her two daughters a sense of stability. Chelsea's girl friend, Barbara,* had already picked up her girls and another buddy, Tyrone Thomas,* planned to meet them at one o'clock sharp for graduation practice at the Howze Theater, located just one hundred feet west of the SRP Center.

Chelsea ran a few errands, polished her nails, and prettied up her hair. She looked at her kitchen clock. How did it get so late? She grabbed her purse and car keys and when she was about halfway to the theater she called Tyrone to tell him that she was running a few minutes late.

* indicates pseudonym

"Don't come in here, someone's shooting," Tyrone sounded uncharacteristically frantic when he answered Chelsea's call. He could hear gunfire outside and he gingerly opened the theater side door. A bloody soldier fell on him.[45]

"What are you talking about?" Chelsea heard "popping" sounds in the background that she attributed to firecrackers.

"No, No, Chelsea. Don't come, don't come. Whatever you do don't come up here. Go back."

Tyrone handed off the wounded soldier to someone more prepared to manage a medical emergency.

"Stay in the parking lot, Chelsea. I'll come get you." He tried to control the quiver in his voice. He didn't want Chelsea to panic.

Chelsea dismissed Tyrone's pleas and got out of her car. She has vivid recollections of walking across the abandoned parking lot to the theater.

> I remember having an eerie feeling that something was wrong. There was a strange calm. Then I heard firecrackers, pop, pop, pop. People were huddled under the theater awning. They were dressed in street clothes and I assumed that they were family members of the graduates. I looked around the parking lot and the hair on the back of my neck stood up. It was too quiet, and deserted. Then I saw Tyrone run halfway down the theater steps. I walked toward him smiling, but he wouldn't come into the parking lot. He just beckoned to me. I couldn't understand what he wanted. Then when I met him on the steps he grabbed my arm and pulled me up the stairs and said there were gunmen shooting. That's when it finally started sinking in why the people were huddling. Something bad was happening and I had to hurry up and go inside.[46]

When Chelsea walked into the building a non-commissioned officer (NCO) was calling for "anyone with medical knowledge" to come with him. Four of the prospective graduates, all of them dressed in caps and gowns, gathered around the officer. They immediately intuited that this was not a drill or mass casualty exercise. Something serious was in the offing.

"I literally walked in one door and out the other," Chelsea recalls.

She asked Tyrone to look after her children and followed the NCO out of the back door of the Howze Theater. After the doors slammed behind them, she thought, *Oh God, my children, I didn't even get to see them or say goodbye to them. Did they see me? I hope this isn't the last image they had of me.*

They ran up a slight rise that separates the Howze Theater from the SRP complex. The NCO instructed them to remove their caps and gowns before entering the building.

> The damage had already been done. I walked into a war zone. One moment I was in jubilee, ready to walk the stage in my cap and gown and the next minute I was slipping on blood and brain matter. For a few seconds I didn't believe it was real. Maybe they were having a mass casualty exercise in order to judge our reactions. I thought that it was staged, that these soldiers had been done up with moulage kits. I remember kneeling down next to a young man. I checked his neck and felt for a pulse but he was gone. I covered him up. Then I noticed that several bodies had already been covered. There were chucks over their faces.[47]

Chelsea darted from cubicle to cubicle, searching for life. She remembers thinking that in all of those tiny compartments there was nowhere for the soldiers to run. They were sitting ducks.

Fortunately, Chelsea didn't learn until later that one of the chucks covering the faces of the dead obscured the identity of Physician Assistant Michael Cahill. Cahill was Chelsea's personal health care provider. She, like all of Cahill's patients, loved and respected him.

The group of four medics continued to assess their fallen comrades. Lying on the floor near the front doors were two soldiers without a pulse. Chelsea found two more near the west corner of the room who were also obviously dead. She would find out later that one of the young women she tried to save was pregnant with her first child.

After assessing life and injuries, Chelsea ran outside to the field at the south end of the SRP complex where several people were gathered around a staff sergeant lying on the ground. Chelsea quickly examined him and determined that he was conscious and breathing. A fire fighter at the scene would not permit the wounded soldier to be moved until he received instructions from the police. Chelsea was afraid that he wouldn't make it.

> I could see he had three bullet wounds—one in upper left chest, one under the nipple, and one on his lateral side. His belly was getting bigger, more distended as time went on. The fireman shouted "the son-of-a-bitch is still shooting." My friend Nancy, who had been at the ceremony with me, screamed, "why aren't we moving him?" Then the fireman yelled back at her, "I have control of this scene and I'm not moving until I get instructions from the police."[48]

The firefighter looked around the building to see if the shooter was coming. They could still hear gunfire. Chelsea shielded the staff sergeant's body with her own and stroked his hair and told him to hang on, he was going to be OK.

They finally got permission to move him and they loaded him on a stretcher and ran with him to the rally point in the parking lot where the ambulance waited.

> After the ambulance drove off I looked for more people to help. There were so many walking wounded, and I saw a woman with a shot to her leg and I offered to go get her a stretcher because she was limping. She declined and told me to save it for someone who really needed it. Then two people came on either side of her and helped support her weight, so she had assistance walking off. In the southwest corner of the complex I saw a man in ACU's with his top off and his tan T-shirt on. I saw no obvious blood but he was lying supine; he was Caucasian, bald, skinny, about six feet tall. I saw another man who wore navy pants and a navy top, like a uniform, but without patches or insignia and he appeared to be in charge of the situation. A medic in ACU's was bent over working on the Caucasian guy. He looked out-of-place—he wasn't an MP. He was kneeling on one leg with a weapon, a small handgun, in front of his leg in the ready position. Another man stood close by and appeared to be observing the situation. As I approached them I saw

that the observer was talking to the Caucasian man on the ground. The man in the navy uniform held up his hand to me when I offered to help, and he said, "We got a handle on this," and turned back to the man on the ground. Then my medic friend, Nancy, ran up to me and yelled "let the son-of-a-bitch die, he's the shooter." I asked her how she knew he was the shooter and she said, "don't you see the gun lying on the ground next to him?" and I told her that I didn't care because I'm a medic. I craned my neck around her and saw a long, big, black military-looking rifle, not the kind used for hunting or that civilians would use, lying on the ground next to him. Nancy grabbed me by the arm and pulled me away.[49]

SGT. MIKE EVERS* AND SSGT. STEVE JOHNSON* WERE BEST FRIENDS, battle buddies, and the ultimate blood brothers. While serving in Iraq together they were seriously injured. Both of them eventually regained their outward physical health but, like so many of the wounded, they suffered traumatic brain injuries. They were reunited at Fort Hood's Traumatic Brain Injury (TBI) program and on November 5, 2009, at 1330 hours the two recovering soldiers were in a therapy session at the TBI Center complex next door to the SRP Center.[50] Among the individuals present in the group room were speech therapist Diana White, wheel-chair bound Sfc. Victor Garcia,* Sgt. Jerry Reid*, Sgt. Kevin Whitehead*, and Sgt. Danny Houston.* Maj. Leslie Parrish, whose office was in the SRP Center, was the OIC that day, and she was working in her office when she heard the gunshots. Parrish kicked out her window, crawled through the broken glass, and ran the few steps to the TBI Center to warn Diana White and the others that there was at least one shooter on the loose. At Parrish's insistence, everyone was instructed to leave the TBI building. Because Sfc. Garcia was confined to a wheel chair, Reid stayed behind and hastily pushed him and his wheel chair inside a closet and covered him with boxes.[51]

With bullets flying by her legs as she ran toward a hedge, White wondered if she would make it to safety. She managed to dial 9-1-1, but hesitated. What could she tell the operator—that she was running for cover behind a row of bushes? She and another soldier finally took cover behind a truck. White had been connected to emergency dispatch for two minutes and twenty-three seconds and the shooting continued for several more minutes. She and the other soldier sprinted to the Howze Theater where they were picked up and taken to Carl R. Darnell Medical Center. She says that she was being fired upon by at least two shooters.[52]

Evers and Johnson were the last two to leave the group room, and as they were fleeing Johnson looked back over his shoulder and saw a gunman. The face of the shooter will be forever etched in his mind—a six-foot-tall, Caucasian bald man with a gun that looked to be a Desert Eagle.[53] Just as the two sprinted to the back door of the building, Johnson heard the gunman cry "Allah open the door! Allah open the door!"[54]

Johnson glanced at the shooter and they locked eyes. He and Evers believed that they were taking fire from multiple directions and ran outside as fast as they could. Johnson stumbled and rolled on the ground and Evers stopped to grab him and pull him up. When Evers turned to help Johnson, he saw a bald-headed Caucasian man fumbling with the magazine of his gun. It had a laser sight on it and Evers could see the red light on it. They spotted a pickup truck and jumped into the bed. The driver dropped them off at the closest MP station where they met up with several of their combat buddies.[55] Although they survived physical injuries, they will forever bear the mental torment and trauma.

PANDEMONIUM QUICKLY SPREAD THROUGHOUT THE SRP COMPLEX. Inside the dental building, technician Salvatore Sanchez heard commotion in the lobby but he paid little attention to it. A certain amount of rowdiness was to be expected from an assemblage of soldiers soon departing for war. Fort Hood and the processing center were the warriors' final sanctuary before being transported to desperate and deadly environs.

When Sanchez heard screams he turned to see a soldier in a bloody uniform run inside the building.[56]

The soldier, saturated with the blood from his fallen comrades, had been a witness to the violence and was not physically injured. He told Sanchez that he originally thought that the shooter was firing blanks but when he saw the blood he realized that the massacre-in-progress was real.

Sanchez and other personnel in the building attended to the wounded as best they could until paramedics arrived. In the meantime Fort Hood was locked down and all communications systems, including cell phones, were disabled. But Facebook and Twitter still worked and several times during the ordeal Sanchez ran to his computer and quickly sent out Twitter messages to let the outside world know what was going on.[57]

> if your [sic] OFFPOST right now don't come to base, multiple shootings, several casualties, possible terrorist suspects...FT HOOD TX
>
> a soldier I treated here said he was waiting in line @SRP when another soldier stood up and started shooting
>
> wow...umm the entire FORT HOOD just restricted all CELL PHONE usage, unless its gov authorized...twolla @ me yall
>
> GET OUT OF HERE!!!!there were children in the theatre!!!thank God they're fine!! We have them here in the clinic.
>
> Army post is a mess right now, lots of traffic...everyone in a hurry to get off post and pick up their kids or get home to their loved ones.

At midnight, "tired and dehydrated" Sanchez's next "tweet" reflected upon the calamitous day. "The SRP is the last place a person should get shot!"[58]

And the last person shot was the gunman himself, Major Nidal Malik Hasan, U.S. Army Medical Corps.

The aftermath of George Hennard's shooting rampage at Luby's in Killeen, Texas.
Photo courtesy of *The Temple Daily Telegram*.

2. King of the Hill

05 November 2009
1635 hours
City Hall, Killeen, Texas

Those who are bent on wrongdoing will in time come to know
how evil a turn their destinies are bound to take!
~Inspire Magazine

Minutes after the shooting began at the SRP Center, Fort Hood was locked down. Without access to the base, reporters descended on the Killeen City Hall where spokeswoman Hilary Shine briefed them on the unfolding situation.

"Unfortunately, this is a day we had dreaded, we are in an emergency situation," Ms. Shine said in a statement to the media. "Every time you hear of a mass casualty situation in Killeen, you think of Luby's and twenty-six people who were killed. Here in City Hall, it's panic."[1]

"We know the terrible impact and not knowing how it will end is gut wrenching right now. Fort Hood is set up as its own city, they have their own fire, police, SWAT...they have asked for EMT and ambulance assistance." Shine added that the ambulances were having "issues" getting on and off base.[2]

"The first shooting took place at the SRC [*sic*] Building 42000 at 75th and Battalion Avenue, at about 1:30 p.m., according to Army officials," Ms. Shine told reporters. "A second shooting took place at a Howze Theater on Battalion Avenue."[3]

"This tragedy will have a long-lasting effect," reflected state Congressman Sid Miller of Stephenville, Texas, about the Fort Hood shooting. "This community is still reeling from the 1991 Luby's shooting."[4]

THE GULF, COLORADO & SANTA FE RAILROAD, chartered by a group of Galveston, Texas, businessmen to transport cotton from central Texas to the Gulf Coast, established the towns of Killeen and Temple in 1881.[5] The railroad also built a small hospital in Temple and hired Dr. Arthur Carroll Scott and Dr. Raleigh R. White to take care of ill and injured workers.[6]

The first train rumbled through Killeen, population forty, in 1882. A mostly agricultural area, in just two years its population swelled to 350 residents. With two gristmills, two cotton gins, several shops, a saloon, and a school, the town supported the farming industry in central Texas for many years. The small community suffered great adversity during the Great Depression, however, but its economy rebounded with Roosevelt's New Deal, which provided funding for the construction of U.S. Highway 190 through the region.[7]

The entry of the United States into World War II turned central Texas upside down when a military base, Camp Hood, was established in 1942 as a soldier and tank training center. With very little notice, 300 of the farms and ranches in the area were forced to cease operations in order to accommodate the needs of the base. Hundreds of contractors and carpenters moved into the Killeen area to work in construction jobs in anticipation of the influx of new residents. The demand for housing was so great that creative newcomers rented hen houses to sleep in and a tent city was hastily erected for sheltering a thousand people. New businesses opened to service the requirements of the soldiers and support personnel stationed at the expanded Camp Hood. Toward the end of the war the base also served as an internment camp for German prisoners.[8]

Central Texas struggled through a serious recession after the war, but when Fort Hood was made permanent in 1951, Killeen and the surrounding areas recovered economically and flourished. The relationship between the city of Killeen and Fort Hood evolved to an association of co-dependence; so much so that in the late 1980's the city initiated a public relations campaign that created the slogan, "Tanks for the Memories." By this time Killeen had reached a population peak of 65,000 residents.[9]

While central Texas was suffering economically during the Great Depression, a San Antonio, Texas, cafeteria chain was making money hand over fist. Luby's restaurants served "good food at reasonable prices" and catered to shoppers, church-goers, civic groups, and soldiers. In the mid-1980s Luby's opened a cafeteria in Killeen. In a 1990 *Forbes* magazine article, William Barrett notes, "They say you have to beat the Baptists out of church on Sunday to get a seat at Luby's."[10]

Robert Earl Keen, a popular Texas troubadour, wrote a song about spending Sunday mornings during his college years at Texas A&M serenading the Presbyterians on their way to Luby's.[11] Luby's became so ubiquitous that "it seemed like there was a cafeteria on every corner." The Fox TV satire about Texas, *King of the Hill*, even named one of its characters, Luanne Platter, after the Luby's popular Lu Ann Platter.[12]

Business was brisk and the atmosphere festive at the Killeen Luby's on "Bosses Day," Wednesday, October 16, 1991. At 12:45 p.m., George (Jo-Jo) Hennard, rammed his 1987 blue Ford Ranger pickup through the crowded cafeteria's plate-glass front window and leaped out of his truck while firing a semi-automatic pistol in each hand. A lit cigarette dangled from his lips as he shouted epithets and shot at the 150 stunned patrons.[13]

"It's payback day," bellowed Hennard as the panic-stricken diners dove under tables. "Take that," he ranted, firing both weapons at one person after another. He targeted the serving line, then turned to the tables. As he mechanically picked out and murdered diners in the lunch crowd, he shouted "Is it all worth it, what they have done to me in Texas and Belton? All women of Killeen and Belton are vipers!" he shouted.[14]

A chiropractor from the nearby community of Harker Heights recalls Hennard's macabre affect. "His whole face was completely relaxed, no emotion at all."[15] He watched as Hennard walked over to a patron hiding under a table and shot him at point-blank range. A surreal calm enveloped the room, broken only by Hennard's rants and shots from his pistols. One of the diners summed up the killings as "the silence of death. I guess everyone was waiting their turn."[16]

Hennard walked up to a table of three—an elderly woman with her daughter and four-year-old granddaughter—and delivered two fatal shots to the older woman, then brandished his pistols at the young mother and her daughter and told them to leave.

On the other side of the dining room, Tommy Vaughn, an auto mechanic, threw himself repeatedly into a plate glass window until it shattered. Vaughn assisted diners in escaping through the jagged glass and is credited with saving more than fifty lives. He was later treated for deep lacerations on his shoulder. One kitchen worker was found twelve hours later hidden in a dishwasher—another one ran inside the freezer and stayed long enough to suffer frost bite.[17]

Firefighter/paramedic Robert Kelley was one of the initial first responders on the grisly scene. He says he "went numb" and that he was not prepared for the hecatomb that lay before him. Kelley quickly began checking victims for signs of life and placed green dinner napkins over the faces of the dead.[18]

"I wondered about the people as they sat there eating when the truck came crashing through the window. I cannot imagine. I wondered about the people who crawled under the tables, only to have him reach under and shoot them."[19]

Unlike Nidal Hasan, Hennard grew up a troubled young man in nearby Belton. He and his Swiss father, Georges Marcel Hennard, frequently locked horns. Georges Hennard, an orthopedist, practiced medicine at various military installations around the country. Hennard also frequently fought with his domineering mother. A classmate from one of the high schools that "Jo-Jo" Hennard attended described him as a loner who had few friends, who didn't date, and who harbored a deep-seated hatred for his mother.[20] Hennard's childhood was turbulent and unstable.

Like Hasan, George "Jo-Jo" Hennard joined the military following high school graduation in 1974 and, after completing his three-year obligation, he signed on with the Merchant Marine. He was caught smoking marijuana on duty and was promptly discharged. Hennard appealed his dismissal, but failed in his effort to be reinstated as a seaman.[21]

Hennard's parents divorced in 1983 and he lived for a short time with his mother in Nevada. His father moved to Houston, Texas, where he became embroiled in a weight-loss clinic scheme and was subsequently disciplined by the Texas Medical Board.[22]

Hennard tried again to find work as a seaman, but was once more denied a position in the Merchant Marine because of his substance abuse history. In 1989, Hennard fell into a contemptuous, unbalanced state of paranoid delusions in which he voiced his abhorrence of women. He told anyone who would listen to him that his mother was a "snake." He was a frustrated, bitter, and delusional man—a time bomb that could explode at any moment.[23]

Hennard returned to Belton and moved into his mother's vacant upscale house and found a menial job at a local cement company. He was fastidious and kept the house, pool, and yard in perfect order. Neighbors recall that he yelled obscenities at garbage collectors who left litter strewn about on the curb.[24]

According to Katherine Ramsland of TruTV, the thought of committing a mass murder in a restaurant as an expression of his anger first occurred to Hennard when he viewed a TV documentary called *Acts of Violence* about the San Ysidro, California, McDonald's shooting. Ramsland argued that Hennard was influenced by the actions of James Huberty, a malcontent who killed twenty-one people and injured nineteen others in the mass shooting in 1984.[25]

A few months before his shooting at Luby's, Hennard purchased two handguns—a Glock 17 and a Ruger P-89, both semi-automatic pistols designed to deliver rapid bursts of ammunition. Just ten days before the massacre, he abruptly quit his job with the cement company. On his birthday, one day before his rampage, patrons at a restaurant in Belton witnessed Hennard explode with rage at a news story on the dining room television about Clarence Thomas' Supreme Court confirmation hearings. When an interview with Anita Hill was aired, Hennard erupted in an angry tirade of profanity.[26]

Hennard had developed a crush on two sisters in his neighborhood, ages nineteen and twenty-three, and had written a five-page, disjointed letter to them the previous June. It read, in part,

> It is very ironic about Belton, Texas. I found the best and worst in women there. You and sister are the one side. Then the abundance of evil women that make up the worst on the other side...I will, no matter what, prevail over the female vipers in those two rinky-dink towns in Texas.[27]

The sisters' mother was so alarmed by the letter that she sought help from the Belton Police Department, but they declined to take action. She enlisted the assistance of her husband, a hospital administrator who, in turn, gave it to a staff psychiatrist who proffered the opinion that the author exhibited a great deal of anger and frustration. Furthermore, he speculated that the writer of the letter could be dangerous. On the morning of the shooting, the local newspaper, coincidentally, ran a front page story about Hennard's bizarre letter.[28]

Hennard's rampage lasted fifteen minutes. He killed twenty-three people and injured twenty-seven others. After being wounded by police he ran to the restroom area and turned one of the guns on himself. His reasons for perpetrating the mass killing followed him to his grave. A ticket stub from the movie *The Fisher King*, a story about a mass murder at a restaurant, was found in one of Hennard's pockets. The Luby's massacre was the worst mass killing in the United States until the Virginia Tech shooter murdered thirty-three people in April 2007.[29]

That day at Luby's one of the couples killed was enjoying a casual lunch with their daughter Suzanna Gratia-Hupp. The tragedy motivated her to run for the Texas legislature where she was instrumental in the passage of the Texas concealed carry law. [30]

The state statutes, however, do not apply to military installations such as Fort Hood that are obligated to follow the federal law that prohibits transporting guns onto a base without a permit, either openly or concealed. This policy was instituted in February 1992 under President George H. W. Bush. The directive authorized only specific designated soldiers to carry firearms on base who have a reasonable expectation that life or Department of Defense assets could be jeopardized if they were not allowed to possess weapons. Other personnel are prohibited from carrying firearms on base.[31]

As soon as they heard the news about the shooting, the Luby's president and several top executives flew to Killeen to offer their assistance to the community. Governor Ann Richards attended the memorial service, flags flew at half staff, and a "Thirty Days of Unity" campaign was initiated by the City of Killeen. Residents freely gave blood for the survivors. Grief counselors offered solace as the community struggled to regain a state of normalcy. When asked how they would ever be able to get past the tragedy, Mayor Major Blair responded, "You don't really ever overcome it. You begin to do what you think is necessary to cause people to mellow and get a hold of their life… we've gotten stronger because of it."[32]

When Luby's re-opened two months later it was packed with diners. In time, however, support for the restaurant dwindled and business declined substantially. Luby's cafeteria closed and a few months later reopened as the Yank Sing restaurant, popular to this day for its nine dollar all-you-can-eat Chinese buffet.[33]

Despite the fact that Killeen and Fort Hood are next-door neighbors, at the time of the Luby's shooting it was inconceivable that military personnel could have been called upon to assist Killeen's civilian emergency response to Hennard's rampage. Now, eighteen years later, Killeen was again facing the devastating repercussions of a mass killing, a horror that no city should have to contend with even once. Their resources would be tested again, but this time they were ready to handle a crisis of major proportion. No one had ever considered that the Army would need help from the city of Killeen and Bell County in dealing with another mass shooting.

Walter Reed Army Medical Center
Photo courtesy of the U.S. Navy

3. American Dream

All that is necessary for the triumph of evil
is that good men do nothing.

~Edmund Burke

Nidal Malik Hasan was born to Palestinian immigrants in Arlington, Virginia, on September 8, 1970. Nidal's father, Malik Awadallah Hasan, emigrated to the United States in 1962 at age sixteen and his mother, Hanan Ismail (Nora), followed in 1963. The couple enjoyed a large close-knit extended family in Virginia and was very quickly indoctrinated in all things "American."[1]

One year and two days after Nidal's birth, the Hasans welcomed Anas Malik to the family and settled into an apartment on Lancelot Lane in northwest Roanoke. Eleven years later the Hasans' third son, Eyad Malik, was born. Nidal and Eyad adopted American names— Michael and Eddie.[2]

In an interview with *ABC News*, Nidal Hasan's cousin, Nader Hasan, maintained that he and his cousin experienced "a typical American upbringing in suburban Virginia, from birthday parties to playing sports to Santa at Christmas." Nader Hasan characterized their childhoods as the "perfect American Dream, growing up, being American, being a kid," and stated that neither of them spoke Arabic nor were they particularly religious.[3]

In 1987 Malik and Nora Hasan opened the Capitol Restaurant in the historic Roanoke City Market, the "oldest continuously operating open-air market in the Commonwealth of Virginia."[4] According to the *Roanoke Times*, the Hasans' restaurant "was a dive beer hall and diner with a bad reputation and a lot of down-and-out regulars" and a place where "patrons enjoyed greasy, blue-plate specials and sipped on Old Milwaukees...while a jukebox played Motown."[5]

Nidal Hasan as a teenager. Photo courtesy of the *Roanoke Times*.

The Hasans embarked on several other enterprises in Roanoke: Hot Dog Queen on Church Avenue, Parrish Grocery on Fourth Street, Community Grocery on Elm Avenue, and, in 1995, after closing the Capitol Restaurant, they opened the upscale Mount Olive Bar and Grill. Malik had a reputation for his "cheerfulness, honesty, and kindness toward everyone." Nora Hasan "became infamous in Roanoke for her leadership in running the...restaurant" and was known for keeping order when the patrons became rowdy. She, like her husband, was known for her kindness in providing meals for those who would have otherwise gone without.[6]

Soon after the Hasans opened the Capitol Restaurant, they bought a traditional two-story white house at 666 Ramada Road in the Roanoke suburb of Vinton. Nidal, a senior at William Fleming High School, is remembered by neighbors as an isolated, studious child. One Ramada Road resident in particular remembers that "Michael was more school and less play. He'd get home and he'd have his book bag, and he'd go straight inside." Nidal apparently did not participate in any extra-curricular or social activities.[7] He and his brothers grew up working in the family restaurant as bus boys, dishwashers, cooks, and cashiers.[8]

One of Nidal's William Fleming High School classmates, Robert Jordan, characterized him as a normal, laid-back teenager who liked to joke. Once, the two shopped for a birthday present for their history teacher. Jordan also remembers that Nidal studied hard and helped out with his family's businesses. Jordan remembers Nidal as being intelligent and says he never knew him to be violent. Soon after the shooting, Jordan gave the *Roanoke Times* a 1988 video that he had taped of Nidal attempting to tell an off-color joke in Arabic. Jordan was shocked when he heard the news that his old friend had killed and wounded his fellow soldiers in a cold-blooded shooting spree.[9]

"It's just amazing how much people can change in twenty years," Jordan remarked when he heard about the Fort Hood shooting. WDBJ television in Roanoke contacted the teacher who received the gift, who recalls Nidal as a "very bright, outgoing, fine young man" and called the shooting "tragic."[10]

Nidal Hasan's senior yearbook photo at William Flemming High School In Roanoke. Photo courtesy of the *Roanoke Times.*

Over the objections of his parents, Nidal joined the Army immediately after graduating from high school in 1988 and was dispatched to Fort Benning, Georgia, for infantry training. After successful completion, he was assigned to Fort Irwin, California.[11] Through an agreement with Barstow Community College, Fort Irwin offers college classes on base at its education center and Nidal enrolled in the 1989 spring semester. A straight A student who made the Dean's list, he took classes through the spring semester of 1990. According to a Barstow spokesperson, his classes included English, algebra, political science, and biology. He did not take any psychology courses.[12]

Upon leaving Fort Irwin, Nidal's active military service was deferred and he returned to Roanoke where he enrolled in Virginia Western Community College. He graduated summa cum laude with an associate degree in science in 1992.[13]

With the Army footing his tab, Nidal enrolled in Virginia Technical Institute in Blacksburg in 1992 for the second summer session. A good student with a proven track record, he majored in biochemistry with minors in biology and chemistry.[14]

In the fall semester of 1993, Nidal approached biochemistry professor, Dr. George E. Bunce, with a request to participate in undergraduate research for credit in Bunce's lab. Bunce has the following recollections.

Usually students begin undergraduate research as juniors but students in good standing academically were allowed to begin as freshmen or sophomores. I remember him as being quiet and respectful in his initial meeting with me. I allowed him to work on a research project…[that] was part of a larger program. After a month or so of work, [his lab instructor] Kathryn Simon, complained to me that Nidal was not using good technique and as a consequence, many of the cultures were becoming contaminated with bacteria. Worse, she said that he was not cooperative in taking her advice on how to improve. I called Nidal into my office and told him that he would have to accept Ms. Simon's directions or we would have to remove him from the project. As I recall, he grudgingly agreed and finished the semester. He chose not to re-enroll in this activity with me for the next semester. Nidal was from a Palestinian refugee family. I attributed his attitude… as a part of his cultural reluctance to taking direction from a female.[15]

Kathryn Simon, the aforementioned lab instructor, has vivid recollections of her interactions with Nidal.

Nidal wanted to work with cell cultures. He was put under my direct supervision and I explained to him the research we were doing and he was very interested in learning. As for my day-to-day interactions with him, I would spend several hours with him in the lab, go over different instructions. Personally he was very interested in learning but at the same time he was hesitant to take direction. He thought he knew better ways to do things and didn't necessarily want to follow the instructions or follow any of the guidance or direction that I gave him. That's when I went to Dr. Bunce and explained the situation. He did speak with him and I remember very vividly after that conversation when Nidal came to the lab he was very confrontational with me. It was very much that he would not take responsibility.[16]

When asked if she believed that the problems she encountered with Nidal had anything to do with her being female, she stated emphatically that she was convinced Nidal had a problem taking direction from a woman.[17]

Nidal did not engage in social activities at any of the three colleges that he attended. Bunce remarked that "Nidal had a demanding academic schedule and worked in his family's restaurant on the weekends so he did not have much time for a social life."[18]

Roanoke is a fifty-minute drive from Blacksburg, an easy commute that allowed Nidal to live at home. Simon had no recollections of any social involvements Nidal may have had as a student. The faculty and the students in the Virginia Tech biochemistry department often got together.

> We would go out and socialize—we worked a lot of very crazy hours, so a lot of us would go to some of the local restaurants and bars in the evening and would invite all the undergrads as well as graduate students, and he did not participate in any of those…sometimes we would just go out on social events— the movies, various activities—and he never participated. He seemed to be a very private person and did not, for whatever reason, want to socialize.[19]

Although Bunce and Simon encountered work problems with Nidal, his pattern of behavior was not, in Bunce's opinion, pathological.

> Nidal seemed to me to be a hard-working but not an especially imaginative young man. He was not out-going but neither did he appear to be antisocial. I did not detect (and was not looking for) any pathological characteristics. He gave no indication of being either particularly religious or hostile. I was surprised to learn of Nidal's actions. There was nothing that I observed in his behavior to indicate that his life would take such a tragic turn.[20]

Nidal Hasan graduated with honors from Virginia Tech with a degree in biochemistry in 1995.[21] Following graduation he was placed on active duty with the Army and was assigned to Fort Sam Houston in San Antonio for "medical training."[22]

Three months after his stint at Fort Sam, Nidal, back in Roanoke, applied for a permit to carry a concealed weapon. He passed a required background check but was notified in writing on January 2, 1996, that his application was on hold due to his failure to complete a firearms training program. Nidal did not respond to the notice and was sent another one on March 11, 1996. He enrolled in a National Rifle Association personal protection course and was granted a certificate of completion on March 24, 1996. His license to carry a concealed firearm was issued two weeks later on the condition that he make a personal appearance at the clerk's office and present a photo ID, which he did. Six months later, on September 3, 1996, he reported his wallet stolen and requested a replacement permit. His driver's license during this time listed his parents' Ramada Road home as his official address.[23]

A Family Disrupted

Life was uneventful for Nidal until April 1998 when his father, at age fifty-one, died suddenly of a heart attack inside the Ramada Road home. It is not known if Nidal was present at the time of Malik Hasan's death. Soon after his father's passing, Nidal began escorting his mother to the Dar al-Hijrah Mosque and Islamic Center—the same mosque that the radical Anwar al Awlaki, an American-born Yemeni cleric, would assume leadership of as imam in 2001. Alawki would serve as spiritual advisor to three of the World Trade Center terrorists responsible for the 9/11 attacks. A gifted preacher, Alawki wielded a great deal of influence upon Nidal.[24]

The Hasan family sold the Ramada Road home shortly after the death of their patriarch. A neighbor commented that the elder Mr. Hasan had been the "backbone of the family." According to the same neighbor, the Hasans told him that they were returning to Palestine.[25] Nidal moved to an apartment in the Washington, D.C. suburb of Kensington, Maryland.[26]

Around the time of his father's abrupt death, Nidal was accepted by the F. Edward Hebert School of Medicine of the Uniformed Services University of the Health Sciences (USUHS) in Bethesda, Maryland. The next few years would have a formidable impact upon the manner in which he would adapt to changing circumstances and how his beliefs about the role of Muslims in American society would be transformed.

Just months after her husband's death, Nora Hasan was diagnosed with cancer. Nidal took a hiatus from medical school and moved her into his one-bedroom apartment in Kensington. His daily activities revolved around his increasing preoccupation with Islam and his commitment to caring for his mother. When she was able, Nora accompanied him to prayers. Nidal dutifully read and memorized the Qur'an, prayed five times a day, and attended services at the Dar al-Hijrah Mosque.[27]

Nora Hasan died on Wednesday, May 30, 2001, a gray, windy, drizzly day four months before the September 11, 2001, attacks on the World Trade Center and the Pentagon. Nidal arranged a traditional Muslim *salat-l-janazh*, or funeral prayers, at Dar al-Hijrah the next day after a "crowded Thursday prayer." According to Islam, the number of heavenly favors bestowed upon the dead depends upon the number of people who pray for the deceased. There is quite a contrast between the final services for Nidal's father and mother: Malik Hasan's memorial was held at a local non-denominational funeral home while his mother's was conducted at the mosque at a time when there would be a large number of people present to pray for her.[28]

After Nora Hasan's death, for the first time in his life Nidal was alone in the world without the guidance and encouragement of his parents. Although he had joined the military without their blessing, for the most part Nidal had always acquiesced to his parents' wishes and relied upon their judgments. And now, the two people who had kept his moral compass on a straight and honorable path were gone. He, alone, owned his future. In his grief, he moved into another apartment building and turned to Allah.

Nidal's cousin, Nader, told ABC reporter Bob Woodruff that Nidal's mother's greatest wish had been for her son to "know God… [and] so he started praying more and becoming more pious…then all of a sudden, four months later, September 11 happens. Now you might see that as your first challenge is how much do you believe in your faith," Nader Hasan continued, "but who knows what was going on in his head."[29]

Less than one month after September 11, the United States invaded Afghanistan. From Nidal's perspective, his country was waging war against Islam.

Refiq Hammad, Nidal's maternal uncle, a resident of al-Bireh in the West Bank, tells of taunts and abuses that his nephew endured as a Muslim after September 11 and emphasizes that Nidal "was not the type who acted out of revenge, nor was he a man who could have been driven to multiple murder by religious conviction."[30]

Mr. Hammad talks freely about his nephew's sensitivity and often relates a story of the death of Nidal's pet bird that he accidentally killed when he rolled over on it.

"He used to have this bird. He would feed it from his mouth to its. For three months he mourned the bird. He made a grave for it and used to visit it."[31] Nidal's uncle Hammad also remembers Nidal telling him of an incident where someone put a diaper on his car with a note that it was his "headdress." Others called him a camel jockey and worse.[32]

There is no disputing the fact that the September 11, 2001, terror attacks had a profound effect upon Nidal Hasan. An internal battle of powerful opposing ideologies left him riddled with questions and doubts about his country and his faith. On the one hand he loved America and wanted to openly demonstrate his loyalty through his military service; on the other, he was being taunted and accused of sedition because of his ethnicity and Muslim faith.

Nidal graduated from USUHS F. Edward Hebert School of Medicine in 2003 and was promoted to captain. He stayed on at Walter Reed for his internship, residency, and a fellowship in which he worked

Nidal Hasan in medical school. Photo courtesy of the U.S. Army.

as a "liason between wounded soldiers and the hospital's psychiatry staff."[33] Nidal's decision to specialize in psychiatry came about for two reasons. First, early in his medical education he attended a birth and fainted. He did not have the temperament or the disposition to provide hands-on medical care. Second, one of his commanding officers would have failed him as an intern but decided to allow him to continue since "he was going into psychiatry and would not be doing any real patient care."[34]

By 2003, Nidal was fully entrenched in the study and practice of Islam. He became even more convinced that the wars in Iraq and Afghanistan were assaults against his religion and he petitioned the military for an early release as a conscientious objector. When his request was denied, Nidal sought the advice of an attorney and offered to repay the Army for his educational expenses. Again, his petition to leave the military was denied. The typical length of service required to repay the U.S. government for a degree in medicine is seven years. Nidal not only had to repay his medical training but his entire college education, as well. According to his cousin, Nader, he resigned himself to remaining in the Army until his time was up.[35] Nidal had ceased to care about his medical education and the pride that came with being a top student was replaced by his desire to save his Muslim brothers fighting American soldiers in Iraq and Afghanistan.[36]

The Camp Pennsylvania Connection

During Nidal's internship and residency at Walter Reed Army Hospital he became increasingly vocal about his condemnation of the Iraq and Afghanistan wars. He proselytized openly to his colleagues and his patients about the evil deeds of American infidels and urged them to seek the Islamic way. One of his fellow students, Naomi Surman, recalls an incident in which Nidal asked her if she knew anything about Islam. When she replied that she did not, he told her that she would burn for eternity in the afterlife. She replied that Islam didn't sound like something that she wanted to hear about and avoided Nidal for the remainder of her residency.[37]

On March 23, 2003, Sgt. Hasan Akbar, a thirty-four-year-old Muslim from Los Angeles, went on a murderous rampage at Camp Pennsylvania in Kuwait. One night Akbar tossed grenades into officers' tents while they slept, then shot them in cold blood as they ran from the fire and flying shrapnel. Two officers were killed and fourteen others were wounded. Akbar kept a computer diary for thirteen years and his writings were used against him at his murder trial. In 1992 he wrote, "I made a promise that if I am not able to achieve success because of some Caucasians, I will kill as many of them as possible." In 1993, in one of his diary entries, he expressed his feelings about Islam—"A Muslim should see himself as a Muslim only. His loyalty should be to Islam only." Another of his diary entries emphasized that destroying America was his greatest goal.[38]

Like Nidal Hasan, in his youth Akbar was an introverted loner with few friends. He was bright, a good student who stayed out of the way of his classmates and teachers, and he spent most of his time studying and attending prayers at his neighborhood mosque. Both Akbar's and Nidal's lives were defined by a lack of engagement with others and a strong preoccupation with ideology. Also like Nidal, after September 11, 2001, Akbar was harassed by fellow soldiers for his Islamic beliefs. Anti-Muslim slurs were common at Camp Pennsylvania. It was reported that command computers had circulated an email cartoon with President Bush allegedly commenting to "tell those with the dirty laundry on their heads that it is wash day."[39]

When Akbar was arrested he blurted out that he had been afraid that the soldiers in his unit were going to "kill and rape Muslims." At the conclusion of his trial, after a brief, mumbled apology, it took a jury only a few hours to convict him of premeditated murder and to sentence him to death. He was the first soldier since the Viet Nam conflict to be convicted of murdering a fellow soldier during war time.[40]

The acts of violence perpetrated by Hasan Akbar sparked the interest of Nidal Hasan. As to the degree of influence, if any, upon Nidal's shooting spree, one can only speculate. NPR's Daniel Zwerdling reported that he was told by one of Nidal's supervisors/professors that he "was obsessed with this case and actually wanted to study the minds of Muslim soldiers who committed fratricide, even though his supervisors said there was no evidence that they knew of that there were any more cases like that."[41]

Nidal's primary clinical responsibility during his residency at Walter Reed was to counsel and treat returning soldiers from Iraq who had developed post traumatic stress disorder (PTSD). He preached Islam to his patients and appended charts with "Allah willing." After attempting to convert a patient, Nidal was counseled for "inappropriately discussing religious topics with his assigned patients" and he also required remediation for not properly documenting an "[emergency room] encounter with a homicidal patient who subsequently eloped from the ER." The *Residency Administrative Handbook* defines "remediation" as follows.[42]

> If any supervisor of a resident identifies problems of resident's performance, the supervisor will inform the resident of the problems by providing either verbal and/or written feedback and the action needed to correct the problematic

behavior. Should the problems persist or are of a serious nature, the supervisor will notify the resident that the matter will be taken to the Program Director for formal counseling and the need for in-program remedial training. The Program Director may formally counsel the resident and develop a plan for remediation with the resident's input and agreement. Also, the Program Director may forward the matter to the policy committee and may recommend a formal in-program remediation plan to the NCC Policy Committee for review and concurrence.[43]

Second-year residents are required to take and pass the "United States Medical Licensing Examination." Nidal didn't bother to show up on the day that it was administered and he was put on probation. As a result, he was not promoted to his third year of residency with his class. He did finally obtain his medical license and was allowed to continue. Nidal's failure to sit for his licensing exam was an indicator of his overall lack of engagement with the program. He began skipping classes and was consistently late to the required morning report, a "multi-disciplinary meeting of all faculty and staff where cases are discussed for both teaching and supervision."[44]

Nidal also failed to show up for the annual required "Psychiatry Resident In-service Training Examination" (PRITE) one year and performed poorly another year. The *Residency Administrative Handbook* describes the PRITE as a written examination that

allows [students] to compare [their] level of knowledge on a variety of subjects with the medical knowledge of residents throughout the country. Results are used by the Program Director to help plan the program as a whole and the individual medical knowledge development of each resident. If a resident's score on the PRITE is significantly below expectations, the resident is required to develop a personalized program to address the particular deficiency.[45]

This required test is considered important enough that "during the annual PRITE administration, every resident will be afforded a call-free night prior to his/her examination(s). Make-up dates will be arranged for those residents required to stand call on the nights prior to the examination(s)."[46]

Later, Nidal missed a night on call and failed to respond to pages and telephone calls, leaving patients unattended. Additionally, he was found to have too much body fat, and, therefore, failed to meet height/weight requirements.[47] Both faculty and students characterized him as "disconnected, aloof, paranoid, belligerent, and schizoid."[48] Nidal "stopped caring about being a top student."[49]

Despite repeated counseling and probation, Nidal's downward spiral continued to the point where he was only seeing one patient per week. He was castigated by Program Director Scott Moran, M.D.

> He demonstrates a pattern of poor judgment and a lack of professionalism. Taken together, these issues demonstrate a lack of professionalism and work ethics. He is able to self-correct with supervision. However, at this point he should not need so much supervision. In spite of all this, I am not able to say he is not competent to graduate.[50]

Two weeks later Dr. Moran wrote a favorable letter of recommendation for Nidal to the American Board of Psychiatry and Neurology, the organization that certifies psychiatrists in the U.S., stating that there was "no documented evidence of unethical or unprofessional behavior, nor any serious question regarding clinical competence during his residency."[51]

In the wake of the letter of reference written by Moran, just a few weeks later in June 2007, Nidal presented a fifty-slide Power Point lecture on the implications of military Muslims fighting America's wars against fellow Muslims. The presentation, titled "The Koranic World View As It Relates to Muslims in the U.S. Military," was delivered by Nidal to a stunned room full of senior military doctors. According to Dana Priest, a *Washington Post* investigative reporter who managed to obtain a copy of the slides, one of the staff members told her that Nidal's audience looked very troubled. Other students had talked about medications and psychiatric illnesses, yet, Nidal Hasan deemed it appropriate to discuss Islam, suicide bombings, "offensive jihad," and Osama bin Laden.[52]

One of the objectives of Nidal's presentation was to "describe the nature of the religious conflicts that Muslims may have with the current wars ..." One slide stated, "It's getting harder and harder for Muslims in the service to morally justify being in a military that seems constantly engaged against fellow Muslims," and another slide characterized Hasan Akbar's Camp Pennsylvania attack as an "adverse event." He talked about hajj, the Muslim pilgrimage to Mecca in Saudi Arabia which all Muslims are encouraged to undertake at least once in their lives (Nidal travelled to Mecca while he was a student); another slide stated that believing in "predestination" was an "Article of Faith." Two slides listed the rewards of complete submission to Islam—the assurance of Paradise with "round vessels of silver and cups of crystal" and "round them will [serve] boys of everlasting youth." He concluded with a slide that declared "fighting to establish an Islamic State to please God, even by force, is condoned by the Islam," and "Muslims Soldiers [*sic*] should not serve in any capacity that renders them at risk to hurting/killing believers unjustly→ will vary!" and ends with the recommendation that "Muslims Soldiers" [*sic*] should be given the option of release from the military as "Conscientious objectors" in order to decrease "adverse events." One of the final slides in his presentation, under "Comments," stated that "We love death more then [*sic*] you love life."[53]

One of Nidal's advisors recognized that, over time, Nidal's views about the military and the Iraq and Afghanistan wars were becoming increasingly extreme. He pulled Nidal aside one day and told him "I don't think you and the military will fit." He offered to help Nidal resign, "to just say goodbye," but unless Nidal could be assured that he would get an honorable discharge, he insisted he wanted to remain in school and in the Army.[54]

During this same time period his official Army rating described his performance as outstanding with the recommendation "must promote; best qualified; a star officer."[55] Despite his dismal performance, political correctness dictated that his rating reflect excellence in achievement. Nidal's poor performance can be easily explained. He had switched sides. He was a Muslim first and he felt compelled to help his Muslim brothers overseas. He was finding it impossible to justify being a good Muslim while serving in the U.S. military.[56]

The Call to Islam

After his mother's death Nidal began attending the Silver Springs, Maryland, Muslim Community Center, often five times a day, dressed in his Army fatigues. Imam Fazul Kahn was in charge of that mosque during the time Nidal was enrolled in the Walter Reed medical residency program. Imam Kahn, who has a social services background and is a marriage counselor as well as the Director of the Interfaith Coalition Against Domestic Violence, remembers him well.

> I met him when he was about thirty-three years old, about seven years before he committed that act. He used to come in his Army uniform. It definitely identified him. He would come to the mosque and chat a little bit about Islam, Muslims, and what-not. I would say that he was an introvert; he was not at all out-going. He was not a very social person. He was not very outwardly accessible to other people. He would sit by himself and read the Qur'an in the mosque. He was not very actively involved with any of the programs at the mosque.[57]

Shortly after Nidal began worshiping at the Silver Springs Muslim Community Center, he enlisted Imam's Kahn's help in finding a wife.

> He was interested in getting married and I offer a matrimonial service here at the mosque. That's where I got to know him a little better. He would come here and look at the files for a wife. He attended our seminars once or twice and there was really no one that was pious enough for him.[58]

On a matrimonial questionnaire Hasan characterized himself as "reserved" and "funny" and he listed "Palestinian" as his nationality.

Nidal wanted and expected a traditional Muslim wife who followed Islam and strictly adhered to the text of the Qur'an, prayed five times a day, and wore a hijab, the traditional Muslim female head covering. A few women were interested in dating Nidal, but he did not find any of them to his liking.

While Imam Kahn believed Nidal Hasan to be eccentric, he did not pick up any signals that would lead him to believe that he was dangerous. He was shocked when he found out that his congregant had engaged in a mass shooting.

He never showed any signs of dysfunction. He seemed very stable, very much reserved but very much aware of what's happening and in tune with world events. Part of the reason that I was surprised was because he never discussed any ideas at all about radicalism or extremism in Islam. That was surprising. It was all about himself.[59]

The Governor's Servant

After barely squeaking by in his residency, Nidal was accepted into a fellowship in Preventive/Disaster Psychiatry at USUHS. At some point during the postdoctoral program, Nidal adopted an additional name, *Abduwali*, which appeared on his official military record as "Nidal Abduwali Hasan." In Arabic "*Abduwali*" means "servant of the governor."[60] In all likelihood Nidal took the name to honor Abduwali Quiri Mirzoyev, a radical Wahhabi cleric from Central Asia who had ties to the Soviet Union prior to its fall.

Abduwali Quri Mirzoyev was one of the founders of the Wahhabi radical Islam movement in the Ferghana Valley in Central Asia. The roots of the sect lie within the core of Saudi Arabian extremism and in the intransigent Uzbekistan guerrillas, the Islamic Movement of Uzbekistan (IMU). Caught in a secular war, some members of this group were forced to relocate abroad and were absorbed into the al Qaeda terrorist organization.[61]

After the collapse of the Soviet Union, Central Asia became a hotbed for terrorists looking for refuge. The Taliban offered the IMU sanctuary with a goal of toppling the government of Uzbekistan and eventually all of Central Asia. The IMU also made contact with Osama bin Laden in Afghanistan and "the two became supportive of each other."[62]

In a Senate Subcommittee on Terrorism, Technology and Homeland Security hearing on June 26, 2003, Chairman Jon Kyl spoke of the ongoing threat of the Wahhabi terrorist movement in his opening statement.

Nearly twenty-two months have passed since the atrocity of September 11th. Since then, many questions have been asked about the role in that day's terrible events and in other challenges we face in the war against terror of Saudi Arabia and its official sect, a separatist, exclusionary and violent form of Islam known as Wahhabism. It is widely recognized that all of the nineteen suicide pilots were Wahhabi followers. In addition, fifteen of the nineteen were Saudi subjects. Journalists and experts, as well as spokespeople of the world, have said that Wahhabism is the source of the overwhelming majority of terrorist atrocities in today's world, from Morocco to Indonesia, via Israel, Saudi Arabia, Chechnya.[63]

Senator Kyl continued with a comment on a story published in *Newsweek* magazine's June 26, 2003, issue stating that, "al Qaeda, which experts have described as a Wahhabi movement, has overhauled its approach to penetrating the United States, and I just want to quote this one paragraph before I conclude:"[64]

> To foil the heightened security after 9/11, al Qaeda began to rely on operatives who would be harder to detect. They recruited U.S. citizens or people with legitimate Western passports who could move freely in the United States. They used women and family members as support personnel, and they made an effort to find African-American Muslims who would be sympathetic to Islamic extremism, using mosques, prisons, and universities throughout the United States.[65]

Stephen Schwartz, former Senior Fellow with the Foundation for the Defense of Democracies, a Washington, D.C. think-tank, testified at that same Senate sub-committee meeting that,

> Wahhabi Saudi policy has always been two-faced. That is, at the same time as the Wahhabis preach hostility and violence, first against non-Wahhabi Muslims, they maintain a policy of alliance with Western military powers, Britain, then the U.S. and France, to ensure their control over the Arabian Peninsula.[66]

Schwartz believes that many Islamic organizations, such as the Islamic Society of North America, or ISNA; the Council on American-Islamic Relations, CAIR; the Muslim Students' Organization, the

American Muslim Council, AMC; the American Muslim Alliance; and other Islamic groups that he refers to as the "Wahhabi lobby," exert domination over mosques and their congregants through control of everything from ownership of property to the content of sermons. Schwartz asserts that there is Wahhabi control over the training for imams, the content of information disseminated at local Muslim community centers, organizational fund raising, and even material displayed on mosque bulletin boards.

Schwartz said in his testimony, "Similar influence extends to prison and military chaplaincies, Islamic elementary and secondary schools or academies, college campus activity, endowment of academic chairs and programs in Middle East studies, and most notoriously, charities ostensibly helping Muslims abroad, many of which have been linked to or designated as sponsors of terrorism."[67]

Nidal Hasan during his fellowship at Walter Reed Army Hospital. Photo courtesy of the U.S. Army.

Perhaps the most notable point that Schwartz makes is that the Islamic Development Bank, a Wahhabi organization, funded the "Bilal Islamic primary and secondary school in California in 1999," an institution with which Hasan Akbar, a person of great interest to Nidal, had ties.[68]

NIDAL BEGAN HIS FELLOWSHIP IN PREVENTIVE/DISASTER PSYCHIATRY in July 2007, where he had previously studied, USUHS. This two-year program trains psychiatrists to use their behavioral health skills to respond to mass casualties such as terrorist attacks; weather disasters like Hurricane Katrina; earthquakes, floods, and the like; epidemics; and other dire situations where the public-at-large is endangered and rapid intervention is essential. During the first year of the program students must successfully meet the requirements for a master's degree in public health.[69]

Even though Nidal had barely made it through his residency at

Walter Reed, he was back to his old patterns of behavior very shortly after entering the Preventive/Disaster Psychiatry program. One of his classmates, Dr. Val Finnell, remembers an environmental health class where Nidal made a presentation on the U.S. involvement on the "war on Islam." Other students followed the class syllabus and presented topics on mold remediation, air quality, ozone, and other environmental concerns. Nidal's material created quite a stir. Finnell and another student raised their hands during and after the presentation and questioned the instructor about the appropriateness of the material. The professor did not try to question or stop Nidal during his talk.[70]

"Dr. Hasan made it a point to be very vocal in his beliefs, he was very extreme in his view....Military officers take an oath to uphold the constitution and to defend the U.S. against all enemies, foreign and domestic. So you have to wonder, what was someone this conflicted doing as a military officer?" asked Finnell in a CNN interview.[71]

Finnell also told Anderson Cooper that one of the students in the class approached a faculty member about Hasan, calling him a "ticking time bomb." Another student, in a *New York Times* story, dismissed Hasan as a "chubby, bald guy" and said that it had not occurred to him that he might be dangerous. A classmate remarked that there were a lot of people at Walter Reed who opposed the wars.[72] Nidal told one of his classmates, Anthony Bonfiglio, that his "primary reason for wanting to do a fellowship was to stay in training and thus delay deployment."[73]

Nidal was a steady poor performer and he was ranked in the bottom 25 percent of his class. Despite his deplorable performance, his Officer Evaluation Report for 2007-2008 stated that he was

> among the better disaster and psychiatry fellows to have completed the MPH at the Uniformed Services University; he had focused his efforts on illuminating the role of culture and Islamic faith within the Global War on Terrorism; his unique interests have captured the interest and attention of peers and mentors alike.[74]

In July 2008, Nidal began attending a series of round-table discussions at the Homeland Security Policy Institute, a not-for-profit George Washington University think tank whose mission is to find solutions for dealing with terrorist threats.[75] HSPI Director Frank Cilluffo remembers Nidal Hasan very well. He had to cut him off at one of the conferences because he wouldn't stop talking.[76]

By this time Nidal's radical views about defending the tenets of Islam in the most rigorous sense were so internalized that he could not separate them from his everyday life. His every thought, his every action was colored by the strict Wahhabi and Salafi interpretation of the Qur'an. He even initiated combative conversations at his mosque and fiercely defended the concept of "jihad" with a fellow congregant. To most Muslims, jihad is an inner struggle but Nidal maintained that jihad is a holy war that one must fight when Islam is threatened. He defended killing anyone who was doing a Muslim "wrong."[77]

This fellow churchgoer engaged in many conversations with Nidal. "I was trying to modernize him," he says. "I tried my best. He used to hate America as a whole. He was more anti-American than American. I couldn't get through to him. He was a typical fundamentalist Muslim."[78]

Nidal also used the Internet to vent his frustrations. In a comment about an article that castigates suicide bombings on *Scribd.com* he posited "suicide bombers whose intention, by sacrificing their lives, is to help save Muslims by killing enemy soldiers. If one suicide bomber can kill 100 enemy soldiers because they were caught off guard that would be considered a strategic victory." In this lengthy post he likened World War II Japanese Kamikaze pilots to radical jihad suicide bombers declaring that they died defending their homeland and, therefore, suicide was justified and honorable. He ended his post by asserting "so the scholars [*sic*] main point is that 'IT SEEMS AS THOUGH YOUR INTENTION IS THE MAIN ISSUE' and Allah (SWT) knows best."[79]

Once again, while Nidal was studying in the Preventive/Disaster Psychiatry program, he chose to give a USUHS class presentation on Islam instead of an appropriate medical topic. During his talk he stated that "non-believers should be beheaded and have boiling oil poured down their throats." He also told his audience of doctors that "non-muslims were infidels condemned to hell who should be set on fire."[80]

The Pen and the Sword

Six months after he began attending the Homeland Security Policy Institute's events, Nidal Hasan initiated a series of sixteen email messages to his former imam, Anwar al Awlaki, who by this time had fled to Yemen and was on the State Department's terrorist watch list.

On December 17, 2008, Hasan contacted Awlaki through his website and expressed his concern that some soldiers who convert to Islam develop internal conflicts about fighting in wars where the enemy is Muslim. He asked Awlaki his views on somone like Hasan Akbar, who murdered fellow soldiers in order to prevent them from killing Muslims. Would he consider Hasan Akbar a "shaheed," a martyr who dies fighting jihad?[81]

Awlaki had been under investigation by the San Diego FBI's Joint Terrorism Task Force since 2006 and the message was intercepted and marked as a "product of interest" because it referenced the military. The agent who analyzed the message sent it to three other JTTF members asking, "Can we check to see if this guy is a military member? Also, I would like your input, from the military standpoint, on whether or not this should be disseminated further." For some unknown reason, unfortunately Hasan's military connection was not discovered until later.[82]

On January 1, 2009, Hasan sent Awlaki a second message with his personal observation that Israelis lump all Muslims together. "Is it better for Muslims to say I am just Muslim and not Sunni or Shia which seems to divide us?" Hasan asked. The agent who intercepted the message marked it as "Not a Product of Interest" and noted,

> Though [*Agent's Name Redacted*]'s research indicates that Nidal is not a military member, I still think this would make a good [Intelligence Information Report]. There might be other information out there that links him to the military in some way…[*Agent's Name Redacted*]—did you check to see what other Hasan's are in the military? If not, I can have our guy run just the last name.[83]

Additional checks revealed that there was a "Nidal Hasan" in the military. He was an Army officer stationed at Walter Reed Army Medical Center in Washington, D.C. In a printed report, Nidal's official title was abbreviated "Comm Officer" which was misinterpreted as "Communications Officer." Since Hasan's home base was Washington, D.C., the two messages were sent to the Washington field office for resolution with an Electronic Communication (EC) advisory message.

> The individual is likely an Army communications officer stationed at Walter Reed. I would recommend that this not be disseminated as an IIR (Intelligence Information Report), since he may have access to message traffic. If this needs to get to the military, WFO (Washington Field Office) might have to do it internally....While email contact with Aulaqi does not necessarily indicate participation in terrorist-related matters, Aulaqi's reputation, background, and anti-U.S. sentiments are well known. Although the content of these messages was not overtly nefarious, this type of contact with Aulaqi would be of concern if the writer is actually the individual identified above. [84]

On January 16, 2009, Hasan sent a third, very long, rambling message in which he asked Awlaki,

> Is it permissible to Fire Unguided Rockets into Israel. There is no question that firing unguided rockets into Israel has the potential of indiscriminately killing civilians. The real question is why Hamas would do such a thing. Can one envision a scenario where it would be acceptable to so. Well, what if Israel was and continues to indiscriminately kill and hurt civilians and commit other atrocities in the Gaza territory to serve their expansionary ambitions. One can then begin to at least understand why the Palestinians would do such a thing. In fact it is probably one of the only things they can do to in an attempt to avenge themselves and repulse the enemy.[85]

He compared the firing of rockets into Israel to a mosquito bite—"annoying but not a real threat" and wondered if it would be considered a transgression against Allah. He goes on to rationalize violence against Israel with quotations from the Qur'an.[86]

In his next even lengthier message of 920 words, on January 18,

2009, Hasan continued his tirade against Israel and expressed his unbridled support of Hamas. This was his fourth message and Awlaki had not responded to any of them. He waited a month to contact Awlaki again, and on February 16, 2009, he sent the sheik a short message through his website. "Please have alternative to donate to your web site. For example, checks/money orders may be sent to [redacted]. This can assure privacy for some who are concerned."

Anwar al-Awlaki. Photo courtesy of the U.S. Department of Homeland Security.

Two minutes later, he emailed an almost identical note. "Please have alternative methods to donate to your web site. For example, checks/money orders may be sent to [redacted]. This can assure privacy for some who are concerned and maximize the amount given."[87]

A few minutes later Hasan tried again, asking Awlaki if he could possibly come to the U.S. to award a prize for an essay contest to be held in the imam's honor. Hasan had attempted to initiate a personal relationship with Awlaki under the guise of asking for his advice. This time, the ruse was flattery.

> Insha Allah, A $5,000 scholarship prize is being awarded for the best essay/piece entitled "Why is Anwar Al Awlaki a great activist and leader." We would be honored if you would award the prize. If you have any questions, concerns, or potential modifications, please e-mail me. Advertisement will be posted in the Muslim link, in the March 2009 issue. Jazakallah Khair, ViR Nidal PS-We met briefly a very long time ago when you were the Imam at Dar al-Hijra. I doubt if you remember me. In any case I have since graduated medical school and finished residency training.[88]

There was, of course, no essay contest. Hasan was desperate to establish a personal relationship with Awlaki. He was infatuated with the imam and had elevated him to almost the same level of worship as Allah. The Army had failed Hasan as a substitute parental figure; unbeknownst to Awlaki, Hasan had chosen him to fulfill that role. His hoax worked. The next day, February 19, 2009, Awlaki answered Hasan's email.

Assalamu alaykum Br Nidal,

I pray this message reaches you at the best state of emaan [*sic*] and health. Jazakum Allahu khairan for thinking good of me. I don't travel so I wont be able to physically award the prize and I am too "embarrassed" for a lack of the better word to award it anyway. May Allah assist you in your efforts.

Assalamu alaykum

Your Brother

Anwar Awlaki[89]

A few hours later, Hasan backpedaled in his reply to Awlaki and told him that the essay contest had been cancelled and blamed it on circumstances beyond his control. First, however, he expressed his elation over receiving Awlaki's email. "It's nice to hear your voice even if its email."[90] He explains that there were "obstacles" from

Muslims in the community that are petrified by potential repercussions. Allah willing everything will work out in such a way that pleases Allah (SWT). You have a very huge following but even among those there seems to be a large majority that are paralyzed by fear of losing some aspect of dunya. They would prefer to keep their admiration for you in their hearts.[91]

He concludes his message with an offer to donate money to Awlaki's website and he requested the imam's assistance in finding a wife.

If you need any assistance, Allah willing I will be able to help. I believe my biggest strength is my financial situation...Allah (SWT) forgives us for our short coming, forbids our body from touching the Hell-Fire, allows plenty of shade on the day of reckoning, and hastens our entrance into Jannah where we will see each other [in Jannah] sipping on non-intoxicating wine in reclined thrones and in absolute and unending happiness.

PS: I'm looking for a wife that is willing to strive with me to please Allah SWT. I will strongly consider a recommendation coming from you.[92]

Hasan's predilection toward magical thinking is apparent in this email. He was in search of a relationship and, if necessary, would pay for it. For Hasan, Awlaki could fulfill a dual role—friendship and eternal salvation.

A JTTF agent in San Diego reviewed the email thread and evaluated it as "Not a Product of Interest."[93]

Awlaki responded to Hasan's message on February 22, 2009:

> Believe it or not I kind of felt that the contest would end up running into red tape. People in that part of the world are becoming very timid and it doesn't look it's getting any better. Thanks for the offer for help. Well it is needed but I just don't know how to do it. There are poor people, orphans, widows, dawa projects, and the list goes on. So if you have any ideas on how to get help across and in accordance to law in a climate that is strict to start with please let me know. Tell more about yourself. I will keep an eye for a sister.[94]

> Assalamu alaykum

> Anwar

Hasan wrote to Awlaki a few hours later with a very lengthy email.

> I will keep trying. If Allah (SWT) wants something to occur no one can stop it. My job is to put in the effort and have patience. Your various works force the controversial issues to surface and be addressed. If there is going to be a resolution between Islam and the West the difficult issues have to be brought up. I think this is important. It may take many generations before people realize the gift that Allah (SWT) has given them through your work. But, I see the value now and don't have to wait for your death....My goal is Jannat Firdaus and I praise and thank Allah (SWT) for giving me the ability to strive, to see the truth, to beg for his forgiveness, and ask for his guidance.

> If people truly understood the peace they could have by really believing that Allah (SWT) is in control and that he is just testing to see who is the best among us, it would be a lot easier to see through Shaitans promises of poverty and destruction.

> I want to be with those who are the best. Imam, if you have any specific projects that you feel are important to get on their feet let me know. I will read up on them and Inshallah I will

please Allah (SWT). In regards to a sister for marriage, my name is Nidal Hasan. If you Google CSTS and Nidal Hasan you will see a picture of me. I currently reside in Silver Spring MD;[telephone number redacted]. I was born and raised in the U.S. Both of my parents are from Palestine but have both passed away. I joined the U.S. military at age 17 as an infantryman. I subsequently received a BS in Biochemistry Degree in medicine with residency training in psychiatry, and am just finishing up my fellowship training in Disaster and Preventive Psychiatry.

During my working career I have been a bus boy, a dishwasher, a cook, a cashier, a lab technician, a researcher, and entrepreneur. Allah (SWT) lifted the veil from my eyes about 8-9 years ago and I have been striving for Jannat Firdaus ever since. I hope, Inshallah, my endeavor will be realized. If you know someone that you feel that will be compatible and complement my endeavors to please Allah(SWT) please let me know.[95]

Again, the messages were marked by a San Diego JTTF agent as "Not a Product of Interest." This was the second and final message that Hasan would receive from Awlaki.[96]

Hasan's goal, of course, was to secure a place in heaven. His pathway to the afterlife was through Allah. By allowing Allah to use him for his purposes, Hasan believed that he was assured a place in paradise. The only requirements were that he supply the effort required to fulfill Allah's quest and to be patient. This message is significant because it indicates that, at this point in his life, Hasan had internalized and codified a justification for any acts of violence that he might commit in Allah's name.

On February 25, 2009, two months after it had been received, an agent in the FBI Washington Field Office read the discretionary lead and the first two of Hasan's emails to Awlaki that had been forwarded by the San Diego office. Because of his military status, a special agent was instructed to perform an assessment of Hasan's initial two emails. The San Diego office had failed to forward the subsequent seven communications from Hasan to Awlaki and the two emails written by Awlaki to Hasan. The agent was not given a deadline for the completion of the assessment.[97]

On February 28, 2009, Hasan emailed a report to Awlaki entitled "Public Opinion in the Islamic World on Terrorism, al Qaeda, and U.S. Policies," with a short note, "most Muslims feel that US is trying to undermine Islam. It substantiates an earlier study it did as well as other studies by other organizations. I think you will find it interesting." This message, like the others, was captured by the San Diego office and marked "Not a Product of Interest."[98] It was not forwarded to the Washington office.

A few hours after sending the public opinion report to Awlaki, Hasan emailed the sheikh a link to a newspaper article about Imam Yayha Hendi, noting "He is well known in the Greater Washington Area and serves the U.S. military as imam for the Bethesda medical center. A true vision of what the government views as a good role model for all Muslims."[99]

The San Diego agent who intercepted the message marked it as a "Product of Interest," and also identified it as potential foreign intelligence correspondence.[100]

On March 3, 2009, Hasan sent another email to Awlaki offering to pay the domain fee for the imam's website. He asked him for his preferred payment method and offered to send money through PayPal. A San Diego agent marked the communication as a "Product of Interest" but noted that it was "Non-Pertinent."[101]

Four days later, on March 7, 2009, Hasan wrote to Awlaki and told him that he realized that the imam was very busy and asked him to "keep me in your rolodex [sic] in case you find me useful and feel free to call me collect." He included his contact information in the message. The San Diego agent who intercepted the communication marked it "Reasonably Appears to be Foreign Intelligence."[102]

Hasan did not write to Awlaki again until three months later when he was promoted to major. On May 25 Hasan sent a message to the imam through his website.

> Brother Anwar don't fear the blame of the blamers! When I
> read this verse (below) I think of you. Most of us have turned
> back for fear…of this life. We have thus suspended our crit-

ical Judgment for a small price. Allah (SWT) makes it clear that most won't believe and of those that do; the ones who struggle for his cause are greater in his sight then those who sit back and pray.

0 you who believe! Whoever from among you turns back from his religion (Islam), Allah will bring a people (like Anwar Al Awalaki) whom He will love and they will love Him; humble towards the believers, stern towards the disbelievers, fighting in the Way of Allah, and never fear of the blame of the blamers. That is the Grace of Allah which He bestows on whom He wills. And Allah is All Sufficient for His creatures' needs, All-Knower.

Your Brother Nidal[103]

This was Hasan's final message to Awlaki. It was not until May 27, 2009, that the Washington, D.C., JTTF agent who had been assigned Hasan's initial two messages to Awlaki looked at the original two messages from Hasan to Awlaki. The suspect emails had been sitting in the WFO for five months, and Hasan had come to the end of his "personal" relationship with the cleric. Information that could have led to an investigation of Hasan was split between the FBI's San Diego and Washington, D.C., offices and there was no coordination and little communication between the two divisions about Hasan's case. Later, in hindsight, deputy security advisor Juan Zarate remarked that it was "very difficult in the moment for analysts and agents...to piece this together and see they had a ticking time bomb on their hands."[104]

Despite Hasan's odious behavior, shoddy performance, and questionable loyalty to his country, he completed his Preventive/Disaster Psychiatry fellowship and was promoted to major in May 2009.[105] His Officer Evaluation Report for July 2008 through June 2009, commended his "keen interest in Islamic culture and faith and his shown capacity to contribute to our psychological understanding of Islamic nationalism and how it may relate to events of national security and Army interest in the Middle East and Asia." In the category of "unique skills" was listed Islamic studies. The only negative mark on any of Nidal's performance evaluations during his tenure at Walter Reed was a notation that he failed to pass a fitness test. Other than that, there was not one disparaging remark, not a single criticism in any of his evaluations.[106]

Two months later, Nidal Hasan was on his way to Fort Hood, Texas, the largest military installation in the country, to minister to vulnerable warriors' broken psyches. Hasan's advisor at Walter Reed told Col. Kimberly Kesling at Fort Hood, "You're getting our worst."[107]

WELCOME TO
III CORPS & FORT HOOD
"THE GREAT PLACE"

Photo by John Porterfield

4. The Great Place
July 2009

A man is but the product of his thoughts—
what he thinks, he becomes.
~Mahatma Gandhi

Nidal Hasan must have wondered if he had been transported into Dante's inferno when he arrived in Killeen, Texas, in July 2009. It was a blistering month with daytime high temperatures registering in the low 100's. The wide expanses of concrete freeways and parking lots coupled with a paucity of vegetation were reminiscent of an alien desert when compared to the verdant rolling hills and mild weather that he left behind in Maryland.

Like the Washington, D.C. area, Killeen and its bedroom communities are diverse in population and culture—the abundance of ethnic restaurants is a testament to the melting pot typical of a city where soldiers tend to stay put when they leave the military. But Killeen is not cosmopolitan in its politics, social mores, or in its cultural acceptance. Political affiliations flourish right of center—liberal ideologies are not tolerated, uniformity is celebrated, and individual differences are ostracized. This fundamental conservatism can be traced back to central Texas's early Christian heritage.

Spanish Roman Catholic missionaries first came to central Texas in the early seventeenth century to provide religious instruction to Native Americans. Spain declared Catholicism the official religion of Texas in 1820 and all protestant affiliations were outlawed. Despite the Catholic church's efforts to keep them out, by the early eighteen hundreds protestant clergy flowed into Texas—first circuit-riding Methodists who preached in private homes, then Baptists who arrived by wagon train, followed by Presbyterians. Protestant colleges sprang up in central Texas, namely Baylor University in Waco, University of Mary Hardin-Baylor in Belton, and Southwestern University in Georgetown.[1]

Central Texas also spawned noteworthy evangelical cults like the Sanctified Sisters in Belton who believed in the revolutionary concept of womens' equality, and the Davidians, an Adventist reform splinter group of the 1920s which gave rise to the fundamentalist Branch Davidians. In the early 1990s, members of the Branch Davidians awaited Armageddon on their commune just northeast of Waco and fifty miles northeast of Killeen. Their leader, David Koresh, allegedly amassed an enormous illegal munitions cache for which the federal government issued an arrest warrant. Just after sunrise on April 19, 1993, after a fifty-one-day stand-off with federal agents, the FBI fired tear gas canisters into the Branch Davidian compound. Instead of evacuating the buildings as the FBI had expected, Koresh instructed his followers to pour accelerants throughout the interior of the enclosures and then to set fires inside the buildings. The arsenal inside the compound exploded, killing eighty-one residents, many of them women and children. Oklahoma City bomber Timothy McVeigh blamed the FBI for the Branch Davidians' loss of life and cited the incident as a motive for bombing the Alfred P. Murrah Federal Building in downtown Oklahoma City exactly two years later.[2]

Muslims also have a storied history in Texas. After the Mexican-American War ended in 1848, Lt. George Crosman and Maj. Henry Wayne convinced Sen. Jefferson Davis that camels could play an important role in westward expansion to California. Imagine the amazement of early Texas settlers who spotted caravans of strange looking animals with long necks and humps on their backs trotting down the trails from Indianola to Camp Verde, flanked by their exotic Middle Eastern handlers. Syrian-born Hajj Ali, a Muslim who came to be known as Hi Jolly, is legendary for his role in facilitating the use of camels in the movement west. Hi Jolly eventually married an American woman and became a citizen of this country.[3]

Today, Texas has the eighth largest Muslim population in the United States, most of whom reside in large metropolitan areas. There are about one hundred families who make up the Islamic community of Greater Killeen, some of whom were born into Islam, others who are converts.[4]

A central Texas handgun instructor, Crockett Keller, made headlines in 2011 for refusing to teach classes to Muslims and non-Christian Arabs, stating that "You've already proven that you cannot make a knowledgeable and prudent decision as required under the law." He also discouraged "socialist liberals" and supporters of President Obama from enrolling in his firearms course. Keller paid $175 for an ad espousing his views on a local radio station and posted it on YouTube. It went viral and made national news.[5]

By and large, however, Muslims in Killeen have been silently assimilated into the central Texas sociocultural milieu. Osman Danquah, founder of the Killeen masjid, or mosque, is a retired Jamaican Army sergeant who championed the construction of the red brick building on South Fort Hood Street that serves as the Islamic community's place of worship.[6]

The central Texas economy is inextricably tied to Fort Hood. A self-contained city in its own right, Fort Hood is the largest military installation in the United States and it covers 335 square miles. It is home to more than 70,000 people. By contrast, the City of Killeen's physical area covers just over 100 square miles. Fort Hood's buildings and structures contain thirty-four million square feet and it is the largest armored military installation in the United States. Home to III Corps, it is the only base capable of housing and training the First Cavalry division and the Thirteenth Sustainment Command.[7] Fort Hood contributes over seven billion dollars annually to the central Texas economy.[8]

Fort Hood was named for John Bell Hood, a Civil War swashbuckler who climbed the ranks of the Confederate army from a lieutenant to major general in a span of only two years. General Hood sustained massive losses in the siege of Atlanta and his ensuing descent was as rapid as his rise.[9]

Elvis Presley, Fort Hood's most legendary soldier, was drafted into the U.S. Army in 1958. It seems fitting that Presley was assigned to Fort Hood's Second Armored Division's "Hell On Wheels" unit, formerly led by General George Patton in World War II. Presley's parents accompanied him to Killeen where the three of them lived in a rented house.[10]

Fort Hood offers a rich quality of life to the soldiers and civilian workers who live and work there. Modern housing, restaurants, an entertainment complex, high quality health care, and exemplary schools provide stability and foster solidarity in its community, thus its nickname "The Great Place."[11]

Hasan found a vacant upstairs apartment at Casa Del Norte through a classified ad in a local newspaper. It was a run-down, nondescript, twenty-seven unit apartment building located in a seedy part of town so close to the base that Hasan could hear morning reveille from the courtyard. The complex's dilapidated buildings had deteriorated over the years and showed no signs of having been updated, remodeled, or even routinely maintained. Some of the letters on the sign out front had fallen off and were held in place with duct tape. A dingy streamer greeted residents and guests: "Welcome Home Fort Hood Heroes—We're Proud of You!" Hasan moved into apartment number nine.[12]

In 2011, the Bell County Appraisal District valued Casa Del Norte at $337,810. With an annual salary and housing allowance approaching one-third of the value of the entire complex, Hasan had ample means to live in much more comfortable quarters either on or off post. He had other ideas, however, of how he wanted to spend his money. He donated twenty-to-thirty thousand dollars a year to Islamic charities—fronts for money laundering operations funneled to terrorist organizations.[13]

Hasan signed a six month lease and paid the $350 per month rent up front with a cashiers check. He told apartment complex owner Jose Padilla that under no circumstances could anyone enter his apartment without his express permission and then, only if he was home at the time.[14]

With little furniture and few belongings, Hasan's sparse apartment felt larger than its cramped 650 square feet. He ate his meals and worked at a flimsy card table covered with a white tablecloth; an inexpensive framed mirror hung on his living room wall with two small decorative shelves placed on either side; a paper shredder was tucked into a corner with his prayer rug; a small shelving unit held a few books; and an air mattress was positioned directly on the floor in the bedroom.[15]

Hasan's neighbors sometimes sat at a picnic table outside in the evenings, drinking beer and gossiping to pass the time. They referred to Hasan as "Number Nine" and sniggered at him when he arrived home in the evenings wearing Islamic prayer clothes. Most of the tenants agreed that while their neighbor, Hasan, was friendly and easy-going, he made few attempts to befriend any of the Casa Del Norte residents. One of his next door neighbors, Willie Bell, however, thought very highly of Hasan.[16]

"The first day he moved in, he offered to give me a ride to work," says Bell. "He'd give you the shoes and shirt and pants off him if you need it. Nicest guy you'd want to meet."[17]

Fractured Egos

At Fort Hood, Hasan was provided an office in the Behavioral Health Department on the fifth floor of Darnall Medical Center. He also saw patients at the Resiliency and Restoration (R&R) Center, a walk-in psychiatry clinic located next-door to the hospital. The R&R Center is the busiest outpatient psychiatric clinic in the world and more patients are seen there than in the Darnall Medical Center Emergency Room.

Hasan transferred to Fort Hood from Walter Reed with former classmate Capt. Naomi Surman, who was now his supervisor. He had been promoted to the rank of major shortly before reporting for duty at Fort Hood but Surman, an exemplary student and psychiatrist, was passed over.

Hasan and Captain Surman arrived at Fort Hood on the heels of an internal AR 15-6 administrative investigation into inappropriate conduct by the chief of the Behavioral Health Department, Ltc. Ben Kirk Phillips, and his second-in-command Ltc. Sharette Gray. Phillips and Gray were accused of cultivating a hostile work environment of intimidation and bullying. In sworn statements, personnel complained of staff shortages, overwork with no overtime pay or compensatory time off, intimidation, name-calling, tantrums, and managerial interference.[18] One staff member accused Phillips of being "heavy-handed" and intimidating. Another complained of his constant "yelling" at behavioral health personnel and remembered that "meetings quickly deteriorated into dysfunctional and emotional events," "altercations" so loud that they could be heard out in the hallway, and "verbal attacks that resulted in significant anxiety and chaos."[19]

One physician who held a leadership position and who had suffered a heart attack used accrued sick leave to recuperate. When he returned to work he found that, unbeknownst to him, he had been relieved of his position and relegated to regular staff.[20]

Ltc. Sharette Gray was characterized as "interfering with the day-to-day running of the clinic" and "undermining clinic leadership." Several of the staff complained that she "detailed" clinic personnel for her personal use. Another stated that she was "fault-finding, condescending, and demoralizing. I do my best to avoid her." All of the respondents expressed a fear of retaliation if either Ltc. Phillips or Gray read their sworn statements. "I feel her capacity for reprisal is unlimited," stated one of the staff; another said, "I am afraid this statement will end badly for me, nonetheless, I must do what I think is right."[21]

Turnover was high in the Behavioral Health Department. According to one clinician, at least two psychiatrists stated as their reason for leaving "negative interactions with Ltc. Gray." Others cited that "she often ate while completing rounds with them," that she was frequently "not in proper uniform." One physician claimed that because of Ltc. Gray's "yelling" he planned to transfer out of the department to "any low-level job just to get out."[22]

In the midst of this turmoil, several staff psychiatrists who observed Hasan's orientation sessions recalled that he showed little enthusiasm about his new job. They reported that he was apathetic and disinterested in his new job duties which consisted of counseling soldiers returning from the wars, ordering consults with specialists, and reviewing medical records for severing medically disabled soldiers from the Army.[23]

Col. Kimberly Kesling, chief of medical staff at Darnall Medical Center, had been forewarned about the problems with Hasan at Walter Reed. She discussed these concerns with him and made it clear that he had better behave in a manner befitting an officer and health care provider. In a CNN article, Colonel Kesling admitted that although she was concerned about his unsatisfactory conduct at Walter Reed, the report did not raise any red flags. Her approach was to integrate Hasan into the existing staff. Aside from her talk with him upon his arrival, she had almost no contact with him during his five month tenure at Fort Hood.[24]

The major focus of Hasan's job was to evaluate soldiers returning from Iraq and Afghanistan for psychological injuries such as PTSD. Hasan, among other psychiatrists, determined if these incoming soldiers were capable of further duty and, if not, made recommendations to a Medical Evaluation Board (MEB) for their dispositions. He also took turns with other staff psychiatrists for after-hours emergency calls at the base hospital. While most of the workers in his department were cordial to him, there were some who overtly resented him for being Muslim and made it clear that they didn't trust him.[25]

One of Hasan's co-workers described him as having a round cartoon-like head with large, flat ears, and an almost bald head. He was chubby and always looked like he needed a shave. He walked with a slow and awkward gait, as if he was uncertain of his direction and his close-set eyes were generally fixed on the floor. He was introverted, demure, reserved, and a loner who did not participate in any social activities and never joined in any office functions.[26]

The Fort Hood Behavioral Health Department was wrought with turf wars and personal battles among the command staff who openly displayed short tempers with some of their staff and favoritism toward others. One of the departmental psychiatrists recalls a confrontation with Ltc. Ben Phillips, M.D., chief of behavioral health services, in which he ordered that psychiatrist to falsify time sheets. The department uses a system of relative value units (RVU's), a performance based system that utilizes work accomplished versus actual time spent with a patient. Phillips would look bad to his superiors if any of the staff documented more than their allotted RVU's. While some of the staff did falsify their time sheets, others refused to do so.[27]

In the meantime, Hasan was becoming acquainted with Killeen. Osman Danquah, co-founder of the Killeen mosque, invited Hasan to his home for dinner. The young major reached out to the cleric and asked him for his counsel regarding a "hypothetical" situation where a Muslim soldier might express reluctance in deploying to a war zone in which he would be required to kill enemy soldiers of the Islamic faith. Danquah advised Hasan that the soldier should tell his chain of command about his reservations. Danquah, a veteran, had spent several months in the Middle East during the first Gulf War and saw no conflict between service to his country and his religious beliefs.[28]

Photo by John Porterfield

Soldier of Allah

Soon after moving to Killeen, Hasan ordered business cards from an Internet site. Centered at the top of the card was "Behavioral Heatlh [sic] – Mental Health – Life Skills." Underneath, on the left side of the card, was his name and titles, Nidal Hasan, MD, MPH, and under his name, "SoA(SWT)." The third line was "Psychiatrist." The bottom right listed Hasan's cell phone number, a Maryland exchange, and his email address. There was no mention of his military affiliation. "SoA" is an acronym for "Soldier of Allah;" "SWT" is short for "Subhanahu Wa Ta'ala" and recognizes that Allah is "exalted."[29]

There has been speculation that Hasan wanted to establish a private psychiatric practice on the side, but with such a small Muslim population to market his skills, a more logical explanation suggests that he was continuing to search for a wife and wanted to distribute the cards to male worshipers at the Killeen mosque for referrals. He frequently, and inappropriately, asked members of the Islamic Community Center with whom he was barely acquainted if they knew of a Muslim woman that he might marry.[30]

Just two weeks after Hasan moved to Killeen he purchased a Belgian-made semi-automatic FN Five-Seven high-velocity handgun from Frederick Brannon, a salesman at the local gun shop, Guns Galore. Brannon recalls Hasan's first visit to the store:

> His initial interest was in the most high-tech hand gun we had. I wasn't the salesman talking to him that day but the guy who did showed him the gun and gave him some information on it. Maj. Hasan left and came back the next day. He had researched the gun on the Internet. He wanted to buy *that one*, an FN Five-Seven. We showed him how to load it, how to operate it, take it apart for cleaning, and so on. He videotaped everything with his cell phone so that he could review it later. I've never seen anyone do that before but the impression that we had was that he was an Army major and that he wasn't into any kind of sports like [target shooting]. This was something new and he was interested in doing it all *right*. I don't want to use a term like egghead but when you have somebody who has absolutely no experience with something and decides to get into it, they're immediately over their head and they do things to try and catch up. That's what he did so we went along with it.[31]

Hasan also asked the clerk about hydrostatic shock, a controversial theory that suggests that the shockwave caused by a penetrating bullet causes collateral damage in the body that cannot be accounted for by the bullet alone.[32]

While Hasan was handling the FN Five-Seven pistol, a fellow soldier from Fort Hood, Spc. William Gilbert, approached him and gave his personal recommendation for the gun. He spent more than thirty minutes instructing Hasan on the proper handling of the pistol—"a full tactical demonstration."[33]

Originally intended for the military and law enforcement, the FN Five-Seven is a lightweight, low recoil, high velocity weapon. This particular handgun was featured in the August 2009 movie, *GI Joe: The Rise of Cobra*.[34] Two weeks after Hasan arrived at Fort Hood and one week prior to its public release, *GI Joe: The Rise of Cobra* was shown at a Fort Hood theater. Despite heated objections from gun control advocates, sales of the pistol to the public were approved in 2004. In early 2005 Brady Campaign staff purchased a FN Five-Seven and ammunition from a Virginia gun dealer and test fired it. It penetrated a Kevlar bullet-proof vest.[35] The FN Five-Seven is not an inexpensive weapon—it retails for one thousand dollars. Hasan didn't flinch at the price. Shortly before his shooting spree the armor-penetrating ammunition for that handgun was taken off of the public market. Gun shops were allowed, however, to sell their remaining stocks.[36]

FN Five-Seven Courtesy of *Bear Arms Gun Shop*, Boerne, Texas. Photo by John Porterfield

For Hasan, one of the attractive features of the FN Five-Seven was its expandable magazines that increased the factory-specified ten rounds to twenty or thirty rounds of ammunition. Frederick Brannon asked him why he needed so many twenty and thirty-round magazines and Hasan told him that he didn't like to waste time reloading at the range. He preferred to fill the extra magazines while watching television at home in the evenings. Hasan also purchased both red and green laser sights for $275 each, extra magazines, and lots of ammo at twenty-four dollars per box of fifty rounds. After Spc. Gilbert gave him the name of a handgun instructor, Hasan became a regular at Guns Galore and over the next two months spent a considerable amount of money on magazines and ammunition.[37]

Weapons expert Lindsey Bertomen believes that Hasan chose the ideal hand gun for committing a mass shooting in close quarters when he purchased the FN Five-Seven. Although it is not generally characterized as a "high power" pistol, it is a high velocity handgun. At about twenty-one ounces unloaded, it is light with not much recoil. It fires as rapidly as a small caliber rifle and can incapacitate a crowd very quickly. Its bullets are capable of exiting one target and entering another. Due to its low recoil, it is also more accurate than most other close-quarter hand guns. Because of its light weight, The FN Five-Seven is easy to conceal in a pocket or belt.[38]

Hasan purchased a membership at Stan's Shooting Range and practiced target shooting a couple of times a week with silhouette targets rather than the usual "bull's-eyes," aiming at heads and torsos and practicing rapid exchanges of magazines. John Choats, co-owner of the range, teaches a concealed handgun course and remembers that Hasan and five others attended a class on October 10, 2009. According to Choats, Hasan improved his accuracy and with his FN Five-Seven pistol was "consistently putting bullets in the chest and head of silhouette targets."[39]

Within a few weeks after arriving at Fort Hood, Hasan had established a routine. He left his apartment between five and six o'clock

Killeen Islamic Community Center
Photo by John Porterfield

every morning, prayed at the masjid, stopped at a neighborhood convenience store for coffee and hash browns to-go, and then reported for duty at Darnall Medical Center. One of the clerical workers in the Behavioral Health Department, Angela Gomez,* routinely arrived at the hospital at the same time as Hasan and usually rode the elevator with him to the fifth floor.

"He always wore a white Muslim cap," Gomez remembers. "He would take it off as soon as he walked into his office. I asked him about it once. He told me that he was Muslim and that the hat was a prayer cap."[40]

Gomez also recalls that that Ltc. Philips had a strong dislike of Hasan and frequently shouted at him.

> Phillips used to yell at Dr. Hasan a lot. Dr. Hasan asked me and two other clerical staff to be his personal witnesses. I remember one time that Dr. Hasan went to Phillips because he had counseled a patient who had killed a Muslim baby over in Iraq. He asked Phillips to assign someone else to the case because it was so upsetting. I knew what Hasan was talking about and I heard Phillips yelling at him. He shouted 'You've got a fucking job to do, now go do your fucking job.' Dr. Hasan came out of Phillips's office in tears. A little while later I went into Dr. Hasan's office to see how he was doing. He wasn't crying any more but he was still upset.[41]

Gomez also witnessed Hasan in tears on two other occasions.

A FEW MINUTES AFTER MIDNIGHT ON AUGUST 16, 2009, the manager of Casa Del Norte knocked on Hasan's door and informed him that one of his neighbors, John Van de Walker, had damaged his car with a sharp object. Hasan called the Killeen Police Department and an officer came out and filed a report. When asked why he had damaged Hasan's car, Van de Walker stated that when he got home from work he noticed an "Allah is love" bumper sticker on Hasan's Honda Civic and was offended. He became angry, ripped off the sticker, and scratched the car with one of his keys. Damage was assessed between $500 and $1,500.

On September 30, Hasan signed a notarized offense report stating that Van de Walker committed the vandalism. A week later, on October 8, 2009, Van de Walker was arrested and jailed for criminal mischief. Bail was set at $3,000. One of Hasan's neighbors asked him if he was angry with Van de Walker for scratching his car. Hasan responded that it was Ramadan and he had forgiven him.[42]

Gomez remembers that Hasan's car was also "keyed" in the Darnall Medical Center parking lot. "He suffered a lot of abuse," she remembered.[43]

A month after his dinner with Osman Danquah, Hasan reciprocated with an invitation to dine at the Golden Corral restaurant. Hasan once again broached the subject of the ethical dilemma of a "hypothetical" soldier killing fellow Muslims during wartime. Danquah answered Hasan's question with a question of his own. Would Hasan actually expect this same question to have a different answer now? Danquah came away from their dinner with the feeling that Hasan suffered severe emotional problems.[44]

Muslim prayer services were held on base as well as at the community center. Hasan approached the Fort Hood spiritual leader about becoming a lay preacher. In turn, the Fort Hood imam asked Osman Danquah his opinion about Hasan serving as a spiritual guide. Danquah responded with "No. There's something wrong with him."[45]

Although Hasan prayed at the Killeen mosque several times a day, he was painfully reserved and made few friends. Victor Benjamin, a member of the Killeen Community Center, talked to Hasan several times after services. He used an analogy of an abused dog who flinches when its master simply moves his hand to describe Hasan. "You can see it in the eyes," he said. "That was Hasan." Benjamin regarded Hasan as a "misfit" who could not find brotherhood or acceptance in the military so he looked for friendship and camaraderie in the mosque.[46]

By September 2009, Hasan finally found a friend in another member of the Killeen masjid, Duane Reasoner, an eighteen-year-old substitute school teacher and Muslim convert who had a strong Internet presence on jihadist web sites. Hasan often treated Reasoner to fish dinners at the Golden Corral restaurant in the evenings after attending services at the Islamic Community Center. Reasoner used the moniker "ooklepookle" on the Internet and characterized himself in an online profile as an extremist, fundamentalist Muslim.[47] Hasan assumed the role of mentor in his relationship with Reasoner.

While on duty at Darnall Medical Center on Sunday, October 17,

2009, Hasan attempted to treat a highly disturbed, psychotic patient. Contrary to Darnall's psychiatric protocols, he removed the soldier's restraints before determining his mental condition. According to one of the physicians who observed the incident, the patient began acting out and a code green[48] was called. The physician-onlooker read the patient's chart and noted that Hasan had not even performed a routine assessment. The physician-onlooker accused Hasan of improper handling of the patient and Hasan lost his temper. Several hospital staff members heard him threaten that if the military ever deployed him to a war zone he would do something to make them regret it.[49] One of the family practice physicians who also reported that Hasan made threatening remarks about deployment, Tonya Kosminski, said that he told her if he was ever deployed, "They will pay!"[50]

On several occasions while on hospital duty, Hasan chatted with an inpatient psychiatric nurse. The two of them were frequently on duty together on weekends and she commented that Hasan "hung out" at the hospital, as if "he had no other place to go."

"He would hang with us on the unit," she remembers, "and one day he noticed family photos on my screen saver. He asked if my husband was Arabic, given his coloration, but he is black. That got us talking about my family and he seemed interested." From that day forward the two enjoyed a positive working relationship.[51]

War is Hell

It is not possible to work in any behavioral health capacity at Fort Hood and not be affected by the horrors experienced by soldiers at war. Hasan was steeped in his patients' gruesome stories about killing Iraqi and Afghani soldiers, civilians, and even children. For years he had openly opposed the wars, had attempted to get out of the Army as a conscientious objector, and had vowed that he would never allow himself to be deployed. As tortured as he was, he became even more tormented when he listened to his patients' accounts of killing Muslims.

One of Hasan's patients who had been diagnosed with PTSD told him that he had been ordered to find and kill an Iraqi insurgent. The soldier found the insurgent's home and upon entering came face-to-face with his wife. He killed both the Iraqi soldier and his wife. These were not isolated incidents—there were others and Hasan communicated his concerns in writing. He felt strongly that these incidents were serious enough to be classified as war crimes.

Hasan contacted a senior staff psychiatrist and insisted that several of his patients be arrested and tried for crimes against humanity. When that psychiatrist told him that it was not possible to arrest post-deployment soldiers suffering from PTSD for war crimes, Hasan approached another senior staffer and his supervisor, Capt. Naomi Surman, in an attempt to gain their support for filing such charges.[52]

On October 23, 2009, less than two weeks before the shooting, Hasan sent Ben Phillips an email outlining his concerns about "atrocities" committed by soldiers deployed to Iraq and Afghanistan.

From: Hasan, Nidal M Maj MIL USA MEDCOM WRAMC

Sent: Friday, October 23, 2009 11:31 AM

To: Phillips, Ben K LTC MIL USA MEDCOM WRAMC

Cc: Manuele, Gary M Mr CIV USA MEDCOM CRDAMC; Anthony Febbo; Robert J Dr CTR USA MEDCOM CRDAMC; Surman, Naomi E CPT MIL USA MEDCOM WRAMC; Shehan, John B. MAJ MIL USA MEDCOM CRDAMC; Staton, Robert S Dr CTR USA MEDCOM CRDAMC

Subject: Acquiring adverse information-What to do?

Good morning fellow colleagues,

I had an issue that came up and I thought the answer to my question would be helpful to all of us writing MEB's.

During a number of encounters I have come across situations where the soldier expresses guilt/anger about events that can be quite disturbing. I happened to be at Mr. Manuele's (legal consultant) office with Dr. Shehan for another case. Since I was there I asked him about one of our soldiers complaining/having guilt about our troops pouring 50 gallon [sic] of fuel in the Iraqi water supply as revenge for some adverse events that occurred. He stated that was a war crime and if I gave that information to him he would have to report it. He subsequently gave me numbers to contact to pursue this. I called the DSJA (LTC Febba) who couldn't give me an answer at that particular time. However, his eventual response will be beneficial to all of us writing MEB's or encountering similar situations.

V/R,

Nidal Hasan, MD, MPH MAJ, MC. USA

Hospital and Administrative Psychiatry

Carl R. Darnall Army Medical Center

"All praises and thanks go to Allah, The Cherisher and Sustainer of all the worlds"

Qur'an, Chapter 1, verse 2[53]

On November 2, 2009, three days before the shooting, Hasan sent Phillips another email.

From: Hasan, Nidal M Maj MIL USA MEDCOM WRAMC

Sent: Mon 11/2/2009 10:18 AM

To: Hasan, Nidal M Maj MIL USA MEDCOM WRAMC; Phillips, Ben K LTC MIL USA CRDAMC

Cc: Manuele, Gary M Mr CIV USA MEDCOM CRDAMC; Febbo, Anthony LTC MIL USA; Surman, Naomi E CPT MIL USA MEDCOM WRAMC; Shehan, John B. MAJ MIL USA MEDCOM CRDAMC;

Subject: RE: Acquiring adverse information-What to do?

Sir, thanks for talking with me and communicating to me how to proceed. I have attached the name of the soldier and his unit with a description as requested. I am also attaching Dr. Phillips (Chief of the dept), Dr. Shehan (inpatient chief), and Dr. Surman who are in positions [of] authority/responsibility and can help while I'm deployed. I will also try to get a hold of the soldiers to let them know ahead of time as you requested [redacted name of soldier]. He describes our troops pouring 50 gallons of fuel in the Iraqi water supply as revenge. To continue, I'm still not clear on the exact guidelines of when and what to report. Mr. Manuele your legal expertise will be helpful for reassurance. I think I need a lot of reassurance for the first few times I come across these. I believe my colleagues feel the same. So, I have also attached 2 other cases for your review.

2. [redacted name of soldier]. He describes calling in an air evac for an injured insurgent where our medics than [*sic*] proceeded to kill the insurgent—I would like to think it was some type of mercy killing because of the severity of insurgents [*sic*] injuries.

3. [redacted name of soldier]. He describes intentionally killing a woman because she was at the wrong place at the wrong time—he reports he was ordered to kill anything that approached the specific site to include dogs, etc.

V/R,

Nidal Hasan, MD, MPH

MAJ, MC. USA

Hospital and Administrative Psychiatry

Carl R. Darnall Army Medical Center

"All praises and thanks go to Allah, The Cherisher and Sustainer of all the worlds"

Qur'an, Chapter 1, verse 2[54]

ARMY RESERVE UNITS HAVE PLAYED AN IMPORTANT ROLE in the Iraq and Afghanistan wars and they rotate in and out of Fort Hood with regularity. The Wisconsin-based 467th Medical Detachment's combat stress control reserve unit, a small specialized cadre comprised of mental health professionals who serve on the front lines and treat traumatized soldiers on the battlefield, was scheduled for deployment in early December 2009. They would be arriving at Fort Hood on November 4 for pre-deployment training and processing. It is customary for active duty soldiers to fill vacancies in the reserve units and, according to two clerical workers in the department, Ltc. John Shehan, a staff psychiatrist, was given orders to deploy to Afghanistan with the 467th Medical Detachment. Shehan called his friend, colleague, and Georgetown neighbor, Ben Phillips, and asked if Phillips could pull some strings and find someone else to fill his slot. Phillips was happy to oblige—he could substitute Hasan for Shehan—and get rid of a psychiatrist that he despised while at the same time doing a favor for a friend.[55]

One day in mid-October while Hasan was counseling a soldier, Phillips burst into his office and handed him a piece of paper. He loudly informed Hasan, in front of his patient, that he would be shipping out to Afghanistan in early December with the 467th Medical Detachment's combat stress control reserve unit. To Philips, it was just an insignificant piece of paper. To Hasan, Phillips dealt him a death warrant. Angela Gomez was a witness to the confrontation.

"He blew up at Hasan," she says. "He was yelling at him 'what's right is right and what's fair is fair'." Hasan was aghast and excused his patient. As a clerical worker, Gomez routinely handled military orders as they filtered into the department. She was the first to find out about Hasan's deployment to Afghanistan.

Later that day a co-worker observed Hasan crying as he worked at a computer at Ltc. John Shehan's desk. She asked him if he was all right and he told her that Phillips had yelled at him.[56]

In an instant Hasan's worst nightmare had become a reality and his world disintegrated. For him the war in Afghanistan metamorphosed from an ideological brawl to a deadly reality game where life is cheap and survival isn't always reserved for the fittest.

"I was shocked," Hasan later told the Sanity Board that examined him after the shooting. "I wasn't expecting [to deploy] this soon." His commanders had led him to believe that he would not deploy for one to two years. He quickly came to the conclusion that getting his deployment orders was a "task from God to speed up his actions." His "Oath to God" was overriding his "Oath to America."[57]

Hasan would be allowed take a week's vacation leave and visit his relatives in Virginia followed by a month of training and pre-deployment processing at Fort Benning, Georgia. He did not tell his colleagues and co-workers about his new assignment. He did inform Edgar Booker, a retired soldier who worked in one of the cafeterias. Booker said he asked Hasan how he felt about going over there "with their religion and everything," and Hasan told him, "It's going to be interesting."[58]

In the meantime, Phillips was tasked with writing an Officer Evaluation Report (OER) prior to Hasan's deployment. On November 3, 2009, he completed a glowing evaluation of Hasan's performance.

In addition to giving Hasan the highest ratings for possessing honor, integrity, courage, loyalty, respect, selfless service, and duty, Phillips wrote, in part.

> MAJ Hasan performed all duties as a staff psychiatrist at Carl R. Darnall Army Medical Center in a superb manner. In the four months since his arrival, MAJ Hasan's strong work ethic, professionalism, sound judgment and willingness to take on various responsibilities and tasks have been critical in the overall delivery of behavioral health care at the largest behavioral health department in the U.S. Army.... MAJ Hasan repeatedly demonstrated his willingness to be a team player by taking on significant additional duties....MAJ Hasan is an outstanding physician who has the potential to excel within the AMEDD. He should be selected for positions of increasing responsibility. Promote now.[59]

Phillips' comments on Hasan's performance potential were even more effusive.

> MAJ Hasan has been a significant addition to the psychiatric staff. He has taken on the mission of MEB and additional patient care. He has enthusiastically jumped into his role as provider and administrative physician. He is learning his new administrative duties and will be a significant contributor in the future. He has unlimited potential for advancement and leadership and should be groomed for those roles. Promote now and select for Intermediate Level Education in residence.[60]

A notation followed: "Soldier is unavailable for signature." Hasan was on pre-deployment leave.

Phillips had made it known from the day that Hasan arrived at Fort Hood from Walter Reed that he didn't like him and he considered his job performance to be marginal, at best. But he had to make sure that Hasan's new commander in Afghanistan would accept him with open arms—that was the only way that he could get rid of him, so writing a very favorable performance evaluation was necessary.

Other psychiatrists in the department felt that Phillips dealt a very heavy hand when it came to their performance evaluations.[61] He used his position of power to control their destinies. Merit was not a consideration. Later, at trial, Phillips admitted that any other rating would have been a "career killer" for Hasan.[62]

5. Rage Against the Machine

I will do such things,
What they are, yet I know not: but they shall be
The terrors of the earth.
~King Lear, Act II, Scene IV

Nidal Hasan may not have been successful in finding a wife but he certainly demonstrated his appreciation of the female form when he visited the Killeen strip club, Starz, on the evenings of Thursday, October 29 and Friday, October 30. He had visited Starz before and he knew that he would not be able to buy alcoholic beverages there. He stopped at a convenience store on his way and bought a couple of six packs of Bud Lite—not for himself, but for the ten dancers who curled their bodies around floor-to-ceiling poles and performed nude. He also stopped at his bank and got a wad of five dollar bills. Hasan preferred to go to Starz because the people with whom he worked did not frequent this particular club.[1]

Starz is a non-descript, shabby strip joint located just down the street from the main gate at Fort Hood and next door to Guns Galore. It's smaller and noisier than most of the other clubs that dot the area around Fort Hood. Hasan pulled into the Starz parking lot at half past six, just thirty minutes after it opened, and handed manager Matthew Jones the fifteen dollar cover. He bought a bucket of ice to keep the beer cold and settled down alone at a rear table. As each girl finished her dance Hasan politely got up and walked to the stage, tipped her five dollars and handed her a beer. He took quite a liking to a blonde stripper named Paige. He asked her for a three-song nude lap dance in a private room and paid the fifty dollar charge without hesitation. He purchased a total of three lap dances during his two visits, two from Paige and one from another stripper.[2]

According to Paige, Hasan preferred blondes. "He wasn't too loud like some of our other customers, or sleazy. He didn't try to take us home and he was respectful." Hasan told Paige that he was a medic and would be deploying soon. He asked the performers a lot of questions.

"He asked us why we were working at the strip club, if we liked the lifestyle, if we had kids. It was right before Halloween so he asked what our kids were dressing up as," says Paige.[3]

On Friday, October 30, Hasan wrote to his brother Anas who lived in Palestine at the time.

> Anas, I'm not sure if Eyad told you but I am leaving for Afghanistan next month. I will be leaving sometime next week to visit Eyad and his family in Virginia and then head towards Georgia for some final training before flying out. In any case, I have transferred 21,000 dollars that I owe you into the business account. We are now even—of course you take the 4,000 that you have of mine also for a total of 25,000. Please take it out ASAP, I don't like things floating and if you lose it for any reason it's your fault.
>
> I have filled out a power of attorney so that you may handle my affairs in case I need something done during the 6 months I'm in Afghanistan or if I die, etc—I'm not sure if it will work for everything but I will give a copy to Eyad to hold when I visit him. In the event that I am incapacitated or not able to use my money/property i.e. captured by the enemy—please donate my money/property to the poor as soon as possible— use your judgment but you know I'm trying to maximize my

rewards. If I happen to die, obviously split it according to the Islamic inheritance law and give the maximum allowable amount to a charity/sadaqa jariah etc—I think its 1/3 of my wealth. I am not aware of any psychiatrists that have died in Iraq/Afghanistan by enemy fire however it's always good to be prepared.[4]

On Sunday, November 1, 2009, Hasan received an email from Anas with the subject "Cair: Houston Texas office." The body of the email contained only a link to the CAIR web site that contained a form to report a hate crime.[5] Perhaps Hasan wanted to report Jon Van de Walker's vandalism of his car and asked Anas, an attorney, to assist him.

Hasan's official pre-deployment leave began on Monday, November 2, 2009. He did not travel to Virginia to visit relatives as he had told his co-workers, but remained in Killeen. He contacted a superior officer, Col. Anthony Febbo, twice that day about his desire to file war crimes charges against some of his patients.[6]

On Tuesday, November 3, after worshiping at the Community Center of Greater Killeen, Hasan stopped at a neighborhood 7-11 convenience store for his customary coffee and hash brown potatoes. The store's surveillance camera recorded him wearing hospital scrubs, his corpulent form a focal point in each frame.[7] Because the Middle Eastern store owner did not speak fluent English, Hasan often attempted conversation with him in his clumsy Arabic. The proprietor had grown tired of Hasan's whining about not having a wife, his admonitions about attending Friday prayers, and most recently his confession that he did not want to go to Afghanistan. "Muslims should not kill Muslims," Hasan told him. The owner of the convenience store began evading him whenever possible.[8]

Later that morning, on the way to Stan's Shooting Range, Hasan stopped at Radio Shack and bought extra batteries for his pistol's laser sights. At the range he purchased ten targets and fired more than two hundred rounds at human torso silhouettes.[9] He also closed out his Bank of America safe deposit box and told a bank employee "You'll never see me again."[10]

That evening, after prayers at the community center, Hasan treated his young friend, Duane Reasoner, to a fish dinner at the Golden Corral Restaurant. They dined in a rear booth and after discussing religion Hasan confided to Reasoner that he didn't want to go to Afghanistan. He counseled Reasoner not to ever join the military because "obviously Muslims shouldn't kill Muslims."[11] After dinner, the two men stopped briefly at Hasan's apartment and were seen leaving a few minutes later. Manager Alice Thompson commented that she had never observed a visitor entering Hasan's apartment prior to the evening of November 3. Reasoner was a memorable figure—tall, dark complexioned, moustached and bearded, and wearing Islamic prayer clothing.[12]

Wednesday, November 4, was a busy day. Early that morning Hasan's neighbors observed him throwing large garbage bags of trash into the apartment complex's dumpsters. He chatted with a few of the Casa Del Norte residents and told them that he was shipping out to Afghanistan the next morning. Wednesday afternoon he knocked on Patricia Villa's door and handed her two bags of frozen vegetables and a box of frozen veggie burgers. He peered inside her apartment and noticed that she had very little furniture. A few minutes later he brought her a clothes steamer, men's clothing for her husband (tee shirts, a jacket encased in dry cleaner's plastic, and several other items), and a Spanish-language Qur'an. When Villa told him that she did not speak Spanish, he immediately replaced it with an English version. Hasan also gave another neighbor, a devout Christian, a Qur'an and urged her to read it. "In my religion," he told her, "we'll do anything to be closer to God."[13]

Hasan worked late into the night shredding papers, including his medical school diploma, and boxing up his belongings. At 2:37 a.m., he called his next-door neighbor, Willie Bell, to ask him to turn on his Internet Wi-Fi connection. Bell did not answer his phone.[14]

He called Bell again at 5:30 a.m. and left a message. "Nice knowing you, friend. I wish you'd plug in your Internet system so I could get online. Goodbye, good buddy, I'll be moving."[15]

The next morning, Thursday, November 5, 2009, Hasan, dressed in Islamic prayer clothes, dumped several more bags of trash in a Casa Del Norte dumpster and drove to the masjid for morning prayers. When Pat Sonti, one of the congregants, picked up the microphone to call for morning prayers, Hasan abruptly grabbed the mike from him and uncharacteristically took control. At the end of the service he bid the audience farewell and told them that he was going home.[16]

On the way back to his apartment Hasan stopped at the neighborhood 7-11 for coffee and hash browns. The proprietor saw Hasan pull into the parking lot and slipped into the back room of the store to avoid him. The 7-11 surveillance cameras recorded a relaxed and smiling Hasan who looked as though he hadn't a care in the world, dressed in a white flowing robe, white trousers, and a prayer cap. On his way out of the store Hasan remarked to another customer that "something big" was going to happen at Fort Hood at one-thirty that afternoon. "Be prepared," he warned him.[17]

Hasan drove back to his apartment, changed into his Army combat uniform (ACU) and threw out several more plastic bags full of trash. He knocked on Patricia Villa's door.

"Hi. How're you doing?" she asked him.

"I'm blessed," he told her.[18]

Hasan gave Villa his air mattress and handed her sixty dollars in cash and asked her to clean his apartment. He told her that he didn't want to make the manager angry by leaving it dirty.[19]

Villa offered Hasan some homemade tamales. At first he declined, commenting that he did not eat meat. When she explained to him that they were sweet tamales made from pineapple, he helped himself to two of the treats. That was the last time Villa saw her neighbor.[20]

Hasan didn't look back when he pulled out of the Casa Del Norte parking lot between 9:30 and 10:00 that morning. He drove straight to Darnall Medical Center, rode the elevator up to the fifth floor and walked directly to Ltc. Ben Phillips' office, ostensibly to pick up his pre-deployment performance rating. Phillips was not there and after a few minutes of pacing outside of his office, Hasan approached one of the clerical staff and asked her to check Phillips' schedule. He peered over her shoulder while she pulled up Phillips' calendar on her computer. He was on leave and was not scheduled to return to Fort Hood until the following week.[21]

Hasan took the elevator down to the Credentialing Office in the basement where he ran into a fellow psychiatrist. They exchanged pleasantries and talked for a few minutes. When his co-worker asked him what he was doing in the basement, Hasan told him that he was checking the status of his transfer brief on one of the basement computers.[22]

The Department of Defense (DoD) maintains a sophisticated electronic privileging system for tracking and verifying health care providers' credentials; for monitoring quality of patient care (quality assurance); and for evaluating and assessing the risk of patient morbidity and/or mortality. Whenever a physician or other health care provider is assigned to a temporary duty station or is deployed to a medical facility or unit overseas, that physician must first have his credentials evaluated, checked, and accepted by the receiving facility through an inter-facility transfer. At the same time, the transferring facility must certify that the physician (in this case Hasan) is both mentally and physically fit and is capable of adequately performing the duties required by the new assignment. The resulting file is called a transfer brief. Hasan's performance evaluation was an important document in the file.[23]

After spending a few minutes in the hospital's basement, Hasan rode the elevator back up to the fifth floor where he, again, approached a member of the clerical staff and asked her if she was certain that

Fort Hood Behavioral Health Department
Fifth Floor, Carl R. Darnall Hospital

Elevators	
Office	Employee Break Room	Nidal Hasan's Office
Office	Secretarial and Administrative Support	Office
Office		Office
	Reception Area	
Office		Waiting Area
Col. Philip's Office	Physician Charting	Office
Office		Office
Office	Physician Charting	Office
Office		Waiting Area
Conference Rooms		

Illustration based upon descriptions from various employees

Phillips would not be on base that day. She assured him that Phillips would not be back in his office until the following week.[24]

Frustrated, Hasan called Phillips on his cell phone and left a voice mail asking him to return the call. He sat at his desk and read an on-line "jihadist" article that quoted a Taliban leader urging his mujahideen followers to be brave and not show cowardice.[25] He waited around until Phillips called back. Hasan bluntly asked Phillips to give him his physical location. Phillips told him that he was on vacation in Arizona. Hasan asked him about his performance evaluation which was due that day. Phillips told him that it was his "best ever" and not to worry about it.

Hasan's demeanor underwent a radical alteration during his conversation with Phillips. His usual acquiescent, passive affect and shuffling gait were transformed to a demeanor of petulance, annoyance, and agitation. According to the clerical workers who witnessed the conversation between Hasan and Phillips, Hasan didn't seem to fully comprehend at first that Phillips was not on base. He stormed down the hall toward the department's kitchenette, glared at the occupants, then strode angrily back to Philips' office before leaving the building shortly before noon.[26]

Hasan drove back to the mosque for noon prayers and returned to his office at Fort Hood where he put his .357 handgun in the right front pocket of his ACU blouse and stuck his FN Five-Seven pistol in the waistband of his pants. He wrapped twenty or thirty loaded magazines in paper towels to muffle any noise they might make clinking together and stashed them in his left ACU blouse pocket. He quickly drove to the SRP Center and parked in the parking lot. He inserted earplugs in each ear and when he got out of his car, held his cell phone to his ear and pretended to carry on a conversation while he walked up the sidewalk to the building. He didn't want to be interrupted by anyone. Hasan was in warrior mode and he needed to concentrate on his plan. He was on a mission of great importance.[27]

Hasan failed to notice a man with a video camera, Steven Bennett, who was standing on the steps of the Howze Theater just a few yards away. He was setting up to record the graduation that was due to begin in a few minutes. He pointed his camera in Hasan's direction and recorded him at 1:15 p.m. "casing" the TBI, rehabilitation, and the automated neuropsychological assessment metrics (ANAM) build-ings. Hasan then walked calmly into the SRP Center and sat down in a folding chair at the back of the room for about five minutes before approaching Latoya Williams at the check-in desk. He told her that Maj. Parrish had an emergency and needed to see her. After she got up and started walking toward Maj. Parrish's office, he walked behind the desk, shouted "Allahu Akbar" and opened fire.[28]

First responders use a table as a stretcher to transport a wounded soldier to an awaiting ambulance at Fort Hood on Nov. 5, 2009. Photo by Sgt. Jason R. Krawczyk, III Corp, courtesy of the U.S. Army.

6. A Kick in the Gut

Show me a hero and I will write you a tragedy.
~F. Scott Fitzgerald

Soldiers responded to the shooting as they had been trained to do in a combat zone—they jumped inside the line of fire and risked their own lives so that they could rescue their battle buddies felled by Nidal Hasan's bullets. They dragged and carried the wounded to sheltered areas and ripped their own clothing into makeshift tourniquets, bandages, and slings. They performed CPR and comforted the victims. Several of the rescuers were wounded or killed attempting to save the lives of their fellow soldiers. When the bullets stopped, they loaded up the injured survivors in their own cars and trucks and drove them the two miles to Carl R. Darnall Medical Center. One soldier grabbed a wounded friend, threw him over his shoulders in a fireman's carry, and ran almost two miles to the hospital, never once slowing down.[1]

Pfc. Jeffrey Pearsall was sitting in his truck in the SRP Center parking lot waiting for his buddy, Marquest Smith, who had gone in for a quick allergy shot. Smith was filling out paperwork for his injection when he heard a yell followed by the unmistakable sound of gunfire. He grabbed the clerk who was helping him and pushed her under a desk. When there was a lull in the barrage, Smith cautiously emerged

Detectives assigned to the Fort Hood Directorate of Emergency Sevices respond Nov. 5, 2009, to Nidal Hasan shooting rampage in the post's deployment readiness center. Photo by Andrew Evans, courtesy of the U.S. Army.

from the cubicle. He saw a sea of bodies—he estimates twenty to thirty—and tables and chairs strewn around the room. He quickly surveyed the wounded and dead soldiers and began pulling the injured out of the building. Several medics whose graduation was interrupted at the Howze Theater next door rushed into the center and began treating the wounded. Smith suddenly realized that the shooter was still inside the building and had spotted him. "He turned towards me and started shooting. I had my back turned towards him and I ran to the door. I could hear bullets going past me," Smith says. He later found a bullet lodged in the heel of his right combat boot.[2]

When Smith's buddy, Jeffrey Pearsall, saw wounded soldiers spilling out of the Center he pulled his truck in as close to the entrance as possible, jumped out and started loading wounded soldiers in the bed.[3]

Nurse Shemaka L. Hairston was in the middle of administering a vaccination to a soldier at Station Twelve when she heard a loud yell that sounded to her like "Allah."

"Then I heard what sounded like firecrackers," Hairston says. "I tried to peer over the partition but it was too high and I couldn't see anything...I saw a lot of smoke and, the smell, it smelled like ammunition...it smelled like you were at a shooting range."[4]

Hairston grabbed her phone and dove under a desk. Two other soldiers squeezed in with her. She dialed 9-1-1.

"What's your emergency?" the call center dispatcher asked.

"Shooting at Fort Hood site," Hairston sobbed into her phone.[5]

Hairston stayed on the line while the dispatcher called Fort Hood's Directorate of Emergency Services (DES). The county's emergency call center was not allowed to dispatch Fort Hood public safety personnel directly. Operators were required to contact DES which, in turn, dispatches its own police, fire, and ambulance services.

"Is he still there? Ma'am, get down low, ma'am. Just stay on the ground. "Is he still there? Ma'am...get down, stay down. Is the shooter still there?"[6]

"I don't know...there are two people down. A soldier just started shooting. We don't know who he is. Some guy with a weapon just started randomly shooting."[7]

The DES dispatcher radioed patrol officers.

The gunfire was closing in on Hairston and the two soldiers with her under the desk. The shooter was so close that she could hear his footsteps. Hairston stayed put until the shooting stopped. The two soldiers with her under the desk were killed.[8]

Registered Nurse Kimberly Huseman was in her office in the SRP Center taking care of routine emails when she heard a cry and "pop pop pop." A sergeant burst through Huseman's office door, slammed it closed, and stood with her back against the door as Huseman dialed 9-1-1.

"We're getting help on the way," the dispatcher told her.

"Oh my God, people are shot, oh God," Huseman sobbed.

"We're inside the building...oh my God, there are about fifteen down, probably more than that...oh my God," Huseman screamed. "I don't know who he is. He's wearing ACU's."[9]

The 9-1-1 operator heard commotion in the background and shouts of "He's down, the shooter's down."[10]

Still on the phone Huseman cautiously opened her office door and walked out into the hallway. "You have at least ten more who are injured," Huseman told the operator.[11]

Records show that Huseman was on the line with the Bell County Communications Center for eight minutes.[12]

Hairston and Huseman were not the only persons to call 9-1-1. For the first time in its history there were so many incoming calls that the communications center couldn't handle the traffic and, instead of a dispatcher, callers got a "busy" signal.

Spec. Elliot Valdez, a Fort Hood photographer, was setting up his equipment inside the Howze Theater when he heard screaming from outside the building. He grabbed a camcorder and ran across the parking lot to the SRP area.

"They already had people out in the grass and the field—working on people. A lot of people had their ACU tops off, using them as bandages, wraps—trying to stabilize people....It was pretty noisy—a lot of people running...from inside running to the parking lot."[13]

When Staff Sgt. Zackary Filip pulled into the SRP Center parking lot and got out of his truck, he heard gunshots. He ran toward the noise and saw Hasan shooting at a female police officer. He was behind her and realized that bullets were flying in his direction. A combat medic, Filip knew what blood smelled like. When Munley hit the ground, Filip saw blood spurting from her leg. He recognized that a bullet had penetrated an artery and he ripped off his belt and pulled it tight against her wound. He was in "medic mode" and treated at least twenty injured soldiers.[14]

Next door in the TBI building Dana Hoeff,* a therapist who had stayed behind after most of her staff sprinted to safety, attempted to reach 9-1-1 several times on a land line and got "busy" signals. She called the hospital switchboard and, again, the lines were "busy." She tried her cell phone, but could not reach either the Bell County Communications Center or the hospital. Believing that the telephone lines were either jammed or cut, Hoeff called the Resilience and Restoration (R&R) Center next door to the hospital and a clerk answered the phone. Relieved, Hoeff hastily told her that there was a shooting in progress at the SRP complex and that it wasn't a drill. She told the clerk to "run with your feet—don't call" the hospital and apprise the emergency department OIC of the shooting. Instead of notifying the ER of the mass casualty (MASCAL), the R&R staff locked down their building. When the first seriously injured casualties arrived at the Darnall emergency room, the staff members weren't prepared for them. They were outside smoking cigarettes and telling jokes.[15]

Ten minutes after the rampage began, base commanders announced that an act of terrorism was in progress on Fort Hood and a Force Protection Condition (FPC) Delta, the most serious FPC, was declared.[16] Security personnel directed the closure of all gates and "Big Voice," Fort Hood's post-2001 loud speaker system, wailed for a full minute before instructing all persons on base to take cover, lock their doors, and to close and stay away from windows. Automated emails flashed pre-recorded messages on every computer monitor on the base and at the same time carefully scripted robo-calls were automatically placed to every telephone on Fort Hood stating that a "Code Gray" mass casualty event was in progress. A blackout rendered landlines and cell phones silent. All base daycare centers and schools were immediately locked down and frightened parents were unable to contact their children.[17]

Tammy Biggers lived only a mile from the shooting and was outside playing with her dog when the "Big Voice" ordered her to go inside her house and lock her doors. Biggers tried to reach her daughter, a tenth-grader at one of the high schools on base, but couldn't get through.[18]

"It's just nerve-wracking," says Biggers. "They did the overhead warnings for everyone to seek shelter immediately."[19]

Pam Stephenson, who lived in base housing with her husband and young children, was leaving for the grocery store when the "Big Voice" ordered her to find shelter. She flipped on the television and was distressed to find out that one or more shooters had opened fire on base.[20]

"When you hear it's soldiers gone crazy, you don't know what kind of ammunition or guns they have," she told CNN.[21]

Stephenson's first impulse was to pick up her young child from day care but she knew that with the base on lockdown she wouldn't be able to leave her house. It wasn't until later that night that she was able to bring her toddler home.[22]

When he picked up a transmission about a shooting on base, Special Agent Duane Lloyd Mitchell, chief of Fort Hood's Criminal Investigative Division, ran to the SRP complex and darted through the spaces between the buildings. He spotted the gunman lying on the ground. Major Steven Richter was administering first aid and Mitchell ran over to them and grabbed the discarded FN Five-Seven pistol. He emptied the shooter's uniform pockets and found a second handgun and one hundred seventy-seven unexpended rounds of ammunition contained in twenty-round extended magazines. He and Special Agent Kelly Jameson, chief investigator, recovered one-hundred-forty spent shell casings for a FN Five-Seven handgun from inside the SRP Center and seventy-six on the surrounding grounds, including the TBI buildings. Hasan had carried four-hundred-twenty rounds of ammunition with him inside the SRP Center.[23]

On the other end of Fort Hood the Third Calvary Unit was quickly mobilized and personnel were instructed to search for one of the shooters who had escaped capture—a slender, blonde, Caucasian man wearing a bloody tee shirt and jeans. Gate security guards were given the suspected second shooter's description and were instructed to search the cars of anyone attempting to leave the base.[24]

The Golden Hour

Chief Dalton Cross is proud of the Bell County Communications Center (BCCC), and rightfully so. As Director of the countywide emergency call agency, Cross was instrumental in the conception-to-completion process of making the dream of a few county visionaries come to fruition. The BCCC was the first emergency communications center in the United States charged with dispatching all county emergency services and public safety units from one single location.[25] The 12,000 square foot steel and concrete structure opened its doors in 1999. Built to withstand tornados and terrorist attacks, the BCCC serves thirty-one law enforcement agencies, twenty-two volunteer and paid Fire Department/EMS agencies, and dispatches calls for rural law enforcement agencies as well as schools and colleges. The center handles over 200,000 calls each year.[26] The BCCC utilizes technologically advanced location identification equipment which qualifies it as an enhanced system. Many county and city dispatch centers continue to utilize basic 9-1-1 services where only the caller's name and telephone number are displayed. In an enhanced system such as Bell County's, additional information such as physical address, cross streets, other phone numbers and types of telephones associated with the caller's name, and in some systems even pertinent medical information is provided to the dispatcher on a computer monitor. Cell phone location information is now available in most enhanced 9-1-1 systems.

First responders prepare the wounded for transport in waiting ambulances near Fort Hood's Soldier Readiness Processing Center Nov. 5., 2009. Photo by Jeramie Sivley, courtesy of the U.S. Army.

Centralized communications like the Bell County center are the backbone of emergency services systems. With its origins in military field medicine, Emergency Medical Services (EMS) came into its own in the late 1970's when Dr. David Boyd pioneered the first trauma systems in Illinois at Cook County Hospital and at the University of Maryland's Shock/Trauma unit. Recognized as the father of EMS, Boyd conceptualized a rapid, systematic, coordinated approach to emergency medical care. He adopted R. Adams Cowley's concept of the golden hour, a small window of time available for achieving successful patient outcomes in critical medical situations, as a pre-hospital care model and travelled around the country preaching the gospel of efficacious trauma care. Boyd advanced the idea that patient stabilization at the scene prior to transport to high-quality definitive medical/trauma care would improve patient outcomes. He was appointed by President Gerald R. Ford as the first National Director of Emergency Medical Services Systems. Along with innovators such as Tulane University trauma surgeon Dr. Norman McSwain in Louisiana and James O. Page in North Carolina and California, Boyd advocated the training of ambulance attendants as emergency medical technicians and promoted the designation of hospital trauma centers.[27]

"Trauma care is an amazingly complex and demanding field," Boyd explains. "Every case is different. People get shot differently, they are critically injured, you have to think fast and have a rapid, accurate response to their situation."[28]

By the early 1980's the establishment of EMS systems had become a contentious issue in many communities in the United States and turf wars among health providers almost brought this innovative, new industry to a halt. Even the installation of 9-1-1 communications systems, which everyone in this country now uniformly take for granted, became a political hot potato. Thirty years ago, if one had an emergency, the options were to dial "O" and speak to a telephone operator who would either transfer the call to a police station or provide the telephone number for law enforcement. Generally, police would respond by sending out a patrol officer who would then radio for an ambulance if there was a medical emergency. Ambulance services were often operated by funeral homes.

With local support, "scoop and run" ambulance services gradually gave way to highly trained emergency medical technicians, 9-1-1 emergency call centers took the place of telephone operator assistance, and hospital emergency rooms transitioned into fully equipped and professionally staffed trauma centers. Regional quasi-governmental EMS councils flourished under the auspices of state emergency management offices and received federal grant money to dole out to local ambulance providers and first responders for EMT training and for the purchase of medical and communications equipment.

By the late 1980's federal EMS funds dried up and many state emergency medical services offices were either downgraded to departmental level sections or eliminated altogether. In 1989, the State of Texas, however, passed the Omnibus Rural Health Care Rescue Act which provided funding and administrative support for the continued development and perpetuation of coordinated regional EMS systems. Funding has been allocated every year since.[29] Most states, including Texas, utilize the American College of Surgeons criteria for verification of trauma centers, with Level I facilities providing the highest level of care, to Level V hospitals that offer minimal care.[30]

Today, the emergency medical services community is a fully functioning, vital member of the modern health care team. In addition to paid personnel, a cadre of dedicated volunteers in many parts of the state, especially in rural areas, wholeheartedly support the tenets of EMS and adhere to national training and equipment standards. It is because of this high level of commitment and perseverance of these volunteer firefighters and paramedics that EMS systems have achieved the kind of success that Dr. David Boyd envisioned more than forty years ago.

ON NOVEMBER 5, 2009, BELL COUNTY, TEXAS, WAS FORTUNATE to have a state-of-the-art 9-1-1 communications center. Within seconds after Nidal Hasan opened fire the BCCC was flooded with calls. It logged in sixty-three contacts in just eleven minutes. The BCCC was able to activate the regional EMS system within seconds by dispatching law enforcement, ambulances, and fire personnel simultaneously.[31]

"It was hectic," says Dalton Cross, director of the multifaceted call center. "Our people handled it very well. Several of our dispatchers are military wives and, at that time, there were two or three dispatchers who had family on Fort Hood. The initial call was a lady who was right there involved in the shooting and she [told] us what was going on at the scene at the time."[32]

Bell County not only has a state-of-the-art communications system, Scott & White Medical Center in nearby Temple, Texas, is a world-class trauma center. Just twenty-five miles north of Fort Hood, Scott & White was also able to immediately mobilize its emergency medical resources. The only Level I trauma center between Austin and

Dallas, Scott & White dispatched ambulances equipped with trauma teams and cutting-edge equipment while a specialized line-up of emergency physicians, trauma surgeons, and critical care staff readied the emergency room bays, operating rooms, and critical care units. Wary that Scott & White might be a secondary target in a full-fledged terrorist attack, hospital administrators decided to close their facility to the public. In anticipation of mass casualties, the hospital called upon the community for blood donations. Over 1,000 prospective blood donors responded and stood in line for hours. The hospital roped off an entrance specifically for the blood donors and checked their identification outside before they were allowed to enter the facility.[33]

Medical Control

Written triage and treatment protocols are step-by-step instructions utilized by pre-hospital care personnel to ensure uniformity and continuity of care in the field setting. But it is not always possible to fit patients into a rigid category and use a "recipe" to provide medical care. In many cases EMT's and paramedics need to talk to a physician or trauma nurse to determine appropriate treatment. As a Level I trauma center, Scott & White is required to have available in-house physicians who are knowledgeable in emergency medicine and trauma care. These specialists must be available twenty four hours per day to personally direct paramedics in the field. Generally, medical control is provided by the Level I trauma center to all providers of emergency medical services in the regional EMS system. Not only does the medical control physician direct field care, he or she determines the hospital to which the patient will be transported based upon the seriousness of the patient's condition and the capabilities of the facility. Most upper-tiered hospitals monitor public safety on dedicated radio channels. Scott & White is no exception and their first clue about the Fort Hood shooting was picked up on their scanner.

Patient triage, or classification of injury and illness according to severity, is one of the key elements of an EMS system. Patients are matched to the capabilities of area hospitals with the most critically injured transported to Level I trauma centers while patients with less severe injuries are delivered to facilities with more limited resources. The goal of emergency medical services systems is to get the patient to the right hospital within an appropriate length of time in order to reduce disability and death.[34]

The situation at Fort Hood was of such magnitude that it required countywide response from EMS, law enforcement, and fire department first responders. Fortunately, there were written agreements in place among Fort Hood and Bell County emergency management agencies that provided for the mobilization and sharing of emergency management resources. These mutual aid agreements are essential in insuring an adequate response to mass casualties and disaster situations. After the BCCC issued a countywide call for EMS, fire, and law enforcement, imagine the first responders' shock and bewilderment when they rolled up to locked gates.

There were several minutes of confusion before ambulances and other public safety vehicles were allowed to drive onto Fort Hood. Victims of the shooting were first transported from the SRP Center to Darnall Medical Center about two miles away. Darnall is a Level III facility and lacks the resources to competently care for critically injured patients. There was not adequate triage performed at the scene and as a result, "it became more of a scoop and run procedure than a choreographed plan with transport of the most critically first, consciously spreading them out between area hospitals."[35]

It very quickly became obvious that the Darnall Medical Center could not take care of all of the patients that it received. Many of those who had been transported to the hospital in private vehicles required transfer to a more technologically sophisticated facility. The medical staff contacted Scott & White and told them to prepare for a deluge of Army choppers loaded with critical trauma patients. The ten most urgent cases and a comatose Nidal Hasan were airlifted to Scott & White. All eleven were treated in the same critical care area of the hospital and a special area for family members was set up just a few steps away. Family members of the wounded had no idea that the person who had tried to kill their loved ones, Nidal Hasan, lay unconscious nearby.[36]

Officer Kimberly Munley and seven shooting victims were transported to the Killeen Metroplex Hospital, one-half mile from Fort Hood, and two patients were taken to Seton Hospital, a 181 bed facility in Round Rock, about forty miles south of Killeen.[37]

No matter how many drills and rehearsals, people who are unfortunate enough to be caught up in a mass casualty like the Fort Hood shooting are overwhelmed by the incongruity of the situation. The perception of one's safety and security is shattered and reality acquires a surreal aspect. Because the actual facts surrounding the shooting were largely unknown at first and open to speculation and conjecture, central Texas residents had no other place to turn but to the media. National and local television stations interrupted regular programming very quickly after the shooting began and reported that there were several locations at Fort Hood where attacks were taking place. The media also announced that multiple shooters were involved and broadcast that one of the gunmen had been killed. These inaccurate reports contributed to confusion on and off the base. CNN announced Scott & White's command center referral telephone number and the hospital received 1,300 calls in one hour, crippling their telephone system.[38]

Administrators at Darnall Medical Center desperately needed off-duty staff to report back to the facility but because Fort Hood's mass casualty protocols dictated that telephone lines be shut down, medical personnel could not be reached. Many of Darnall's providers had heard the news about the shooting and knew to get back to the hospital, but had problems getting through Fort Hood's closed gates.[39]

Metroplex Hospital in Killeen, a Level IV facility, also experienced overload problems with telephone lines, and like Darnall, Metroplex could not reach off-duty personnel. Ambulances delivered eight patients to Metroplex only to find three physicians in house—two general surgeons and one emergency physician. Although a radio was available for emergency communications, none of the staff knew how to operate it. As a result, as soon as transportation was available, two patients were hurriedly transferred out of the region.[40]

Sgt. Howard Appleby reported to the Behavioral Health Department at Darnall Medical Center early in the afternoon on November 5 for a scheduled psychiatric consultation but his appointment had been abruptly cancelled. When Appleby left the hospital and noticed the commotion outside of the emergency department, he walked over to investigate. Without a word he pitched in and helped treat the wounded.[41]

"It was just like being back in Iraq," Appleby says.[42]

Twenty-seven patients were seen in the Darnall Emergency Room. Four patients required at least one surgical procedure and one soldier died.[43]

As for the non-wounded survivors and bystanders, they were quickly herded into the Sports Dome just west of the SRP/TBI complex where they were locked down with the rest of the base. Their sequestration lasted for ten excruciating hours. Chelsea Garrett, whose earlier graduation ceremony at the Howze Theater had been interrupted, was among those who were told to wait for an "all clear."

> I can't say for sure how many people were sent over to the dome, but the room where I was had about eighty or so people crammed around one TV. We were getting live news feeds and that is when I first saw a televised photo of Hasan. I was floored because I did not recognize him as the person I saw on the ground earlier. We had plenty of food (MRE's) and water. I had no word about my children and cell phones did not work—not even texts. I finally got fed up waiting to be released and left on my own accord to be with my children around 10:00 p.m. I was surprised that no one attempted to stop me, so I continued, barefoot, over to the theater to find my children.[44]

Silver Stars and Six Guns

On November 5, 2009, Waco-based Texas Rangers Kirby Dendy and Frank Malinak happened to hear a news bulletin broadcast on CNN about a mass shooting on Fort Hood. They sprinted to their car and at speeds upwards of 100 miles per hour made it to Fort Hood in a record thirty minutes.[45]

Ranger Dendy says it was "crazy and hectic." "The base was on lockdown and at that time it was still undetermined whether there was only one shooter or others. For reasons I've never understood, other people on post had reported shootings in separate locations."[46]

Fort Hood is a federal installation and the Texas Rangers don't have jurisdiction over a military base.

"As far as why [we responded]," Dendy says, "it's a federal facility but it's still in the State of Texas. When you have a shooting in progress, the primary response from law enforcement, regardless of location, is to neutralize the threat to the citizens. Obviously, if [the military] had said 'No, you can't come on base,' then we would have abided by their decision. They wanted our help and we provided it."[47]

Texas Rangers from surrounding areas—Lampasas, Temple, and Georgetown—joined Dendy and Malinak.

"By the time it was over," says Dendy, "there were thirty to thirty-five of us."[48] That was one-quarter of their force.

THE TEXAS DEPARTMENT OF EMERGENCY SERVICES released the first official statement about the shooting at 3:30 p.m., just two hours after Hasan's shooting rampage ended. It was a brief confirmation that,

> More than one shooter fired shots into the Soldier Readiness Processing Center and Howze Theater on Fort Hood. Emergency personnel have responded to the scene and evacuated several wounded. Officials cannot at this time confirm the number of fatalities or wounded. Of the shooters, one has been apprehended.

> Media representatives who are interested in covering this event are asked to call the III Corps Public Affairs Office…. Public affairs representatives will meet members of the media at the Fort Hood Main Gate.[49]

The second statement came from Lt. Gen. Bob Cone, commander of III Corps and Fort Hood, at a 3:50 p.m. press conference in which he stated that "a soldier and possibly two more were involved in the shooting that resulted in twelve dead and thirty-one wounded in the general location of the Soldier Readiness Processing Center." Cone also reported that the shooter had used two handguns and was killed at the scene. Cone confirmed that Fort Hood was still locked down.

Twelve minutes after Cone's press conference, President Obama told audience members at a Tribal Nations Conference that there had been "a tragic shooting at the Fort Hood Army base in Texas." He talked about American soldiers being killed and "even more wounded in a horrific outburst of violence." The president asked that "all Americans keep the men and women of Fort Hood in your thoughts and prayers." President Obama pledged to get answers to every single question about the shooting and emphasized that "there's no greater honor but also no greater responsibility for me than to make sure that the extraordinary men and women in uniform are properly cared for and that their safety and security when they are at home is provided for."[50]

Shortly after 6:00 p.m. Glen R. Couchman, M.D., Chief Medical Officer for Scott & White Healthcare, and Robert D. Greenberg, M.D., FACEP, Vice-Chair of the Department of Emergency Medicine, Division of Prehospital Medicine at Scott & White, held a press conference where Dr. Couchman told a large group of reporters that the hospital had closed "primarily for safety issues. We've been getting mixed information from security over there [Fort Hood] and over here. We didn't know exactly what was going on. So, first and foremost, we wanted to protect all of our patients and all of our staff here."[51]

Dr. Couchman indicated that the hospital's security personnel were screening patients to double check that everyone inside of the hospital had a legitimate reason to be there and making sure that "the right people are coming through."[52]

Just a few hours after the president's pledge to "get answers" to all of the questions surrounding the massacre, several airplanes filled with federal support personnel headed for Fort Hood. Thirteen teams of spiritual support staff, thirty-five family life consultants, thirty-three behavioral health specialists, seventeen critical-incident stress-management personnel, five combat stress teams, and four Operation Homecoming counselors responded—more than all of Fort Hood's behavioral health personnel combined.[53]

The international press corps wanted answers and they scrambled to get correspondents and camera crews to the scene. Reporters waited impatiently at the Fort Hood gates hoping for statements from officials, victims, and onlookers. CNN and other media outlets pleaded for anyone who had been at the shooting scene to call into their studios and to upload photographs and videos. Finally, a convoy of military vehicles escorted members of the press to a controlled area of the post where limited numbers of first responders, rescuers, and Darnall medical staff made themselves available for questions and comments for a brief period of time.[54]

In a press release about six o'clock that evening the Fort Hood Public Affairs Office announced that a Family Hotline had been set up for information dissemination. The Office also announced that the post was no longer locked down and reaffirmed that there was more than one shooter and that Hasan was killed at the scene.[55]

One of the first Fort Hood officials to give the press a statement about the shooter was Col. Kimberly Kesling, the medical staff chief who had warned Hasan to behave when he first transferred to Fort Hood the preceding summer, she continued to describe him as a "quiet, personable man."[56]

He was "a hardworking, dedicated young man who gave great care to his patients," Kesling told the *Toronto Star*. "I personally had no indication this was something he would choose to do."[57]

In another statement to the *Houston Chronicle*, Kesling praised Hasan's work ethic. "Up to this point I would consider him an asset."[58]

Jabberwocky

The response to the shooting was swift and harsh from the organized Muslim community. As soon as the Council on American-Islamic Relations (CAIR) realized that the Fort Hood killer had an Arabic name, their communications director carefully composed a press release. He held on to it until he received confirmation that the shooter was, indeed, a Muslim, then released their statement.

> We condemn this cowardly attack in the strongest terms possible and ask that the perpetrators be punished to the full extent of the law. No religious or political ideology could ever justify or excuse such wanton and indiscriminate violence. The attack was particularly heinous in that it targeted the all-volunteer army that protects our nation. American Muslims stand with our fellow citizens in offering both prayers for the victims and sincere condolences to the families of those killed or injured.[59]

Nihad Awad, executive director of CAIR, warned "American Muslims, and those who may be perceived to be Muslim, to take appropriate precautions to protect themselves, their families and their religious institutions from possible backlash."[60]

The Muslim Link, a bi-weekly newspaper distributed throughout the Washington, D.C. and Baltimore, Maryland, metropolitan areas, expressed its shock and disbelief when readers recognized Nidal Hasan's photograph on broadcast media. One Muslim reader in Prince George's County said "I would say [greetings of peace] to him and shake his hand, and he would smile and respond. He wouldn't talk much. He seemed like an organized person who put his trips to the masjid in his schedule, he did not hang around or socialize after the prayer."[61]

A Muslim from Laurel, MD, expressed surprise that Hasan was in the Army. "None of us even knew he was in the military. He would come in wearing Pakistani cloths [*sic*] sometimes, so we thought he was from Pakistan."[62]

"He never spoke to any of us about politics, the military, or violence. We had no idea he was even a doctor. He seemed very together yet humble," said another Muslim from the Washington, D.C., area.[63]

State, regional, and local mosques and Muslim organizations all over the country and throughout the world were quick to condemn the massacre and doled out harsh criticisms of Hasan's brutality. One of the leaders of the Killeen masjid, Dr. Manzoor Farooqi expressed his sorrow, an almost word-for-word recitation of CAIR's statement.

"The Islamic community strongly condemns this cowardly attack, which was particularly heinous in that it was directed at the all-volunteer army that protects our nation."[64]

Imam Islam Mossaad from a north Austin, Texas, mosque denounced Hasan's rampage as an act against Islam. "He did not live up to [our] code of conduct—not just in being an American soldier but being a good Muslim," Mossaad said. Police officers were positioned around the perimeter of the mosque in anticipation of possible violence against the Muslim house of worship.[65]

Noel Hasan, Nidal Hasan's aunt, told reporters that "[Hasan] must have snapped. He was not a fighter, even as a child and young man."[66]

Mohammed Hasan, nephew of the accused killer, was completely taken off-guard with the news that his uncle was accused of a mass shooting. He blamed it on the Army's insensitivity to Islam. He told reporter Paula Hancocks, "They don't respect him and there is racism toward him because he's a Muslim, he's an Arab, because he prays."[67]

Nidal Hasan's young friend, Duane Reasoner, told the BBC that he would not condemn Hasan for what he did. About the victims, Reasoner mused that "they were troops who were going to Afghanistan and Iraq to kill Muslims. Honestly, I have no pity for them."[68]

Anwar al Awlaki, the United States-born Yemeni cleric and former charismatic preacher at the Dar al Hijrah Islamic Center in Falls Church, Virginia, had a similar take on Nidal Hasan's murder rampage. On his blog he called Hasan a "hero" and praised him as a "man of conscience" who could not support wars against fellow Muslims.[69]

In an *Al-Jazeera* interview reprinted by the NEFA Foundation, al Awlaki admitted that he had first met Hasan at the Dar al-Hijrah mosque when he served as an imam there. Their email correspondence was initiated by Hasan about a year prior to his shooting rampage.

"Working in the American Army to kill Muslim [*sic*] is a betrayal to Islam. The American Muslim's loyalty is to the Muslim Nation and not to America, and brother Nidal is a proof on that through his blessed operation," Awlaki said.[70]

Awlaki emphasized Hasan's Palestinian roots and stated that "Nidal Hasan…is also from Palestine and he sees what the Jews are doing through oppressing his people under American cover and support."[71]

Awlaki was not the only person to praise Hasan's actions. A Facebook page entitled "Praying for the recovery of Dr. Nidal Malik Hasan," appeared soon after the shooting. It was allegedly created by Khadeeja Nuur, who wrote,

> I work for an Islamic-interest organization, lobbying on behalf of those we represent. Dr. Hasan has not been charged w/ [*sic*] anything! All we know is that he is wounded.[72]

Mussamaldin Hameed posted his admiration for Hasan.

> Nidal Malik is a brave mujahid, he did jihad, he did kill the killers [American soldiers] that was [*sic*] going to Iraq and Afganistan [*sic*] to fight the Islamic nation…my greeting and pray for him, we will never forget you brother Nidal, and I made this video for you.[73]

The Facebook tribute page dedicated to the glory of Nidal Hasan was quickly hijacked by outraged anti-Muslims and the verbal fisticuffs that ensued were hateful and venomous. The name of the group was changed from "Praying for the recovery of Dr. Nidal Malik Hasan," to "Praying for the Victims of Islamic Terrorist Nidal Malik Hasan." Posts such as "I'll pray for him alright. I'll pray he goes straight to hell," and "I pray for Maj. Hasan's quick recovery. Can't hang a man when he's on a ventilator, after all," represent some of the more tame verbage recorded on the site.[74]

And in Lehigh, Florida, Dan Ross contacted a Killeen florist and ordered an arrangement of yellow roses for delivery to Nidal Hasan's hospital room. He requested a card be included bearing the message "Qur'an Chapter 2: Verse 190-3. In God's eye, and those who submit, you are a hero."[75]

The shop's proprietor immediately called the FBI who sent an agent to Ross's home. A Viet Nam veteran, Ross claimed that the "Holy Spirit" told him to send the flowers.[76]

A reporter asked Ross why he would want to send flowers to Hasan. "That's part of Christianity, love your enemies and do good to them," Ross told him.[77]

No Stone Unturned

Within a few hours, a very large investigative force comprised of officials from the Army's Criminal Investigative Division (CID), FBI, Texas Rangers, Texas State Troopers, the Bell County Sheriff's Department, and Killeen Police Department SWAT teams, were combing every square inch of Fort Hood, Killeen, and the Casa Del Norte apartment complex. Federal agents were hard at work at Walter Reed, USUHS, Virginia, Washington, and Maryland, uncovering every moment of Nidal Hasan's life.[78]

Just two hours after the shooting commenced the residents of Casa Del Norte were ordered to leave their apartments immediately until officers could determine the safety of the area. Killeen Police Department SWAT teams, Texas Rangers, and FBI agents swarmed through Hasan's apartment and over the grounds of the complex. Large trucks hauled off the apartment complex's dumpsters and the FBI confiscated Willie Bell's computer. Officers allowed reporters to photograph and shoot video footage of Hasan's apartment before they removed his possessions to their crime lab.[79]

On the afternoon of November 5, Texas Governor Rick Perry called a press conference and emphasized the "important relationship" between the State of Texas and the military. He ordered the state flag flown at half-staff for three days and pledged state resources to Fort Hood to aid in the aftermath of the shooting.[80]

Among the few belongings left behind in Hasan's apartment were Jordanian and Israeli coins; a book on dream interpretation by Allamah Muhammad Bin Streen (R.A.); an old 2004 Psychiatry "Resident In-Training Examination;" a large paper/CD shredder and its box; a white crocheted prayer cap; digital alarm clock; toothbrushes and floss; luggage; old prescriptions including erythromycin and the cough suppressant Tessalon from Walter Reed Army Medical Center; a 2001 prescription of Combivir (an HIV drug) dated 2001 from Wilford Hall Medical Center Pharmacy at Lackland Air Force Base in San Antonio; an all-in-one screwdriver; empty ammunition boxes, an empty laser sight box, and assorted clothing. Print-outs of documents were stacked on a worn, cracked Formica countertop next to the refrigerator.[81]

"It wasn't so much what we saw," said FBI Special Agent Donna Cowling, who headed the team sent to Hasan's apartment. "It was what we didn't see." She said there was no food, no dishes, and no furniture.[82]

Nader Hasan was packing up to leave the golf course when he got a call that his cousin, Nidal, had been injured in a shooting at Fort Hood. *What kind of kook would open fire on a military base?* He drove straight to his mother's house. He found her weeping with the TV tuned to a news channel and he watched in horror as news commentators reported that his cousin was dead. The phone rang. It was Fox News anchor Shepard Smith. Nader agreed to a quick interview. He told Smith that Nidal had once hired a lawyer to get him out of the military; he was afraid to go to a war zone; he had been harassed and ostracized by his peers.[83]

"We're blown away," Nader said. "The guy was born and raised here, my cousin, a good American. Our family is feeling sadness. Our condolences go out." Smith asked him if his cousin was violent. "Him?" asked Nader. "No. Absolutely not."[84]

In a press conference at eight-thirty that night, Lt. Gen. Bob Cone announced that Nidal Hasan was alive, injured, and in stable condition. Three other soldiers-of-interest had been picked up, questioned, and released. Cone acknowledged that the Army and FBI were investigating the shooting.[85]

ON NOVEMBER 6, 2009, THE MORNING AFTER Nidal Hasan's shooting rampage, President Obama signed a proclamation honoring the victims and ordering the American flags flown at half-staff until sunset, Tuesday, November 10, 2009, Veterans Day. The proclamation read, in part,

> Our Nation's thoughts and prayers are with the service members, civilians, and families affected by the tragic events at Fort Hood, Texas. The brave victims, who risked their lives to protect their fellow countrymen, serve as a constant source of strength and inspiration to all Americans.[86]

The president also convened a meeting of his national security team and ordered "an inventory be conducted of all intelligence in U.S. Government files that existed prior to November 6, 2009, relevant to the tragic shooting at Fort Hood, Texas, especially anything having to do with the alleged shooter."[87]

President Obama also met with Robert Mueller, the Director of the FBI, and instructed him to perform an internal investigation.[88]

At one-thirty that afternoon, twenty-four hours after the shooting, U.S. forces throughout the world observed a moment of silence.

Former President George Bush, his wife, Laura, and their security detail slipped quietly through a Fort Hood gate unnoticed and visited with hospitalized shooting victims for two hours. The Bush's Crawford, Texas, ranch is less than thirty miles from the base and they were able to keep their visit low-key and press-free.[89]

A few hours later, after a solemn ceremony, a military honor guard loaded thirteen flag-draped coffins onto a Air Force C-17 Globemaster III aircraft where they were flown to Dover, Maryland, the military's official mortuary, for forensic examination and a rendering of the official causes of death.[90]

Army Sgt. Christopher Williams plays taps during the memorial ceremony honoring the fallen heroes who were killed by Nidal Hasan, Nov. 5, 2009. Photo by Cherie Cullen, photo courtesy of the U.S. Army.

Under heavy guard, a comatose Nidal Hasan was transferred by helicopter from Scott & White Hospital in Temple to Brooke Army Medical Center in San Antoinio. Paralyzed from the waist down, Hasan remained in critical condition. His family retained retired Col. John P. Gallagan, a lawyer and former military judge, to represent him.[91]

General George Casey, U.S. Army Chief of Staff, and Secretary of the Army John McHugh, held a joint press conference Friday afternoon from Fort Hood.

"This was a kick in the gut," Casey told reporters, "not only for the Fort Hood community but for the entire country."[92]

"We have to understand what caused that suspect to act in the way in which he did and ride back from that programs [*sic*] that can make a difference," said McHugh.[93]

A candlelight vigil on Friday night at Hood Stadium intensified the collective grief and sorrow—pain so fresh and raw that its roots could only spring from a soldier's ultimate betrayal.

⊕

On Saturday November 7, Texas Governor Rick Perry visited the hospitalized survivors at Scott & White Medical Center in Temple. After meeting with the victims of the shooting Perry thanked the care-givers and told a large press corps,

> The passage of two days since the violent outburst on Fort Hood has done little to dull the feelings each of us has about the incident. To those whose lives have been shaken by this isolated incident you need to know that it communicates less about the safety of our society or the condition of the human soul and much, much more about the way people look out for their neighbors in trying times.[94]

When *ABC News* correspondent Bob Woodruff, a staunch supporter of U.S. troops in Iraq and Afghanistan, visited the wounded at Carl R. Darnall Medical Center on Monday, November 9, he listened to the victims' survival stories and was impressed by their resilience and determination. Woodruff, who sustained a traumatic brain injury while he was embedded in an Army batallion during the Iraqi war, was the only member of the press allowed into the hospital to speak to the shooting victims.[95]

On Saturday night, next to a funeral wreath set up in their courtard, Hasan's neighbors at the Casa Del Norte apartments lit candles and prayed for the dead.[96]

On Sunday, November 8, three days after Hasan's rampage, a press release issued by III Corps & Fort Hood Public Affairs Office asked that anyone who might have inadvertently left the scene of the shooting with evidence to bring it to command headquarters.[97]

Also on November 8, the Senate Committee on Homeland Security and Governmental Affairs, chaired by Joseph Leiberman and co-chaired by ranking member Susan Collins, initiated an investigation into the events leading up to the shooting.[98]

On Tuesday, November 10, after visiting with the victims of the massacre, President Obama gave a moving eulogy at the Fort Hood memorial service.

We come together filled with sorrow for the thirteen Americans that we have lost, with gratitude for the lives that they led, and with a determination to honor them through the work we carry on. This is a time of war. Yet these Americans did not die on a foreign field of battle. They were killed here, on American soil, in the heart of this great American community. This is the fact that makes the tragedy even more painful, even more incomprehensible….But here is what you must also know: Your loved ones endure through the life of our nation. Their memory will be honored in the places they lived and by the people they touched.[99]

On the dais below the president's podium were thirteen empty pairs of military boots, each holding a rifle that cradled a combat helmet, memorializing the dead.

It is almost incomprehensible how the heinous act of one individual, in mere minutes, could bring this country and its armed forces to their knees.

SRP Center was demolished in February 2014. Photo courtesy of the U.S. Army

7. Judgment Day

The first principle is that you must not fool yourself.
~Richard P. Feynman

While Nidal Hasan lay paralyzed from the waist down in a hospital room at Brooke Army Medical Center in San Antonio, leadership teams from the DoD, the Army, Fort Hood, and the FBI retreated to their respective corners behind closed doors to assess the situation. They were in full damage control mode.

The Senate's Homeland Security Committee convened and ordered an investigation.

Defense Secretary, Robert Gates, called for a fact-finding probe into the events leading to the Fort Hood shooting and appointed two Defense officials, former Army Secretary Togo West and former Navy Chief Vernon Clark, to lead the study. Additionally, he instructed them to make recommendations on ways to prevent another attack in the future.

FBI Director, Robert Mueller, requested assistance from former CIA/FBI Director, Judge William Webster, in conducting an independent assessment of the FBI's strengths and weaknesses in dealing with situations like the Fort Hood shooting.

III Corps and Fort Hood After Action Review (AAR)

Just twelve days after the shooting, Fort Hood issued its "After Action Review," an assessment of its management response to Nidal Hasan's shooting rampage. The report began by focusing upon the first response to the MASCAL and was critical of the Bell County Communications Center and the fact that 9-1-1 calls are handled by a centralized county agency. The report's recommendation regarding emergency calls was to insure that base personnel had the Fort Hood Directorate of Emergency Services (DES) Dispatch in their speed dial (in addition to 9-1-1) in order to bypass the BCCC. At the same time, the review also cited a lack of a "synchronized communications architecture and plan" as problematic because Army personnel relied upon various means of communication, such as a specified FM radio frequency, cell phone, and DES two-way radios. Having no centralized "command net" contributed to the chaos. The report suggests that the Emergency Operations Center (EOC) should serve as command-central and should utilize their pre-established FM communications frequency.[1]

An assessment of the initial response to the MASCAL was mixed. In the months prior to the shooting, Fort Hood police officers were trained to directly confront an active shooter instead of waiting for SWAT and sniper teams. Officers Kimberly Munley and Mark Todd approached Hasan head-on, by themselves, and stopped him in his tracks. There is no doubt that this active shooter response method of dealing with the situation saved many lives. The report pointed out, however, that body armor was not available for any non-law enforcement first responders and there were no rifles or shotguns on hand for military police.[2]

A Crisis Response Battalion (CRB) was deployed to the scene in a timely manner, the review concluded, but there was confusion about who was in charge. Another problem concerned CRB identification. The members of the unit were attending field training at the time of the shooting and reported directly to the scene without first stopping at their headquarters for their uniforms, identification vests, and vehicle placards. Because officers were searching for a second shooter, there was some confusion in accurately identifying the out-of-uniform crisis response team.[3]

Triage at the scene was also criticized as non-existent. Soldiers and SRP personnel "brought patients to the arriving ambulances," the report states, "and it became more of a scoop-and-run procedure than a choreographed plan with transport of the most critically injured first, consciously spreading them out among area hospitals." The report recommended to first "assess the severity of wounds and allow EMS to prioritize transport" in order to "reduce chaos and patient tracking."[4]

Also, with respect to identification, the report noted that Army medical personnel who were off-base during the crisis had a difficult time getting back on Fort Hood after it was locked down. Many of the victims were transported to area hospitals with no ID, and identification problems contributed to the public dissemination of inaccurate information. Nidal Hasan was initially reported to be in the Scott & White morgue. The final head count of forty-three injured victims was incorrect because ID's were not tracked and there were no all-inclusive records kept at any facility regarding patients who were treated and released.

"Further investigation revealed some had superficial or minor GSW [gunshot wounds]," the report states, "but others were seen and released at the scene for stress symptoms without physical injuries. The method of reporting…created confusion in the total number reported." Civilian receiving facilities were reluctant to release patient information because of security concerns for patients and for their hospitals.[5]

Another source of havoc was the lack of logistical support for the large number of multi-agency investigators who swept through the base. There was no centralized depository for evidence and a there was a paucity of liaison officers (LNO) which "overwhelmed the resources of the CID."[6]

The media response to the crisis was fierce. The Fort Hood shooting was the single, most deadly act of violence to ever occur on a military installation inside the borders of this country. According to the "After Action Review," there was a conflict between the "public's desire for information" and preserving the "integrity of sensitive case information that jeopardizes prosecution." Victims, onlookers, and first responders stepped forward to give their accounts of the massacre to the media. In a mass casualty situation, the report concluded, there must be a "balance to satisfy the press's need for information and the Command's desire to appear transparent, while ensuring case-sensitive information is protected. Historically, criminal defense teams use disclosed information to display carelessness and "prosecution in the press." Indeed, Hasan's attorneys filed a motion requesting an expert to gauge the effects of the extensive media coverage on the case. The judge denied their motion but granted their request for an expert to assist with the selection of an unbiased jury.[7]

The Fort Hood "After Action Review" was pragmatic in its approach. It identified areas of deficiency and offered solutions to the problems encountered in effectively managing a mass casualty of such a great magnitude. Its criticism of the Bell County Communications Center, however, was unwarranted. If the 9-1-1 callers had been connected with the Fort Hood DES, there is absolutely no way that it could have centrally dispatched all of the county's emergency providers with the same speed, efficiency, and authority as the BCCC.

Department of Defense "Protecting the Force: Lessons from Fort Hood"

The Department of Defense published its findings in January 2010, two months after the release of the Fort Hood "After Action Review." Much of the DoD report focuses upon the military's inability to identify internal threats.

DoD force protection policies are not optimized for countering internal threats. These policies reflect insufficient knowledge and awareness of the factors required to help identify and address individuals likely to commit violence. This is a key deficiency. The lack of clarity for comprehensive indicators limits commanders' and supervisors' ability to recognize potential threats.[8]

The report recommends that the DoD work with the FBI's Military Violence Unit to develop a methodology for identifying potential personnel who may engage in violence and to train commanders to recognize the behavioral indicators most likely to precede violent acts and radicalization. Additionally, an assessment of soldiers' predilections for violence should be incorporated into pre- and post-deployment health screenings.[9]

Much of "Protecting the Force" pertains to information sharing. It was the absence of interagency communications that allowed Nidal Hasan to complete his medical training at Walter Reed Army Hospital, transfer to Fort Hood, and brutally murder thirteen people. The lack of communications between the San Diego and Washington, D.C. joint terrorism task forces is directly related to their failure to recognize the implications of the emails exchanged between Hasan and al Qaeda terrorist Anwar al Awlaki. Hasan exhibited his radical tendencies many times during his medical training, yet his performance evaluations did not reflect his superiors' concern about his mental health and his pre-occupation with radical Islam. When Hasan was transferred to Fort Hood, therefore, there was no indication in his personnel file that he could pose a threat to the Army. Col. Kimberly Kesling admits to being forewarned that Hasan could potentially cause difficulties at Fort Hood, but she did not take the warning seriously. Most importantly, Ltc. Ben Phillips, Hasan's immediate supervisor, was not informed about Hasan's disturbing behavior at Walter Reed.

When Hasan was promoted to the rank of major, he was required to submit to background and credit checks which he passed. That might not have been the case if his behavior had been documented in his personnel file. "Protecting the Force" addresses these issues with a recommendation that military departments and defense agencies "establish formal information sharing agreements with allied and partner agencies; federal, state, and local law enforcement; and criminal investigation agencies, with clearly established standards regarding scope and timeliness."[10]

Another deficiency within the military that "Protecting the Force" identified was the DoD's failure to implement enhanced 9-1-1 emergency communications. This is especially interesting in light of Fort Hood's "After Action Review" which recommended that the DES telephone number be programmed into the installation's telephone system in order to bypass the regional emergency communications system. "Protecting the Force" points out that "there is no DoD policy implementing public law for a 9-1-1 capability on DoD installations. Failure to implement policy will deny the military community the same level of emergency response as those communities off base."[11]

The DoD recognizes the difficulties in identifying the types of behaviors that can escalate into violence and "Protecting the Force" incorporates various psychological models that can integrate "current knowledge into professional military education" and "provide supervisors and commanders the tools they need to make judgment calls in disciplinary cases and when conducting performance and career counseling."[12]

The DoD made seventy-nine recommendations covering five major areas of command: personnel, force protection, information sharing, emergency response, and health affairs. The Department of the Army immediately implemented twenty-one of the recommendations and stated that they required guidance for the implementation of forty-five others. The remaining thirteen require congressional action before implementation can be effected.[13]

Upon release of the report, John Galligan, Nidal Hasan's defense attorney, was quick to criticize it as being vague.

"This whole report is designed to tell people we need to start looking for internal threats," Galligan told Associated Press reporter Angela K. Brown. "It doesn't say what those threats are…and calls into question people's privacy and constitutional rights."[14]

Fort Hood: Army Internal Review Team

The Department of Defense directed the Army to perform a review and assess its ability to identify internal threats. Army command visited seventeen bases and surveyed more than eighty installation commanders (ICs). In general, they concluded, "the Army has sufficient personnel policy guidance for implementing personnel support programs and services." The installation commanders expressed a need for a more centralized approach for the funding of emergency medical (EM) equipment. Currently, each Army base procures EM equipment locally without a clear funding mechanism. As such, much needed emergency equipment must compete with other line-item funding requests.[15]

The Army Internal Review Team (AIRT) questioned the legal authority for utilization of contract security guards (CSGs). The team found that the legal authority of CSGs to respond to an active shooter threat is unclear. After 9/11 the Army relied upon CSGs but soon after the Fort Hood shooting it began converting its almost seventeen hundred security guard positions to Army personnel. Additionally, increased performance requirements were put into place for the contractors that remained.[16] The officers who responded to the Fort Hood shooting were civilian police employed by Fort Hood, not CSGs, and Officers Munley and Todd lost their jobs because of the re-focusing of military resources.

During the assessment process, there were ten programs and processes, i.e. "quick wins," identified in addition to the seventy-nine recommendations made by the DoD that, if implemented across-the-board, would serve to minimize risk in any future mass killing scenario. These "quick wins" were,

- Adoption of the active shooter scenario used by Officers Munley and Todd during the Fort Hood shooting including and expanding upon a training program.

- Authorization for military police to use jacketed hollow point ammunition to reduce the risk of friendly-fire injuries.

- Revision of General Officer assignment orders to include "senior commander authorities, responsibilities, and duties."

- Training of senior commanders in the Army's emergency management program.

- Revision of the "Subversion and Espionage Directed Toward the Army," regulation AR 381-12 with the new title of "Threat Awareness and Reporting," which would add "indicators for espionage, terrorism, and extremism."

- Implementation of an electronic threat-reporting system that would provide all personnel with a means for reporting suspicious behavior or activities.

- Implementation of an iWATCH program to detect and report terrorist activities on post.

- Standardization of a traumatic event management (TEM) program which would require mental health professionals and ministry teams to attend specialized training.

- Establishment of training programs for management of the unique stressors common to health care professionals.

- Amendment of the FBI Criminal Justice Information System to allow contract security guards to conduct criminal background checks on civilians who attempt to enter a military installation.[17]

The most significant issue identified by the Army Internal Review Team was the lack of control that installation commanders have over "synchronizing policy, establishing priorities, and allocating resources" necessary for securing their bases. The recommendations in the report directly addressed this issue.[18]

"Taken individually," the panel concluded, "no single action would have prevented the tragedy at Fort Hood. However, in the aggregate, the initiatives outlined by the Army's internal review team will significantly improve the Army's ability to mitigate internal threats, ensure force protection, enable emergency response, and provide care for the victims and families."

FBI

Upon release of the DoD "Protecting the Force" report, the FBI responded immediately with a press release. It identified four areas for "immediate adjustment and improvements."

- Protocols with the Department of Defense.
- The FBI agreed to notify the DoD of investigations involving military personnel which would "streamline information-sharing and coordination between the FBI and all components of DoD."
- Additional Levels of Review.
- The FBI agreed to provide a supplemental layer of review at the headquarters level. By bringing in a broader perspective, the risk of human error could be reduced.
- Technological Improvements.
- Improvements to information technology to provide agents and analysts with expanded analytical tools.
- Training for Members of Joint Terrorism Task Forces.
- More stringent training requirements for members of Joint Terrorism Task Forces to ensure more thorough analyses of

critical information and expanded training programs regarding legal issues.[19]

The press release stated that "Judge Webster's review is continuing and will evaluate additional areas, including whether current laws and policies strike an appropriate balance between protecting individuals' privacy rights and civil liberties while detecting threats." The results of Judge Webster's review were not released until July 2012, a few weeks prior to the originally scheduled beginning of Hasan's Court Martial.[20]

Senate Committee on Homeland Security and Governmental Affairs Report: "A Ticking Time Bomb"

The Senate Committee on Homeland Security and Governmental Affairs was quick to place blame for the Fort Hood massacre on the Department of Defense and the FBI. The members concluded:

- The military did not pay proper attention to Nidal Hasan's radicalization and ignored the signs that he was becoming more and more critical of wars that he considered the U.S. to be waging against Islam.

- Hasan attempted to leave the military and at least one of his advisors offered to help him.

- Hasan made several presentations to his classmates and professors that clearly demonstrated his radical views.

The FBI was aware that Hasan was communicating with radical cleric Awlaki but botched their investigation.[21]

Susan Collins, ranking member of the Senate Homeland Security Committee, expressed her dissatisfaction with the DoD report, "Protecting the Force."

"The reports fail to even mention the phrase 'violent Islamist extremism,'" Collins complained. "The administration's reluctance to confront this threat directly is ill-advised and impedes the search for solutions."[22]

The report further accuses the DoD of being "reluctant to confront directly the threat of radicalization to violent Islamist extremism among service members" and of "glossing over evidence of Hasan's radicalization to violent Islamist extremism."

The members of the committee were obviously troubled that the

DoD's failure to use the specific term "violent Islamic extremism" in its report would prevent the military from properly educating its personnel on how to detect and counter the "enemy."

The purpose of the Homeland Security Committee's investigation of the Fort Hood shooting was twofold. First, the panel directed a probe into the nature of the information that the U.S. government possessed regarding Nidal Hasan prior to his mass shooting and the actions it took or failed to take in response to that information. Second, the committee wanted to identify steps necessary to protect the United States against future acts of terrorism by homegrown violent Islamist extremists.

At the outset, the Senate Homeland Security Committee made the presumption that Hasan was a violent, lone-wolf, Islamist terrorist. Their conclusion was that,

> Although neither the DoD nor the FBI had specific information concerning the time, place, or nature of the attack, they collectively had sufficient information to have detected Hasan's radicalization to violent Islamist extremism but failed both to understand and to act on it. Our investigation found specific and systemic failures in the government's handling of the Hasan case and raises additional concerns about what may be broader systemic issues.[23]

Much of the report focused upon Nidal Hasan's email correspondence with extremist Muslim cleric Awlaki which the committee called "a shocking course of conduct for a U.S. military officer.[24] Most of the findings, however, pinpointed the failure of the FBI's Joint Terrorism Task Forces (JTTF's) to ferret out Hasan's self-radicalization, specifically a conflict between the San Diego and Washington JTTF's; a feud between the FBI and the Department of Defense; and the Army's failure to kick Hasan out of the military.

After 9/11 the FBI's mission was expanded from a domestic crime-fighting organization with loosely connected local offices to an "intelligence-driven counterterrorism agency." In testimony before Congress, FBI Director Robert Mueller explained the agency's new approach.

> Today, we are focused on prevention, not simply prosecution. We have shifted from detecting, deterring, and disrupting terrorist enterprises to detecting, penetrating, and dismantling

such enterprises—part of the FBI's larger culture shift to a threat-driven intelligence and law enforcement agency.[25]

The Homeland Security Committee raised "concerns that the FBI headquarters exercised insufficient supervision and coordination of FBI field offices and JTTF's." There are fifty-six FBI field offices located in major cities. The first director of the FBI, J. Edgar Hoover, emphasized the necessity of the field offices retaining a great deal of autonomy. This decentralization of the FBI was reinforced by Director Louis Freeh from 1993 until 2001. The committee cited the lack of cohesion among field offices as the basis for the absence of effective communications between the San Diego and Washington, D.C. JTTF's.[26]

The Joint Terrorism Task Forces are the primary investigative units for terrorist activities and are staffed with FBI agents and representatives from other federal, state, and local agencies. At the time of 9/11 there were thirty-five JTTF's which were increased to one hundred-six by 2010. A national JTTF agency was established to assist with the coordination of investigations among the individual offices.

The San Diego JTTF intercepted Hasan's first email communication with Awlaki in December 2008. The notation "comm. officer" in Hasan's military file was misinterpreted as "communications" officer instead of "commissioned" officer, which would present a threat to national security if Hasan were sending Awlaki military secrets. The San Diego JTTF decided to keep Hasan's communications with Awlaki within its own subset and to not pass on these emails through normal channels.[27]

When a second email to Awlaki was discovered, the San Diego office sent a detailed message to the Washington, D.C. JTTF and requested that an inquiry be performed. The Washington office had led a post-9/11 investigation into Awlaki's activities. The Washington office had no reason to believe that these emails between Hasan and Awlaki were of a terrorist nature and waited six weeks to act upon the San Diego's JTTF's request. The investigation was assigned to a Department of Defense officer who had been detailed to work with the Washington JTTF and whose handling of the case led to a serious problem in the investigation.[28]

After scrutinizing Hasan's military file, the Washington office concluded that Hasan was erroneously labeled a communications officer instead of the correct rank of commissioned officer and that Hasan's research into Islamic culture and beliefs regarding terrorist activities provided a justifiable reason for his communications with Awlaki. The Washington office sent the San Diego JTTF a memo outlining their conclusions. Because the report on Hasan was superficial, the San Diego agent incorrectly surmised that Hasan could possibly be one of the Washington office's confidential informants and did not want to harm that relationship. The investigation went no further and Hasan's superiors and colleagues were never interviewed, as the agency's common practice dictates.[29]

The FBI does not automatically allow all JTTF agents access to their criminal/investigative databases but permits use of their computer systems on a need-to-know basis. The investigator in the Washington office, in fact, was not even aware of the existence of the FBI databases. The investigator in the San Diego office, who did have access to FBI databases, assumed that his counterpart in the Washington office had already performed a thorough inquiry into Hasan's activities. Neither office felt they had reason to investigate Hasan further, and he slipped through the cracks and was not noticed again until he committed his mass murder on November 5, 2009. One of agents who had been involved in the failed investigation saw the early television coverage and called his counterpart in Washington. "Guess what?" he asked. "That's our boy."[30]

The Homeland Security Committee blamed the two respective JTTF offices for protecting their regional turfs and failing to act as a cohesive, singular agency. The committee concluded that "the Hasan inquiry was plagued by disjunction between two field offices and the lack of coordination by FBI headquarters and that the field offices retain too much autonomy." The committee further alleged that the local JTTF offices failed to utilize intelligence analysts and allowed regular agents to perform the investigation of Hasan. "An analysis of the full extent of Hasan's communication would have shown that Hasan's interest in [al Awlaki] belied any conceivable research purposes."[31]

The committee also blamed the failure of the two JTTF's to uncover Hasan's true reasons for contacting Awlaki on a competitive relationship between the FBI and the Department of Defense. The Washington field agent who investigated Hasan was an employee of the DoD who had been detailed to the JTTF. The committee maintained that the JTTF should have notified the DoD of the potential counterterrorism activities by one of their own and accused the two agencies of perpetuating a feud.

"We have found no legal barrier that prevented the JTTF's from notifying DoD counterintelligence officials concerning Hasan's communications and enlisting those officials' expertise in investigating Hasan," chided the committee.

Furthermore, the DoD and FBI had signed a Delimitations Agreement in which the DoD was designated the responsible agency for investigating members of the military. The Delimitations Agreement defined counterintelligence as both classical espionage and international terrorism. The FBI argued that the Delimitations Agreement did not cover counterterrorism and was applicable only in the event of classic counterintelligence such as espionage. In the FBI's view, the JTTF's were the appropriate agencies to investigate Hasan.[32]

The William H. Webster Commission

In response to FBI Director Henry Mueller's request to perform an all-inclusive, independent investigation into the FBI's handling of the agency's dossier on Major Nidal Hassan, Judge William Webster assembled a team of experts who

> conducted investigative interviews of all FBI and other JTTF personnel who handled the Hasan information; conducted on-site visits and interviews with counterterrorism squads and intelligence fusion cells in Northern Virginia, Philadelphia, and Los Angeles that were not involved in the Hasan matter; and performed or supervised comprehensive searches of the FBI's data holdings on Hasan and Aulaqi. To obtain a broad range of perspectives, the Commission also consulted with outside experts on counterterrorism, intelligence operations, information technology, and Islamic radicalism; public interest groups that promote and protect civil liberties and privacy interests; and staff from Congressional committees with FBI oversight responsibilities.[33]

The William H. Webster Commission concluded that JTTF agents mishandled the Hasan/Awlaki communications. The commission found no evidence that any of the mistakes made by individuals working on the case were the result of intentional misconduct or the disregard of their duties. The report stated, in part,

> We find that each Agent, Analyst, and Task Force Officer who handled the Hasan information acted with good intent. We do not find, and do not believe, that anyone is solely responsible for mistakes in handling the information. We do not believe it would be fair to hold these dedicated personnel, who work in a context of constant threats and limited resources, responsible for the tragedy at Fort Hood. We conclude instead that these committed individuals need better policy guidance to know what is expected of them in performing their duties, and better technology, review protocols, and training to navigate the ever-expanding flow of electronic information.[34]

While the commission admitted that JTTF agents mishandled the Hasan/Awlaki communications, it cited reasons why these agents were limited in their abilities to investigate the communications. Among them were,[35]

- Their knowledge of the facts was limited because they did not have DIRECT access to all of the DoD information on Hasan, such as his personnel file and medical licensing records.

- Prior to the shooting, the FBI did not routinely reveal to the DoD their counterterrorism investigations of military and civilian personnel or individuals who had access to DoD installations and facilities.

- There were errors in judgment. The San Diego Field Office knew only that an individual named Nidal Hasan sent two email messages to Awlaki, and that an Army major named Nidal Hasan was stationed in Washington, D.C. The agent who turned the information over to the WFO did not know with certainty that those individuals were one and the same and there was no formal mechanism in place for making that determination.

- The San Diego agent's cover email to the WFO recommended that the information on Hasan not be disseminated widely throughout the agency in the form of an IIR, but, instead, "If this needs to get to the military, WFO might have to do it internally."[36] There was no policy-guidance in drawing these kinds of conclusions.

- There was no "clear ownership" of the lead. The San Diego office believed that the Washington office "owned" the lead and vise-versa. San Diego's prime focus was the acquisition and disposition of information regarding Awlaki. In its opinion, collateral information (i.e. Hasan) was a "fringe benefit."[37]

- The WFO received the lead from San Diego while dealing with threats surrounding President Obama's inauguration. The lead was not labeled as urgent and the WFO dealt with it according to the policy at the time, within ninety days.

- The two San Diego agents who intercepted the Hasan/Awlaki communications were immersed in the Awlaki investigation. According to the report, "The Aulaqi investigation is a stark example of the impact of the data explosion….By November 5, 2009, the date of the Fort Hood shootings, the Aulaqi investigation had required SD-Agent and SD-Analyst to review 29,041 electronic documents - on average, approximately 1,525 a month, or 70 to 75 per work day. At times, the average number of documents reviewed ranged higher than 130 per work day. The complexity of their review task was exacerbated by the diversity of the electronic communications. As these statistics show, the information review demands of the Aulaqi investigation were relentless."[38]

The commission concluded that fault lay with the FBI command structure for not having in place formal policies and procedures. Without clear policy direction, each JTTF office looked to the other as responsible for resolution of the case and as the final decision-maker. "As a result," the report stated, "nothing further was done."[39] The agents who handled the Hasan communications were flailing in the dark.

The Webster Commission Report cited positive internal changes that were implemented after the shooting. It recommended additional operational adjustments in investigative techniques and information flow, technological and information technology improvements, oversight, and legislative authority. Additionally, the commission suggested the implementation of formal policies that address the proper disposition of leads, the resolution of inter-office disagreements, clearinghouse procedures, regular information audits, and procurement of technologically sophisticated computer hardware.

THE ARMY WAS SO FOCUSED ON MAINTAINING THE STATUS QUO that it missed the storm clouds rising on the horizon. Why was Nidal Hasan allowed to squeak through medical school with his record of poor performance and extremist, anti-military beliefs? In a meeting in the spring of 2008, officials at Walter Reed expressed their concerns about Hasan's lack of achievement, outbursts of anger, and emotional instability. His classmates and professors alike were troubled by his behavior—more than one questioned his mental stability.[40] In hindsight, one has to wonder why the military insisted upon hanging onto someone who obviously did not fit organizational expectations.

When he graduated from medical school in 2003, Hasan was commissioned as a captain in the regular Army. His anti-war position on the United States' involvement in the Iraq and Afghanistan conflicts was familiar to his professors and his classmates as was his increasing preoccupation with Islam. Hasan was not the only medical student at USUHS, however, who espoused anti-war views. There was not sufficient reason to question the appropriateness of his initial commission as captain. It was during Hasan's residency that his behavior became troubling—his PowerPoint presentation entitled "The Koranic World View As It Relates to Muslims in the U.S. Military," where he talked about America's wars against Islam, suicide bombings, "offensive jihad," and Osama bin Laden; his appending patients' charts with "Allah willing;" telling classmates that they would burn in hell if they did not convert to Islam; and his proselytizing to patients.

It was also during this time that Hasan's professors raised serious concerns about his performance as well as his obsession with Islam. He was cited for failure to meet fitness standards, his emotional stability was questioned, he missed classes, and he was frequently absent from work.

According to his family, during his residency Hasan hired an attorney to help him obtain a discharge from the Army based upon his status as a conscientious objector which the Selective Service defines as "one who is opposed to serving in the armed forces and/or bearing arms on the grounds of moral or religious principles."[41] Members of the Medical or Chaplain Corps, however, are classified as non-combatants and are not eligible for a military release based upon their religious or moral beliefs.[42]

After Hasan completed his residency, he was the only applicant for the USUHS Preventive/Disaster Psychiatric Fellowship. These fellowships are generally reserved for physicians who excel in their training—there was nothing about Hasan's medical education that could remotely suggest excellence. Even though he did not qualify for the program, his superiors were afraid that they would lose the slot if they didn't fill it. They used Hasan to preserve funding for the fellowship. Hasan confided to a classmate that the reason he applied for the program was to avoid a combat deployment to Iraq or Afghanistan.[43]

The question of Hasan's retention is very perplexing in light of numerous DoD and Army regulations that would make Hasan's release from the military mandatory. These rules pertain to the appointment of commissioned officers, conscientious objection, security clearances, performance ratings, fitness issues, combat deployment, and mental health matters. An examination of DoD regulations demonstrates numerous avenues that were available to the Army for discharging Hasan.

Appointment of Commissioned Officers

Upon successful completion of the Disaster/Preventive Psychiatry Fellowship, Hasan was recommended for promotion to the rank of major. There are several steps involved in the promotion process.[44]

- Candidates must provide proof of citizenship
- Medical fitness standards must be met
- Conscientious objectors are not eligible for an officer commission
- Candidates must have a "SECRET" security clearance
- Candidates must pass age and educational requirements
- Candidates must swear to an oath of loyalty
- Candidates must be a person of good moral character
- Candidates must not be or have been a member of any domestic or foreign group that "seeks to alter the form of the U.S. Government by unconstitutional means"
- Applicants must not have any civil or military criminal convictions
- Candidates must be currently on the Army's rolls

Hasan met the citizenship, age, and educational requirements, but a closer look at medical fitness, including weight control standards, conscientious objector status, security clearances, loyalty; and character standards is warranted.

Medical Fitness Standards

Soldiers are evaluated for both mental and physical fitness and must be certified as fit in order to qualify for a commissioned officer position and are rated as either "medically acceptable" or "medically unacceptable." There are several medically unacceptable categories that may apply to Hasan. His professors and classmates questioned his mental fitness and his outrageous behavior indicated his inability to function appropriately and successfully in academic and military environments. Soldiers who are candidates for promotion as a commissioned officer must be of sound mental health with no history of psychotic or mood disorders such as major depression or bipolar complex. A history of behavioral disorders including "immaturity, instability, personality inadequacy, impulsiveness, or dependency [that] will likely interfere with adjustment in the Armed Forces does not meet the standard."[45]

Hasan obviously displayed behavior consistent with a psychological anomaly. One of his advisors questioned whether he might be symptomatic of a schizoid personality disorder and several others believed that he showed symptoms of depression. His professional conduct was called into question on numerous occasions. All of his advisors and professors agreed that he was not able to adjust to a military environment which provided a mechanism for separating Hasan from the Army.[46]

Behavioral scientists Jack Levin and James Alan Fox do not believe that most mass murderers suffer from psychosis, a serious mental illness in which one exhibits a loss of contact with reality and which is characterized by delusions and/or hallucinations.[47] According to Declercq and Audenaer, most of them display characteristics of personality and mood disorders such as sociopathy, depressive syndromes, and borderline personality disorder.[48] Had Hasan's superiors wanted to pursue a way to separate him from the Army, they could have used his maladjustment as a reason serious enough for him to be discharged. Hasan was never referred to a psychiatrist for evaluation.

Army Weight Control Regulations

Nidal Hasan was overweight. He was cited several times during his medical training for carrying too much body fat. All branches of the military emphasize the importance of fitness and proper weight. The Army asserts that

> An essential function of day-to-day effectiveness and combat readiness of the Army is that all personnel are healthy and physically fit. Self-discipline to maintain proper weight distribution and high standards of appearance is essential to every individual in the Army.[49]

The objective of the Army's Regulation 600-9, "Weight Control Program," is to make sure that all personnel "meet the physical demands of their duties," and "to present a trim military appearance at all times." Excessive body fat, according to the Army weight control policies, "connotes a lack of personal discipline, detracts from military appearance," and might reflect poor health." Additionally, the weight regulations emphasize "personal discipline, operational readiness, optimal physical fitness, and health" and "foster high standards of professional military appearance expected of all personnel."[50]

If a soldier fails to meet the Army's fitness standards, the consequences can be severe. Personnel who are found to be overweight are non-promotable and are not allowed to attend professional military schools, including Hasan's alma mater, the USUHS. Overweight soldiers are immediately put on the Army's weight control program which consists of setting weight loss goals, nutritional and exercise counseling, and monthly weight checks. If weight loss goals are not met, a letter documenting failure is entered into the soldier's official record and he is given six months to demonstrate progress. If after six months the overweight individual has not shown improvement, the soldier is subject to separation from the military.[51]

Nidal Hasan's peers and co-workers consistently described him as a "bald, fat guy." His excess weight had been obvious for years. According to the Army's weight control regulations, he qualified for a discharge from the military.

Conscientious Objection

During his residency Nidal Hasan hired an attorney to help him obtain a discharge from the Army based upon his status as a conscientious objector (CO). He even offered to repay the military for his educational expenses. The Selective Service defines a CO as "one who is opposed to serving in the armed forces and/or bearing arms on the grounds of moral or religious principles." Members of the Medical or Chaplain Corps, however, are classified as non-combatants and are not eligible for a military release based upon their religious or moral beliefs.[52] Because Hasan was pursuing a medical degree, he could not qualify for a discharge based upon conscientious objection. As badly as he wanted to leave the military, Hasan insisted that he would not do so unless he was honorably discharged.

Requirements for a "secret" security clearance

A "secret" clearance is mandatory for commissioned officer candidates.[53] While the Army believes that eligibility for a secret clearance must be "an overall common sense determination based upon all available facts," it also sets forth specific criteria for judging the suitability of a candidate to qualify for one.[54] Some of the disqualifiers for a secret security clearance include engaging in acts which serve the interests of foreign governments; association with terrorists, seditionists, revolutionists, or anarchists; participation in organizations which advocate violence or force that prevents others from exercising their constitutional rights; criminal or dishonest conduct; and any behaviors or illnesses that might interfere with good judgment and reliability. Also, falsification, cover up, concealment, misrepresentation, or omission of a material fact from any written or oral statement, document, or form used by DoD or any other federal agency, or a refusal to submit to a medical or psychological evaluation will disqualify a candidate.[55]

Officer candidates must also submit to a background check consisting of a national agency check, a credit check, and a personal interview conducted by an agent of the Defense Investigative Service (DIS). In Hasan's case, the Department of Defense, concluded that

> The alleged perpetrator held an active and current SECRET security clearance based on a February 2008 National Agency Check with Local Agency and Credit Check of background investigation. Although accomplished in accordance with current guidelines this background investigation did not include a subject interview or interviews with co-workers, supervisors, or expanded character references. We believe that if a more thorough investigation had been accomplished, his security clearance may have been revoked and his continued service and pending deployment would have been subject to increased scrutiny.[56]

The National Agency Check consists of queries to those agencies of the federal government—such as the FBI—that maintain records of a nature that could disqualify an officer candidate. The background check on Hasan, however, was done in February 2008, ten months prior to the interception of his first email message to Awlaki in December 2008.

The Department of the Army admitted to the Senate Homeland Security Committee that it did not conduct an interview of Hasan, as required by their Personnel Security Program, nor did they interview any of Hasan's coworkers, professors, or supervisors. In addition to conducting interviews of coworkers and supervisors, the Army's Personnel Security Program requires three character references who have sufficient knowledge of the candidate's background to judge his or her loyalty. The character witnesses must have known the candidate for at least five years and the character witnesses must be personally interviewed. Had investigators talked face-to-face with Hasan and the people who knew him, in all likelihood they would have concluded that he was a dangerous soldier who posed a threat to the military.

Loyalty

All officer candidates must prove their loyalty to the U.S. government. Regulations pertaining to the appointment of commissioned officers in the Army provide that "an individual must neither be nor have been a member of any foreign or domestic organization, association, movement, or group or any other combination of persons that advocates subversive policy, or seeks to alter the form of the U.S. Government by unconstitutional means."[57]

The first loyalty oath under our constitution was sanctioned by an Act of Congress on September 29, 1789 when Revolutionary War soldiers were required to swear their allegiance to this country. Officers in today's Army must also swear their loyalty to the United States.

> I, [Name], having been appointed an officer in the Army of the United States, as indicated above in the grade of [rank] do solemnly swear [or affirm] that I will support and defend the Constitution of the United States against all enemies, foreign and domestic, that I will bear true faith and allegiance to the same; that I take this obligation freely, without any mental reservation or purpose of evasion; and that I will well and faithfully discharge the duties of the office upon which I am about to enter; So help me God." (DA Form 71, 1 August 1959, for officers.)[58]

Deployment Fitness

Even though Nidal Hasan was retained in the Army and subsequently transferred to Fort Hood, there were other options available to his supervisors for obtaining a mental health separation. According to the Fort Hood policies regarding mental health issues, "a commander suspecting a mental health evaluation may be indicated will contact the appropriate mental health facility to schedule an appointment."[59] If a psychiatrist deems the soldier unfit, a medical evaluation board will proceed to a certification that the individual is not suitable for military life and will order a discharge.

There are also regulations governing deployment fitness. Not only must a soldier be physically able to qualify for combat deployment, he or she must be mentally and emotionally fit. A Pre-Deployment Health Assessment (PDHA) must be completed before a soldier can be sent to a combat zone. Indeed, the soldier readiness process is designed to evaluate soldiers' fitness. Documentable adjustment problems and mood disorders can disqualify personnel from combat or other deployment. Regulations state that persistence or recurrence of psychological symptoms that interfere with "effective military performance" are sufficient to refer a soldier to a Medical Evaluation Board with subsequent separation from the military.[60]

Because Hasan was a deploying physician he was required to complete a "Credentials Transfer Brief" which mandated that he be certified as competent by his transferring facility and that the information in his credentialing file be reviewed and verified by the receiving facility. There were numerous documentable breaches of Army regulations that could have been used to prevent Hasan's deployment which could have possibly prevented the November 2009 shooting.

Col. Kimberly Kesling, Darnall Deputy Commander for Clinical Services, knew about Hasan's problems at Walter Reed. Indeed, she had been told that Fort Hood was getting their "worst." Capt. Naomi Surman, Hasan's immediate supervisor at Fort Hood, was one of Hasan's classmates at Walter Reed and she knew all about his problems. In fact, when they were at Walter Reed, Hasan told Surman that she would burn for eternity because she was not Muslim. Hasan told many of his co-workers, including Dr. Tonya Kosminski with whom he shared emergency call duties, that the military would regret it if he were ever deployed.

No Exit

Despite his obvious failings as a military officer, the most probable reason that Hasan was retained in the Army is because physicians are valued as scarce commodities. There is an across-the-board shortage of mental health providers and the military decided that every psychiatrist was irreplaceable. For example, when one Fort Hood psychiatrist was diagnosed with multiple sclerosis, he was not successful in petitioning the Army for a medical discharge, even when his symptoms were serious enough to prevent him from carrying out his duties.[61]

Eugene R. Fidell, a professor of law at Yale University, told *New York Times* reporter Tamar Lewin that "in the case of people who have received substantial and valuable training, like health care providers or aviators, the military is very loath to allow people out prematurely."[62] Hasan was granted almost two years of leave to care for his dying mother, but with a shortage of psychiatrists and a skyrocketing increase of combat-related mental illnesses and traumatic brain injuries among the troops, the Army would not consider allowing him to be discharged until he completed his required service obligation.

With such myopic vision, it was easy for Hasan to remain a terrorist in training, hiding in plain sight.

Fort Leavenworth, Kansas, the Department of Defense's only maximum security prison and where Nidal Hasan is currently on death row. Photo courtesy of the U.S. Army

8. Ticking Time Bombs

By the work one knows the workman.
~Jean de La Fontaine

Over 14,000 people were murdered in the United States in 2013, a four percent decrease from 2012 and a fourteen percent decline from 2003.[1] The incidence of mass murders also declined with twenty-four occurrences in the past decade, down from forty-three cases in the 1990s.[2] Large-scale mass homicides such as the Fort Hood massacre are rare events that are sensationalized by the national print and broadcast media. Mass killings are so disconcerting and shocking that they become locked into our collective psyche, leading us to believe that there are many more of these events than there actually are. Because multiple homicides are increasingly committed with semi-automatic firearms with high-capacity magazines, there has been an increase in the total numbers of victims killed and injured.[3]

Two grisly multiple killings in 1966 brought mass murder to national attention, leaving a permanent mark on America's collective consciousness.

Bad not Mad

In the summer of 1966, Richard Speck entered a Chicago townhouse and raped and murdered a student nurse. Before leaving, he killed all six of her roommates and a guest. *Time* magazine called the mass killing a "crime of the century."[4]

Two weeks later, on August 1, 1966, twenty-five-year-old Charles Joseph Whitman climbed to the top of the 300 foot University of Texas tower with an arsenal of guns and enough food, water, and supplies to last at least a week. He shot and killed sixteen people and wounded more than thirty others.[5] It was this shooting rampage that defined mass murder and it has continued to serve as an exemplar for all other mass murderers committed since that time.

Charles Whitman was the embodiment of an all-American boy with good looks and excellent grades. He was an accomplished pianist and the youngest Eagle Scout in the world at the time. From outside appearances Charlie and his two brothers lived an idyllic life. The family was quite well off and lived in an upscale home in an upper middle class neighborhood. But, as often is the case, there were serious problems within the Whitman household. Charlie's father, C. A., had endured a rough childhood and had spent time in an orphanage. He was often violent and abused his three boys and his wife. When Charlie celebrated his eighteenth birthday by getting drunk with friends, C. A. roughed him up and threw him in the backyard swimming pool. Charlie almost drowned and retaliated by leaving home. He gave up his college plans and enlisted in the Marines where he thrived in the structured military environment. Charlie very quickly fell in love with guns and gambling.

At the military's expense, Charlie enrolled in the University of Texas at Austin and married a beautiful east Texas girl—an aspiring education major who made good money at her job with the telephone company. Charlie settled into a routine of attending classes, driving his wife, Kathy, to and from work, and obsessing about making huge sums of money. While Charlie harbored ill feelings toward his father, he had no problem accepting cash from him. He was determined to outdo his dad in amassing personal wealth. Like his father, Charlie treated his wife as a possession. His father treated his mother as an object and, not having any other role model, Charlie objectified Kathy.[6]

Charlie knew how to behave but "pretending to be nice proved easier than actually *being* nice."[7] One afternoon he walked into class, found a Middle Eastern student sitting in his chair and assaulted him. He kept weapons in his car and, in acts of road rage, would pull out a gun and threaten other drivers. Once he was arrested for poaching deer on private property. When Charlie's grades plunged, placing him in danger of flunking out, the Marines withdrew their financial support for his college expenses and called him back to Camp Lejeune.[8]

Back at the base, Charlie grew to hate the Marines and became a trouble-maker. After he threatened to assault a fellow soldier, illegal weapons were discovered in his possession. Charlie, court-martialed and locked up for four months, was busted from lance corporal to private. While in jail Charlie developed an obsession with writing and kept a journal entitled "The Daily Record of Charles J. Whitman." He kept an extensive record of his thoughts, feelings, and activities for the remainder of his life.

After serving his time, Charlie moved back to Austin to be with Kathy and re-enrolled at UT. At the same time, he began taking large quantities of an amphetamine [Dexedrine] that kept him awake for days at a time. He consumed enormous amounts of junk food and gained so much weight that his friends teased him. His lack of self-discipline had a deleterious effect on his grades and he came to the realization that flunking out was, once again, a distinct possibility.

Charlie also suffered severe bouts of depression. During one episode he expressed his hatred of his father. "I just despise my father," he said. "I hate him. If my father walked through that door, I'd kill him."[9]

He frequently lost his temper with Kathy and hit her on several occasions—the same behavior that he loathed in his father.[10] She urged him to see a mental health professional and Charlie made an appointment with a psychiatrist at the campus health clinic. During his visit, Charlie told the therapist that he had thought about "going up to the Tower with a deer rifle and shooting people."[11] At the end of their session, the psychiatrist asked Charlie to make an appointment for the following week but Charlie never returned.

Charlie's mother finally had enough of her abusive, controlling husband and pleaded with Charlie to drive to Florida and pick her up.

Angry, frustrated, and depressed, Charlie drove to Florida and moved his mother to Austin. Although C. A. swore he would never strike his wife again, her mind was made up and she filed for divorce.

On Sunday July 31, 1966, Charlie bought provisions: canned foods, a Bowie knife, water, and binoculars. He had made a conscious choice to kill. While Kathy was at work, Charlie typed two letters.

In the first letter, he wrote, "It was after much thought that I decided to kill my wife....I truly do not consider this world worth living in, and am prepared to die, and I do not want to leave her to suffer alone in it."[12]

Charlie wrote a second letter about his intention to kill his mother. He drove to her apartment complex and let himself in. She had retired for the night and Charlie killed her in her sleep. The letter of explanation that he left inside her apartment said, in part, "I have just taken my mother's life" and he blamed his father for "beatings, humiliations, degradation, and tribulations that I am sure no one but she will ever know." Charlie had simply "relieved her from her suffering."

Next, Charlie stabbed Kathy multiple times with a bayonet while she slept. The next morning he loaded up a gun locker, a cooler, a knapsack full of ammunition, and other survival gear and drove to campus dressed as a maintenance man. He managed to convince a gate guard to give him a temporary permit to unload his truck in front of the Tower. He dragged his arsenal and supplies up to the top, fatally wounding a receptionist and two tourists who were in his way. Once outside on the tower balcony, during a ninety-six minute shooting rampage, he shot and killed sixteen people and wounded more than thirty others before he was fatally shot by two Austin police officers.[13]

An autopsy revealed that Charles Whitman had a brain tumor. Medical and forensic experts do not believe that his medical condition precipitated his cold-blooded murders.[14]

In his biography of Charles Whitman, *A Sniper in the Tower*, Gary Lavergne writes "Charlie Whitman had a very troubled childhood. While provided for in the material sense, he had little in the way of an emotional support system....Charlie was never taught how to handle failure; it simply was not an option."[15]

Texas governor John Connelly appointed a special commission to study the Whitman murders. They concluded that he was,

- Shackled by personal turmoil.
- Obsessed with out-doing his father.
- Struggling with the break-up of his parents.
- Emotionally explosive, but covered it up with a "nice" façade.
- Frustrated by his friends' successes and his own failures.[16]

Was Charles Whitman insane? Experts say he was not. While organic brain disease has been associated with sudden, impulsive, outbursts of rage, Whitman's diary entries show that he carefully and meticulously planned his sniping rampage down to the clothes he wore and the provisions he brought to the Tower. Social scientists Jack Levin and James Alan Fox believe that Whitman fits a sociopathic profile of "bad, not mad." He carefully formulated his scenario for multiple murder with "planning, patience, and discipline."[17]

According to Levin and Fox multiple homicide often follows a period of extreme frustration. A precipitating event triggers intense rage. Seldom is serious psychosis or brain disease causally related to a killing rampage. The mass murderer rarely has a serious criminal background and is "extraordinarily ordinary."[18] The break-up of Whitman's parents' marriage was the catalyst that fueled his rage—fury hidden under the surface of a congenial façade—an anger brought upon by the successes of his wife and friends made worse by the humiliation of his own failures.

David Mattson, a Peace Corps trainee, lived in Austin at the time of the Whitman shooting and he likens the tragic event to Thornton Wilder's novel *The Bridge of San Luis Rey*.[19]

"In the book," Mattson says, "people from all walks of life were, for various reasons, drawn together by fate to a critical time and place in space. Everyone was there for a different reason when the bridge, which spans a gorge in Peru, collapses and they fall to their deaths."[20]

Like most victims of mass murder, it was simply a matter of being in the wrong place at the wrong time.

The brutal murders committed by Richard Speck and Charles Whitman in 1966 compelled the American public for the first time to face the fact that in a free society we are all vulnerable to the heinous acts of others, shattering our assumptions that we are safe in public places—even on a military base surrounded by fellow soldiers.

Several high-profile mass murders followed Whitman's shooting rampage. In May 1978, on the Northwestern University campus in Chicago, a bomb was discovered on the desk of Professor Buckley Christ. Fortunately, it was dismantled just before it detonated. This bombing attempt marked the beginning of Ted Kaczynski's seventeen year string of package bombs targeted at individuals who worked in academia and the airlines industry. Kaczynski is responsible for killing a total of three people and injuring twenty-three others.

On April 19, 1995, Timothy McVeigh detonated a fertilizer truck bomb in front of the Alfred P. Murrah federal building in Oklahoma City. One hundred sixty-eight people were killed and over six hundred were injured. One of McVeigh's Army buddies, Terry Nichols, was implicated in the attack. McVeigh was ultimately executed and Nichols remains incarcerated in the federal Supermax prison in Florence, Colorado, along with Ted Kaczynski. The Oklahoma City bombing was designated an act of domestic terrorism by the FBI and was the deadliest mass killing within the United States prior to the September 11, 2001, attacks. It remains the most serious act of domestic terrorism in this country's history.

Nidal Hasan had much in common with Charles Whitman, Ted Kaczynski, Timothy McVeigh, and Luby's mass killer George "Jo-Jo" Hennard all had axes to grind. If you asked any or all of them, they would tell you that they were victims of an evil, punishing society, a country that tolerated, even sanctioned, the exploitation and abuse of the helpless and the disadvantaged. Whitman hated his father with a vengeance so intense that he killed innocent people to get back at him. Both he and McVeigh cultivated a deep-seated anger and animosity toward the military, an institution they felt had rendered both of them powerless and impotent. Kaczynski harbored the conviction that technology was responsible for the ruination of society and directed his rage toward the people and institutions that he blamed for civilization's demise. None of these killers had been properly socialized as children. All were loners who had difficulty establishing and maintaining meaningful relationships. Most people with whom they came in contact throughout their lives did not remember them. But after committing their heinous acts, upon reflection, those who did recall them were not surprised at what they had done.

Always a prolific letter writer, after his incarceration Timothy McVeigh corresponded with numerous individuals. In an article for *Esquire* magazine, journalist Phil Bacharach chronicled his written communications with McVeigh. Like Ted Kaczynski, McVeigh distanced himself from his victims and blamed society and its institutions for the world's problems.[21]

"The public never saw the Davidians' home video of their cute babies, adorable children, loving mothers, or protective fathers," McVeigh wrote, "nor did they see pictures of the charred remains of children's bodies. Therefore, they didn't care when these families died a slow, torturous death at the hands of the FBI."[22] Always a cheerleader for the underdog, McVeigh went to the death house believing that he performed a duty to save society from its own ills and rationalized that his act of mass murder was justified.

Hunting for Humans

On the morning of July 18, 1984, James Huberty appeared in court for a simple traffic violation and the judge let him go with a warning. He and his wife, Etna, ate lunch at a McDonald's restaurant and he told her that "society had had its chance." That afternoon, Jim wrapped a few of his guns in a blanket and stuffed several hundred rounds of ammunition in his pockets. He told Etna that he was going "hunting for humans."[23] On his way out of their apartment, he informed one of his daughters that he wouldn't be back. He went straight to the neighborhood McDonald's, calmly walked inside and opened fire. When it was all over, he had murdered twenty-one people, mostly children, in cold blood and wounded nineteen others before a SWAT team killed him.[24]

In considering the victimology of Huberty's rampage, former FBI profiler John Douglas believes that to Huberty, McDonald's represented the kind of life that he could never have. Families had fun at McDonald's and that kind of enjoyment of life was unattainable for him. It was easy to blame those care-free diners for his dismal existence.[25] Like Charles Whitman, Ted Kaczynski, and Timothy McVeigh, James Huberty had been unable to establish and maintain meaningful relationships at any time in his life, especially during childhood. Although he was married with children, he maintained an emotional distance from his family. Huberty's mass killing was, in all likelihood, the inspiration for Hennard's massacre at the Killeen, Texas, Luby's. These mass murderers had many traits in common.

- They were male.[26]
- They were above average in intelligence.
- They had difficulties bonding with parents and significant others during childhood and displayed signs of an attachment disorder.
- They were unable to appropriately or adequately relate to girls and women.
- They were unable to establish meaningful participation in groups, were socially isolated, and were loners.
- They were subjected to some degree of bullying during childhood/adolescence and were rejected by classmates and others.
- They blamed others for their own shortcomings and did not accept responsibility for their own actions.
- They over-identified with an ideology, perhaps inventing their own set of beliefs, and had an emotionally unhealthy obsession with a societal institution. This led to extremist views and a rationalization that their act(s) would achieve a higher purpose.
- Their rampages were preceded by at least one precipitating or "triggering" event that caused long-term frustration and rage and a sense of having no control over their own destiny.
- They had the ability to disassociate themselves from their victims.
- They were "extraordinarily ordinary;" in hindsight, few people even remember them.[27]
- They were "bad, not mad." Most mass killers are not mentally ill; however, most display characteristics of personality

disorders such as sociopathy, borderline personality disorder, or narcissism.[28] Most experience episodes of depression.

- They left clues about their desires and plans to commit acts of mass murder and kept journals or some kind of record of their thoughts and feelings leading up to their rampages.

- They craved fame and public attention and planned their mass homicides in a manner that garnered maximum media coverage.

Not all mass murderers exhibit all of the characteristics listed above, but most possess many of these traits, as did Nidal Hasan.

All of these killers were socially isolated and had no traditional support systems. All of them blamed others for their misdeeds—Whitman blamed his father, Kaczynski blamed technology, McVeigh blamed the government, Hennard blamed the Merchant Marine, and Huberty blamed authority figures. Nidal Hasan blamed the American military for waging war against Islam. These mass murderers experienced a life-long rejection by others and felt that they had no control over their circumstances and, therefore, no power over their own lives. All had been rejected at some point in their lives by traditional, mainstream organizations and institutions.

Criminology experts such as John Douglas, Park Dietz, Jack Levin, and James Alan Fox believe that mass homicides are preceded by years of frustration and are precipitated by specific triggers, or events, that fuel the killers' rampages. Prolonged frustration leads to anger and feelings of inadequacy and powerlessness which, in turn, bring about a desire to control others. A sudden change in circumstance such as death of a significant other, divorce, or loss of job, and occupational grievances, are common triggers for murderous rampages.

In Nidal Hasan's case, his mother, reportedly the only meaningful person in his life, died from the ravages of cancer. Nora Hasan's death had a profound effect on Hasan, her primary caregiver. As a physician-in-training who was taught to save lives, he most certainly felt as though he had lost all control over his own destiny. The September 11, 2001, terrorist attacks occurred shortly after his mother's death. Hasan and many other Muslims were ostracized, shunned, and made to feel that they were personally responsible for the deaths and destruction that occurred as a result of the terrorist attacks. In response, Hasan immersed himself in extreme ideology and became increasingly convinced that the United States' involvement in the wars in Iraq and Afghanistan were assaults against Islam. From that perspective, Hasan was able to very quickly rationalize that America's offensives against the Middle East were personal affronts against him. Hasan's anger toward the military became obvious to his professors, classmates, and co-workers, but not a single person stepped forward and intervened in his downward spiral.

Nidal Hasan's orders to deploy to Afghanistan served as the trigger that precipitated his shooting rampage. He planned, first, to kill his boss, Ltc. Ben Phillips and possibly other co-workers in the behavioral health department. Because Phillips was not at work that day, he proceeded to the Soldier Processing Center and opened fire. The victimology of the crime scene suggests that he first directed his anger at the members of the Wisconsin-based 467th Medical Detachment's combat stress control reserve unit, the unit with which he had been assigned to deploy and whose members were present at the SRP Center at the time of the shooting; and second, at any armed services personnel who were preparing to deploy to one of the war zones. Physician assistant Michael Cahill was the only civilian killed by Hasan that day, only because he attempted to stop the attack. Hasan's bullets were directed to the service members he believed would be killing his Muslim brothers, not to the civilian workers in the Soldier Processing Center.

Nidal Hasan's cold-blooded detachment was foreshadowed in his *Scribd.com* comment justifying suicide bombings. He posted his statement just a few weeks prior to his transfer to Fort Hood and subsequent to his correspondence with Awlaki. Like other mass killers, Hasan was able to disassociate himself from the act of murder. He assumed the role of passive observer when he wrote,

> If one suicide bomber can kill 100 enemy soldiers because they were caught off guard that would be considered a strategic victory. Their intention is not to die because of some despair... You can call them crazy i [*sic*] you want but their act was not one of suicide that is despised by Islam. So the scholars main point

is that "IT SEEMS AS THOUGH YOUR INTENTION IS THE MAIN ISSUE" and Allah (SWT) knows best.[29]

Going Postal

The various government agencies that analyzed the Fort Hood shooting were confronted with the question of whether it should be classified as domestic or workplace violence. As discussed in more detail below, the classification of the Fort Hood shooting as workplace violence rather than an act of terrorism has had a tremendous impact on the eligibility of victims for combat-related benefits. Such a determination begs the question of when this dichotomy arose. There is no regulation that states that workplace violence cannot be an act of terrorism.

Many people associate workplace violence with the highly publicized post office ("going postal") mass shooting committed by Patrick Henry Sherrill in Edmund, Oklahoma, a suburb of Oklahoma City, on August 20, 1986.

Sherrill was a lonely, alienated, unremarkable man who had no friends and who was obsessed with the military. An ex-Marine sharpshooter and a member of the Air Force Reserves, Sherrill lived alone with his mother in a lower middle class neighborhood in Oklahoma City until she died of Alzheimer's in 1978. After her death he remained in the house and bought himself a pit bull.[30]

Sherrill's neighbors abhorred him and the feeling was mutual. Not only was he caught window-peeping several times, but he made obscene telephone calls around the neighborhood and often bothered residents by mowing his lawn at night. Sherrill was obsessed with guns and the military and wore fatigues much of the time. He worked part-time for the postal service and was frequently reprimanded for his sloppiness in delivering the mail. Nine months prior to the attack his supervisor, Bill Bland, suspended him for seven days for failing to deliver mail in a timely manner. A few months later he was written up for spraying mace on a barking dog. The dog was behind a fence and not a threat to Sherrill, and the dog's owner witnessed Sherrill's abusive act.[31]

On the morning before the shooting, Bill Bland and another supervisor chewed Sherrill out inside a glass-enclosed room in front of other employees. On the morning of the massacre, Sherrill placed

139

three semi-automatic pistols and two-hundred rounds of ammunition in his empty mail bag along with eye protection and ear plugs, and reported to work about 6:30 a.m. Bill Bland, the boss that Sherrill hated, had overslept that morning and was late for work, which undoubtedly saved his life. Sherrill opened fire on his fellow employees killing fifteen co-workers and wounding six others. Before the police could get to him, Sherrill shot and killed himself.[32]

Criminal profiler John Douglas recommends that companies implement a general policy that can help identify potentially violent employees.

> We can't track or intensely monitor every seemingly frustrated, unhappy employee or coworker…how do we assess danger, determine who is merely pissed off, and who is so motivated by anger he doesn't even think about all the innocent people he's going to take out with him?[33]

Mass killings are generally precipitated by an emotionally devastating incident or circumstance that serves as a trigger. Whether it's a job loss or a failure to get a promotion, work problems are common triggers for violence. While multiple homicides in the workplace constitute only a small portion of the total number of mass murders, the FBI's Critical Incident Response Group (CIRG) on workplace violence cites a multitude of factors that lead to violent behavior on the job.

Mass murder on the job by disgruntled employees are media-intensive events. However, these mass murders, while serious, are relatively infrequent events. It is the threats, harassment, bullying, domestic violence, stalking, emotional abuse, intimidation, and other forms of behavior and physical violence that, if left unchecked, may result in more serious violent behavior. These are the behaviors that supervisors and managers have to deal with every day.[34]

The CIRG strongly recommends that employers institute violence prevention programs and the group assists local law enforcement agencies to establish measures that employers can utilize to identify potential threats. Employers can set the standards of behavior in the workplace with written policies and procedures. Employees must feel comfortable in reporting suspicious and threatening behaviors to their supervisors in order for violence prevention programs to work. The

CIRG suggests the use of the following definition of a threat: "an inappropriate behavior, verbal or nonverbal communication, or expression that would lead to the reasonable belief that an act has occurred or may occur which may lead to physical and/or psychological harm to the threatener, to others, or to property."[35]

Nidal Hasan chose his workplace as the location for his shooting rampage. There is little doubt that he intended to kill his supervisor, Ltc. Ben Phillips, and possibly his co-workers, prior to perpetrating his mass homicide at the SRP Center. Like Patrick Sherrill, the disgruntled postal worker, Hasan didn't get the opportunity to murder his boss. Neither one of them hesitated to murder their co-workers when their supervisors were unavailable. There were materials discovered in Hasan's car after the shooting that indicated that he planned to commit additional murders elsewhere on base which would have categorized him as a spree killer.

Hasan's act of mass murder differs from Sherrill's, however, because it also involved an ideological preoccupation with Islam and an irrational obsession with saving Muslims by waging his own jihad against the American military. Although Hasan disliked his supervisor, Ltc. Ben Phillips, his plot became manifest while he was at Walter Reed. Unlike Sherrill, whose rage was a response to his supervisor's reprimand, Hasan's act was driven by his warped belief system.

So many times when a mass shooting or bombing occurs, the killer is characterized as having lost control, or just "snapped." To the contrary, the offender is completely in control and has carefully planned all of the smallest details of the rampage. Most mass murderers do not fit the criteria for insanity, which, by definition, requires that the perpetrator be incapable of discerning right from wrong. In their book, *Mass Murder: America's Growing Menace*, authors Levin and Fox state that a mass killer "is not sick in either a medical or a legal sense... [he] definitely knows right from wrong, definitely realizes he has committed a sinful act, but simply doesn't care about his human prey."

All of the killers discussed in this chapter absolutely knew that their homicidal acts were wrong. They killed because they wanted to.[36]

As a means for rationalizing their bad acts, mass murderers depersonalize their victims in order to be able to look upon them as objects, not as human beings. That's why Timothy McVeigh's actions were such a dichotomy—on the one hand he was emotionally distressed when he saw his neighbor place helpless kittens in a burlap bag and drown them, and he experienced extreme feelings of sorrow after he killed Iraqis in Desert Storm. On the other hand, McVeigh had no problem with murdering one 168 innocent people in Oklahoma City. Nidal Hasan accidentally rolled over on his pet parakeet and killed it. He dug a grave for his bird and visited it often and wept for it. But when it came to murdering fellow soldiers, he was cold, calculating, and determined.

The vast majority of mass murderers express their frustrations and desire to commit violence to at least one other person, or in some way leave clues about their homicidal intentions. Nidal Hasan told several people that the military would regret it if he was ever deployed to a war zone in a Middle Eastern country. He left comments on websites that revealed his belief that retaliation against those who killed Muslims was acceptable, even laudable, behavior. No one took his threats seriously despite the fact that he left plenty of clues. During his trial, he released some of his copious writings to the press.

Most mass killers don't plan to survive their own acts of violence. Suicide is an integral part of their plan—either at their own hand or "suicide by cop." After the shooting, Hasan admitted to military psychiatrists that he had not planned to survive his attack.

Excerpted from *Inspire* magazine

9. Playing With Fire

And inspire the believers to fight.
~Inspire magazine

I t only takes a spark to ignite a combustible material and the silver-tongued preacher, Anwar al Awlaki, lit a fire inside a grieving Nidal Hasan. Five months after Awlaki captivated worshipers at the Dar al-Hijrah mosque with his eloquent sermons, cancer-ravaged Nora Hasan died. Perhaps sensing the darkness that would overcome her son, she made Nidal promise to find God. For Hasan, Awlaki's sermons opened a pathway to Allah.

Anwar al Awlaki was born in Las Cruces, New Mexico, in 1971. His father, Nasser, an agricultural economics student at New Mexico State University, came to the United States from Yemen on a student visa to work on a graduate degree. With his parents rooted in the conservative religious traditions of the nomadic Bedouin Awlak tribe of southern Yemen, young Anwar was more likely to hear stories of martyrs and the mujahideen than Dr. Seuss and Winnie the Pooh.[1]

The Awlaki family moved back to Yemen when Anwar was seven years old. His father served as Yemen's Agriculture Minister as well as holding chancellorships at two universities. He was financially well-off and politically connected which enabled the family to enjoy an upscale lifestyle. Anwar was sent to the best private schools in Yemen and received both academic and religious training. Having spent the first seven years of his life in the United States, he was fluent in English and Arabic, an important skill that would serve him well later in his life.[2]

After high school graduation, in 1991, Awlaki returned to the United States on a foreign student scholarship to study engineering at Colorado State University. Although his family could afford to pay his expenses, Awlaki lied about his U.S. citizenship in order to qualify for financial aid. He lived a typical austere student's life in a one bedroom apartment and drove an old car in serious need of repair. Although he prayed at the Fort Collins mosque, he did not appear to be particularly devout. That changed when he visited Afghanistan in 1993 and saw first-hand the devastation wrought by the Soviets during their ten year war against the mujahideen. The Soviets ravaged the country and left most of its citizens destitute. Awlaki found the plight of the Afghanis depressing.[3]

After graduating with a civil engineering degree in 1994, Awlaki accepted a job as imam of the Denver Islamic Society. It was there he discovered that he had an aptitude for preaching. His extensive knowledge of the Qur'an, his flawless, unaccented English, his personal magnetism, and his gift for storytelling attracted new congregants. He married one of his cousins and they lived in a small cottage on the grounds of the mosque. A pond on the property afforded him the opportunity to engage in one of his favorite pastimes—fishing. Awlaki often shared his catch with his congregation.[4]

After serving as the leader of the Denver Islamic Society for two years, Awlaki moved to a larger mosque in San Diego, California, the Masjid Ar-Ribat al-Islami, where he served as imam. At the same time he also enrolled in a master's degree program at San Diego State University. Most of Awlaki's congregation regarded him as a moderate, soft-spoken, articulate preacher whose message was mainstream. Although married with children, Awlaki, who hesitated to shake hands with women, was arrested twice for soliciting prostitution.[5]

It was in San Diego that Awlaki became acquainted with radical Islamic organizations. He accepted a position on the board of directors of a charitable foundation run by an associate of Osama bin Laden which was later discovered to be a fundraising front for al Qaeda. He also met with a colleague of Omar Abdel Rahman, the "blind sheik," who was successfully prosecuted for seditious conspiracy in the 1993 attack on the World Trade Center. Two of Awlaki's congregants, Khalid al-Mihdar and Nawaf al-Hamzi, who hijacked American Airlines Flight 77, sometimes met with Awlaki behind closed doors. Hamzi commented to other congregants that he considered Awlaki his spiritual advisor.[6]

Awlaki may have preached against vice and sin but not only did he frequent the company of prostitutes, he could not resist his urge to gamble. He participated in several get-rich-quick schemes, even losing $20,000 that he borrowed from relatives to buy into a speculative gold venture. *US News & World Report* magazine claimed that Awlaki also invested in the Yemen honey trade, as did Osama bin Laden.[7] Federal intelligence agents discovered a network of bin Laden-controlled honey shops in the Middle East that were used for operational support in moving weapons, drugs, and operatives from place to place. Yemen, in particular, produces some of the most treasured honey in the region.[8]

In 2001, after five years as leader of the Masjid Ar-Ribat al-Islami in San Diego, Awlaki accepted a position as imam of the Dar al-Hijrah Islamic Community Center in Falls Church, VA. He followed a familiar pattern and enrolled in a doctoral program at George Washington University where he also served as their Muslim chaplain. Awlaki's reputation as a gifted orator attracted new congregants wherever he preached. He motivated and inspired his audiences with sermons that blended secular themes such as an interview with Michael Jackson in which the pop star expressed his desire to "live forever" and frequent references to "Joe Sixpack." Two of the September 11 hijackers, Nawaf al-Hamzi and Hani Hanjour, followed Awlaki to his new mosque in Falls Church from Arizona where they had been enrolled in a pilot training program.[9]

Shortly after moving to Virginia and taking over the Dar al-Hijrah mosque, Awlaki returned to San Diego in August, 2001, to fetch the remainder of his belongings. He knocked on one of his former neighbor's door to tell him goodbye. When the neighbor asked him to stop by and visit the next time he was in the area, Awlaki remarked "I don't think you'll be seeing me. I won't be coming back to San Diego again. Later on you'll find out why." Within the month al Qaeda attacked the Twin Towers and the Pentagon. His neighbor remembered his brief conversation with Awlaki and concluded that the cleric had advance knowledge of 9/11.[10]

Awlaki was quite the social butterfly in the aftermath of September 11. The Congressional Muslim Staff Association (CMSA) invited him to preach at its Friday jummah prayers, and, in an effort to reach out to the Muslim community, officials from the Pentagon invited Awlaki to eat lunch with them.[11] He was called upon frequently by the media for interviews, including a two-part report by *National Geographic News* published just seventeen days after 9/11. In that interview, Awlaki talked about being scrutinized by the FBI and he placed blame on Israel for the attacks. He also issued a veiled threat to the United States, saying "the U.S. needs to be very careful and not have itself perceived as an enemy of Islam." He declared that the reason for the attacks was poverty and lack of freedom.

> There are some people who went through a miserable life. So we need to strive as human beings to improve the situation of everybody on the planet, not just look at ourselves....When there are people who have freedom and people who don't, people who are extremely wealthy and people who are destitute, you get into these conflicts.[12]

The *New York Times* went so far as to label Awlaki a "new generation of Muslim leader capable of merging East and West." Later, the FBI acknowledged his celebrity status and said that "Aulaqi is a prime example of a radicalization leader. He established and sustained an international reputation as a prolix, charismatic imam who provided Islamic guidance in English through sermons, lectures, publications, recordings, and a website."[13]

Although Awlaki's commentary and façade were quite moderate following 9/11, his actual views were extreme. In an article for the *Atlantic*, J. M. Berger traces Awlaki's movements during the two year period of 1999-2001 and concludes that the cleric was deeply involved in the planning of 9/11. An FBI agent told the 9/11 Commission that "if anyone had knowledge of the plot, it was Awlaki."[14]

The FBI had opened a file on Awlaki in 2000 but concluded that he did not "meet the criterion for [further] investigation" and closed it.[15] While they did not have direct information concerning Awlaki's involvement with 9/11, they suspected that he had prior knowledge of the attacks and they wanted to question him again. A warrant for fraud, based upon his falsified passport, was issued while Awlaki was out of the country. About the same time, German intelligence officials found Awlaki's telephone number inside the home of Yemen-born Ramzi Binalshibh, one of the al Qaeda 9/11 conspirators. Upon his arrival back into the United States, Awlaki was detained by the FBI but his arrest warrant was withdrawn on a technicality. The FBI had no choice but to release him.[16]

For months, federal agents had observed Awlaki transporting prostitutes across state lines and thought about detaining him on a little-used 1910 federal statute, the Mann Act, originally aimed at pimps, but he left the country before they could bring him in for questioning.[17] The 9/11 Commission Report indicates that there was not enough information on Awlaki to prove that he was a co-conspirator in the September 11 attacks, but he was certainly a suspect.[18]

Awlaki was angry that he had been labeled a terrorist. In retaliation, he set out on a personal mission to initiate violent jihad against the United States. He declared that the U.S. was waging war against Muslims and argued that unbelievers were "plotting to kill this religion…plotting day and night."[19] At a series of lectures in London in 2003, one of his students characterized him as "the main man who translated the jihad into English."[20] Another of his students, Nidal Hasan, listened to Awlaki's recordings and hung on his every word.

One of Awlaki's congregants suggested that he record his sermons and lectures and sell the recordings. His fifty-three CD's about the life of Muhammad, plus numerous other recordings, were very popular and netted him a good sum of money.[21] In addition to his CD's, Awlaki used YouTube, his blog, social media, and jihadist web sites to get his radical Islam messages out to as many potential followers as possible.

Awlaki's reputation and fame grew in Britain and, while he enjoyed brisk sales of his CD's, he lacked sufficient income to fully support himself and his family. He moved back to Yemen and, when he intervened in a local tribal dispute, was arrested by Yemini authorities. In 2006, Awlaki was imprisoned and his presence on the Internet temporarily ceased.

During Awlaki's incarceration Nidal Hasan continued to actively study Islam. On March 29, 2006, Hasan posted an "Imam Needed" classified ad on an Islamist website.

> Brothers and sisters,
>
> Walter Reed Army Medical Center is in need of an Imam for jumua'ah prayers held at WRAMC in Washington, D.C., as well as to console/make dua for Muslim patients in the Medical Center. This has the option of becoming a full-time position, based on experience and educational qualification. For more information, please contact br. Nidal Hasan at Nidal.Hasan@NA.AMEDD.ARMY.MIL.
>
> May Allah bless your efforts, wassalama alaykum.[22]

It is interesting that Hasan felt comfortable using his military email address for responses to his ad instead of his personal one.

While Awlaki was serving his time, FBI agents traveled to Yemen and questioned him. He was released in 2007 when the FBI informed the Yemini authorities that they did not have sufficient cause to hold him. Awlaki came out of prison a very hardened, angry man and he declared that he would not rest until he witnessed the fall of the United States. It was reported that Awlaki became a fan of Charles Dickens' novels while incarcerated in Yemen.[23]

After his release, Yemeni security forces followed Awlaki's every move. Disgusted over his lack of privacy, Awlaki retreated to family property in the southern province of Shabwa where he tended to his radical jihadi website, his Facebook page, and his blog where he coordinated the training of young holy warriors, the mujahideen, bent on committing jihad in the west—among them, Saudi bomb-making savant Ibrahim Hassan al-Asiri, underwear bomber Umar Farouk Abdulmutallab, and media-savvy Samir Khan.[24] Personal one-on-one terror training had become much more difficult after the September 11 attacks, however, and Awlaki had no choice but to promote self-radicalization through the Internet in addition to training indoctrinees in terrorist camps.

While Nidal Hasan never expressed a desire to travel to Yemen to join the rank and file of the AQAP mujahideen, he, nevertheless, shared situational commonalities and personality traits with many other young men who did seek out a more personal jihadi experience. Hasan joined the hundreds of Islamist converts who immersed themselves in jihadist propaganda through Awlaki's website and mass indoctrination emails.[25]

Not only did Hasan admire Awlaki as a religious leader, he felt a kinship with the imam. Both of them came from countries in the Middle East that shared histories of extreme political turmoil, poverty, and deeply rooted Bedouin cultural traditions. Notably, both countries are terrorist training grounds.

Both Anwar al-Awlaki's and Nidal Hasan's ancestries were rooted in fundamentalist Bedouin tribes comprised of herders and foragers who, for over two thousand years, expended most of their energy searching for food and water for themselves and their herds of sheep, goats, and camels. Bedouin tradition requires that they display faultless hospitality to any visitor—friend or enemy—yet, their interpersonal relationships are marked by generations of blood feuds, and their system of justice is swift and harsh. Cutting off the hand of a thief is viewed more as a deterrent than as a punishment. There is no separation of church and state. Shari'ah law, or fundamentalist Islam, serves as both.[26]

There is an ominous presence of al Qaeda in Yemen's Shabwa province, the ancestral home of Awlaki, where jihadi training camps pepper the stark, harsh landscape. Until recently there had been no paved roads, no electricity, and no functioning schools. In January 2009, the al Qaeda franchise, al Qaeda in the Arabian Peninsula (AQAP), a union of al Qaeda groups in Saudi Arabia and Yemen, took advantage of the social and government unrest in Yemen and officially began operating in Shabwa. That same year Secretary of State Hilary Clinton designated AQAP a terrorist organization. At the time, AQAP was considered to be the most unified and most dangerous al Qaeda franchise in the world. The terrorist group has won the hearts and minds of the south Yemeni people through its efforts to provide schools, teachers, electricity, and other essentials.[27] In this isolated and protective environment, Awlaki was able to devote his time and efforts to recruiting and training a cadre of devoted young followers.

The legacy left by Hasan's mother obligated him to find God. Awlaki was the logical agent through which Hasan could fulfill her wish. Timing and circumstances created a perfect storm that led Hasan down a path to tragedy.

Martyrs and Mayhem

One of Awlaki's most valuable assets was Ibrahim Hassan Tali al-Asiri. Asiri, a native of the Saudi Arabian capital city of Riyadh, was (and continues to be) obsessed with explosives. His father, Hassan, was a career Saudi soldier and his family was religious but did not subscribe to fundamental radical Islam. One of five boys and three girls, Asiri and his brother, Abdullah, were especially pious in their early youth. "Abdullah used to call for prayer at a mosque in the area they were living in and sometimes led the prayer," says his father, Hassan. "In Ramadan he used to stand at traffic lights before the Iftar and hand out food."[28]

Ibrahim and Abdullah became involved in the Saudi al Qaeda franchise and Ibrahim was imprisoned in a Saudi Arabian jail for participating in terrorist activities. When he was released in 2007, he and Abdullah made a bee line for the Saudi-Yemen border and they joined the Yemeni mujahideen. When AQAP was established in January 2009, both boys were happy to become full-fledged members of Awlaki's team.[29]

Asiri found a kindred spirit in Awlaki. Both men had come out of their respective prisons angry, bitter, and determined to get revenge. Asiri quickly demonstrated an aptitude for bomb-making and Awlaki called upon him to use his talent. First, Asiri had a personal matter to take care of. While imprisoned in Saudi Arabia, he had developed an overwhelming hatred for the Saudi royalty responsible for his confinement. In August 2009, he convinced his twenty-three year old brother, Abdullah, to carry out a suicide bombing against the Saudi Deputy Interior Minister Prince Mohammad bin Nayef. Abdullah contacted the prince and told him that he wished to turn himself in to authorities. Asiri fitted his brother with a prototype underwear bomb. Bin Nayef sent a private jet to Yemen to fly Abdullah to Jeddah, Saudi Arabia, where he was given a private audience in the interior ministry offices. When the bomb detonated, the blast blew Abdullah into pieces but barely injured the prince.[30] Several reports of the incident stated that Ibrahim had planted the bomb in Abdullah's rectum; others reported that the bomb was contained in his undergarments. This distinction is important only because recent intelligence suggests that Asiri is currently working with physicians to perfect a surgical method of hiding explosives inside the body. Abdullah was searched prior to boarding Prince bin Nayef's private plane and his implanted bomb was not detected.[31]

Abdullah's parents took the news of his suicide bombing with disbelief. His father accused AQAP of "snatching" his sons. "We were living in Makkah [Mecca] two years ago and were planning to move back to Riyadh, but Abdullah and Ibrahim said they wanted to go to Madina [Medina] before coming back with us," Hassan Asiri said. "Abdullah later contacted us to say he was out of the country, but didn't say where and from that day on we had no more news of him until we saw his and his brother's pictures a few months ago in the media as on the list of wanted people."[32]

Asiri's choice of the explosive PETN, pentaerythritol tetranitrate, is in the same chemical family as nitroglycerin. It is a relatively stable, powerful compound that is available as either a powder, a cord (commonly used in mining operations), or in thin sheets of plasticized material, and it is difficult to accidentally detonate. PETN bombs can be constructed without metal parts, using chemical fuses, making them undetectable in standard airport security systems. According to explosives expert Jimmie Oxley, PhD, professor of chemistry at the University of Rhode Island, PETN is a very dense substance and can only be spotted with certain types of x-rays and full-body scans.[33]

"If your luggage gets swabbed, it can also be detected," she says.[34] "I doubt there's any foolproof [screening] method that we can instigate."[35] PETN can be detonated by chemical heat or shockwaves and it is generally unnoticeable to bomb-sniffing dogs. PETN residue can be identified in human hair, but the TSA does not currently possess the technology to accomplish rapid, widespread sampling of airline passengers' hair follicles—even if it did, terrorists could simply remove their body hair.

PETN has a storied history. It came into the limelight between World Wars I and II and was tested at Los Alamos for use as a detonator in nuclear weapons. PETN was one of the components in the bomb that brought down Flight 103 over Lockerbie, Scotland on December 21, 1988. On December 22, 2001, "shoe bomber" Richard Reid attempted to detonate a PETN bomb hidden in a hollowed-out cavity in the bottom of his shoe, but the fuse was damp, rendering the explosive ineffective. PETN is also used in medical applications as a vasodilator for preventing angina and touted by some as a preventive agent for facial rosacea outbreaks.[36] The explosive is also commonly utilized in hydraulic fracturing.[37]

Word Wars

Samir Khan, another of Awlaki's devotees, became one of the most valuable assets in AQAP. It was Khan's expertise and talent that provided a means for Awlaki to widely distribute his violent jihadi rhetoric.

As a child, Khan, the middle child of Pakistani parents, lived for a time in Saudi Arabia. When the family immigrated to the Long Island, New York, in 1992, Khan was very self-conscious because he didn't look or sound like his classmates. Like Nidal Hasan, Khan was an outsider. Also like Hasan, he was a quiet studious child, socially isolated, and a loner. He spent hours on the Internet and in high school, following 9/11, his mainstream Muslim perspective turned radical. Family friend Steve Elturk, imam of the Islamic Organization of North America, spoke to Khan about his increasingly radical views.[38]

"He developed these militant views through the Internet, and he had arguments with his father about it," Elturk says. "He became very much convinced that America is an imperialist country that supports dictators and supports Israel blindly."[39]

Khan's parents forbade him from accessing the Internet but he found other sources of extremist Islamic ideology. In the tenth grade he began wearing a Kufi, a round Muslim cap, and refused to participate in reciting the Pledge of Allegiance. He did participate in two school activities—he worked on his high school newspaper and, for a brief time, played football on the junior varsity team. Khan displayed no emotion about the loss of life caused by the September 11 attacks. His classmates began to wonder if he was "like them." One of them remarked to him "What's your deal man? You hate America?"[40]

Khan began engaging his classmates in arguments about terrorism and his religious views became increasingly obsessive and radical. He resumed his Internet habits and posted comments on terrorism-related blogs. Under his name in his high school senior yearbook was the single word *Mujahid* (a Muslim engaged in jihad), and underneath *Mujahid* was the phrase, "If you give satan an inch, he'll be a ruler." He wrote, "I'm planning to teach philosophy in religion. During the learning process, I hope to go oversees [*sic*] and study Islamic law in other subjects that deal with Islam."[41]

After graduation, Khan's father, a computer analyst, landed a better job in Charlotte, North Carolina and moved the family to an upscale neighborhood. There Khan resumed his extremist Internet presence. According to an unnamed intelligence official, Khan posted comments about founding an Islamic state. By 2007 he was using the Internet handle of *Insha Allah Shaheed*, which means "God willing to be a martyr." Khan started a website called "Jihad Recollections," which published messages from Osama bin Laden and "other extremists waging holy wars in Islam's name."[42]

Khan's parents were very worried about their son and his father staged an intervention with a local imam, several Muslim community leaders, and Jibril Hough, a spokesman for the Islamic Center of Charlotte. For the most part, Khan listened to the men politely while they urged him to abandon his extremist beliefs. The group met twice and Khan made a feeble attempt to explain his view that Americans should be held accountable for killing and "abusing" Muslims in Afghanistan and Iraq.[43]

In October of 2008, after communicating with Awlaki on the Internet, Khan bought a one-way ticket to Yemen. In the summer of 2010, AQAP released the premier issue of its brand new magazine, *Inspire*. Khan was the editor—his high school newspaper experience had proved valuable. In his "Letter From the Editor" Khan wrote, "Allāh says: And inspire the believers to fight (al-Anfāl:65). It is from this verse that we derive the name of our new magazine."[44]

The al Qaeda media company, Al-Malahem Media Foundation, is listed as the publisher of *Inspire*, an English-only publication designed to appeal to the western aesthetic. In appearance, it looks like a copycat production of the *New York Times Magazine* with its provoking cover, slick and sophisticated design, and photography-driven feature stories.

The premier issue of *Inspire* magazine left no doubt that AQAP was operationally aligned with Osama bin Laden, al Shabab, the September 11 hijackers, and other radical Islamic groups. Yet, in an article written by Awlaki in the first issue, he admits that Nidal Hasan acted alone and without assistance from al Qaeda.

> Nidal Hasan was not recruited by al Qaeda. Nidal Hasan was recruited by American crimes, and this is what America refuses to admit. America refuses to admit that its foreign policies are the reason behind a man like Nidal Hasan, born and raised in the U.S., turning his guns against American soldiers. And the more crimes America commits, the more mujahidin will be recruited to fight against it.[45]

There is no doubt, however, that Awlaki's communications with Hasan influenced his shooting rampage. In an interview with the *Yemen Post* published just prior to the *Summer 2010* release of *Inspire*, Awlaki discussed his email correspondence with Hasan:

> Q: Sheikh Anwar, what is your relationship with Nidal, and when did it start?
>
> A: Brother Nidal…was praying in my mosque when I was the cleric of Dar Al-Hijrah Islamic Center.
>
> Q: When was the first meeting between the both of you?
>
> A: Some nine years ago when I was the cleric of Dar Al-Hijra in Washington, D.C.
>
> Q: Reports revealed that your relations were more than that?
>
> A: Brother Nidal was also contacting me via e-mail over the past year.
>
> Q: When did Nidal's first email contact start?
>
> A: The first message I received from him was on 17, December 2008.
>
> Q: Who began contacting the other, you or him?
>
> A: He started contacting me.

Q: What did he want from you overall?

A: His messages were asking about the Islamic rule of killing a Muslim soldier who served in the U.S. Army. And in other letters he explained his view of killing Israeli civilians and was in favor of this, he mentioned the legal and factual justifications for targeting Jews with rockets. Later, there were some of his letters that asked for a way he can transfer some funds to us, to contribute on charity works.

Q: There are other signs of your relation with him like how you blessed his attack three days after he implemented the operation?

A: The operation done by Hasan was heroic, and I tried to articulate my opinion on what happened because many of the Islamic organizations and preachers in the West condemned the operation.

Q: How can you support what he has done, he betrayed his homeland the U.S.?

A: More importantly than that, he does not betray his religion. Working in the U.S. military to fight Muslims is a betrayal to Islam. America today is the Pharaoh of yesterday, it is the enemy of Islam. A Muslim is not permitted to work in the U.S. military, unless he intends to follow the footsteps of our brother Nidal. Allegiance in Islam is to God (Allah), His Messenger… and the faithful believers, not for a handful of land and dust they call "homeland." An American-Muslim's loyalty is to the Muslim nation, not for America. Hasan has proved that, through his blessed operation; may God richly reward him.

Q: Are you directly related to the incident?

A: I did not advise Hasan, but he was recruited by the U.S. by its crimes and its injustice; this is what America does not want to admit. Yes, I might have a role in the "intellectual guidance" to him, but not more than that.[46]

In the first issue of *Inspire* magazine, Osama bin Laden contributed an article about global warming; Ibrahim al Asiri wrote a tutorial on

"How to Make a Bomb in the Kitchen of Your Mom," complete with numbered instructions and close-up photos of the steps required to construct both chemical and mechanical explosive devices. There are sixty-seven photo-driven pages of how to pack for a jihad, how to send and receive encrypted messages, murder threats against cartoonists who depict caricatures of Mohammed, and even a "Contact Us" page. Inside its slick, professionally edited pages there are numerous direct threats to the United States. The large header on page sixty-six reads "America and the Final Trap," and underneath "With her missile campaigns upon the honorable Muslims of Yemen, America has forced itself into a new front with the steadfast Mujahidin, setting for herself a final trap for annihilation."[47]

Underwear Wars

Nidal Hasan, Ibrahim al Asiri, and Samir Khan were not the only persons to fall into Awlaki's gravitational grip. For AQAP, 2009 and 2010 proved to be very busy years. After Asiri's suicide bombing attempt of Prince Mohammad bin Nayef, a Nigerian graduate student, Umar Farouk Abdulmutallab, traveled to Yemen to seek an audience with Awlaki.

Farouk was a highly educated young man who had grown up in a life of privilege. He abandoned all of his many advantages to travel to Yemen in search of Awlaki. He surrendered all his assets to Awlaki's cause and, without hesitation, agreed to trade his life for martyrdom. After filming a five minute martyrdom video, Farouk was outfitted with one of Asiri's PETN underwear bombs and he zigzagged his way to Amsterdam on a number of flights. During an extraordinary lapse of security he was able to board an Airbus bound for Detroit without a passport on Christmas day, 2009, just six weeks after Hasan's shooting rampage. Awlaki had instructed Farouk that the only requirement was that the bomb be detonated over United States soil.

On the eight hour flight from Amsterdam to Detroit, Farouk fasted and refrained from eating and drinking. Shortly after the wide body Airbus A330 reached Canadian airspace, Farouk, in window seat 19-A, took a fifteen minute trip to one of the bathrooms where he prayed and "purified" himself by washing his hands and body, dousing himself with a perfumed substance, and brushing his teeth. After returning to his seat he prayed for a few moments, then placed a blanket over his head, completely covering his body. According to the trial transcript, when the Airbus entered the Detroit area at 11:38 a.m.,

> He pushed the plunger on the bomb and he set [it] off. And then there was a loud pop. Almost all of the passengers on the plane heard [it]. Many described that it sounded like a fire cracker, and then there was smoke and the smoke was coming from where the defendant was sitting. And then there was a fireball, and the fireball was literally on the defendant. It was on his lap, and it was coming out from inside his clothes. And he was enveloped in the fireball. And then the fireball spread and it started a fire on the seat and the carpeting and some of the other areas of the aircraft, and then all hell broke loose. While that fireball was on him, the defendant sat there. He didn't move. He was expressionless. He was completely blank.[48]

One nearby passenger shouted at Farouk several times, "Dude, your pants are on fire." Several people attempted to put the fire out, but because it was a chemical fire, water and suffocation had no effect. Many of the passengers panicked and believed that the airliner was in jeopardy of crashing. Amidst screams and cries of alarm, flight attendants rushed to Farouk with fire extinguishers and quickly put out the flames.[49]

After the flight crew extinguished the fire, they hustled Farouk to the first seat in the business class, I-G. His pants dragged on the floor and a piece of the bomb fell from his burned underwear. One of the flight attendants pulled his pants and shoes completely off of him and he was given a blanket to cover himself. He quickly and willingly admitted to the crew that he had ignited a bomb with the sole purpose of bringing down the flight. Asked if he was in pain, he nodded his head. He told the crew members that he was working for al Qaeda. The Captain radioed air flight control and asked for emergency assistance. Air space was cleared and Northwest Flight 253 made its descent in record time. Only seven minutes elapsed between the time Farouk ignited his underwear and the flight landed. Had it not been for the sweat that dampened the fuse in his underpants, the aircraft could have very well been blown to pieces.[50] Farouk is currently imprisoned at the federal Supermax facility in Florence, Colorado, in the company of Unabomber Ted Kaczynski, Terry Nichols, and other notorious killers. He will remain there for the rest of his life.

The most important and serious failure by authorities was allowing Farouk to board the flight without a passport. According to passengers who were playing cards near the boarding area in Amsterdam, a middle-aged Indian man walked with Farouk to the ticket agents at the gate and told them that it was imperative that Farouk board the flight because he was a Sudanese refuge. These same passengers looked for the Indian man when all of them were sequestered in Detroit, but did not see him. Another Indian gentleman who was on that flight was handcuffed by federal agents and marched out of the area after dogs identified his luggage as suspicious. Those passengers believe that Farouk did not act alone—they believe that the two Indian men were co-conspirators. There has never been any evidence that was made public that linked the two Indian men to Farouk.[51]

A White House press release dated January 7, 2009, identified the primary failures that permitted Farouk to fly to the United States with a bomb secreted on his person and with the express purpose of bringing the airliner down:

A failure of intelligence analysis, whereby the counterterrorism (CT) community failed before December 25 to identify, correlate, and fuse into a coherent story all of the discrete pieces of intelligence held by the U.S. Government related to an emerging terrorist plot against the U.S. Homeland organized by al Qaeda in the Arabian Peninsula and to Mr. Abdulmutallab, the individual terrorist.

A failure within the CT community, starting with established rules and protocols, to assign responsibility and accountability for follow-up of high priority threat streams, run down all leads, and track them through to completion; and shortcomings of the watchlisting system, whereby the CT community failed to identify intelligence within U.S. government holdings that would have allowed Mr. Abdulmutallab to be watchlisted, and potentially prevented from boarding an aircraft bound for the United States.[52]

Farouk spoke openly and candidly to paramedics and nurses who treated his burns and to the FBI agents who questioned him. He expressed his belief that radical jihad is mandatory for salvation and that "one's obligation for jihad ends only when Muslim lands are free from Western occupation." A nurse asked him "about today on the plane, don't you consider that harming yourself or others?" Farouk replied: "no that is martyrdom." Farouk believed that the innocent bystanders who would have been killed were collateral damage and he was convinced that the attack was "righteous" and transformative and that the mission was sacred.[53]

From the remains of Farouk's underwear bomb, the FBI concluded that it was made from PETN, the same material that was used in the construction of the bomb used in the Saudi Arabia's Prince bin Nayef's assassination attempt. It had all the markings of Asiri's explosive devices. The FBI discovered Asiri's fingerprint on the inside of Farouk's explosive underwear.

While the United States breathed a sigh of relief over the close call of Flight 253, AQAP boasted of Farouk's operational success. In the premier issue of *Inspire*, Farouk was lauded as a hero, as was Nidal Hasan.

> With the grace of Allah alone the heroic martyrdom bomber brother Umar al-Faruq managed to carry out a special operation on an American Airplane, from the Dutch city Amsterdam to the American city Detroit, and this happened during the Christmas holiday, Friday December 25, 2009. He managed to penetrate all devices, modern advanced technology and security check points in the international airports bravely without fear of death...and defying the great myth of the American and international intelligence, and exposing how fragile they are, bringing their nose to the ground, and making them regret all that they spent on security technology.
>
> The mujahidin brothers in the manufacturing department managed with the grace of Allah to make an advanced bomb. The bomb had been tested and proven effective as it has passed through the detector ports...we call on every soldier working in the crusader armies and puppet governments to repent to Allah and follow the example of the heroic mujahid brother Nidal Hassan [*sic*] to stand up and kill all the crusad-

ers by all means available to him. We will come to you with slaughter and have prepared men who love death as you love life.[53]

IN OCTOBER 2010, TWO CARGO AIRPLANES belonging to FedEx and UPS on refueling stops in England and the United Arab Emirates were discovered to be carrying explosives. Authorities were tipped off; otherwise, it is doubtful that the bombs would have been discovered. PETN was packed inside toner cartridges that were placed into printers, and the printers were stowed in containers that were addressed to two Chicago synagogues. The printers contained enough explosive material to destroy an aircraft. One of the parcels actually traveled on two passenger flights for part of its route. One of the bombs contained a cell phone SIMS card as a detonator; the other a timer.[54] A copy of Charles Dickens's *Great Expectations* was tucked inside of one of the boxes.[55] Intelligence officials recognized the printer bombs as the handiwork of AQAP explosives guru Ibrahim Asiri.[56]

Looking back on cargo flights originating from Yemen, intelligence officials believe that AQAP made a dry run just weeks prior to the cargo jet's transport of printer bombs. The *New York Times* reported that "the plotters may have used the information to estimate when cargo planes carrying the parcel bombs would be over Chicago, or another city, to trigger explosions and cause the greatest damage."[57]

A few months after the AQAP parcel bombing failure, in an action to curb the flow of money to Asiri by "blocking all property subject to U.S. jurisdiction in which al-Asiri has an interest and prohibiting all transactions by U.S. persons with al-Asiri,"[58] U.S. Secretary of State Hilary Clinton officially designated the AQAP mad bomber a terrorist. According to the State Department press release.

> Al-Asiri is an AQAP operative and serves as the terrorist organization's primary bomb maker. Before joining AQAP, al-Asiri was part of an al Qaeda affiliated terrorist cell in Saudi Arabia and was involved in planned bombings of oil facilities in the Kingdom. Al-Asiri gained particular notoriety for the recruitment of his younger brother as a suicide bomber in a

failed assassination attempt of Saudi Prince Muhammed bin
Nayif. Although the assassination attempt failed, the brutality,
novelty and sophistication of the plot is illustrative of the
threat posed by al-Asiri.[59]

AQAP responded to the failed bombings with a special issue of
Inspire magazine, which they called "Operation Hemorrhage." AQAP
also claimed that one of their bombs had been successful in causing
the crash of a September 3, 2010 UPS cargo jet bound for Cologne,
Germany from Dubai. The statement released by AQAP stated in part,

> We have been enabled by Allah to blowup [*sic*]a UPS cargo
> plane on the 3rd of September, 2010, after its takeoff from
> Dubai International Airport. We have succeeded in bringing
> down the UPS plane but because the enemy's media did not
> attribute the operation to us we have remained silent so we
> may repeat the operation. This time we sent two explosive
> packages, one was sent through UPS, and the other through
> FedEx....We would like to say to Obama: We have struck
> against your aircrafts [*sic*] twice within one year and we will
> continue directing our blows towards your interests and the
> interests of your allies....Since the two operations have suc-
> ceeded, it is our plan to disseminate the idea to the mujahidin
> worldwide[*sic*]and to expand its deployment.[60]

In another related article, AQAP boasted that "Operation
Hemorrhage" "forced the West to spend billions of dollars to defend
its airplanes" and called the crash of the UPS cargo plane a "brilliant
success." AQAP also claimed that western airport security systems
were incapable of detecting PETN explosives.

> We have researched the various security systems employed
> by airports. We looked into X-Ray scanners, full body scan-
> ners, sniffing dogs and other aspects of security...we were
> confident that...it would pass through the most stringent
> and up-to-date security equipment. We were right....We were
> very optimistic about the outcome of this operation. That is
> why we dropped into one of the boxes a novel titled, *Great
> Expectations.*[61]

In July 2011, TSA Administrator John Pistole told CNN that Asiri was working with physicians to develop explosives that could be surgically implanted in humans. The TSA admitted that it would be difficult, if not impossible, for full-body scanners to detect a surgically implanted bomb. The TSA utilizes "overlapping layers of security" that "include intelligence information about possible plots, equipment that checks for minute traces of explosives, behavior detection officers and canine teams."[62]

The CIA thwarted an AQAP plot in 2012 to bring down an airliner to coincide with the anniversary of the death of Osama bin Laden. John Pistole told the audience at an Aspen, Colorado, security forum that an upgraded underwear bomb was smuggled out of Yemen by a double agent. It contained a different type of explosive and a more refined detonation system.[63]

Fatal Attractions

Belonging to groups is a fundamental human need. The family is an individual's first experience with group interaction and behavior. A physically and mentally healthy family life is critical in the socialization process. Sometimes, however, families are dysfunctional to the point where children are unable to perform within the parameters of societal expectations. These individuals are at risk of becoming socially isolated, frustrated, and angry and may seek violence as a way of acting out their feelings of inferiority. Terrorist organizations target societal rejects who are all too happy to find acceptance and self esteem within their ranks.

If an individual cannot find a socially acceptable organization, formal or informal, with which to become affiliated, he or she will seek out relationships with unorthodox or socially unacceptable groups. Oklahoma bomber, Timothy McVeigh, sought the company of like-minded survivalists by attending gun shows and joining the Ku Klux Klan. Nidal Hasan identified with radical Islam. Unabomber Ted Kaczynski, the consummate loner, attended several conferences held by anti-technology groups and in his "manifesto" he referred to himself as "we" and signed his bombs with "FC" which stood for "Freedom Club." In many cases, a terrorist group such as al Qaeda becomes a substitute family where individual members are welcomed, unconditionally accepted, and where they are treated as valuable, trusted group associates.

Many members of terrorist organizations exhibit similar personality traits as mass murderers: they are frustrated, angry males with a history of social isolation and who adhere to an extremist ideology. Like Nidal Hasan, Ibrahim al Asiri, Farouk Abdulmutallab, and Samir Khan were drawn to radical Islam. They exploited the Koran to rationalize and legitimize their murderous behaviors.

It is the leaders of radical groups, however, who attract and retain followers to their twisted ideological agendas. Awlaki was a charming, charismatic, highly narcissistic preacher who used his followers to gain power and control over others. He convinced his believers that they could achieve immortality through his strict interpretation of Islamic law. Awlaki relied upon proven mind-control methodologies exemplified by cult and pseudo-religious leaders throughout history to manipulate his followers' psyches: isolation from family and friends, constant repetition of ideology, fear, requiring followers to hand over financial resources and possessions to the leader, and testing followers' loyalty through the commission of heinous acts. Leaders of these groups profess to be divine and they typically claim that Armageddon is imminent. They subjugate the individual ego for their personal benefit and they prey upon the universal fear of death in extracting the unyielding loyalty of their adherents. In return, they promise their followers an intangible reward such as immortality or assurances of going to heaven.

When underwear bomber Farouk Abdulmutallab traveled to Yemen seeking an audience with Awlaki, he severed all ties with his family and friends, gave his worldly possessions to the "cause," was completely isolated from all the trappings of civilization, sat through hours upon hours of extremist ideological rhetoric, and in exchange for martyrdom, agreed to become a suicide bomber. In return, Awlaki assured him that he would receive Allah's exaltation in heaven.

Over the past several decades, al Qaeda training camps have sprung up throughout the middle East. Trainees are taught how to use weapons, make IED's, and are thoroughly indoctrinated into extremist ideology. At one time, attendance at these training camps was a mandatory prerequisite for al Qaeda membership. Travel to Middle

Eastern destinations has become more difficult in a post 9/11 world, and smuggling weapons in and out of Western countries is now almost impossible. Al Qaeda has re-oriented its focus from a formal training format to individual indoctrination over the Internet and the establishment of smaller, regional groups, or cells, of like-minded extremists.

Awlaki gave Hasan and his other followers what they perceived to be unconditional love and approval, something that many, if not most, of them had never experienced from their significant others. The military often fulfills the role of a surrogate parent, but, like a rebellious teenager, Hasan rejected the Army's dogma and turned to Awlaki. Awlaki's emails to Hasan provided him with the reassurance he craved and, in turn, gave him an excuse for rationalizing and legitimizing his act of terror.

IN MAY 2010, FAISAL SHAHZAD, a Pakistani immigrant, planted explosives in a Nissan Pathfinder and parked it on the street in Times Square, New York City, in a failed attempt at a suicide bombing. He was believed to have had contact with Awlaki and Osama bin Laden. Two months later, the U.S. Treasury Department designated Awlaki as a "special" global terrorist and blocked his assets. This designation made it a crime for an American citizen to do business with him.[64] Even though he was a U.S. citizen, the Obama administration authorized the targeted assassination of Awlaki. On September 30, 2011, Awlaki and *Inspire* editor, Samir Kahn, were killed by a Hellfire missile fired by an American drone.[65] As one would expect, immediately upon their deaths, Awlaki and Khan were elevated to the status of martyr. In an article for *Inspire*, Yahya Ibrahim issued a threat against the U.S. "As for the blood of Shaykh Anwar and his companions, it is the fuel for the coming mujahideen, while they are at the peace of martyrdom."[66]

SWAT team members approach the Soldier Readiness Processing Center shortly after Nidal Hasan's attack. Photo by Sgt. Jason R. Krawczyk, III Corp, courtesy of the U.S. Army.

10. One Nation's Terrorist is Another Nation's Freedom Fighter

If crime fighters fight crime and firefighters fight fires,
what do freedom fighters fight?
~George Carlin

There is no federal, standardized definition of terrorism. Prior to 1985, the United Nations Security Council (UNSC) avoided using the terms *terrorism* and *terrorist*. Between 1985 and 2005 the council continued to refrain from a definition and, instead, labeled various acts as terrorist.

- hostage-taking and hijacking
- abduction of UN personnel
- unlawful use of plastic explosives
- assassination of heads of State or political leaders
- destruction of, or attacks on, civilian aircraft
- bombings of embassies and civilians
- organized, non-State political violence in peacetime, including attacks on civilian, government and military buildings
- attacks on religious sites in armed conflict[1]

In 2005 the Defense Personnel Security Research Center (DPSRC) defined terrorism as "anyone who [is] sympathetic to, or a member of, a group that could be characterized as both disloyal and hostile toward the U.S. government." The DPSRC included "main foreign (militant jihadists) and domestic groups (White Supremacists, White Nationalists, and domestic militias) whose past and recent actions and current ideologies render them particularly hostile and disloyal toward the U.S. government. The report cited "attempted or actual enlistment of disloyal and hostile persons."[2]

The U.S. Department of State defines terrorism as "premeditated, politically motivated violence perpetrated against noncombatant targets by subnational groups or clandestine agents, usually intended to influence an audience."[3]

The FBI, however, employs a broader definition of terrorism, calling it the "unlawful use of force and violence against persons or property to intimidate or coerce a government, the civilian population, or any segment thereof, in furtherance of political or social objectives."[4] The FBI further categorizes terrorists as domestic or international. Oklahoma City bomber Timothy McVeigh is an example of a domestic terrorist as categorized by the FBI.[5]

At a Department of Defense news briefing at the Pentagon in 2006, Director for Strategic Plans and Policy Lieutenant General Gene Renuart reported on a Multilateral Planners Conference that he had recently attended in Washington, D.C. An audience member asked him if the conference attendees had formulated a definition of terrorism.

"We attempted to reach a common definition of terrorism," said Renuart. "It is a very difficult problem…In one country, organizations will use terrorist techniques even though they may really be insurgents struggling against the government….Are they terrorists or are they rebels; are they insurgents? And that clearly is a very difficult definition to come up with."[6] Although the audience was unable to pin Renuart down on a definition of terrorism, he did indicate that his interpretation of the meaning of terrorism related to religious extremism.

According to the U.S. State Department, Palestinian mortar attacks on Israeli settlements are defined as terroristic; similar Israeli attacks upon Palestine, however, are not considered to be terrorist acts. Evaluating international terrorism depends upon the classification of the country in question as an ally or an enemy. During President George W. Bush's administration, the State Department avoided the establishment of a definition of terrorism by listing specific organizations that it considered terrorist.[7]

Using the State Department's definition of terrorism, Nidal Hasan's shooting on Fort Hood would not have been considered a terrorist act if Hasan had not been Muslim. That same act perpetrated by a radical Caucasian Christian would have been considered workplace violence. There is no consensus, however, on how the Fort Hood shooting should be classified. When the Obama administration characterized the massacre as workplace violence, anti-Muslim blogs and conservative talk-radio hosts castigated him. An unfortunate consequence of Hasan's mass shooting is that the victims have not been able to collect the same benefits as they would have qualified for if the mass murder had been labeled as terrorism.

Another problem arises in defining "radicalization." The National Terrorism Center defines radicalization as the process through which individuals accept the violent jihadist narrative.[8] While the FBI admits that there are numerous definitions of radicalization across the spectrum of governmental and law enforcement agencies, it defines radicalization as "the process by which individuals come to believe their engagement in or facilitation of nonstate violence to achieve social and political change is necessary and justified."[9] Under the FBI definition, Timothy McVeigh, Unabomber Ted Kaczynski, Nidal Hasan, and numerous other mass murderers would fit into the radicalization model.

A joint bulletin issued by the Department of Homeland Security (DHS) and FBI in August 2001, just prior to the September 11 terrorist attacks, defined a homegrown violent extremist (HVE) as,

> A person of any citizenship who has lived and/or operated primarily in the United States or its territories who advocates, is engaged in, or is preparing to engage in ideologically motivated terrorist activities (including providing support to terrorism) in furtherance of political or social objectives promoted by a foreign terrorist organization, but is acting independently of direction by a foreign terrorist organization. HVEs are distinct from traditional domestic terrorists, who

engage in unlawful acts of violence to intimidate civilian populations or attempt to influence domestic policy without direction from or influence by a foreign actor.[10]

In reality, however, in most occurrences of multiple homicide there is no black/white delineation between terrorist acts and mass murders—the boundaries are blurred. Victims of mass murder, no matter what the motive, all feel terrorized and traumatized. There is solid agreement among experts that acts of public mass homicide generate widespread fear. Invariably, when any mass murder event occurs, the media is quick to shout "terrorism." This was certainly the case in the Virginia Tech massacre.

The Silent Killer

The worst mass shooting in United States history occurred just two years before Nidal Hasan's rampage when Seung-Hui Cho opened fire and killed thirty-two people on the campus of Hasan's alma mater, Virginia Polytech Institute and State University. One may wonder if that mass murder influenced Hasan's shooting at the Soldier Processing Center at Fort Hood.

Seung-Hui Cho, the second child of financially-strapped Korean booksellers, was born in South Korea in 1984. At nine months of age he became ill with pertussis and pneumonia and was hospitalized. While there he was diagnosed with a heart defect and later underwent cardiac function tests. Like Ted Kaczynski, Cho returned home with a noticeably different personality. Quiet and withdrawn, he was a sickly, uncommunicative child. In spite of their meager income, Cho's parents managed to save enough money to immigrate to the United States when Cho was eight years old. They settled in Virginia in a close-knit Korean American community. Cho was an unusually quiet child and, except for brief interactions with his sister, he was uncommunicative. If called upon to speak by his parents, he exhibited physical symptoms of extreme anxiety such as sweaty palms and tears.[11]

Cho's unresponsiveness served as a major family stressor and in an effort to cope with their emotionally unreachable child, Cho's parents coddled him. Although at school Cho was enrolled in English as a Second Language program (ESL), his parents did not learn to speak English, resulting in difficult communications with their son's teachers.

Just prior to middle school, Cho's guidance counselor recommended that the parents seek counseling for their son. Although testing revealed that Cho was of above average intelligence, he was diagnosed with severe social anxiety. Other than a nod of his head and an occasional "okay," he spoke to no one. He occasionally communicated with his sister who often served as an interpreter for her parents when they conversed with Cho's teachers and counselors. Cho and his sister sometimes fought and, on occasion, Cho "punched her with shocking violence."[12] Cho's parents worked long hours in the laundry/dry cleaning industry, making it difficult logistically to attend meetings at Cho's school.[13] Unlike other Korean Americans in their community, the Cho family was withdrawn and socially isolated.[14]

Perhaps because of cultural and language barriers, both Cho and his sister were bullied at school. A high school classmate related an incident in which a teacher threatened to give Cho a failing grade if he did not read aloud in class. When Cho responded by reading in a harsh, raspy voice his classmates laughed and shouted at him to "go back to China."[15] A relative in Korea recalled that Cho's mother told her that her son had been diagnosed with autism.[16]

In 1999, in eighth grade, Cho abruptly became more withdrawn and exhibited symptoms of depression. The Columbine massacre sparked his interest and he wrote a paper for his English class in which he stated that he wanted to "repeat Columbine." Cho was sent to a psychiatrist and was diagnosed with "selective mutism" and "major depression, single episode." He was prescribed an antidepressant which he took from June 1999 to July 2000. His condition improved and he seemed to be in a better mood. The doctor believed that the medication had done its job and allowed Cho to discontinue it.[17]

Throughout his high school years, Cho was given "special accommodations" for his mutism. He spent several hours each day on homework and his grades were excellent. His guidance counselor recommended to Cho's parents that their son attend a small community college where he could make a gradual transition into adulthood, but Cho had his sights set on Virginia Tech in Blacksburg. After much deliberation, his parents acquiesced. They paid his entire tab and did not ask or expect Cho to find a job. His mental health records and his special educational accommodations were not transferred to Virginia

Tech with his high school academic records. Cho left home without a single acquaintance at the university, no medication for anxiety or depression, and no personal ties to a counselor.[18] Cho was mute, he suffered from severe social anxiety, and he was totally alone and invisible in an alien environment. He once told his roommate that he had a girlfriend named Jelly, a supermodel who lived on another planet and traveled by spacecraft.[19]

Cho did not adjust well to college and blamed his difficulties on an unsatisfactory roommate. With his parents' help, Cho was able to switch dorm rooms. His freshman grades were good and just before the beginning of his sophomore year, he moved into a condominium with a Virginia Tech senior. Cho's grades fell and he changed his major from business information technology to English, a puzzling choice for a person who had such difficulty in communicating. Cho had taken an entry-level poetry course in a prior semester and contacted the professor who taught the class.[20]

> I was in your poetry class last semester, and I remember you talking about the books you published. I'm looking for a publisher to submit my novel….I was just wondering if you know of a lot of publishers or agents or if you have a good connection with them," Cho wrote. He continued with a description of his book, "My novel is relative [*sic*] short…sort of like Tom Sawyer except that it's really silly and pathetic depending on how you look at it.[21]

Cho's sister later found a rejection letter written to Cho after he submitted a book proposal to a New York publishing company.[22]

Despite his enthusiasm for writing, once again, Cho's grades took a dive and he moved back on campus. Initially, his roommates invited him to social events. At a female student's apartment one evening, Cho began stabbing the carpet with a knife. After that disturbing incident the invitations stopped. Cho had no friends and did not seek out the company of any of his classmates. In his classes, he wore reflector sunglasses and a cap pulled low over his face. He became angry in one of his English classes and in an abrupt change of behavior, he stood before his classmates and with unusual emotion read an essay that he had written in response to a prior class discussion about the consumption of animals:

I don't know which uncouth, low-life planet you come from but you disgust me. In fact, you all disgust me....You low-life barbarians make me sick to the stomach that I wanna barf over my new shoes. If you despicable human beings who are all disgraces to [the] human race keep this up, before you know it you will turn into cannibals—eating little babies, your friends. I hope y'all burn in hell for mass murdering and eating all those little animals.[23]

As was the case with the audience of Hasan's presentation on "The Koranic World View As it Relates to Muslims Serving in the U.S. Military," Cho's professor and his classmates were stunned and horrified. Over the next few weeks the class dwindled. The professor asked a student if he was aware of a reason for the sparse attendance. "It's the boy...everyone's afraid of him," the student told her. Unbeknownst to her, Cho had been taking photos of classmates without their permission. The professor advised Cho to drop the class but he refused. She contacted the department head and told him either to remove Cho from the class or she would resign.[24]

Cho's aberrant behavior continued and he was accused of stalking, paranoid conduct, and sending unwanted, bizarre text messages to female students. He began signing his name with a question mark.[25] His roommate and suite mate found a large knife in one of Cho's desk drawers and disposed of it. One of his professors spoke to Cho and in November 2005, she recommended that he see a counselor. Cho called the campus counseling center and made an appointment but failed to appear. A month later Virginia Tech campus security received a complaint from the father of a female student who reported that Cho was harassing his daughter with disturbing instant messages and Facebook postings. A campus security officer spoke to Cho and told him to avoid further contact with the student. Cho responded with a suicide threat and he was involuntarily hospitalized for twenty-four hours and diagnosed with a non-specific mood disorder. The psychiatrist who saw him noted in his chart that he was a danger to himself but not to others. Cho's high school mental health records were not available to his Virginia Tech health care providers and he was released and advised to undergo counseling. His parents were never notified of the incident.[26]

Cho's violent writings continued and he resumed his mutism. One student reported that Cho "was the kind of guy who might go on a rampage killing."[27] During the spring semester of 2007 Cho bought two semi-automatic weapons: a Glock 19 nine millimeter pistol and a Walther P22 twenty-two caliber and purchased ammunition on several occasions. He rented a van and practiced shooting at a local range. On two separate occasions he checked into local motels for a night, presumably to make the videos that he mailed to NBC just before his shooting rampage.[28]

Early on the morning of April 16, 2007, Cho left his dorm and walked two-minutes to West Ambler Johnston Residence Hall where his mailbox was located. Although it was too early in the morning to gain legal entry into the dorm rooms, he somehow managed to circumvent security. Cho proceeded to the fourth floor where he killed a female student and a residence advisor around 7:15 a.m. Another student heard the shots and called campus police. Cho left West Ambler and walked back to his dorm room where he changed his bloody clothes. At first, law enforcement officers mistakenly concluded that the shooting had been a domestic dispute and did not lock down the university. Authorities have speculated that if Cho had stopped his bloody rampage after he killed the students in West Ambler, he might not have been apprehended.[29]

Cho accessed his campus computer account about 7:25 a.m., erased his email messages and deleted his account. He disconnected his computer's hard drive, left his dorm and disposed of his cell phone and the computer drive. Shortly after nine o'clock he mailed a package to *NBC News* in New York and a letter to the Virginia Tech English Department. He then walked to Norris Hall, the engineering building, arriving just after 9:00 a.m. He chained the doors closed at all three entrances and placed a note on one door stating that a bomb would detonate if the doors were opened. Cho then proceeded to the second floor of the building and, for the next twelve minutes, walked into occupied classrooms and opened fire. After expending two hundred rounds of ammunition, thirty-one students and professors lay dead and twenty-six more were wounded. When Cho heard police officers break through the chained doors he turned his gun on himself.[30]

From the moment that the news of the Virginia Tech shooting reached the media, there was speculation that Cho was an Islamic terrorist. After NBC received Cho's package containing his written statement, graphic video clips, and still photographs, the media became consumed with the Virginia Tech massacre. Cho's statement, often referred to as a manifesto, was riddled with profanities and was violent to the extreme. Out of respect for the victims, NBC only broadcast excerpts. The following is a representative sample of Cho's statement:[31]

> You had a hundred billion chances and ways to have avoided today, but you decided to spill my blood. You forced me into a corner and gave me only one option. The decision was yours. Now you have blood on your hands that will never wash off, you Apostles of Sin....Thanks to you, I die, like Jesus Christ, to inspire generations of the Weak and Defenseless people – my Brothers, Sisters, and Children....Thanks to you Sinners, you Spillers of Blood, I set the example of the century for my Children to follow....You may stand steadfast on the battlefield of your life's dedication to eternal terrorism American Al-Qaeda....By the power greater than God we will hunt you down, you Lovers of Terrorism, and we will kill you.[32]

In very short order Cho's entire statement was leaked to the media. One reporter discovered that Cho's father had worked for a time in Saudi Arabia and incorrectly concluded that Cho had committed an act of Islamic-inspired terrorism.[33] In the following days, the Virginia Tech tragedy garnered 63 percent of cable and talk radio airtime and 51 percent of overall coverage. It was the top news story of the year.[34]

Before the VT shooting, Cho was virtually invisible. Like most mass killers, his frustration and rage had escalated to such an extreme level that he could not resist the urge to act out his murderous fantasies. On April 16, 2007, the final semester of his senior year was rapidly coming to an end. In a few short weeks Cho would graduate with no hope of finding a job, no coping skills to survive in a competitive world, and he would undoubtedly bring shame to his parents. He blamed his classmates and his professors for his failures and inadequacies. He demanded that the world understand that his problems were not of his making, that he had been horribly abused, that his dignity had been stolen, and that he had every right to be consumed with rage. In an attempt to elicit global guilt for and complicity in his situation, Cho fixed his attention on the media. The Virginia Tech massacre provided him with the fame and recognition that he needed and wanted, and, in his mind, absolved him from personal responsibility for his actions.

With his extreme silence Cho personified the lone wolf. While he did not tell anyone that he was planning to commit mass murder, like most of these killers he left behind a trail of clues and red flags that should have set off alarms. There was general consensus by Cho's classmates, teachers, and mental health care providers that there was "something wrong" with him. Cho displayed the characteristics shared by most mass killers and, as with the majority of them, his potential for engagement in extreme violence went unrecognized. Because of his mental health issues, Cho was not eligible to purchase firearms, but he easily passed a background check which gave no indication of his mental health history.

By most definitions, Cho's shooting rampage was not considered an act of terrorism. While his egregious acts of violence were expressions of personal rage, his "manifesto" reveals a cultural/societal angst that contributed to his feelings of inadequacy and loneliness.

But it was pilot Joseph Stack's attack on the Echelon Building in Austin, Texas, in 2010, that sparked the greatest number of internal discussions among editorial writers, commentators, and journalists regarding the definition of terrorism.

Stacked Deck

When Joseph Stack's parents died in the early 1960s, he and his young siblings were sent to the Milton Hershey Orphanage and School in Hershey, Pennsylvania.[36] The school was established in 1909 through an endowment from Milton and Kitty Hershey who wished to found a school for "poor, healthy white, male orphans between the ages of 8 through 18 years of age."[37] From its first two students in 1910 to the time that Stack completed high school, thousands of needy children had been provided homes and education at the school.

After high school graduation Stack enrolled briefly in a local community college, then headed for Colorado with a hundred dollars in his pocket, a suitcase full of new clothes, and a tool kit. He closed the doors on his tragic childhood and his high school class of 1974. After graduating college with a degree in electronic engineering technology from Southern Colorado University in 1979, Stack moved to California where he worked as a contract software developer and he joined a local band. When a former classmate located him in 2000, Stack made it clear that he wanted nothing to do with his past.[38]

Stack was angered by the amount of his income that he was required to pay in federal income taxes. He joined a discussion group of like-minded individuals engaged in the study of the tax code to find legitimate ways to reduce their income tax burdens. Stack and his wife, Ginger, established a franchise of the tax-exempt Universal Life Church which they believed would eliminate their tax obligations. The IRS took issue with the Stacks' tax-avoidance scheme and sent the couple a large bill. Joe and Ginger Stack defended their tax-exempt status and filed suit against the U.S. government. Stack became even angrier when a government ruling was established in 1986 that prevented contract software developers from taking advantage of certain loopholes that, in the past, had reduced their tax burdens.[39]

By the time Stack realized that there was nothing he could do to win his case against the IRS, he claimed that he had spent about $5,000 and 1,000 hours "writing, printing, and mailing to any senator, congressman, governor, or slug that might listen; none did, and they universally treated me as if I was wasting their time." He lamented that with all of the hours he expended fighting the IRS he lost valuable time and money by not working and billing clients. [40]

Once again, Stack walked away from his life. He bought a small Piper Cherokee airplane, divorced his wife of eighteen years, and moved to Austin, Texas, where the cost of living was cheaper, the job market better, and where the music scene was thriving. He left behind a hefty tax bill. Stack put together a band that he called "The Last Straw," married for the second time, and bought an upscale suburban house.[41]

Soon after Stack married his second wife, Sheryl, he received a certified letter from the IRS informing him that he and his wife's tax return had been chosen for audit. Stack's accountant had failed to report Sheryl's $12,000 income. Stack became enraged and he and Sheryl entered a tension-filled period in their married life. They frequently argued and bickered with Stack blaming Sheryl and her teenage daughter for all of their problems. On the evening of February 17, 2010, Stack's wife and step-daughter became alarmed over his increasingly bizarre rhetoric and stayed in a motel for the night. The next morning Sheryl returned to the smoldering ruin of her house. "I saw the smoke billowing and I said, oh, my god, he's burned the house down," Sheryl told an arson investigator at the scene. "And then I figured he was in it because he's suicidal....once I realized he burned down our house and everything in it, I hope he's in the house because if he's not, he's still at large, and I have to be afraid for my life because he's mad at me for ruining his life."[42]

Sheryl took refuge at a neighbor's house where she and friends watched the news coverage of the fire. The television report, however, was interrupted with a story of her husband's small airplane flying into the Austin building that housed the offices of the Internal Revenue Service. Sheryl watched helplessly as images of the aftermath of her husband's violent act appeared on the screen. Her heart sank when clouds of billowing black smoke conveyed the likelihood that human beings in the building had perished at the hands of her spouse.[43]

On his web site, Joe Stack left behind a rant against the IRS and the U.S. government.

> Violence not only is the answer, it is the only answer....I saw it written once that the definition of insanity is repeating the same process over and over and expecting the outcome to suddenly be different. I am finally ready to stop this insanity. Well, Mr. Big Brother IRS man, let's try something different; take my pound of flesh and sleep well.[44]

Stack's intention was to kill a large number of IRS employees. Fortunately, only one other person died—sadly, that fact provided little consolation to the victim's family. The mainstream media generally focuses upon the victims of mass murders, but in this case, Vietnam hero Vernon Hunter was all but forgotten by reporters. Joseph Stack garnered almost all of the public's attention.[45]

Congressman Steve King of Iowa commented that Stack's issues with the IRS were "legitimate" and he called for the dissolution of the federal agency. Massachusetts Senator Scott Brown claimed that the attack was proof that "American people want transparency in government."[46]

While American televisions flashed the news of Stack's airplane flying into Austin's Echelon Building, several groups of tax protesters were meeting at a Conservative Political Action Conference (CPAC) in Washington, D.C. The day that Stack flew into the IRS offices marked the first day of CPAC's online tax revolt. Debra Arab, member of the *FairTax* organization, said that Stack "was in a bad situation and made a poor life choice."[47]

Just a few hours after Stack's stunt, a Facebook fan page appeared declaring him a hero. The founder of the site posted "Finally an American man took a stand against our tyrannical government that no longer follows the Constitution." Another Facebook post said "His sacrifice was for all of us." A *tweet* called Joe Stack an American hero and said "we need more of you to make a stand."[48]

While he may have been a hero to tax protesters, Stack was instantly labeled a terrorist by the media. In a press conference just a few hours after Stack's aerial attack, Chief of Police Art Acevedo and Congressman Mike McCaul described the event as domestic terrorism.[49]

"I think when you fly an airplane into a federal building to kill people, it depends on how you define terrorism, but it sounds like it to me," McCaul told a local television reporter.[50]

"The bottom line: terrorism and criminal misconduct, street criminals commit terror every day in our streets and our neighborhoods," said Acevedo.[51]

University of Texas associate professor of Government and Middle Eastern Studies Ami Pedahzur stated that he believed there were elements of terrorism in Stack's IRS attack, but he didn't believe that overall it could qualify as an act of terrorism. Stack's motivation was fueled by anger, desperation, and revenge but lacked the element of creating panic and fear within the general public.[52]

In an interview with *Time Warner Cable News* in Austin, Pedahzur said that Stack committed a "criminal act that incorporated elements of terrorism." He believes that his target, the IRS building, was highly symbolic and that Stack's "modus operandi was a copycat of the 911 terror attack of the World Trade Center."[53]

Pedahzur believes that Stack's manifesto shows a build-up of anger aimed at the government. "Sometimes it's just the easy way out, to find someone to blame," Pedahzur said, "But I think it was another event that was the trigger for [the attack]. It was an ongoing process that came to the point of explosion."[54]

Newsweek/Daily Beast staffers initiated a fierce debate among themselves about the correctness of labeling Stack a terrorist. Their email discussion was not intended for public eyes, but after several days of dialogue, the publisher of the *Daily Beast* aired their heated internal disagreement.

- *Newsweek* editor Devin Gordon wondered if any of the staff had read a comparison of "our ho-hum reaction to a guy who successfully crashed a plane into a government building versus the media's full-throated insanity over the underpants bomber who didn't hurt anyone but himself."[55]

- Multimedia editor Kathy Jones, wondered if the terrorist labeling of Timothy McVeigh, Ted Kaczynski, and various members of white supremacist groups had survived over time.

- Patrick Enright, Senior Articles Editor, believed that the branding of a murderous act is dependent upon the target— if, like Stack and the IRS, the attack is against someone or something perceived to have wronged you, it can be classified as a protest, but if you indiscriminately kill innocent people, you're a terrorist.[56]

- Reporter Jeneen Interlandi commented, "right or wrong, we definitely reserve the label 'terrorist' for foreign attackers."[57]

- Investigative correspondent Michael Isikoff observed that the underwear bomber was "dispatched and equipped by a foreign enemy—Al Qaeda in the Arabian Peninsula....the Fort Hood shooter may have been a disturbed "lone wolf" but he was in ideological alignment...with a member of the same foreign enemy. That makes them both terrorists." Not Stack.[58]

- Isikoff recognized that domestic violence doesn't garner

as much media attention as foreign-inspired terrorist acts, especially those committed by members of al Qaeda, because their acts of violence are less clear-cut. The difference between a domestic terrorist and a dissident is sometimes difficult to distinguish.[59]

- Staffer Ben Adler pointed out that it is "easier to keep explosives off of commercial jets," than to prevent a lone individual from flying his private plane into a skyscraper. "There is something about dying in an explosion or crash on a plane," he said, "that Americans find uniquely terrifying."[60]

If *Newsweek/Daily Beast* staffers and federal agencies cannot reach a consensus on a definition of a terrorist act versus a generic episode of mass murder, then how can we, as a society, reach an agreement on a definition of terrorism?

Spin

Criminal profiler Pat Brown believes that too much attention is paid to labeling mass murderers. "We should be focusing the discussion where it counts—prevention—not on labeling. It's distracting and we lose sight of the issue. Some of these people are psychopaths looking for something to hang their hats on."[61] Brown distinguishes terrorist acts from other types of violence by looking at motive.

"It's an interesting dilemma," Brown says. "There are some people who want to believe that anyone who engages in an act of mass violence and who is also a Muslim, is a terrorist. I believe in analyzing the motive behind [the violent act] and look at how it was carried out so that we are able to identify future mass murderers and terrorists." Mass murderers, "terrorist" or not, often use a political or religious ideology to justify their violent acts.[62]

In Nidal Hasan's case, Brown believes that it was intense rage that mobilized him to kill his workmates. Islam provided the justification that he needed to legitimize his brutal shooting. Leaders of terrorist groups like al Qaeda understand the radicalization and rationalization processes and use them to their benefit by preying on psychologically disturbed individuals. A tightened global security has prompted terrorist groups to find and recruit lone wolves willing to act out their violent fantasies. It is much more difficult to identify a single individual and prevent a terrorist act than it is to ferret out members of violent extremist organizations.

Terrorist acts are public and extremists exploit the media to spread fear—mass murderers use the publicity surrounding their acts for instant fame. Timothy McVeigh chose Oklahoma City, in part, because the downtown area provided plenty of space for the deluge of reporters that he correctly predicted would cover the bombing. Unabomber Ted Kaczynski exploited the print media for publication of his manifesto. Charles Whitman knew that he would achieve instant fame for his University of Texas tower shooting, and the 9/11 terrorists chose their targets to garner maximum media exposure. Mass murders, no matter what the motive, are public events for a reason—that is unless you live in China.

After the Boston Marathon bombing, a Chinese netizen[63] explained. "Terrorist attack works in the U.S., but not in China. With no immediate press conference and all information blocked, the terrorists would have no proof that they indeed attacked."[64]

Ethnicity is also important in considering the reporting of mass murders. In July 2012, Professor of Journalism, Angie Chuang, published a report on the media's response to the ethnic backgrounds of mass shooters. She discovered that killers with "foreign" ethnic backgrounds are portrayed by the media as un-American. Chuang examined murders committed by Seung-Hui Cho at Virginia Tech and by Jiverly Wong in Birmingham, New York.[65]

"We are seeing people's ethnicity being blamed for these incidents," says Chuang. "There is a sense that the media blames the person's foreign background for what has happened and there is a lack of critical thinking on the part of the media as to the real motivations behind these actions."[66]

When the name of the Fort Hood shooter was released to the media, there was an instantaneous supposition that Nidal Hasan was a terrorist because of his Arab ethnicity. But the DoD and the Army classified Hasan's shooting rampage as workplace violence and denied benefits to the victims that they would otherwise have automatically received if they suffered death or disability in a war zone.[67]

"The truth is, we don't know, and we may never know, exactly what drove this senseless act," says Chuang. "In the absence of factual explanations, we all—journalists especially—are driven to speculate.

When the perpetrator has…an unusual name, we are quick to seek reasons to label him or her "not like us."[68]

Keith Woods, dean of faculty at the Poynter Institute and diversity expert, says that "race and ethnicity never truly describe. Connecting faith, race or ethnicity to motive without proof is reckless journalism."[69]

Was Nidal Hasan's lone wolf act of mass homicide terrorism? Hasan used Awlaki and radical Islam as a justification for violent retaliation against the military. His shooting rampage was a politically motivated act designed to further his ideological objectives. Hasan's mass shooting was also fueled by rage. When his supervisor, Col. Ben Phillips, handed him his orders to deploy to Afghanistan, Hasan's intent to kill enemies of Islam was given wings.

In their 2011 second edition of their book *Extreme Killing: Understanding Serial and Mass Murder*, James Alan Fox and Jack Levin discuss Hasan's shooting rampage. They believe that there are elements of both terrorism and workplace violence "as indicated by Hasan's Muslim affiliation, his Middle Eastern-style clothing, and reports of his having shouted 'Allahu Akbar,' an expression of praise to God. He had also communicated by email with an imam who declared Hasan a hero for shooting down 13 people." At the same time, Fox and Levin describe the shooting within the parameters of workplace violence.

> Hasan's rampage was also a classic case of workplace homicide, even though a military base would seem to be an unusual location…Despite its unique function, Fort Hood is indeed a workplace, the U.S. Army an employer, and Hasan a disgruntled worker attempting to avenge perceived unfair treatment on the job. His rampage was selective, not indiscriminate. He chose the location—his workplace—and then apparently singled out certain co-workers for death.[70]

In November 2011, attorney Neal Sher filed a 750 million dollar lawsuit on behalf of eighty-three victims and their families against the Secretary of the Army, the Secretary of Defense, the Director of the FBI, six John Does who are members of the Army, Nidal Hasan, and the official representative of Awlaki's estate for wrongful death, survivorship, assault and battery, due process violations, loss of consortium, civil conspiracy, violation of negligence, and intentional misrepresentations.[71]

The lawsuit asserts that,

> At all times relevant, Al-Qaeda—established by Osama bin Laden—was a designated Foreign Terrorist Organization operating through a global network of terror cells, members, associates and supporters (like Hasan) dedicated to the establishment of a pan-Islamic caliphate worldwide. In February, 1998, Al-Qaeda issued a religious pronouncement titled "the World Islamic Front for Jihad against Jews and Crusaders"saying it was the duty of Muslims to kill Americans – civilians and military – and their allies everywhere. This is what Aulaqi and Hasan believed and this is what Hasan did at Fort Hood.[72]

The suit refers to the Senate Committee on Homeland Security report, A Ticking Time Bomb, and the FBI Final Report of the William H. Webster Commission on the Events at Fort Hood, Texas, and alleges that,

> These reports prove the government defendants knew to a moral certainty that Hasan was a radical extremist who supported violent jihad against the United States and who considered himself a devoted fellow-traveler and "soldier" of al Qaeda and Aulaqi. They also prove that the government defendants knew to a moral certainty both that Hasan's conduct and beliefs rendered him unfit to serve as an officer in the U.S. Army, and that he was a "ticking time bomb" who posed an unreasonable risk of harm to plaintiffs.[73]

The suit claims that it was because of political correctness that Army officials awarded Hasan a fellowship that he did not earn; sanitized and falsified his Officer Evaluation Reports ("OERs") to hide both his Islamist jihadi ideology and his professional incompetence; intentionally ignored his constant violations of Army regulations and professional standards; wrongfully and intentionally disregarded, or "spiked," the multiple reports from his peers calling him a security risk and a "ticking time bomb;" promoted him to Major; chose not to discipline, prosecute, discharge and/or imprison him; and terminated the security investigation into his ties to Aulaqi and al Qaeda without a personal interview, an appropriate database review or the disclosure of the fact and content of his communications with this international terrorist chieftain to his commanding officers.[74]

The petition also cites examples of victims' injuries that were neglected by the Army which led to catastrophic consequences.

> Many of the seriously wounded and injured plaintiffs were left abandoned to their own means and devices to obtain decent medical care. One injured soldier was able to obtain proper treatment for a traumatic brain injury caused by a bullet to the head only because the treatment was paid for by a private benefactor. In multiple cases, the Army has refused to admit the seriousness [of] the Fort Hood victims' injuries. For example, one soldier, who was diagnosed with crippling post traumatic stress syndrome, was denied treatment and a medical discharge by a Captain who specifically refused to sign the appropriate certifications because his injuries were sustained at Fort Hood.[75]

> In another case, a soldier was kept on active duty despite doctors' recommendations that he be transferred to a wounded warrior unit if not discharged from the Army on disability entirely. After the last of several major surgeries, he had to enlist the help of his brigade surgeon in begging his brigade commander to approve surgery to remove a bullet...that could have caused internal bleeding from the axilla artery leading to death. His medical care has been so inadequate that he has been forced to get civilian care off base.[76]

> Another soldier who was shot by Hasan five times and almost died due to medical neglect of his head and belly wounds at Darnall Army Hospital and has been in a Wounded Warrior unit for over two years. Although he is unable to lift anything heavy, or walk more than a short distance, or even ride a bicycle, he has been denied a medical discharge and been taunted by his commanders. He has been told that if he had been

wounded in Iraq, he would have been retired and deemed disabled long ago. However, because the DoD views his injuries as a workplace violence matter, he remains in limbo.[77]

Another soldier, whom the Veterans' Administration has since diagnosed with post traumatic stress disorder so severe that he cannot work, drive a car, or even bathe himself, was sent to Iraq immediately after the Fort Hood attack without any treatment whatsoever. Upon returning from Iraq, he had a breakdown and requested treatment. The Army refused and instead put him on a punitive duty that involved 24-48 hour shifts. He was not allowed off base, and was forced to sleep in a hallway on a cot for 3 weeks. When he was allowed to return home he received discharge papers and was told that he was lucky to have an honorable discharge because he was such an embarrassment to his company. Since he was not medically discharged as he should have been, his family went without any income for two years, until in August 2012 the VA classified him 100% disabled. But for assistance from his mother and mother-in-law, this soldier and his family would have been homeless.[78]

The lawsuit cites additional cases, but perhaps the most egregious concerns a soldier who had been shot in the neck by Hasan, lying unconscious and near death, and was loaded into a medevac helicopter for immediate transport to a medical facility. Armed FBI agents ordered that he be taken off of the helicopter so that Nidal Hasan could be transported to Scott and White Medical Center in his place.[79]

Bills have been introduced in both houses of Congress to re-classify the Fort Hood shooting as a terrorist act.

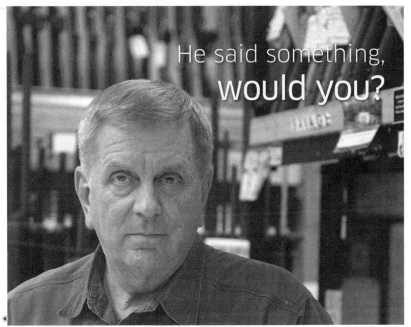

He said something, **would you?**

Greg Ebert, an employee of Guns Galore in Killeen, thwarted a terrorist plot.
Photo courtesy of the U.S. Department of Homeland Security

11. Hide and Seek

An ounce of prevention is worth a pound of cure.
~Benjamin Franklin

The death of Malik Hasan in 1998 initiated a string of unfortunate events beyond Nidal Hasan's control. His childhood home was hastily sold and within a few months his mother was diagnosed with cancer, dying just three months before 9/11. During this tumultuous time an embittered Hasan turned to Islam and seemingly found comfort in its teachings. His escalating hatred for the U.S. Army was not lost on his professors, classmates, and co-workers. But not one individual took him seriously enough to make certain that he never had an opportunity to act on his threats. Not one individual reported his behavior to a commander or to law enforcement. Hasan's enmity toward the military intensified and his inclination to commit violent acts was obvious to his classmates, co-workers, and superiors. When his commander, Col. Ben Phillips, handed him his deployment orders to Afghanistan, Hasan erupted in an angry burst of gunfire. Why didn't someone stop him?

One of Hasan's classmates told a journalist that he did not report him because he felt sorry for him.[1]

Another student remarked "Sir, why should I have to when the faculty heard all of these things firsthand?"[2]

One of Hasan's colleagues approached multiple faculty members about Hasan's rants but no action was taken. "Political correctness squelched any opportunity to confront him," the colleague remarked.[3]

The failure to report Hasan as a "ticking time bomb"[4] by members of the groups with which Hasan was affiliated can be explained by the phenomenon of *diffusion of responsibility* in which members of a group feel less compelled to take action or intercede than they would if they were acting alone. The responsibility to intervene in a situation is shared by members of the group making it easy to rationalize inaction with the attitude "let someone else get involved."[5]

Hasan's professors, classmates, and colleagues at Walter Reed did not wish to become entwined in a potentially venomous situation. At Fort Hood, Hasan had his first "real" job. His honeymoon wasn't over—he had only been in his new position for three months. His co-workers may or may not have recognized that he was capable of murder but they certainly were not going to initiate an effort to have him investigated. His supervisor, Col. Ben Phillips was trying to mitigate infighting within his staff and chose to bully Hasan instead of seeking help for him.

As a psychiatrist, Hasan was a valuable asset to the department, not because he was a particularly good therapist, but because there was a shortage of mental health providers in the Army. Col. Phillips would have stirred up a hornet's nest if he had changed the status quo. As difficult as it may be for co-workers to report suspicious activity, it can be even more difficult for a family member to do so.

Blind Eyes

Mass killer Adam Lanza was characterized by residents of his neighborhood as "dark and disturbed, a deeply troubled boy from a wealthy family who unnerved his neighbors and classmates."[6]

It was Lanza's mother who purchased the semi-automatic weapon that he used to murder her as she slept before killing twenty second graders and six adults at Sandy Hook Elementary School on December 14, 2012.[7] Lanza appeared to be a very intelligent, normally adjusted student until age thirteen when he began suffering such severe anxiety that his mother took him to a hospital emergency room. Lanza's anxiety became pathological and escalated to such an extreme level that she removed him permanently from school.[8]

Mrs. Lanza did not, however, recognize that her son was capable of violence or, if she did, she did not vocalize her misgivings to others. After his shooting rampage, a huge cache of weapons, ammunition, samurai swords, and photographs of a bloody corpse were discovered by law enforcement in Lanza's basement living area. Along with these grisly items was a holiday card with a check signed by his mother to be used to purchase another firearm.[9]

There are numerous reasons for the reluctance of family members and friends to warn authorities about their loved-one's capacity or intention to commit violent acts. In a report by a national summit on multiple casualty shootings in 2012, experts determined that people close to a marginalized family member or friend who has the potential to carry out violent acts are reluctant to warn authorities for numerous reasons: fear of embarrassment, fear of being ostracized, fear of losing the trust of the troubled loved one, and denial. In many cases, the friend or loved one rationalizes that their significant other is just having a rough period in his or her life and will snap back into normalcy.[10]

Nidal Hasan's family knew that he was unhappy serving in the army. They were aware that he had hired an attorney to assist him in leaving the military. His relatives told reporters that his shooting was an act of "lunacy" from being forced to fight an unjust war in Afghanistan. One of Hasan's cousins said "We're not trying to make excuses for him but what we were told was that he was under a lot of pressure."[11]

Hasan's family probably did not have enough information concerning the extent of his dissatisfaction to adequately predict his act of violence. His classmates and co-workers, however, did possess the knowledge that he was a time bomb waiting for a trigger to set him off.

Even in cases like Hasan's where the perpetrator is known by the mental health community to be capable of violence, there is an institutional reluctance to report that individual to law enforcement. The Virginia Tech mass killer, Seung-Hui Cho, was involuntarily committed overnight to an on-campus medical facility and was known by campus security and several faculty members to be mentally unstable. His involuntary commitment papers stated that he was mentally ill, yet he was not tagged as a potential perpetrator of violence by mental health professionals, even though his actions supported it.

In another high profile case, Amy Loughner, mother of Jared Loughner, knew that there was something wrong with her son. His erratic and increasingly strange behavior set off emotional alarms and she feared that he was taking drugs. Her husband was so concerned about Jared that he took his shotgun away from him and on many nights disabled his car. When Jared was kicked out of the community college he was attending, the Loughners were told that their son could not re-enroll until he received counseling for his aberrant, frightening behavior.

The Loughners did not seek treatment for Jared and on January 8, 2011, he took a taxi to a Tucson, Arizona, Safeway supermarket where U.S. Congresswoman Gabrielle Giffords was holding a meet-and-greet for her constituents. Loughner moved close to Giffords and pulled out his legally obtained Glock and opened fire. Giffords sustained a serious brain injury and almost succumbed to her wounds. Six bystanders died, including a federal judge and a nine-year-old child, and nine persons were wounded.[12]

For several months prior to the shooting Loughner had posted disturbing videos on YouTube in which he referred to himself as a terrorist. He often voiced his hatred of Giffords to his friends. The night before the shooting, he posted a photo of a Glock semi-automatic pistol placed on an American history textbook. Loughner's shooting rampage in Tucson, Arizona, is a tragic testament against keeping silent in the face of imminent violence.[13]

Duty to Protect/Warn

Not only are significant others and members of groups reluctant to report individuals likely to commit acts of violence, the medical community is often unwilling to report homicidal patients to authorities. Prior to his 1966 shooting rampage, Charles Whitman sought help from a campus clinic psychiatrist. He confided to the therapist that he fantasized about taking his deer rifle up to the University of Texas Tower and opening fire on the people below. The psychiatrist told no one about Whitman's homicidal ideation and Whitman acted upon his impulse to engage in a mass shooting.

Ten years after Whitman's shooting, in 1976, the first "Duty to Warn" law in the United States originated in California in response to a state Supreme Court decision, *Tarasoff v. Regents* of the University of California. A psychologist's patient, Mr. Poddar, articulated his intention to kill "an unnamed but readily identifiable woman, Tatiania Tarasoff." The therapist believed that his patient should be involuntarily committed to a mental hospital but his supervisor disagreed. Tarasoff was not warned of Poddar's intent and Poddar murdered the woman. The court held that when

> a therapist determines, or pursuant to the standards of his profession should determine, that his patient presents a serious danger of violence to another, he incurs an obligation to use reasonable care to protect the intended victim against such danger. The discharge of this duty may require the therapist to take one or more of various steps, depending upon the nature of the case. Thus it may call for him to warn the intended victim or others likely to apprise the victim of the danger, to notify the police, or to take whatever other steps are reasonably necessary under the circumstances.[14]

Since the passage of the California Tarasoff statute, most states have enacted their own versions of the law, ranging from discretionary reporting of violent patients in some states to mandatory reporting in others. These laws provide immunity from prosecution for mental health professionals who warn law enforcement and/or potential victims of their patient's violent intentions.[15]

One particularly egregious case is that of James Holmes, the Aurora, Colorado, theater shooter. Holmes, once a bright, promising neuroscience doctoral student at the University of Colorado-Denver, told campus psychiatrist Dr. Lynne Fenton on June 11, 2012, one day after withdrawing from the university, that he "fantasized about killing 'a lot of people.'"[16]

Fenton declined to issue an involuntary commitment order for Holmes, but instead contacted campus police and reported that Holmes was a danger to the public. Fenton refused to schedule follow-up therapy sessions with him and Holmes countered by peppering her with harassing texts and emails. Again, Fenton contacted campus law enforcement. Officer Lynn Whitten responded by deactivating Holmes' campus key card. Other than running a background check on Holmes, campus police failed to follow up or take action.

Two days after seeing Fenton, Holmes purchased a 100 round magazine for his AR-15 assault rifle. One week later, at 12:38 a.m., Holmes burst into the premier of the Batman movie, *The Dark Knight Rises*, tossed a canister of tear gas into the crowd and opened fire, killing twelve people and injuring fifty-eight.[17]

A widow of one of the mortally wounded victims, Chantel L. Blunk, filed suit against Dr. Lynne Fenton, Colorado University, and five additional unnamed defendants. In her complaint, Blunk alleges that

> Defendant Fenton knew that James Holmes was dangerous. Defendant Fenton had a duty to use reasonable care to protect the public at large from James Holmes. Defendant Fenton was presented with the opportunity to use such reasonable care when the Colorado University Police offered to apprehend James Holmes on a psychiatric hold. Defendant Fenton breached her duty to use reasonable care.[18]

Eleven other victims and/or survivors of victims have also filed lawsuits against Fenton and Colorado University.[19]

In a French case, psychiatrist Daniele Canarelli received a one year suspended prison sentence and was fined 8,500 Euros (about $11,000) after one of her patients, Joel Gaillard, murdered an eighty-year-old man. Gaillard had been confined in a mental hospital but escaped after a session with Canarelli and attacked his grandmother's partner with an axe. Canarelli warned authorities about Gaillard, but the French court contended that Canarelli was "blind" to her patient's risk and should have referred him to more specialized care, such as a forensic psychiatrist.

This case was closely followed throughout the western world and has broad implications for psychiatrists in the United States and Europe. According to Dr. Sohom Das, "If the French court's ruling set a precedent, then I fear that we have troubled times ahead. If psychiatrists are forced to act in such a defensive manner to avoid incarceration, there is a real risk that we have to act in an extremely overcautious manner."[20]

The French psychiatrists' union commented that the verdict was "worrying and risked scapegoating the profession over a complex case."[21] On the first day of the trial, mental health clinicians protested outside the court with posters and banners. One proclaimed, "Dark day for psychiatry."[21]

Nidal Hasan worked in Fort Hood's mental health department. Many of his psychiatrist and psychologist co-workers recognized his potential for violence. He even articulated his intentions to several of the medical staff. While he did not have a formal patient-physician relationship with any of his peers, as medical professionals they were obligated to inform their chain-of-command.

Homeland Security Begins With Hometown Security

While reporting dangerous individuals who pose an imminent threat to life is mandatory for clinicians under most of the individual state Tarasoff statutes, ordinary citizens are under no such obligation. If would-be terrorists and mass murderers are to be foiled before they kill, the public must feel free to report questionable activity.

In July 2010, the Department of Homeland Security (DHS) launched a national "See Something, Say Something"™ campaign borrowed from a similar program implemented by the New York City Metropolitan Transit Authority. The goal of "See Something, Say Something" is to "raise public awareness of indicators of terrorism and terrorism-related crime, and to emphasize the importance of reporting suspicious activity to the proper state and local law enforcement authorities."[22]

The program emphasizes that only suspicious behavior and situations such as noticing an unattended backpack or package in a public place, or other behaviors indicative of criminal activity related to terrorism will be investigated. The campaign was designed to be publicized locally using the concept that "homeland security begins with hometown security."[23]

The "See Something, Say Something" campaign was launched as a sister program to the Nationwide Suspicious Activity Reporting Initiative (NSI). The "9/11 Commission" cited breakdowns in communications and failure to share information among federal agencies as key factors in the failure to prevent the 9/11 terrorist attacks. In response to the Commission's report,

- Congress mandated an information-sharing environment that provided a mechanism for the sharing of terrorism information across federal agencies, state and local government, and private sector entities through the development and use of policy guidelines and technologies.

- States and urban areas established fusion centers that coordinated and integrated the gathering, analysis, and dissemination of information across law enforcement agencies, public safety organizations, homeland security, and terrorism intelligence entities.

- Data mining programs were established in order to uncover terrorism plots using "pattern-based queries, searches, or other analyses of one or more electronic databases."[24]

Suspicious activity reporting (SAR) is limited in its scope and only focuses upon behaviors and activities that have been historically linked to planning and carrying out terrorist attacks or criminal acts. Reports cannot be based on race, gender, ethnic, religious, or socioeconomic factors. Some of the behaviors or activities that the NSI has tagged as suspicious are

- "Uses binoculars or cameras.
- Takes measurements.
- Takes pictures or video footage.
- Draws diagrams or takes notes.
- Pursues specific training or education that indicate suspicious motives (flight training, weapons training, etc).

- Espouses extremist views."[25]

The American Civil Liberties Union (ACLU) argued that the behaviors and activities outlined in SAR are overly broad and include routine, day-to-day activities performed by many innocent people.[26] Because of protests from the ACLU and other privacy organizations, the SAR reporting guidelines were revised by refining the definition of suspicious activity as "observed behavior reasonably indicative of pre-operational planning related to terrorism or other criminal activity."[26] The revision also distinguishes between "Defined Criminal Activity and Potentially Criminal or Non-Criminal Activity requiring additional factual information before investigation."[27] Additionally, the updated guidelines clarified activities that are protected under the First Amendment and prohibited their use unless backed up by specific facts and circumstances that would support the suspicion that the observed behaviors would reasonably indicate criminal activity associated with terrorism.[28]

The suspicious activity reporting (SAR) system is designed to begin with a locally-based fusion center in which SAR information is entered into a computer system and shared with other local, state, and federal law enforcement operations—a "shared spaces concept" that encourages but does not require that the center share all of its information. Over the past few decades the role of local law enforcement has evolved from crime-fighting to "first preventers" of terrorism. Without intelligence information, police officers are seriously hampered in their attempts to ferret out would-be terrorists.

State-of-the-art computer systems are critical in storing and analyzing large quantities of data. The sharing of that information provides a cohesive assimilation process for locating and tracking individuals involved in criminal and terrorist plots. In the days before the 9/11 attacks, three of the hijackers were stopped locally for traffic violations and cited for violations in their immigration status. Had there been an integrated system in place and had the data been shared with the FBI, federal agents would have been aware that suspected al Qaeda operatives were present in the Washington, D.C., area. Perhaps the attacks could have been prevented. [29]

Greg Ebert, an employee of Guns Galore in Killeen, actual-

ly thwarted a plot cooked up by Muslim-convert Naser Jason Abdo
to blow up a local restaurant packed with Fort Hood soldiers. Abdo
claimed that he was inspired by Nidal Hasan's shooting rampage.

Less than a week after Hasan's arraignment, Abdo, an AWOL private from Fort Campbell, Kentucky, purchased six one-pound containers of smokeless gunpowder, three boxes of shotgun shells, and
an extended magazine for a handgun from Guns Galore in Killeen.
Ebert became suspicious when his customer began asking too many
naïve questions about the gunpowder. When Abdo paid cash, left in a
hurry, and did not take his change or receipt, Ebert and Guns Galore
management decided to call law enforcement.

By the time police found Abdo at a local motel, he had also purchased an Army combat uniform at a local surplus store. His plan was
to detonate bombs at a restaurant frequented by Fort Hood soldiers
and to shoot any survivors. Law enforcement personnel discovered
the *Inspire* magazine article "How to Make A Bomb in the Kitchen of
Your Mom" in Abdo's backpack. Two pressure cookers were found in
Abdo's motel room as well as two clocks, wiring, batteries, and other materials that could be used in the construction of an explosive
device.[30]

While at Fort Campbell, Abdo refused to deploy to Afghanistan
with his unit on the basis that he was a conscientious objector.
After being turned down initially, one of his commanding officers
managed to pull some strings and eventually obtained a CO designation for him. One of Abdo's superior officers discovered child
pornography on his government-issued computer, however, and
Abdo walked away from Fort Campbell when an investigation was
initiated.

Abdo was incensed and insisted that the pornography was deliberately placed on his computer by the Army. He decided to take
revenge and attempted to purchase a handgun at a local gun store.
Abdo's aberrant behavior alarmed the clerk who refused to sell him
a weapon. Abdo had planned to abduct one of his commanding
officers and murder him on video. When his plans were thwarted,
Abdo decided to go to Fort Hood and murder soldiers at a local
restaurant.[31]

During his arraignment Abdo shouted "Abeer Quassim al Janvi"

[Al Janvi was a fourteen-year-old girl raped in Iraq by soldiers from the 101st Airborne Division out of Fort Campbell in 2006] and "Nidal Hasan—2009."[32] Like Nidal Hasan, Abdo believed that the United States had declared war on Islam. Abdo was determined that he was not going to be put in a position of having to kill his fellow Muslims.

Abdo was born in Garland, Texas in 1990. His father was a Jordanian Muslim, his mother an American Christian. They had two children—Naser Jason and his younger sister. His parents split up when Abdo was three years old and he and his sister remained with their father. Their mother was a substance abuser and moved out of the home. When Abdo was fourteen years old, his father was arrested for soliciting sex with a minor on the Internet. He was subsequently deported back to Jordan. Abdo and his sister moved in with their mother.[33]

Naser Jason Abdo's mug shot after being arrested on charges of attempted murder and attempted use of weapons of mass destruction. Photo courtesy of the *Temple Daily Telegram*.

Like Hasan, Abdo was a misfit loner who did not have any friends. He did not fit in with social groups in his school and community and classmates referred to him as "weird." Although Abdo was familiar with Islam from observing his father's religious practices, he did not officially become a member of the Muslim faith until he was seventeen. Two years later he enlisted in the Army so that he could defend the rights of his Muslim brothers and sisters in Iraq and Afghanistan. Abdo claimed that during his time in the military he was harassed and discriminated against because of his religion and could not pray five times a day and fast during religious holidays.[34]

During his fight to obtain a CO release from the Army, Abdo travelled to New York to participate in an anti-war vigil in support of Pfc. Bradley Manning, who was alleged at the time to have provided classified information to Wikileaks. During this trip, Abdo spoke freely to reporters about his anti-war views. He also made anti-American statements during a language class at Fort Campbell. Army investigators deny that they had enough information about Abdo to foresee an attack.[35]

Abdo freely confessed to law enforcement that he wanted to die a martyr. He had planned to die in a shoot-out with police after setting off bombs in the restaurant and then shooting soldiers as they exited the building. Even more, Abdo wanted to surpass Hasan's body count. During his trial he said that he lived in Hasan's shadow despite "efforts to outdo him." Abdo also said he would continue his jihad "until the day the dead are called to account for their deeds." "I do not ask the court to give me mercy," Abdo told the court, "for Allah is the one that gives me mercy."[36]

Abdo was ultimately sentenced to two consecutive life sentences plus sixty years. It took jurors less than an hour to arrive at their verdict.[37]

Greg Ebert's picture appeared on a widely distributed poster during Hasan's trial with the caption "He said something; would you?"[38]

On November 5, 2009, three years after the congressionally-mandated shared information system, neither the DoD nor the NIS Suspicious Activity Reporting System had identified Nidal Hasan as a threat to national security. An FBI Joint Terrorism Task Force had intercepted Hasan's email correspondence with terrorist cleric Awlaki and passed it off as job-related and irrelevant.

In a perfect world, would-be terrorists and mass murderers would be caught before they killed. Even with our billion-dollar computer systems, data mining operations, and laws mandating the reporting of dangerous persons, Nidal Hasan, Jared Loughner, James Holmes, Adam Lanza, and many others have been able to commit their atrocities with impunity.

Silence is Golden

One result of the recent mass murders is the predominance of gun control as a topic of public debate. While there is great disagreement in approaches to preventing acts of terrorism and mass murder and, at the same time preserving individual freedom, ninety per cent of Americans agree that background checks should be performed on all persons prior to purchasing a firearm.[39] In theory, a background check prevents persons with violent criminal histories, or recent involuntary confinements to mental hospitals, or individuals judged to be a threat to themselves and others from having access to firearms. Unfortunately, background checks do not apply to all gun purchases.

Following the tragic assassinations of President John Kennedy, Dr. Martin Luther King, Jr., and Senator Robert Kennedy the Gun Control Act of 1968 was enacted. It prohibited the sale or transfer of firearms to anyone "who has been adjudicated as a mental defective or who has been committed to a mental institution."[40] This was the first law passed in the United States that regulated the sellers of firearms, controlled interstate commerce of guns, and regulated gun imports.[41]

After a seven-year congressional battle, the Brady Handgun Violence Prevention Act of 1993 was enacted. The Brady Law mandated background checks for all purchasers of handguns. Investigations into the eligibility of applicants to purchase firearms were carried out by local law enforcement. The FBI's NICS was established in 1998 and provided the mechanism for electronic background checks for states that elected to participate in the system.[42] Since the passage of the Brady Law, about two million applicants have been prevented from purchasing a firearm.[43]

Because states were not compelled to utilize the NICS, in 2007 Congress passed another statute to facilitate compliance with the 1968 law. This legislation offered substantial federal grants for states to update their computer systems so that the required prohibitor information could be easily transmitted to the NICS. The legislation uses the Virginia Tech shooting to illustrate the rationale for encouraging individual states to provide information to the NICS stating that the "shooter was able to purchase the two firearms used in the shooting. Improved coordination between State and Federal authorities could have ensured that the shooter's disqualifying mental health information was available to NICS."[44]

These federal laws require background checks on firearms purchased from federally licensed gun dealers. Only nine states require background checks on guns purchased at gun shows. Six states require checks for handguns only. Private sellers are not required to perform background checks if they do not rely on gun sales as their principal livelihood.[45]

The Health Insurance Portability and Accountability Act of 1996 (HIPAA) is a barrier to many states reporting the identities of persons subject to the mental health prohibitor to the NICS. HIPAA requires the protection and confidential handling of health information. Some states, such as California, Colorado, and Connecticut comply with federal requirements for background checks and have worked around the HIPAA constraints. Other states, such as Alaska, Arizona, and Utah have almost no requirements for purchasing firearms.[46]

A 2010 study conducted by the National Center for State Courts revealed that there should be twice as many mental health records in the NICS database than there currently are. According to the FBI, there are over one million people in the database who are prohibited from purchasing firearms due to mental illness—just 0.74 per cent of all gun purchase denials. Almost three-quarters of denials are due to criminal records and domestic violence convictions.[47]

As a workaround to HIPAA barriers, in April 2013, President Obama announced a proposed rule change that would ease the current impediments to NICS reporting.[48] Additionally, the president pledged to take a series of steps to end gun violence by

- Requiring background checks for all gun sales.
- Strengthening the background check system for gun sales.
- Passing a new, stronger legislation banning assault weapons.
- Limiting magazine capacity to ten rounds.
- Getting armor-piercing bullets off the streets.
- Giving law enforcement agencies additional tools to prevent and prosecute gun crime.
- Ending the freeze on gun violence research.
- Making our schools safer with new resource officers and counselors, better emergency response plans, and more nurturing school climates.
- Ensuring quality coverage of mental health treatment, particularly for young people.[49]

Just one month prior to the president's proposed rule change, however, sweeping changes to the HIPAA laws were enacted, strengthening privacy and security protection of medical records and imposing greater penalties for breaches of patient confidentiality.[50] With this tightening of HIPAA, loosening of gun laws in many states, and the contentious political climate throughout the country, it appears doubtful that compliance with federal requirements for background checks will improve in the near future.

The Future

David Eagleman, PhD, a neuroscience researcher affiliated with the Baylor College for Medicine in Houston, Texas, believes that Charles Whitman's shooting rampage was triggered by his nickel-sized brain tumor. Whitman's tumor, a glioblastoma, radiated from the thalamus and encroached upon the hypothalamus and the amygdala. According to Eagleman, because the amygdala is involved in the regulation of fear and aggression, Whitman's gut reaction that something in his brain was affecting his behavior was correct. Eagleman cites researchers Heinrich Kluver and Paul Bucy, who found that damage to the amygdala in monkeys led to a cluster of symptoms that could explain Whitman's behavior.[51]

"Changes in the balance of brain chemistry, even small ones, can also cause large and unexpected changes in behavior," says Eagleman. He relates the case of a sixty-eight year-old man with Parkinson's disease who, after being prescribed a drug that mimics the body's natural release of dopamine, became a compulsive gambler who amassed losses in excess of $200,000 in just six months. Fortunately, when his physician discontinued this medication, his symptoms subsided. This same gambling behavior in conjunction with this particular drug has been documented in a number of patients.[52]

Eagleman believes that the lesson in these cases is that we cannot separate behavior and biology.[53] We are not all operating from a level playing field—people's brains are strikingly different. Our laws are based upon the premise that mentally competent adults behave rationally and can foresee the consequences of their actions. Eagleman believes that "acts cannot be understood separately from the biology of the actors," and the law must be forward-looking "informed by scientific insights into the brain." Eagleman does not suggest allowing biological factors to dictate the consequences of criminal acts, but argues that an understanding of the science behind behavior will give us the tools we need to change it. Through science, one day we may even be able to prevent violent acts.

Most mass killers are not psychotic but many of them display signs and symptoms of personality disorders such as narcissism and sociopathy. Sociopaths are difficult to recognize during childhood and are usually not diagnosed until the individual's late teen or young adult years. These children are often referred to as callous-unemotional children by behavioral scientists. By the time antisocial behaviors are identified as sociopathy, they are extremely difficult to change.

Professor Mark Dadds of the University of New South Wales, acknowledges that it is difficult and inappropriate to label a young child a psychopath. One study that followed 3,000 children over a twenty-five year period found that signs of sociopathy were recognizable in children as young as three years old. Dadds believes that early intervention may offer a means for callous-unemotional children to change course.[54] Researchers are hopeful that if treatment is established at an early age it may be possible to rewire the brain.[54]

According to Jennifer Khan, faculty member at UC Berkley and a notable science writer, sociopaths make up a small portion of our total population, about one per cent, but they comprise about one-quarter of prison populations and are responsible for an incommensurate number of brutal crimes, including murder.[55] Neuroscientist Kent Kiehl estimates the annual cost of sociopathy at $460 million per year.[56]

It may be the firearms industry and not science, however, that provides the ultimate solution to keeping guns out of the hands of violent criminals and would-be terrorists. Several companies have introduced smart guns that use biometrics or radio-frequency identification (RFID). Michael Recce, an associate professor at the New Jersey Institute of Technology, has been working on the design of a smart gun since 1999. His prototype uses dynamic grip recognition that prevents persons other than the owner from firing the weapon.[57]

In 2002, New Jersey was the first state to pass legislation requiring new handguns to contain a computer microchip that recognizes gun owners and is non-functional to anyone else. In the event the New Jersey attorney general determines that the prototype is safe and commercially available, the law will go into effect three years from that date.[58]

One smart gun model is currently available for gun shops to sell, the iP1. In anticipation of the New Jersey law taking effect, the National Rifle Association (NRA) has forged a campaign against smart guns. In a November 13, 2013, post on their legislative agenda web site, the NRA voiced its opposition to smart guns.

> "Smart Guns" is a made-up term for a conceptual firearm that incorporates technology that theoretically permits the gun to be fired only by the authorized user....NRA does not oppose new technological developments in firearms; however, we are opposed to government mandates that require the use of expensive, unreliable features, such as grips that would read your fingerprints before the gun will fire. And NRA recognizes that the "smart guns" issue clearly has the potential to mesh with the anti-gunner's agenda, opening the door to a ban on all guns that do not possess the government-required technology.[59]

There are other players in the race to corner the market on smart guns. SafeGun Technology uses a biometric fingerprint recognition architecture and plans to produce a retrofit kit that will sell for less than $150.[60] An Irish company, Trigger Smart, uses RFID technology to customize a gun to its owner. A tiny high-frequency RFID reader in the handle of the weapon is activated by a transponder worn by gun owner.[61]

In the meantime, the Army plans to implement yet another program—a computer monitoring system called ADAMS (Anomaly Detection at Multiple Scales)—to identify insider threats. ADAMS sifts through massive amounts of data in which "malevolent (or possibly inadvertent) actions by a trusted individual are detected against a background of everyday network activity."[62]

Ideally, the program will pinpoint the time and place where a good soldier becomes an internal threat capable of homicide or suicide. ADAMS uses actual data from the Fort Hood shooting—Hasan's emails and text messages—to rank threats. The proposal for ADAMS poses the question "can we pick up the trail before the fact, giving us time to intervene and prevent an incident? Why is that so hard?"[63]

Photo by John Porterfield

12. The System

Delay is preferable to error.
~Thomas Jefferson

Alex* opened his eyes and tried to squint away the brain fog that clouded his mind. He didn't know how long he had been out and he vaguely remembered being rolled into surgery. He tried to sit up but an IV in each arm kept him tethered to the narrow, hard bed. He surveyed his tiny room. It was barely larger than a jail cell with camo green walls and an irritating, flickering fluorescent light overhead. One wall didn't go all the way to the floor and he could hear the shuffling of footsteps and see several pairs of feet on the other side. There were moans and muffled conversation along with sounds of water splashing into a basin.

Despite all efforts to get rid of it, a small sore on Alex's right arm had begun spreading and eating away at his flesh. He was a surgical tech at Darnall Medical Center at Fort Hood and he assumed that he picked up his infection in the operating room. When the wound didn't respond to antibiotics, his doctor had him moved by ambulance to Brooke Army Medical Center in San Antonio where he had surgery to clean out the infection. He would be on intravenous antibiotics for at least a week, maybe two, and would bear scars that would last a lifetime.

There was a gentle knock at the door and Alex immediately recognized the nurse who walked in. "Hey, Julie.* Long time, no see."

"Hi, Alex. I didn't know you were here. How are you feeling?" Julie walked over to him and began pulling at his bandage. "What do you think about your high profile neighbor?" she asked him.

"High profile?"

"Yes, Nidal Hasan. The shooter."

"That's a joke, right?"

"No joke. It's him. Really! He has a security detail and armed guards at his door. They walled off most of the unit and he has a huge area for all of his machinery. A special spinal cord injury team was flown in—they're not using BAMC staff to take care of him. One of their nurses has been complaining that she doesn't think that she and the other RNs should have to wash his feet five times a day."[1]

Alex knew Hasan from working weekend call at Darnall Medical Center. One Sunday afternoon, Alex was on duty in the emergency room when one of Hasan's psych patients became uncontrollable. Hasan had removed the patient's restraints before properly subduing him and a code had to be called. Another one of the ER docs who witnessed the whole incident criticized Hasan in front of several other physicians who were there and Hasan became infuriated. His patient had been diagnosed with PTSD and the subject of the United States' involvement in Middle Eastern wars came up. Hasan said that if he were ever deployed to Iraq or Afghanistan, he would get even.

ON THE OTHER SIDE OF THE WALL, Major Nidal Hasan, supine in his hospital bed and surrounded by a team of renowned spinal cord injury specialists, breathed laboriously while his attorney, John Galligan, a retired Army colonel, spoke quietly with him. Hasan's brother, Eyad, hired Galligan, who is well-respected for defending soldiers in high-profile military cases. As soon as he agreed to represent Hasan, Galligan charged out of the chute on the offensive, talking to the national media and questioning his client's mental capacity. He feared that Hasan could not get a fair trial at Fort Hood because of the wall-to-wall television, radio, Internet, and print coverage.[2]

Brooke Army Medical Center in San Antonio is a five-hour round trip drive from Fort Hood and Galligan complained of the long distance between him and his client. In mid-December, 2009, when he was told that Hasan required at least two more months of hospital care, he filed a motion to have his client moved to a hospital closer to Killeen. That never happened.[3]

Hasan's Article 32 hearing was scheduled to begin on March 1, 2010. A military Article 32 is an evidentiary hearing similar to a civilian grand jury proceeding, except that the accused attends the hearing and is allowed to inspect all evidence presented. Because Hasan remained hospitalized at BAMC, the proceedings were delayed until June 1, 2010.[4]

In the meantime, Bell County was quietly preparing for a special new prisoner and on March 22, 2010, Bell County Sheriff Dan Smith released a statement to the press.

> Today's action by the Bell County Commissioner's Court formalizes contract negotiations which have been ongoing with Ft. Hood authorities for the past several weeks. Today's court action paves the way for the Bell County Jail to receive Major Nidal Hasan. The extraordinary circumstances surrounding this inmate require unusual and extraordinary security measures....Once Hasan is secured in our jail facility, I will be conducting a press conference to provide additional comments and answer questions. However, until that time, neither I or my staff will be receiving any media inquiries or answering questions.[5]

At four o'clock in the morning of April 9, 2010, a security detail and a medical team quietly loaded Hasan into a military helicopter and flew him to Fort Hood where he was quickly whisked away in a medical van to the Bell County Jail. Despite the paralysis that bridled Hasan from the chest down, he was handcuffed and shackled for the duration of the trip. When he realized that he was being moved to the jail, he asked to call his attorney and a family member but his request was denied. No one was provided advance notice that he was being transferred to the Bell County Detention Center.[6] In a twist of irony, it was Hasan's deployment unit—the twenty-first Combat Aviation Brigade—that moved him from BAMC to Fort Hood.

"He has very unique needs and no matter how good the staff is here, and how new the facility is, it's not a hospital," said Galligan to the press. "I venture to guess if you were to ask where in the history of this jail or even the earlier jail, they have had to deal with a person with his medical needs, they'd be very hard pressed."[7]

In a press conference that afternoon, Sheriff Smith was quick to report that the jail's contract physician had inspected his room in the jail infirmary and had judged that the facility was adequate for Hasan's needs. Smith assured the media that except for security, Hasan would be treated "just like any other military inmate."[8]

Confined in a twelve-by-fifteen foot infirmary cell, Hasan had a private bathroom, a handicap accessible shower, and a hospital bed with an air mattress. He was provided a television (no news reports allowed), a Qur'an (only a printed version, not the electronic one he requested), and his family was allowed to provide prepared meals for him. Like any other Bell County jail prisoner, two twenty-minute visits with his family and friends were permissible by teleconference on pre-determined dates and times posted on the Bell County Detention website.[9] Hasan's defense attorneys were allowed one-on-one access to their client. Guards were on round-the-clock duty in three eight-hour shifts in a small anteroom adjacent to Hasan's cell.[10]

"The majority of the cost associated with this are because of the need I believe we have to assign a jailer to him, twenty-four hours a day, seven days a week," said Smith to the clutch of reporters. "I've assured the military that we will evaluate that policy as time goes back [sic], and if it's in everybody's interest to cut back on that, we will do that."[11]

The six-month contract that Bell County signed with Fort Hood for housing Hasan included $24,393.90 for 183 days—a daily rate substantially higher than a "regular" inmate. As an Inmate of High Value (IHV), Hasan garnered $133.30 per day in comparison to a regular prisoner who is housed at a cost of $60.00 per day. Additional charges for security ($152,402.40), and reimbursable costs for supplies to meet his medical needs($30,000.00) totaled $206,796.30.[12]

"Bell County is in receipt of $207,000 taxpayer dollars to accommodate a person that I think could have easily been placed in a medical ward unit at Darnall, or in a hospital facility. And that money, in my opinion, was wasted," Galligan quipped to reporters.[13] By the time the trial was over and Hasan was transferred to Fort Leavenworth military prison, the Army had paid the Bell County Sheriff's Office $650,000 to house him.[14]

Galligan quickly put Hasan's brother, Anas, on the defense team. After obtaining a law degree in the United States, Anas had moved to Ramallah, Palestine, to join relatives who settled there many years ago. Galligan flew Anas to San Antonio so that he could be near his brother. This accomplished two things: Anas was hoping to find any facts or circumstances that would mitigate his brother's culpability for killing thirteen people and wounding forty-three others.[15] Second, including Anas on the defense team gave him unlimited one-on-one access to his incarcerated brother.

According to Paul Romer, a reporter for the *Temple Daily Telegram*, "The brother of Maj. Nidal M. Hasan continues to be the accused mass murderer's most frequent visitor in Bell County Jail, averaging a visit nearly every other day during the fifteen months Hasan has spent in the infirmary." Jail records indicate that Anas visited his brother 207 times.[16]

As soon as he felt that Hasan could handle it, Galligan arranged for a sanity hearing. In all probability, his client would be facing capital punishment and Galligan wanted to explore all available avenues to mitigate his guilt. If the Sanity Board judged Hasan to be mentally unfit to stand trial, he would be placed in a psychiatric hospital until the time that he could be tried as a rational human being. [17]

Maj. Kaustubh G. Joshi headed up the team of specialists that evaluated Hasan's mental state at the time of the shooting. The Board had planned to wrap up its investigation by the end of February 2010, prior to Hasan's preliminary hearing scheduled for June, but Galligan petitioned the court for a continuance. He needed more time to piece together the evidence that Hasan was suffering from "lack of mental responsibility at the time he committed the murders."[18]

Article 32

On June 1, 2010, looking polished and demure with a clean-shaven face, a beanie over his closely cropped hair, and wearing crisply ironed fatigues, Hasan wheeled himself into the Lawrence J. Williams Judicial Center accompanied by John Galligan and several other defense attorneys. This hearing marked the first of a long string of court appearances and delays. Earlier that morning, officials had cleared the road next to the courthouse and waited for Hasan's arrival with bomb-sniffing dogs in the parking lot.[19]

Inside the courtroom, Hasan shivered and one of his lawyers wrapped a green blanket around his shoulders. Because of his paraplegia, his body could not regulate his body temperature adequately and he constantly complained of being cold. The judge asked Hasan several direct questions. He responded with a barely audible, meek, "Yes sir" or "I understand, sir," and pulled the blanket tightly around his head and neck. Galligan asked for a continuance because the defense team had not received several critical documents, such as the FBI ballistics report and a government review of the shooting.[20] Hasan had not yet undergone his Sanity Board evaluation, and, over lead prosecutor Col. Michael Mulligan's objection, a continuance was granted and the Article 32 hearing was reset for October 4, 2010.[21]

Mike Mulligan had successfully prosecuted the capital case against Hasan Akbar, Hasan's hero who had killed two officers and wounded sixteen others in Kuwait. Akbar's and Hasan's cases were similar in that Akbar's motive for his rampage was to prevent U.S. troops from killing Muslims. Akbar is currently on death row in Fort Leavenworth, Kansas.[22]

The October 4, 2010, Article 32 hearing was delayed until October 12 because of the government's inability to secure funding for the numerous prosecution witnesses. The proceeding was scheduled to last for more than three weeks, but the fifty-six witnesses who were called completed their testimony in only eight days.[23] The cost to American taxpayers for housing the witnesses during the hearing was $65,600.[24]

The first victim to testify was Sgt. Alonzo Lunsford. At six feet nine inches tall, he was a formidable presence in the courtroom. While on the witness stand he locked eyes with Hasan and never blinked. Following Lunsford, a procession of victims described the horrible scene that they had believed, at first, was a training exercise. Some remembered the clicking sound of Hasan's boots—the crevices in them had picked up spent shell casings. All of them described the utter chaos and terror as they witnessed their colleagues and buddies die at the hands of Nidal Hasan. Civilian witness Theodore Coukoulis compared the scene to a horror movie.[25]

Michelle Harper sobbed as her recorded 9-1-1 call was played. Witness Amber Behr testified that she dragged two soldiers outside and loaded them in the bed of a pickup and then climbed in behind them. She didn't realize that she had been shot in the back. Matthew Cooke ran outside and jumped into the truck with Behr. It took a few minutes for him to discover that he had been shot four times—including one bullet in his head. Witness after witness told their stories of blood, mayhem, death, and destruction.[26]

Captain Melissa Kale, via video conference in Afghanistan, said that she was talking to her sister on her phone when she heard gunfire. She thought that she was in the thick of a training scenario and dove under an overturned desk. She spotted a wounded soldier bleeding on the floor and heard Sgt. Crooker shout that she had been shot. She tried to drag Crooker out of the building but finally left her when she realized she was dead. Kale sobbed during the entire time she was on the witness stand.[27]

Throughout the graphic, emotionally-charged testimony of fifty-six witnesses Hasan sat expressionless in his wheelchair, hunched down in his blanket. He never flinched or spoke. The Article 32 hearing for the deadliest mass shooting on an American military base came to an abrupt halt in mid-November when the defense team announced that it would not be presenting witnesses. Col. Morgan Lamb, the special convening authority, recommended that Hasan face a general court-martial with a consideration of capital punishment. Hasan's arraignment date was set for July 20, 2011, in the case of *United States vs. Maj. Nidal Malik Hasan.*[28]

On July 18, 2011, Hasan gave a twenty-minute jailhouse telephone interview to an Al-Jazeera reporter. The following is a partial transcript of that interview recorded by the Bell County Detention Center and transcribed by the FBI.

I would like to begin by repenting to Almighty Allah and apologize to the Muhadageen [*sic*]...the believers ...and the innocent. I ask for their forgiveness and their prayers. I ask for their forgiveness for participating in the illegal and immoral aggression against Muslims...their religion...and deception of many innocent men...women...and children. As a United States Army Psychiatrist...my job was to "conserve the fighting strength" of military armed forces personnel and by deceit "to win the hearts and minds" of Muslims throughout the world. Using American Muslim soldiers such as myself to help win the hearts and minds of naïve and desperate Muslims around the world is a powerful strategy...indeed...I saw and heard how we would give money to Muslim politicians and support projects like the building of schools and mosques... so we could ultimately dictate what is said...read...and done...and I am too ashamed to even mention the clandestine and covert operations that have already occurred...or are still in progress about the Muslim world. My complicity was on behalf of a government that openly acknowledges that it would hate for the law of Almighty Allah to be the supreme law of the land.

I would like to thank those champions of Islam for awakening me from my slumber...for educating and inspiring me for trying to establish the law of Almighty Allah as supreme for future generations...and for serving as role models on how Muslims should stand up against tyranny and aggression...these champions of Islam or the Mujahideen [*sic*]... they are spread out across the globe in Afghanistan...Iraq... Pakistan...and other parts of the world. I ask Almighty Allah to unite the believers as one solid fighting structure and not allow the enemies of His plan divide us.[29]

Two days later, on July 20, 2011, one year and eight months after the shooting, Hasan entered the courtroom for his arraignment without his defense counsel, John Galligan. Hasan had informed Fort Hood's chief circuit judge, Col. Gregory Gross, a few days prior to the proceeding that he had decided he would prefer representation by military lawyers from the Army Trial Defense Service. They had been assisting Galligan and were familiar with the case. There was no public reason given for Hasan firing his lead defense attorney.[30]

Hasan wheeled himself into the courtroom. His headwear of choice for this occasion was a loosely-woven green fleece cap which he removed before Judge Gross entered the courtroom. Gross had complained about Hasan's cap and blanket on several occasions.[31]

Hasan could have entered a plea at that time but he chose not to. Defendants in military capital cases are not allowed to enter a guilty plea and so his choices were limited to "not guilty" or "not guilty for lack of mental responsibility." The prosecution asked to read the charges against Hasan to the court, but one of Hasan's defense lawyers told the judge that the defendant waived the reading. The trial date was set for March 5, 2012.[32]

The media wasted no time in tracking down Hasan's former attorney, John Galligan after the hearing.

"Today marks my leave of absence as a member of the Hasan defense team," Galligan wrote in a press release issued from his Belton office. "I will not at this time detail the reasons prompting this development....I have consistently argued that Major Hasan has not been treated fairly. I maintain that belief....Major Hasan fully understands that I stand ready and anxious to resume an active role."[33]

Buying Time

The eight month interval between Hasan's arraignment and his trial was necessary for each side to develop a witness list, request documents and materials from the opposing team, argue the admissibility of evidence, and take care of housekeeping matters that, if left undone, could disrupt the trial. Pre-trial hearings were scheduled at frequent intervals and the first was conducted on October 27, 2011.

During this first pre-trial hearing Judge Gross issued an order requested by the prosecution to Yahoo! to produce documents. He went over the trial schedule and heard a defense motion for the government to provide funding for a media consultant expert and a panel selection expert (the military panel is comparable to a jury in a civilian trial). The prosecution objected on the basis that the experts were not necessary and hiring them was a foolish waste of money and time. The defense asked Judge Gross to recuse himself because he had been present on the base during the shooting which, according to the defense team, created a potential for personal bias. Gross took all of the matters presented during the hearing under advisement.[34]

From November 30, 2011, to June 6, 2012, there were six pre-trial hearings. The defense continued to ask Judge Gross to step down because of personal bias. At each request, the judge refused. The defense also questioned the constitutionality of the death penalty in military capital cases because the accused is not afforded the same rights as in parallel civilian cases. Gross denied the defense team's request for a pre-trial publicity expert but granted the hiring of a panel selection expert. In February, Judge Gross agreed to a three month continuance of the trial from March 5, 2012, until June 12. In April, another trial delay was approved and set for October 9, 2012.[35]

Whisker Wars

When Hasan showed up for a pre-trial hearing on June 8, 2012, with a full beard, Judge Gross displayed his displeasure with an on-the-record statement that the appearance of the accused was a disruption to the court proceedings. He delayed pre-trial motions until a future date and ordered Hasan to shave off his beard or be prepared to watch the hearings from outside of the courtroom. The defense stated its plan to file for a religious accommodation exception.[36]

Hasan appeared in court eleven days later on June 19, 2012, with his full beard. Judge Gross stated on the record,

> The accused again appeared in court with a beard, and continues to be in violation of Army Regulation 670-1 and Rules for Court-Martial 804(e) (1). The appearance of the accused continues to disrupt the court proceedings and the accused will view court proceedings via a closed-circuit feed in a trailer adjacent to the courthouse. Unless the accused conforms to Army regulations or is granted an exception to policy for religious accommodation by the Department of the Army, he will continue to view the proceedings via closed-circuit feed.[37]

A bailiff escorted Hasan out of the courtroom and wheeled him into a small trailer outside where he could communicate with the court over closed circuit television. There was a switch on the AV equipment so that Hasan could turn off the video connection but the audio feed could not be adjusted.[38] That trailer cost the Army $8,000 a month for sixteen months, almost $128,000 dollars plus the AV equipment and closed circuit television which cost $185,000 part of a $3,508,072.56 grant from the Troubled Asset Relief Program (TARP) after the country's financial collapse in 2008.[39]

Lead defense attorney Lt. Col. Kris Poppe argued that Hasan grew the beard as a "deeply sincere expression of his Islamic faith and because he has a premonition he will die soon" and indicated that they would file an appeal and ask for a stay from the Army Court of Criminal Appeals.[40]

Several motions were considered and Judge Gross approved a defense request for an expert neurologist paid for by the U.S. government.[41] After the hearing, lead defense attorney Lt. Col. Kris Poppe released a letter on behalf of Hasan to his former attorney, John Galligan: "Please be clear, as of July 20, 2011, at 2:30 p.m. you were no longer my attorney and do not represent me in any capacity."[42]

At the June 19 hearing, the a government prosecutor stated,

> At the time the crime was committed, the accused was clean-shaven; at the article 32 hearing, multiple witnesses came in, tried to identify him, and successfully did so...now on the eve of the trial, the accused grows a beard. We believe his motive, if anything, is to disguise himself and to thwart in-court identification at trial.[43]

Hasan's attorneys argued that the chaplain who had spent many hours with Hasan believed that he grew a beard for religious reasons. Overall, Hasan was well-groomed and appeared in court in proper uniform, had a fresh haircut, and adhered to proper courtroom decorum.

On June 29, 2012, Hasan's defense team petitioned the court for another continuance until December 2012, and Judge Gross refused. The current trial schedule for August 20, 2012, would remain. The judge brought up a sensitive issue about Hasan's use of the men's restroom that serviced the courtroom. He had discovered a soiled adult diaper on the floor of the bathroom "with feces spread on the floor and a biohazard bag on the floor."[44] He assumed that it was left there by Hasan and ordered the defense team to clean up the mess and told them to keep their client out of that restroom. It was later determined, however, that it was not human waste on the floor but mud tracked into the men's room by someone from DES.[45] After the incident was investigated, the diaper and biohazard bag were never mentioned again in court and it is doubtful that they ever existed.

Judge Gross also announced at the June 29 hearing that Army Court of Criminal Appeals(ACCA)refused to hear Hasan's appeal.[46] Hasan's defense team quickly filed another appeal.[47]

Contemporary Islamic scholars disagree with Hasan's opinion that as a faithful, devoted Muslim he is required to wear a beard as an outward demonstration of his commitment to Islam. Hasan told the court that he had a premonition that his death was imminent and that he would not be afforded the luxuries of heaven if he died clean shaven. According to Islamic scholar Imam Abduljalil, "Going without a beard became a sign of modernity. In the 1960s and 1970s, you saw more Muslims shaving off their beards."[48]

It is the Taliban, the group with whom Hasan most closely identifies, that requires men to grow beards. The Taliban enforces the most severe dogma of Islamic governance, Shari'a law. It administers harsh and cruel punishments such as public executions where "criminals" are buried chest-deep in sand and stoned to death in a stadium full of the faithful. It directs the amputations of limbs of thieves and performs acts of cruelty that are considered primitive and cruel in most other cultures. The Taliban has banned television, movies, and music and prohibits the education of girls past the age of ten. It was the Taliban that provided shelter to Osama bin Laden and has consistently supported the al Qaeda movement. The Taliban maintains strict enforcement of the male beard and the female Burka.[49]

Hasan's July 6 and July 12 hearings were routine. A preliminary questionnaire for the panel pool was approved by both sides and Hasan continued to watch the proceedings from his trailer.[50]

At a July 25, 2012, pre-trial hearing, Judge Gross allowed Hasan to sit in the courtroom and addressed him directly.

"Maj. Hasan, I am considering whether you should be held in contempt for willfully disobeying the court order to be clean shaven…I will now give you the opportunity to tell me anything about whether or not you should be held in contempt."[51]

Through his attorney, Kris Poppe, Hasan asserted the Religious Freedom Restoration Act (RFRA) as his defense to the contempt charge. Poppe argued, "Major Hasan's desire to have a beard and refusal to shave is a sincerely held religious belief."[52] He denied that the order to shave was a compelling governmental interest or the least restrictive means available to ensure compliance with the judge's order. Poppe emphasized the fact that the accused was not in any way disrupting the court.[53]

Judge Gross again found Hasan in contempt of court, fined him $1,000, and had him removed from the courtroom. "At some point before we start, what I consider the more critical stages of the trial," the judge said, "I am going to force him to be shaved; if he doesn't do it voluntarily. At this point, that's my plan." He then indicated that he would have Hasan shaved before the start of his trial on August 20, 2012.[54]

At that same hearing, the defense requested experts on religious conversion and social science methodology. Judge Gross deferred his decision on funding for those experts but approved additional funds for previously appointed defense experts in jury selection and mitigation.[55]

On August 6, 2012, Hasan filed a request for a review with the ACCA.[56]

On August 9 and August 14, Judge Gross held contempt hearings over the issue of Hasan's beard. Each time Hasan refused to shave, Gross fined him $1,000. With the trial scheduled to commence in just a few days and with no resolution on the beard issue, lead defense attorney Poppe requested a continuance until October. Gross refused to grant another delay and also denied defense motions to exclude the testimony of the government's terrorism expert, Evan Kohlmann, and to have the government produce daily transcripts during panel selection. He also denied a defense request for a special instruction on note-taking by panel members during the court martial. Gross also heard arguments on defense motions regarding panel selection and prosecutorial misconduct. Judge Gross announced that there would be two additional pre-trial hearings prior to the start of the trial.[57]

On August 27, 2012, The Court of Criminal Appeals denied Hasan's appeal without prejudice because the military judge had not yet issued a definitive order for Hasan to be forcibly shaved. If and when Judge Gross formalized his intent to have Hasan's beard removed through an official order, he could re-file his appeal.[58]

Tug of War

Just five days before the commencement of the trial, the Army Appellate Court ordered an indefinite stay. That didn't stop Judge Gross, however, from holding hearings and finding Hasan in contempt of court. The defense requested that the judge consider a sworn affidavit from the accused dated September 5, 2012. Hasan stated in his affidavit that his two-and-a-half year confinement in the Bell County Detention Center had enabled him to reach a deeper understanding of his Muslim faith which, in turn, led him to a strong belief that as a Muslim man, he must wear a beard. He concluded,

> My situation has led me to make a firmer commitment to my faith, including my resolve to not shave in accordance with my understanding of Islamic requirements. I am a paraplegic and, therefore, more susceptible to life-threatening illness. Further, I am convinced the authorities believe someone may try to kill me....I determined that I couldn't risk death without having taken this mandatory step along a pious Islamic path. Regardless of how long I live or when I may die, I believe my faith requires me to grow a beard.[59]

Hasan's defense team reminded Judge Gross that Hasan was willing to plead guilty to the charges and accept full responsibility for his actions. The prosecution accused Hasan of trying to disguise himself so that witnesses could not identify him. They also argued that Hasan was not expressing authentic religious beliefs and backed up their claim with the transcript of Hasan's telephone interview with Al-Jezeera. After considering the evidence, Judge Gross ruled that "the defense has not demonstrated that requiring the accused to shave, or forcibly shaving the accused, substantially burdens his exercise of religion." The judge ultimately concluded that the defense did not prove that Hasan was sincere. In his ruling, Gross wrote,

> Based on all the evidence, it is equally likely the accused is growing the beard at this time for purely secular reasons and is using his religious beliefs as a cover. For example, the evidence suggests it is equally likely the accused's refusal to shave is an action of defiance toward the U.S. Army and the Court; or was done to frustrate his in-court identification.[60]

Judge Gross then ordered Hasan to be forcibly shaved and told him to sign a non-disclosure agreement.[61] The next time Hasan entered the courtroom he would be clean shaven and no one would know if he had been voluntarily or forcibly shaved.

On September 19, 2012, Hasan's defense team once again attempted to have the judge reconsider his findings on Hasan's sincerity about his religion. A paralegal examined daily activity logs kept by the Bell County Jail. These logs showed that at the time Hasan grew his beard, he was praying more than four hours per day, one hour longer than when he first arrived at the Bell County Detention Center and one-half hour more than the months preceding his growing a beard. Defense attorneys also presented an affidavit written by Hasan describing his religious piety and refusing to sign the judge's nondisclosure order.

> Since being ordered into pre-trial confinement, through the study of the Qur'an, the hadiths, and discussions with two Imams, I have learned much about the importance as a Muslim of strictly keeping our covenants (promises)....It is important to me, in my desire to live my life as a faithful Muslim and abide by the requirements of Islam....I am very concerned about entering into an express written covenant mandated by the Military Judge....I do not believe it is necessary as I already want to take responsibility for my actions and plead guilty.[62]

Hasan's willingness to publicly confess his guilt effectively removed his beard as a barrier to his identification by witnesses and victims. Judge Gross denied the motion on September 26, 2012, without consideration.[63]

Hasan made news headlines again in late September 2012, when the Fort Hood Press Center announced that he had been taken by ambulance to Darnall Medical Center. The post spokesman, Chris Haug, did not provide details but said he was in good condition and was expected to have a short stay.[64]

John Galligan, Hasan's former attorney, publicly disagreed. Galligan had been complaining about Hasan's jail cell since he was first taken to the Bell County Detention Center and he told reporters that Hasan's condition was serious.[65] He said that Hasan was suffering health consequences as a result of his unsanitary surroundings including problems with his catheter which caused blood in his urine. Galligan reported that Hasan's bathroom was not properly equipped for a paraplegic inmate and he was forced to use a waste basket as a toilet. He said that jailers washed the trash can in Hasan's sink and didn't clean it afterwards, leading to an infectious environment.[66] Amid speculation that Hasan was on his deathbed in Darnall Medical Center, he was released forty-eight hours after his admission without comment.[67]

Pre-trial litigation continued with the Army Court of Criminal Appeals scheduling oral arguments for October 11, 2012. The defense team based its position on the RFRA.[68] At the same time, they also argued for the court to replace Judge Gross because of his personal bias against Hasan.[69]

On December 3, 2012, the appellate court ruled to remove Judge Gross on the basis of an appearance of bias. The court also vacated Gross' order to forcibly shave Hasan and voided the six contempt citations against him. The opinion said, in part,

> Thus, taken together, the decision to remove Appellant from the courtroom, the contempt citations, and the decision to order Appellant's forcible shaving in the absence of any command action to do the same, could lead an objective observer to conclude that the military judge was not impartial towards Appellant. In light of these rulings, and the military judge's accusations regarding the latrine, it could reasonably appear to an objective observer that the military judge had allowed the proceedings to become a duel of wills between himself and Appellant rather than an ad-

judication of the serious offenses with which Appellant is charged. Moreover, we are cognizant that the military judge and his family were present at Fort Hood on the day of the shootings. While this fact alone is not disqualifying, when viewed in light of the factors identified above, an objective observer might reasonably question the military judge's impartiality.[70]

As an example, the appellate court cited the case of the first judge who presided over the trial of the Oklahoma City bombers. He was removed because his court was only one block away from the explosion and was damaged by the blast. The blast also injured a member of his staff, as well as other court personnel and their families. Even if he were not biased or prejudiced, his personal circumstances would lead the public to believe that he harbored a personal bias.[71]

Because of Judge Gross' bench-war over Hasan's beard, the trial was delayed and American taxpayers footed the $106,700 bill for reserved hotel suites for witnesses at the Shilo Inn in Killeen.[72]

THE APPEALS COURT NAMED COL. TARA ABBEY OSBORN to replace Judge Gregory Gross on December 4, 2012. A Judge Advocate General at Fort Bragg, she was all business and wasted no time in assuming control over the trial. She held her first pre-trial hearing at Fort Hood on December 18, 2012. It was an information-sharing meeting and both teams brought her up to date on the status of the case. Osborn asked both parties to submit a proposed trial schedule by the end of the month. She briefly discussed Hasan's beard and asked him if he wore the beard "of his own free will and if he agreed to waive issues surrounding the beard and panel selection." Hasan responded that he agreed.[73]

Over the next five months Osborn held numerous routine pre-trial hearings where questions of expert witnesses, rules of evidence, and matters that impacted what the panel would see and hear were litigated.[74]

Hasan threw another monkey wrench into the works in late May, just one week prior to selection of the panel, when he announced to the judge that he had decided to fire his team of defense attorneys and represent himself. Osborn postponed panel selection for one week. She did not rule immediately—her decision to allow Hasan to act as his own attorney would be based on a number of factors including his physical status. On several occasions Hasan's lead defense attorney, Lt. Col. Kris Poppe, had brought up Hasan's inability to sit for long periods of time as an issue. Osborn was not certain that Hasan had the stamina to act as his own attorney.[75] She ordered a physical exam and asked for a report from the examining physician regarding his physical ability to conduct his own defense. He was sent back to Brook Army Medical Center, renamed San Antonio Military Medical Center(SAMMC),[76] for his physical. He passed without any problems.[77]

On June 4, 2013, Osborn agreed to allow Hasan to proceed pro se, without defense council, but instructed the defense team to remain on standby in the event that Hasan needed help. She instructed them to provide any assistance that Hasan required, including legal research and advice. She also directed Hasan's commander to find office space for him to work including a computer, legal software, and paralegal assistance.[78]

Hasan asked for another trial delay but Osborn didn't budge. The trial was going to commence as scheduled. When Hasan argued that he needed extra time to prepare his defense, based upon the legal doctrine of the *defense of others*, Osborn gave him until noon, July 5, 2012, to provide sufficient facts about his proposed strategy to justify a continuance.[79]

The doctrine of "defense of others" compels a person to intervene in a situation in which another party would be injured or killed if not for his or her intervention. This is a defense that is commonly used to justify the overturning of *Roe v. Wade* and many states use "defense of others" as a rationale for instituting more stringent abortion laws. This defense strategy is rarely used and even more rarely used successfully.[80]

Hasan claimed that "defense of others" was a valid approach to defending his case because he had "switched sides" and was protecting the Taliban from being murdered by the hands of the U.S. Army soldiers. Hasan's hatred of American soldiers was not new to his defense team. His Sanity Board Report had been released to the defense attorneys but was withheld from the prosecution. Hasan released the report to the media in mid-August, well after the commencement of his trial. In the margins, written in his own hand, he justified his actions and provided the basis for defending his rampage.

> Since the wars in Afghanistan and Iraq are illegal/unconstitutional according to many legal experts, I don't understand why members of the Muslim community cry that my actions went against Islam, because they say, I broke my oath of office. My oath at the very least is irrelevant but I could argue my oath compels me to at least speak out against these illegal and unconstitutional wars.[81]

Hasan's defense team reacted strongly to their client's proposed trial strategy and refused to help him articulate his defense in a legal brief. Hasan complained to the judge during the next pre-trial hearing. "By helping me, they believe that crosses an ethical line."[82]

Lead defense attorney Poppe told Osborn that her order created an ethical conflict and turned the standby counsel into "shadow counsel."[83]

"It becomes clear his goal is to remove impediments or obstacles to the death penalty and is working toward a death penalty," Poppe told Osborn. He called Hasan's strategy "repugnant to defense counsel and contrary to our professional obligations."[84]

Prosecutor Mike Mulligan defended Hasan's approach. "I'm really perplexed as to how it's caused such a moral dilemma," he told the judge.[85]

Judge Osborne ruled against Hasan's proposed defense, stating that there was no evidence to support an immediate threat by anyone at Fort Hood to anyone in Afghanistan. Further, she ruled that as a member of the U.S. armed forces, Hasan had no justification for killing other soldiers. Osborn would not allow Hasan to present any evidence or arguments relating to the defense of others and she would not permit another trial delay.[86]

Panel selection was scheduled to commence on Tuesday, July 9, 2013, and without his "defense of others" trial strategy, Hasan had no legal representation and no plan. Former U.S. Attorney General Ramsey Clark stepped up to the plate and offered to represent him.

Clark, an eighty-five year old Texan with the reputation for jumping into the middle of trouble, was attorney general under President Lyndon Johnson and is a staunch opponent of capital punishment. Clouded in controversy, Clark is a globe-trotter who has represented some of the most notorious criminals and terrorists in the world—among them Saddam Hussein, Slobodan Milosevic, and the blind sheik Omar Abdel-Rahman who was one of the leaders in the 1993 bombing of the New York World Trade Center.[87]

Hasan again petitioned Judge Osborn for a three-day trial delay so that he could consider Clark's offer. Osborn stood steadfast—there would be no delays, no matter the reason. Clark withdrew his offer because there was not enough time to adequately prepare for the trial. He left open the option to step in, especially if Hasan needed him for the sentencing phase of the trial.[88]

On the eve of panel selection, the Lawrence J. Williams Judicial Center was transformed both literally and figuratively into a combat zone. Conex industrial containers, concrete highway barriers, and Hesco Concertainers[89] filled with sand and gravel girdled the courthouse and were stacked to the roof. Armed guards with M-4 rifles patrolled the perimeter twenty-four hours a day, and all persons entering the courthouse were required to pass through a metal detector flanked by armed MPs. Only relatives of the victims were permitted to sit in the courtroom along with ten journalists chosen by lottery. An overflow room held other media representatives who viewed the trial via closed circuit television.[90]

From Murderer to Martyr

"I can't take any pride in wearing this uniform. I think it represents an enemy of Islam. I'm being forced to wear it," Hasan angrily announced during the final pre-trial hearing before his trial began that afternoon, July 9, 2013. He demanded that Judge Osborn instruct the panel that he was being forced to wear his uniform in court.[91]

Everyone was a bit testy that morning. With the trial date put off repeatedly, many of the witnesses complained that they had missed vacations, family reunions, and other events. They were tired of waiting and were worn out before the trial began.[92]

"I'll believe it when it happens," said retired staff sergeant Shawn Manning, "We've been given a window on and off since 2010."[93]

An irritated Judge Osborne chewed out Hasan for leaking his "defense of others" trial strategy to the local newspaper, the *Killeen Daily Herald*, and to *Fox News*. In his own handwriting, Hasan asked three questions about his motive, his oath of office, and his relationship with Awlaki. Following the three questions were two-and-a-half single-spaced typewritten pages entitled "Is Preferring an American Democracy Over Shari'ah (Islamic Governance) Permissible?"[94] Hasan was determined to circumvent Judge Osborn's order that he was forbidden to use his "defense of others" at trial, so he decided to try his case with the public.

Hasan's first question in his "defense of others" document was "What was your motive on November 5?" His answer was that he was defending his religion.

> It is one thing for the United States to say 'we dont [*sic*] want shari'ah (God's SWT) law to govern us but its [*sic*] not acceptable to have a foreign policy that tries to replace shari'ah law for a more secular form of government. Fledging [*sic*] Islamic States like Afghanistan need help to better govern their people under shari'ah law. We are imperfect Muslims trying to establish the perfect religion of All-Mighty God.[95]

His second point was a statement from the perspective of the Muslim community that had accused Hasan of going against the teachings of Islam for breaking his oath of office.

> Many reputable scholars in the legal field like Frances Boyle have clearly explained why the wars in Iraq and Afghanistan are illegal and unconstitutional. So I would argue participating in these wars breaks ones [*sic*] oath of office not the other way around. At best you could argue I broke a law. My brief on the defense of others can help explain this in more detail.[96]

His third question asked about his relationship with Awlaki.

> He was my teacher and mentor and Friend. May All-Mighty Allah accept him as a martyr. We are imperfect Muslims try-

ing to establish the perfect religion of All-Mighty Allah as supreme on the land.[97]

Hasan's typewritten diatribe on "Preferring an American Democracy Over Shari'ah" opens with a simple sentence. "The answer is simply No." His rationalization, was, in part,

> There is an inherent and irreconcilable conflict. American democracy places the sovereignty of man over the sovereignty of All-Mighty God….In Islam, our leaders are expected to govern by what All-Mighty God has determined to be right or wrong, and judge by His rules and injunctions, or else those leaders are referred to as unbelievers, transgressors, and/or defiant. Muslims are expected to completely submit to All-Mighty God….The religion of Islam was brought to prevail over all other religions not to be co-equal with them and certainly not to be subservient to them.[98]

Hasan states his view of polygamy "Currently a man can't marry more than one wife without getting arrested but that same man can marry another man and have multiple mistresses without fear of being arrested."[99]

He was equally adamant about twelve-year-old girls and marriage. "The law allows a 12 year old (or perhaps even younger) to have sexual relations in middle school with multiple partners and in some cases the state provides free forms of 'protection.' However she can't get married with the permission of her parents."[100]

Hasan's views on punishment were quite severe, as well. "Also, a man cannot justly discipline his wife but the state can discipline its citizens (men and women) with force if need be and is especially apparent in the prison system….It would be considered 'cruel or unusual punishment' to punish a person by a punishment that All-Mighty God has ordained like the flogging of a fornicator or severing the hand of a thief."[101]

Hasan concluded his polemic thesis with, "The constitution of the United States can be seen as a man made God competing with the All-Mighty Allah's sovereignty."[102]

IT WAS EXPECTED THAT PANEL SELECTION WOULD TAKE SEVERAL WEEKS. Both the prosecution and defense were allowed to question each of the 150 potential panelists and Judge Osborn had estimated that six officers per day could be queried. The completed panel would consist of thirteen officers of a higher rank than Hasan.[103]

Judge Osborn explained to the group of prospective panelists that Hasan wore his fatigues rather than a dress uniform because of his physical limitations. She also instructed them to not hold his beard against him because he had it for religious reasons.[104]

First, twenty officers from across the country were questioned as a group and six of them were dismissed based on their answers to a pre-trial questionnaire. One of the prosecutors asked the group if they agreed that "the defendant's choice of weapon and a motive could show premeditation." Everyone in the group nodded yes.[105] They also indicated that they had no problem with imposing the death penalty but most did not believe that execution was the only means of punishing a convicted mass murderer.[106]

At taxpayer expense, the defense team had arranged for a jury selection consultant to assist them in evaluating the suitability of each of the pooled panel members, but Hasan was his own boss now and did not want to rely upon an expert. He had submitted to Judge Osborn more than 100 questions that he planned to ask the individual panelists. Osborne had thrown out one-third of them, especially the questions that referred to his defunct "defense of others" trial strategy. She quickly eliminated questions such as, "Do you feel that killing twelve soldiers and a retired soldier was a horrific act?" and a question about the Boston Marathon bombing. Consequently, he abandoned his plan and questioned very few of the panel pool, limiting his queries to questions that reflected their feelings about Islam.[107]

Hasan declined to question the prospective panelists as a group. Individual members of the pool, however, were not ignored by him. He told one officer that Abdulhakim Muhammad, now serving a life sentence for shooting a soldier outside a Little Rock, Arkansas, recruiting station, was his friend. Hasan asked another if the fact that the Qur'an justifies killing would prevent that panelist from being objective.[108]

Judge Osborn reminded Hasan several times to stop telling the prospective jurors his personal beliefs. He asked one colonel why he wrote on the pre-trial questionnaire that he held a somewhat unfavorable opinion of Muslims. The officer said that during a deployment to Saudi Arabia he witnessed the "excesses" of the Saudi royal family. Hasan liked that answer and responded by saying, "You basically called the Saudis on their hypocrisy. Thank you for that on behalf of all Muslims."[109]

Hasan asked another panelist if he would hold it against him if he told him that the Taliban, in establishing Shari'ah law, "were imperfect Muslims trying to establish a perfect religion of almighty Allah." Another prospective panelist said that he had attempted not to form an opinion about the shooting and that he was "ninety-five percent successful."[110]

Hasan asked a female officer why she responded to her questionnaire that she had an unfavorable view of Shari'ah law. "I'm no expert in Shari'ah law, but it certainly seems like something I would not want to live under," she told Hasan. "I think it would pretty much suck."[111]

One thing was very apparent—it would be difficult, if not impossible, to find panelists who had not already formed an opinion of the case.[112]

Although it was expected that the panel selection would take several months, in five days a jury was seated. Could a competent, unbiased jury be seated in a capital punishment trial in just five days? Except for questioning three or four prospective panelists, Hasan was more of a disinterested onlooker than a participant in choosing a group of officers who would hold his life in their hands. By the end of the selection process, nine colonels, three lieutenant colonels, and one major would determine Hasan's fate. These thirteen panelists represented the fields of engineering, logistics, military intelligence, aviation, chemicals, ordnance, air defense artillery, and the signal corps. Many had served in combat zones and all but two had command experience. The highest ranking officer, a female, would serve as president of the panel.[113]

Acting on behalf of Hasan, a few days prior to the start of the trial, John Galligan forwarded a packet of Hasan's writings to *Fox News*. In a letter to Fox, Galligan verified the authenticity of the documents.[114]

"He represented to me that he either personally wrote in longhand or typed the statements at issue. All of the documents were prepared by Major Nidal Hasan and were sent, at his specific request, to your network."[115]

If there were any doubts as to Hasan's state of mind when he carried out his shooting rampage, the materials he sent to *Fox News* removed all speculation. In a handwritten statement dated October 18, 2012, Hasan wrote,

> In the name of All-Mighty Allah, the most gracious and the most merciful, I, Nidal Malik Hasan, am compelled to renounce any oaths of allegiances that require me to support/ defend any man made constitution (like the Constitution of the United States) over the commandments mandated in Islam (Quran and Sunnah). The sovereignty of All-Mighty God must always prevail over the sovereignty of man. I, therefore, renounce my oath of office as well as any other implicit or explicit oaths I have made in the past that associate partners with All-Mighty God. This includes my oath of U.S. citizenship.[116]

Hasan also included his essay "Is Preferring an American Democracy Over Shari'ah (Islamic Governance) Permissible?" and two of the questions/answers that he had mailed to the *Killeen Daily Herald*, plus the question, "Do you have any closing statements?" to which he answered,

> I invite the world to read the book of All-Mighty Allah and decide for themselves if it is the truth from their Lord. My desire is to help people attain heaven by the mercy of their Lord. If I have made any mistakes I ask for forgiveness and understanding.[117]

Staff Sgt. Shawn Manning, one of the plaintiffs in litigation to have the shooting categorized as a terrorist act by the U.S. Department of Justice, told *Fox News*, "The government has tried to deny that this was an act of terrorism. I think that, I hope that, if people hear the words from Hasan's own mouth that they will understand that this was an act of terrorism."[118]

"The evidence will clearly show," Hasan began in his opening statement, "that I am the shooter. The evidence will also show that I was on the wrong side. I then switched sides."[119]

Hasan's words hung in the air like the stench of gunpowder in the SRP Center almost four years before.

"We, the Mujahideen, are imperfect Muslims trying to create the perfect religion," he continued and nodded at the prosecutors.[120]

The prosecution laid out their case by relating the evidence to the murders. Hasan deliberately attacked fellow soldiers in a mass shooting that was premeditated to kill as many soldiers as possible, they asserted. His magazines contained more than 400 rounds of ammunition; investigators found 146 spent casings inside the SRP Center and sixty-eight outside, and Hasan targeted uniformed soldiers and avoided shooting civilians, except for Michael Cahill who tried to stop him.[121]

The prosecution called twelve witnesses on August 6, 2013, the first day of testimony in the trial. Among them were employees from Guns Galore and Stan's Shooting Range, two neighbors, the FBI agent who processed Hasan's apartment, retired Lt. Col. Ben Phillips, Hasan's former supervisor, two congregants from the Killeen Islamic Center, retired Staff Sgt. Alonzo Lunsford, a victim who was shot seven times, and phlebotomist Michelle Harper who was the first to call 911.[122]

Judge Osborn instructed all of the witnesses to limit their testimony to the events that occurred on the day of the shooting and immediately afterward. Prosecutor Mike Mulligan threatened that there would be severe consequences if any of the victims talked to the press after they testified.[123]

The prosecution's first witness was Staff Sgt. Alonzo Lunsford, who lost an eye and half of his intestines, had undergone six painful surgeries, including facial reconstruction, and had been diagnosed with PTSD and traumatic brain injury. He admitted to the *Los Angeles Times* that he harbors a lot of anger. Despite his limitations he coaches an Army wheelchair basketball team. He wanted to tell Hasan that he failed in his mission. "I took his best blows and I'm still here," he said. Lunsford didn't get the opportunity to take on Hasan in court. Hasan chose not to ask him any questions.[124]

Of the dozen witnesses who testified on August 6, Hasan cross examined two. Obviously nervous when he quizzed his former boss, retired Lt. Col. Ben Philips, about the glowing performance evaluation he wrote about Hasan and his work, including "bears true faith and allegiance to the U.S. Constitution, the Army, the unit, and the soldier;" "employs sound judgment, logical reasoning and uses resources wisely;" "promotes dignity, consideration, fairness;" and "places Army priorities before self." Phillips said that any other grade would have ended Hasan's military career. "Everyone gets the same evaluation," Phillips said.[125]

Hasan also asked Philips about two emails he had sent him regarding atrocities committed by U.S. soldiers in Iraq and Afghanistan. Before Phillips could answer, Judge Osborn jumped in and stopped the line of questioning. It was too close to the "defense of others" that Hasan wanted to use.[126]

It isn't clear why Hasan cross examined Pat Sonti, a fellow worshiper at the Killeen Islamic Center. Sonti described the morning of November 5, 2009, when Hasan took the microphone from him and said goodbye to the congregation.[127]

Hasan's standby defense team was livid. The next morning, on August 7, before the panel was ushered in, Col. Kris Poppe approached Judge Osborne and told her that Hasan was "acting in concert with the prosecution to guarantee a death sentence."[128]

"It's become clear," said Poppe, "his goal is to remove impediments or obstacles to the death penalty."[129]

"I object," Hasan said. "That's a twist of the facts."[130]

Poppe told Judge Osborn that she either needed to put Hasan's defense team back in charge or let them resign as counsel. When he handed her a written motion to that effect, she had little recourse but to clear the courtroom and recess the trial for the remainder of the day.[131]

Hasan continued to voice his objections to Judge Osborn about the defense team's indignance. She finally shut him down and told him to go home and put his objections in writing. He told her he wouldn't do that. She spoke to him briefly by himself in her chambers.[132]

Poppe and the other members of the team believed that acting as standby counsel with no actual role to play in advising Hasan put them in an ethical dilemma. Poppe said that he found it morally repugnant to participate in a capital murder trial and be forced to support the accused in his quest for execution. He told the judge that if he and the other members of the team were not allowed to either step down or resume control of the defense, he would file an appeal.[133]

When court came to order the following morning, August 8, 2013, Judge Osborn informed the defense team that she was denying their motion. They would remain as standby council. "That relieves you of any ethical liability," she told them. "If I am wrong, which I am not, you're acting on a specific order of the court."[134]

Testimony resumed. As the victims recounted the horror and brutality they experienced at the hands of Hasan, he sat expressionless and disinterested as he watched and listened to Spc. Megan Martinez tell the court that she watched Hasan slowly walk back and forth in the SRP Center, shooting as he walked. Pfc. George Stratton recounted the sight of bloody grass outside the Center where wounded soldiers had crawled out of the door, Spc. Matthew Cooke said that Hasan shot him five times as he ran from the building, Sgt. First Class Maria Guerra told of hearing Pfc. Francheska Velez yelling, "Please don't, please don't, my baby, my baby."[135]

Hasan voiced an objection. "Would you remind Sgt. First Class Guerra that she's under oath?" he asked the judge.[136]

One of the prosecutors asked Guerra if she would like to change any of her testimony. "No, sir," she said softly.[137]

In all, there were fifteen heartbreaking stories recounted that day. Hasan did not cross examine any of the witnesses.[138]

Testimony continued at a rapid pace through the first week. Both the defense and the prosecution had estimated that the trial would take three to four months. With Hasan's lack of engagement, it appeared that the proceedings would be over in just a few weeks.

The victims who testified became increasingly disconcerted because of Judge Osborn's directive to limit their testimonies to the circumstances during and immediately after the shooting. Attorney Neal Sher, who had earlier filed a civil lawsuit against the DoD and the Army on behalf of the victims, filed an ex-parte motion alleging that the judge's restrictions were unconstitutional because they violated free speech. Sher did not win his motion and the witnesses remained constrained.

"They want to talk about the manner in which they've been mistreated by the Army and the government ever since the attack took place," Sher said.[139]

When Shemeka Hairston took the stand the prosecution re-played her call to 9-1-1. She couldn't bear to hear it and her sobs were audible in a hallway outside of the courtroom.

Lt. Col. Randy Royer slowly and deliberately made his way to the witness stand with the help of a cane. Although he was seriously injured from two gunshot wounds, he didn't have surgery until the next day because soldiers with more serious injuries were treated first. Royer was also diagnosed with PTSD. "One of the worst times is when I have to go to the pharmacy," he told the court. "They have all the chairs lined up in there [as in the SRP Center] and I don't do well."[140]

During this week of testimony, Hasan released more pages of his sanity board report to the *New York Times*. In it, Hasan told the examiners, "I'm paraplegic and could be in jail for the rest of my life. However, if I died by lethal injection I would still be a martyr."[141]

The prosecution had not read the full report, only a short synopsis of it and the fact that it was now in the public domain caused a disruption in the courtroom. Judge Osborn asked Hasan if he sent the report of his own free will and he told her that he did. Obviously displeased, she asked him if he was aware of the consequences of releasing the report.[142]

"Did you understand that by disclosing it to a third party that you could waive the right to keep the full sanity report away from the trial counsel?" the judge asked him.[143]

Hasan answered her in the affirmative.

Despite the fact that Hasan wanted to turn the report over to them, Judge Osborn instructed the prosecution not to read it.

"I'm not going to give it to them until we've had a chance to fully address the matter on the record," Judge Osborn told Hasan.[144]

"We will do our best to avoid it," prosecutor Steve Henricks told the judge.

Standby defense attorney Poppe renewed his request to either step in as lead counsel or break all ties with the case. Judge Osborn wouldn't allow it.[145]

The media had a field day with Hasan's sanity board report and the next day newspaper headlines suggested that Hasan had a death wish. Hasan's former attorney, John Galligan, assured reporters that Hasan was being "realistic."

"Major Hasan doesn't have a death wish," Galligan told reporters. "He believes he's been effectively foreclosed from making any meaningful defense."[146]

The court continued with the business of trying Hasan. Medical examiner Capt. Edward Reedy confirmed to the court that the autopsies of the mortally wounded were performed at Dover Air Force Base and that he had examined two of the deceased, Michael Cahill and Pfc. Kham S. Xiong. Cahill had sustained six gunshot wounds and Xiong three. Two other forensic pathologists testified that many of the deceased were shot in the back while they lay on the floor.[147]

FBI special agents testified about their examinations of hundreds of pieces of evidence. Numerous photos of the scene and the evidence were shown to the panel—the more graphic images were displayed on the attorneys' and panel's monitors and not to observers in the proceedings. Several other experts testified on trajectory analysis and evidence collection. FBI Special Agent Mills called the SRP Center in the aftermath of the shooting "the worst scene I've ever seen." He had re-created more than fifty-eight trajectories from five separate shooting locations. Agent Jameson testified that Hasan's medical file, recently generated when he went through his pre-deployment counseling, was discovered in the center with a notation on the back of it that called Station Thirteen "very busy."[148]

Spec. Frederick Greene, one of the victims who attempted to stop Hasan, was shot more times than any of the others. Lt. Col. Phillip Berran testified that Greene had twelve bullets in him and from the varied angles of the entry wounds it was determined that, like Cahill and Gaffaney, he was shot while charging Hasan.[149]

"There was a dynamic interaction between the shooter and Greene," said Berran. "It wasn't static; there was movement between the two."[150]

Judge Osborn thought that some of Greene's autopsy and evidence photos were too graphic to display or show in the courtroom and she asked that they be modified. Because of the sheer volume of evidence, the trial had slowed considerably, but by the eighth day of the proceedings, seventy-three witnesses had testified.[151]

On Friday, August 16, former police officer Kimberly Munley took the stand. Because of changes in the Army's use of civilian security personnel, Munley lost her job in 2011. Prosecutors played a four-minute dashboard cam video of the area outside the SRP Center. Afterward, Munley described in detail the gunfight that she had with Hasan who shot her three times. When she was felled by one of his bullets, lying on the ground wounded, she aimed her pistol at him and pulled the trigger. Her weapon jammed and Hasan, running toward her while continuing to fire, kicked her gun away from her. Hasan's weapon also jammed and, if not for that, he certainly would have killed her. A high-capacity thirty-round magazine was discovered close to the spot where Munley lay. A sweet taste of irony—until he fired at Munley, Hasan had avoided using the thirty-round magazines because they were prone to jam.[152]

When the trial resumed on Monday, August 19, the prosecution called Staff Sgt. Juan Alvarado, a Fort Hood police officer, who witnessed the exchange of gunfire between Hasan and Munley. Alvarado testified that he saw Hasan continue to fire at Munley after she was disarmed. Hasan uncharacteristically cross examined Alvarado.[153]

"Are you saying after it was clear that she was disarmed that I continued to fire at her?" he asked in disbelief. He was obviously uncomfortable.

"Yes," Alvarado answered.

"No questions. No further questions." Hasan said.[154]

JUDGE OSBORN HELD AN EVIDENTIARY HEARING on August 19, 2013. She ruled that the prosecution could not introduce several pieces of their key evidence that they planned to use to show Hasan's motive for his shooting rampage. First, she ruled that there would be no references to Hasan Akbar, Hasan's hero who murdered several Army officers in Kuwait because they killed Muslims, because it would cause "confusion of issues, unfair prejudice, [and a] waste of time and delay." Second, the prosecution could not introduce Hasan's former interest in obtaining conscientious objector status. Third, there could be no discussion of Hasan's inflammatory medical school presentations, citing that they were too old and irrelevant, and, finally, prosecutors could not introduce Hasan's email correspondence with Awlaki. They would be permitted, however, to introduce evidence that in the days before the shooting Hasan used his computer to retrieve information from jihadi websites.[155]

Hasan, who had remained mute for most of the trial, had a request that day for Judge Osborn. He asked her to instruct the panel to accept his definitions of "jihad" and "Allahu Akbar." He handed her a sheet of paper with his hand-written interpretation of the terms. The prosecution voiced no objection.

> *Jihad*, under Islam, the central doctrine that calls on believers to combat the enemies of their religion. According to the Qur'an and the Hadith, jihad is a duty that may be fulfilled in four ways: by the heart, the tongue, the hand, or the sword. The first way involves and [*sic*] inner hatred for those evils that cannot be overcome by the other 3 ways. The ways of the tongue and hand call for verbal defense and right actions. The jihad of the sword involves waging war against enemies of Islam. Believers contend that those who die fighting in All-Mighty Allah's cause are guaranteed a place in paradise as well as a special status. *Allahu Akbar* or *Alluh o Akbar* is an Islamic phrase meaning "God is Greater" or "God is the Greatest." It is used in many situations. Its recital is necessary in the Muslim prayer ritual, but is popularly used as a battle cry of the Mujahideen when fighting the enemies of Islam.[156]

After eleven days of testimony from eighty-nine witnesses, the prosecution rested its case. Hasan had only two people on his witness list: Dr. Lewis Rambo, a religious conversion expert, and Dr. Timothy Semmerly, a mitigation specialist. Hasan told Judge Osborn that he no longer wanted testimony from either of the experts, but she insisted that Dr. Rambo be present and available in the courtroom in the event that Hasan changed his mind.[157]

When court reconvened the following morning, August 21, 2013, Judge Osborn clarified her earlier gag order that prevented witnesses speaking to the press. It was a temporary order, she told them, and once the court-martial was over, they could speak freely about the case.[158]

There had been much speculation in the media about Hasan's defense. As a pro se defendant, Hasan would be required to ask himself questions and then answer them. He would not be allowed to make speeches or to proselytize. When the time came, without hesitation, he said, "The defense rests."[159]

Before the closing arguments began, Judge Osborn read every charge Hasan faced—thirteen counts of premeditated murder and thirty-two counts of attempted premeditated murder—and recited the names of all of the victims. "Each of you must resolve the ultimate question of whether the accused is guilty or not guilty based on the evidence and the instruction I will give you," she told the panel. She directed the panelists to consider each and every charge independently. A verdict of "guilty" on one charge did not equate to a "guilty" verdict on the others. The panel was required to reach a unanimous guilty verdict for Hasan to qualify for the death penalty.[160]

Prosecutor Col. Steve Henricks gave his team's ninety-minute closing statement in which he told the panel that Hasan believed he had a jihadi duty to kill. He said that Hasan chose the SRP Center because he knew that there were two units being processed that day and it would be crowded. Henricks called the waiting area Hasan's "personal kill station." He re-played one of the 9-1-1 calls and a bloody crime scene video before recounting the stories of the pain and trauma experienced by the victims.[161]

When it was his turn to make a final argument, Hasan simply said, "The defense chooses not to make a closing statement."[162]

After the closing arguments, Judge Osborn asked both sides if they believed that the evidence offered during the trial called for the lesser defense of voluntary manslaughter. Both the prosecution and Hasan agreed that the lesser offense was not merited.[163]

Judge Osborn made one final attempt to persuade Hasan that he would be in better stead if he allowed his standby counsel to represent him and present a closing statement. She asked him if his decisions to act as his own attorney and to forego a closing argument were "free and voluntary."[164]

"In other words," Osborn told him, "you are the captain of your own ship. Do you understand that?"[165]

Hasan said he did.

The prosecution had flown through its witnesses while Hasan sat meekly in the background. A trial that was predicted to last several months was concluded in eleven days. During the sentencing phase of the proceeding, Hasan's fate would rest in the hands of thirteen senior officers. Their decision as to how he would be punished would either permit him to marginally exist in a small prison cell for the remainder of his life or would have him perish from a lethal injection. Either way, he would soon be forgotten and his martyrdom and notoriety would fade into the annals of criminal history. There, Nidal Malik Hasan would forever be known as the miscreant who committed the worst atrocity ever on a United States military installation.

While the panel deliberated for two and one-half hours on Thursday afternoon, August 22, 2013, Hasan rested on a cot in his trailer where, months before, Judge Gross had banished him for refusing to shave his beard. The following morning, after only four hours of deliberation, the panel returned to the courtroom where the president (foreman) read the unanimous guilty verdict.

Hasan looked straight at the panel, his head forward and slightly bowed. He showed no reaction as the verdict was read. Some of the victims wept silently, others grinned and patted each other on the back. There had never been any question of Hasan's guilt—his execution was the linchpin of the case.[166]

As soon as he was delivered back to the Bell County jail, Hasan called John Galligan to make sure that he had heard the verdict. Galligan told reporters that the jury did not hear all of the facts because Judge Osborn would not permit key pieces of evidence to be used.[167]

"Right or wrong, strong or weak, the facts are the facts," Galligan said. "The jury we heard from only got half the facts."[168]

Hasan's refusal to participate in his own defense in a trial that would surely find him guilty and probably mete out the death penalty caused a great deal of speculation that he had a death wish and wanted capital punishment.

Galligan disagreed. "He doesn't have a death wish. I fully understand why he has maintained the position that he wants to represent himself in light of the comments that were made by some of his defense team."[169]

Galligan maintains that Hasan had taken a realistic view of the proceedings in declining to mount a defense in an "almost a ludicrous show trial." He credits Judge Osborn's refusal to allow Hasan's "defense of others" as an impediment in Hasan's ability to defend himself.[170]

The End of the Line

Attempted suicides—admissions to mental hospitals—slow deaths—broken hearts—undeleted cell phone messages and greetings—unread books on bedroom end tables where no one sleeps anymore. These represent the shattered lives of the victims of Nidal Hasan's shooting rampage. The physical and emotional toll on the family members of innocents gunned down in the name of Allah is incalculable—the shock of lives extinguished in a surreal moment at the hands of a delusional soldier who believed that he was doing Islam a favor by killing them will never fade.

Patrick Zeigler was the first to testify at the sentencing phase of Hasan's murder trial. With a labored limp, Zeigler made his way to the witness stand unassisted. After ten surgeries to repair his broken head, his doctors didn't think he would live, or if he did, they believed that he would remain in a vegetative state from the loss of twenty percent of his brain.[171]

"Because of brain injury, my left side is paralyzed," Zeigler told the court. He also suffers from PTSD and traumatic brain injury. "I'm a lot angrier, darker than I used to be."[172]

One of Hasan's bullets tore open an artery in former Pfc. Mick Engnehl's neck. Engnehl is grateful to be alive. The twenty-three year old is medically retired from the Army and jobless. "Nobody is going to hire a paralyzed mechanic," he told the court.[173]

Jeri Krueger, the mother of slain soldier Amy Krueger, said that her daughter was inspired to join the Army after 9/11. "You can't take it on by yourself," she told Amy.[174]

"Watch me!" Amy replied.

"It's like there's a part of you missing. I live with that every day," Jeri Krueger told the court.[175]

Maj. Libardo Caraveo's widow, Angela, refused to turn off her husband's cell phone. She and other family members called his number just to hear his voice until a change in their provider's software erased it.[176]

Juan Velez, the father of Francheska Velez, his twenty-one year old pregnant daughter killed in the shooting, said that Hasan did not just kill thirteen people. He killed fifteen. "He killed my grandson and he killed me."[177]

Shoua Her, widow of Pfc. Kham Xiong, said that she and her husband talked often about growing old together. She lamented that the other side of the bed was now empty and cold. "Our daughter will not have her dad to walk her down the aisle," she said. "My two sons will never have their dad to take them fishing…or [teach them] how to be a gentleman."[178]

Pfc. Frederick Greene's widow, Christi, said through sobs, "I can't explain how hard it's been. You open a box, looking at a picture. It hurts so bad. It's all you're ever going to have."[179]

Joleen Cahill, widow of the only civilian killed in Hasan's rampage, Michael Cahill, told the court that she was so emotionally upset after finding out that her husband was dead that she had to be hospitalized for an asthma attack. She said her family fell apart after the massacre because it was her husband who held the family together.[180]

When Philip Warman heard about the shooting, he wasn't worried at first. He wasn't certain that his wife, Juanita, a lieutenant colonel, had arrived yet at Fort Hood. At nine o'clock that night two officers in dress uniforms rang his doorbell. "It was like I had something ripped out of me," he testified. Warman began drinking and his binge lasted until the following June. He's sober now and he takes the coins he has earned at AA to Arlington National Cemetery where his wife is buried and pushes them into the soil covering her grave.[181]

In all, nineteen emotionally-charged, heart-breaking stories were heard during the two day sentencing phase of the trial. Prosecutor Mike Mulligan, in his closing statement, argued that Hasan "should not be punished for his religion, he should be punished for his hate."[182] Hasan elected not to provide a closing argument.

After two hours of deliberation, Hasan sat expressionless as the president of the panel, reflecting a unanimous vote, recommended that he be executed for his crimes. Additionally, the panel stripped him of his military rank and pay and gave him a dishonorable discharge.[183]

Strangely enough, Nidal Hasan had expended enormous energies defending his beard and none defending himself.

Casa Del Norte transformed. Photo by John Porterfield.

Epilogue

A nondescript apartment complex on the run-down side of Killeen has a fresh coat of paint and a new name—Las Palmas. The courtyard is lined on each side with new sidewalks and a narrow strip of grass interspersed with small palm trees. The management is the same and 'Number Nine', sans a paste-on number to match the other units, has served as home to several soldiers since November 5, 2009.[1]

The impact of Nidal Hasan's shooting rampage has faded into the public background but it remains as fresh and raw to the victims as it was on the day it occurred. The Soldier Readiness Processing Center and its memorial wall are gone, as is Hasan's beard.[2] In the months after the conclusion of the trial, the Pentagon quietly released new regulations that relaxed the military's rules against beards, headgear, tattoos, and piercings for soldiers whose religious practices require them.[3]

In an unlikely alliance, Hasan's cousin, Nader Hasan, has teamed up with Kerry Cahill, daughter of slain civilian physician's assistant Michael Cahill, and through his Nawal Foundation they promote peace and understanding at interfaith conferences, schools, and community organizations.[4]

When Jessica Zeigler, wife of critically injured Patrick Zeigler, first saw Hasan in court she admits that she felt sorry for him. "I think the first thing I felt was probably some sympathy for him, which is surprising. A lot of the families told me that, too. They'd go in there and think they're about to see this really evil person. And instead you see this shell of a man hunched over. He was very polite in court. He wasn't mean. He didn't have any outbursts."[5]

Shortly after Nader Hasan launched his Nawal Foundation, Jessica emailed him and told him that she admired his peace efforts. That started a series of emails and telephone calls. When Patrick had an appointment at Walter Reed Army Hospital in Washington, the Zeiglers and Nader Hasan got together for dinner.[6]

Jessica had not expected that Patrick would want to spend time with the cousin of the man who almost killed him, but, to her surprise, Patrick wanted to go. "Right away, we all hugged and embraced and there were tears. It was really a beautiful dinner."[7]

Patrick, who has a steel plate the size of the twenty per cent of his brain that had to be removed, continues to recover. He works with veterans and does some public speaking. He has made great progress but realizes that there are still obstacles ahead.[8]

After raising almost a million dollars to benefit the victims of Hasan's rampage, the Central Texas-Fort Hood Chapter of the Association of the U.S. Army (AUSA), a charitable organization, quietly closed out the fund at the end of 2013. In response to a March 13, 2014, email query, the Fort Hood-AUSA president Bobby Hoxworth wrote,

> On January 28, 2014, the Central Texas/Fort Hood Chapter of the Association of the United States Army (AUSA) as administrators of the Community Response to 11/5 Fund announced that it had concluded the process of dissolving the fund with a final disbursement to the survivors and Next of Kin who were directly impacted by the tragic events at Fort Hood on November 5, 2009. During a four-year period, the Chapter provided just over $970,000 in assistance. It has been the Chapter's pleasure to perform this solemn duty, and to be able to provide critically important financial resources to fulfill the unmet needs of those affected.[9]

Several survivors reported that the AUSA fund donated $500 to victims for help with travel expenses to Hasan's court-martial. One survivor said that AUSA reimbursed her for badly needed car repairs.[10]

Kim Munley, one of the Fort Hood police officers who helped take down Hasan, also created a non-profit charitable foundation for the benefit of the survivors, as did shooting survivor Christopher Royal who founded the *Thirty-Two Still Standing*, a non-profit organization and website dedicated to helping the victims and their families through cash gifts. Royal raises money by getting sponsors for various marathon runs. In 2012 he ran from Fort Hood to the Texas state Capitol in Austin. He plans to run in all fifty states.[11]

The victims of the Fort Hood tragedy came together in a Coalition of Fort Hood Heroes and established a website, *The Truth About Fort Hood*, where they post status reports of their lawsuit, letters they have written to various legislators and their responses, and gut-wrenching videos made by individuals of their group in which they talk about what has happened to them since the shooting. There is also a petition posted that invites the general public to join their cause to have the shooting re-classified from workplace violence to an act of terrorism.[12]

Prior to committing his mass murder, Nidal Hasan closed out his bank account. He didn't expect to survive the shooting. Afterwards, his attorney, John Galligan, attempted to open another account for him but he could not find a single bank that would accept Hasan's business. During the four years that Hasan was incarcerated in the Bell County jail, he amassed $278,000 in Army pay. The survivors and the next-of-kin had hoped to somehow have that money confiscated and used for the benefit of the victims. Under the Uniform Code of Military Justice (UCMJ) a defendant's salary remains in effect until that individual is sentenced. Immediately after the conclusion of Hasan's trial John Galligan told reporters, "The great bulk of his income has been donated to charity. There's really virtually no money in any bank that I'm aware of. There's really no property holdings." If Hasan had been a civilian defense department employee, the Army could have suspended his pay.[13]

Even more troubling is the lack of physical and mental health services available to some of the survivors and a corresponding lack of combat-related benefits. Many of the wounded were reservists and the unofficial spokesperson for the group, Shawn Manning, explains why they are suffering. When a reservist is activated, the military makes up the difference in pay that the soldier makes as a civilian. After they were wounded in Hasan's shooting spree, the Army stopped paying that salary difference. Most of the survivors were too badly injured to return to their civilian jobs and, therefore, suffered a substantial pay loss. Most were also not able to return to the military.[14]

"Because I was shot," Manning says, "I was immediately disqualified from that difference in pay because it wasn't considered a terrorist attack. They looked at it like I was injured in the same way as if I had been walking down the street. If I had been injured in training, I would still be paid, but because they never called it a terrorist attack they essentially stopped my pay."[15]

When the wounded soldiers returned to their home towns after the shooting they were greeted as heroes. Many times community organizations came together to offer assistance to the survivors, such as building a house, purchasing a prosthesis, or giving a gift of cash. These survivors, however, were not allowed to accept gifts in excess of fifty dollars because their injuries were not combat related.[16]

The classification of the Fort Hood shooting as workplace violence has also jeopardized these soldiers' healthcare. Combat veterans are placed into a higher priority group and receive medical services ahead of non-combat veterans. Wait times for appointments can be very lengthy. Non-combat injuries also require a co-pay, whereas medical services for combat vets are free.[17]

Virtually all of the soldiers and civilian contractors who survived Nidal Hasan's mass shooting suffer from PTSD. Because they are not on a high-priority list for mental health services, they do not always receive treatment in a timely manner. Take the case of Josh Berry.

Berry was present in the SRP Center when the shooting began and the only physical injury he sustained in fleeing the building was a dislocated shoulder. Berry had just returned from a deployment in Afghanistan and he had exhibited some early signs of PTSD. After the shooting, he was never the same.[18]

"The guy that came home was not the guy I talked to the night before [the shooting] and he was never the same," explains Josh's father, Howard Berry…."He was in a war zone 24-7. He honestly was. He was never at peace."[19]

According to friends and family members, John obsessed over the treatment afforded Hasan compared to the Fort Hood survivors. He constantly talked about the trial delays and the refusal of the government to classify the shooting as a terrorist attack.[20]

Josh Berry committed suicide in August 2013. He was thirty-six.

"The number that died shouldn't be thirteen, it should be fourteen. That's what I feel. I feel Josh's name should be added to the list of those on the memorial because that was it. It just took him three and a half years to die," Howard Berry says.[21]

Berry has continued his son's fight. He has written hundreds of letters to his legislators urging them to re-classify the shooting as combat-related terrorism.[22]

Bitter Irony

Mass murder reared its ugly head again on April 2, 2014, when thirty four year old Specialist Ivan A. Lopez opened fire inside the Fort Hood Administrative Office of the 49th Transportation Battalion. Lopez killed one soldier and wounded nine others. He then drove his own vehicle to the motor pool where he worked and fired through the open window at two soldiers who were simply standing outside. One was wounded. At the motor pool he killed one of his co-workers and wounded two others. Lopez again returned to his car and began driving. As another vehicle approached his slow-moving car, he fired at its windshield, wounding a passenger. He continued on to the First Medical Brigade building where he shot another soldier who was simply standing outside. He walked inside the building and killed a soldier sitting at the entry desk.[23]

Lopez returned to his car and drove a few more blocks where he pulled into a parking lot and exited his vehicle. As he walked down the sidewalk he was confronted by a female military police officer. When Lopez pulled out his gun, she fired at him, but missed. Instead of aiming at the officer, Lopez pointed the gun at his head and fired.

He died instantly. No one can be certain of his motive, but it was re-ported that he had an escalating altercation with other soldiers in his unit just prior to the shooting.[24]

Lopez had attempted to file for leave on the morning of the shoot-ing but was told to come back the following day. He had also run into problems in obtaining leave to attend his mother's funeral in Puerto Rico a year earlier. Lopez was being treated for depression, anxiety, and a sleep disorder and was undergoing evaluation for post traumatic stress disorder following a four month non-combat tour in Iraq. He had been prescribed Ambien for sleep and an anti-depressive medication.[25]

Lopez's posts on his family-only Facebook account offers insights into his deteriorating mental condition. "My spiritual peace...has gone away, I am full of hate," he wrote in one; in another "two flacos" [dudes] stole something from him; and "plaka, plaka, plaka [bang, bang, bang in Spanish]. But other postings were more specifically aimed at the Army. He railed about his time in Iraq and focused on the problems he encountered in obtaining leave to attend his mother's funeral.[26]

There were no components of terrorism in Ivan Lopez's shooting rampage, but like most mass killers, there were similarities to Nidal Hasan's attack. Both men had axes to grind with the military and both men exhibited signs of emotional disorders. Each smuggled handguns purchased from Guns Galore in Killeen onto the base without regis-tering them. Hasan treated returning soldiers with PTSD and Lopez had sought, but had not yet received, such treatment. Had Hasan not committed his act of terror, he could have very well been the treating physician for Lopez's emotional problems.

From his death row prison cell at Fort Leavenworth, in August 2014, Nidal Hasan sent a hand-written letter to ISIS leader Abu Bakr Baghdadi and requested citizenship with the terrorist group. "It would be an honor for any believer to be an obedient citizen soldier," Hasan wrote in his letter.[27]

IN SEPTEMBER 2014, SENATOR JOHN CORNYN asked new FBI Director James Comey in a Senate Judiciary Committee meeting if he believed that the Fort Hood shooting was inspired by al Qaeda.

"Yes, sir," Comey answered. "Based on everything I've read. Again, I wasn't in office at the time, but I've read about it since, and I do."[28]

Comey believes that the Internet is a "breeding ground" for extremist radicalization.

"Those people...can be inspired by al-Qaida to kill innocents without having to be directed because the Internet...offers them access to poisonous information, both to inspire them and to tell them how to carry out the attacks they wish to carry out," Comey said.

Rep. Mike Conaway from Midland, Texas, shares Comey's belief that Nidal Hasan acted upon his self-radicalized beliefs.

"The service members who lost their lives on Nov. 5, 2009, were fighting a terrorist," Conaway said. "As we know too well, the battlefield in the war on terror is not limited to foreign lands."[29]

In December 2014, Congress quietly passed a bill that would make victims of the massacre eligible to receive the Purple Heart or the Defense of Freedom medal for civilians. They will also be eligible to receive combat-related compensation upon retirement and burial at Arlington National Cemetery.[30]

On January 29, 2015, almost eighteen months after the death penalty was imposed on Nidal Hasan, he appeared in court at Fort Leavenworth, Kansas, where he has been incarcerated on death row since the conclusion of his military capital court-martial.

Lt. Gen. Sean McFarland, the commanding general at Fort Hood, has yet to review and sign off on Hasan's conviction, delaying Hasan's lengthy appeals process. When Hasan's death sentence is approved, there will be at least two mandatory appeals and possibly one additional proceeding before the U.S. Supreme Court.

A clean-shaven Hasan appeared at the hearing with the legal counsel he fired during his trial, Lt. Col. Kris Poppe. Col. Tara Osborn, the judge who presided over Hasan's court-martial, was a familiar presence in the court. She has since been elevated to chief trial judge of the Army. Hasan appeared sharp and alert and openly joked with his military lawyers. The issue in question is whether there are conflicts of interest if Poppe, in his position as a subordinate judge to Osborn, continues to represent Hasan. As appellate counsel, Poppe's job is to find mistakes with Osborn's handling of Hasan's trial. Osborn articulated her concern that Poppe now works for her.

Poppe wants to continue to represent Hasan and believes he can function simultaneously as Hasan's legal counsel and a military judge. Hasan told Osborn that he did not want her to appoint another attorney to represent him. Osborn asked the prosecution and defense to submit written briefs in a week.[31]

Spontaneous tributes placed on the barbed wire fence erected around the SRP Center.
Photo by John Porterfield

Afterword

On a cold, December day at the Pentagon, during a routine office cleaning in 2003, an old and faded handwritten document entitled *Executed Death Cases Before 1951* was discovered lodged behind a filing cabinet. Several sections of the list had deteriorated over time and were illegible. Statistics on the actual numbers of military personnel put to death before 1951 are sketchy.[1] Prior to that year, there was no uniformity in the enforcement of law and regulations among the branches of the military. Individual commanding officers were responsible for solving legal and regulatory breaches.

Soon after the Second World War ended, there was a public outcry over the two million courts-martial of American troops, or the one out of every eight servicemen court-martialed— more than one hundred executed and forty-five thousand service members imprisoned. In response to public pressure, Congress established the UCMJ which was signed into law by President Harry S. Truman in 1950.[2]

The UCMJ standardized the enforcement of military law and provided protections to service members charged with criminal acts, including the right to be informed of any charges against them; the right to remain silent; the right to know that anything said about the crime could be used in legal proceedings (established prior to the civilian Miranda law counterpart), the right to no-cost defense counsel in serious cases, the right to plead guilty, not-guilty, or not-guilty by reason of lack of mental responsibility, the right to a trial before a military panel, or jury, and the right to appeal.[3]

The UCMJ also created a three-tiered courts-martial system. A summary court-martial was established for minor offenses and carried a thirty-day maximum confinement. Second, a special court-martial was created to adjudicate misdemeanor charges with a one-year maximum confinement. Third, a general court-martial, the most serious trial in the military, was designed to handle felony offenses including capital murder cases.

For the most serious offenses, the accused may request defense counsel, military or civilian, at no expense to the defendant. In both the special and general courts-martial an automatic appeal is triggered if a sentence includes imprisonment for one year or more, a bad conduct or dishonorable discharge, death, or the dismissal of a commissioned officer.[4]

Since the establishment of the UCMJ, there have been ten military executions. All ten were carried out by hanging at Fort Leavenworth, the military's only long-term prison, and all of the executed had been found guilty of murder, except for John Bennett, who was convicted of raping an eleven-year-old girl. All were African-American. There has not been a military execution since Bennett was hanged in 1961.

The death penalty was the primary driver of Nidal Hasan's case. In the course of American history, there is no record of an execution of a commissioned military officer since the Civil War. If Hasan receives the lethal injection that was ordered in his court-martial, he will be the first.

Hasan released a stream of personal documents throughout the trial. The report issued by Hasan's sanity board revealed that he had assumed that he would die at the scene of his shooting rampage and would become a martyr for the cause. It is Hasan's belief that martyrdom will now come with execution and it was obvious during his trial that he was working in accordance with the prosecution to make sure that happened.

If Nidal Hasan is, indeed, executed, it won't occur in the near future. There are automatic appeals and he will not be allowed to represent himself. As to whether his pro se defense will have a bearing on the outcome of his appeals, only time will tell. He will have five other death row neighbors at Fort Leavenworth prison who are at various stages of their long appellate processes.

Former Fort Bragg Army Specialist Ronald Gray, who has lived on death row the longest of the five, was convicted of premeditated murder and rape in 1988. Although President George W. Bush signed off on his execution, a federal judge stayed his lethal injection so that he could continue to pursue his appeals.[5]

Former Private Dwight Loving, on death row since his conviction in 1989, was stationed at Fort Hood when he murdered and robbed two taxi drivers. Loving freely confessed on videotape. He has not exhausted his appeals.[6]

Hasan's hero, former Sergeant Hasan Akbar, was convicted in 2005 of the premeditated murders of two Army officers and the wounding of sixteen others at Camp Pennsylvania in Kuwait. His reason for the attack was to prevent American soldiers from killing Muslims in Iraq.[7]

Former Air Force senior airman Andrew Witt was convicted in 2005 for two counts of premeditated murder and one count of attempted murder at Robins Air Force Base in Georgia. Witt's sentence was overturned during Nidal Hasan's trial for having ineffective counsel but was reinstated a year later.[8]

Timothy Hennis, a former master sergeant at Fort Bragg, was convicted in 1986 in a civilian court of murdering and raping a woman and her two children. After three years on death row, his conviction was overturned and he was re-tried and acquitted in 1989. When DNA testing became a trusted investigative tool, crime scene evidence showed that Hennis was the killer. He could not be re-tried in civilian court because of double jeopardy, but the Army recalled him to active duty and then arrested, tried, and convicted him in 2010, almost a quarter century after he was sentenced the first time.[9]

Since the execution of John Bennett over fifty years ago, there has been a reluctance by military and federal judges to actually carry out a sentence of capital punishment. If Hasan is executed, it will happen many years into the future. Hanging is no longer the favored method of execution in the military. Fort Leavenworth does not have a facility for performing a lethal injection and, if his appeals are exhausted, Hasan will be moved to the Supermax federal prison in Terre Haute, Indiana, after the president signs his death warrant.

The *New York Times* estimated that Hasan has cost U.S. taxpayers about $5 million.[10] In reality, the final tab will total over $15 million. There is no assurance that Hasan will get the penalty that he believes will make him a martyr. It is interesting to note that if Hasan had been allowed to plead guilty and had been sentenced to life imprisonment without the possibility of parole, the cost of his incarceration would be substantially less than what has been spent thus far. He would have to live to be 546 years old to equal the public cost of his capital prosecution.[11]

The toll of the shooting on the victims is immeasurable. The Department of Defense and the Army categorized Hasan's massacre of unarmed, unprepared soldiers as workplace violence, depriving the victims of the benefits that would be afforded to them if the massacre had occurred in a combat zone or if the rampage had been classified as a terrorist act. While Hasan received state-of-the-art medical care, irrespective of the cost, the victims have reported that much of the care that they have received has been sub-standard.

Perhaps the most tragic and disturbing consequence of the Fort Hood shooting is the shattered illusion that a military base on American soil is a place that soldiers can rely upon to be a safe harbor.

Acknowledgments

W e were honored to have worked with a group of talent- ed, dedicated individuals who generously contributed their time and expertise to this project. Without them, this book could not have been written.

Virginia Tech Professor Emeritus of Biochemistry George E. Bunce read and critiqued the manuscript and, having known Nidal Hasan when he was a biochemistry student at Virginia Tech, shared his recollections of interactions with him. We greatly appreciate his observations, his wisdom, and his perspective.

We relied heavily on weapons expert Lindsey Bertomen who test- ed an FN Five-Seven identical to the one used by Nidal Hasan. An adjunct professor of criminal justice at Hartnell College in Salinas, California, Army veteran, and retired police officer, he was able to give us a perspective that we greatly appreciated.

We were fortunate to have the help of Dani Volmer, English and creative writing teacher of twenty years who can catch the smallest grammatical and syntax errors. Dani did much more than proofread the book. She also gave us some great suggestions.

Chelsea Garrett, one of the many unsung first-responder heroes who left her own graduation ceremony and ran to the scene without hesitation, drove us around Fort Hood and shared her experiences. She was also an early reader of the manuscript. Chelsea is a talented writer and we hope that she will someday write a book.

Suzan Pitman was one of our manuscript readers. Her attention to detail was a great help in preparing the manuscript and her enthusiasm and encouragement were appreciated.

Some of the most valuable contributions to this book were made by confidential sources who wanted nothing more than to tell the truth but who were afraid of retribution by the Army if they used their real names.

Many thanks to Tony Brackett of *ABC News* and Bob Bunch, general manager of *KWTX-TV* (CBS) in Waco, Texas, for allowing us to freely use some of the news stories broadcast and published by their television networks. We greatly appreciate the permissions of the Anti-Defamation League and the Southern Poverty Law Center to use materials on their websites.

Michael Haynes of *Public Intelligence*, an international, collaborative research project, has amassed an impressive archive of documents relating to terrorism and has posted the entire collection on his website *publicintelligence.net*, including all of the issues of *Inspire* magazine, the official publication of al Qaeda in the Arabian Peninsula. We appreciate the use of these materials.

Imam Faizul Kahn, thank you for taking the time to talk to us about Nidal Hasan and Islam. Many thanks to criminal profiler Pat Brown who spent a great deal of time sharing her knowledge and expertise. Kimon Ianetta, *trialrun.com*, one of this country's foremost authorities on the analysis and interpretation of handwriting, also devoted time and effort in examining Nidal Hasan's handwriting, Neal Sher, attorney for the victims, shared information, and Senator John Cornyn assisted us with FOIA requests. Texas Rangers Kirby Dendy and Frank Malinak guided us through their first hours as responders to the shooting.

Thanks to Dalton Cross, director of the Bell County Communications Center, for his time in explaining inner workings of the dispatch center and for going into a great deal of detail about how the events of Nov. 5, 2009, impacted his operations.

We appreciate Don White allowing us to photograph his FN Five-Seven handgun, Michael Stowe's permission to use photographs from the *Roanoke Times*, and Jim Painter and the *Temple Daily Telegram* allowing us to use their photos as well.

We thank Frederick Brannon, the clerk at Guns Galore who sold Nidal Hasan the FN Five-Seven used in the shooting for talking with us and Paul Romer, reporter for the Temple Daily Telegraph.

Ken Willey and David Richardson, thanks for your support and expertise. And thank you Matthew Pitman for bringing order out of chaos by organizing our research materials.

And our deep gratitude goes to Ronald Chrisman, Director of the University of North Texas Press, without whom this book would not be possible. We appreciate the great work of Paula Oates, Bonnie Stufflebeam, Karen DeVinney, and Aprell Feagin.

We also express our appreciation to the members of our Mayborn Literary Nonfiction Conference workshop in Dallas, Texas, which we attended in the summer of 2014. We were honored to participate in the book manuscript workshop led by Doug Swanson. We received valuable feedback from Doug and our nine fellow workshop members.

In Memoriam

Cahill, Michael, 62, Cameron, Texas
Fort Hood Civilian Employee

Caraveo, Major Libardo, 52, Woodbridge, Virginia
467th Medical Detachment, Madison, Wisconsin

Decrow, Staff Sergeant Justin, 32, Plymouth, Indiana
16th Signal Company, Fort Hood, Texas

Gaffaney, Captain John P., 54, San Diego, California
1908th Medical Co., Independence, Missouri

**Greene, Specialist Frederick, 29,
Mountain City, Tennessee**
16th Signal Co., Fort Hood, Texas

Hunt, Specialist Jason, 22, Tillman, Oklahoma
1st Brigade, Fort Hood, Texas

Krueger, Sergeant Amy, 29, Kiel, Wisconsin
467th Medical Company, Madison, Wisconsin

**Nemelka, Private First Class Aaron, 19,
West Jordan, Utah**
510th Engineer Company, 20th Engineer Battalion,
Fort Hood, Texas

**Pearson, Private First Class Michael, 22,
Bolinbrook, Illinois**
510th Engineer Company, 20th Engineer Battalion,
Fort Hood, Texas

Seager, Captain Russell, 41, Racine, Wisconsin
467th Medical Co., Madison, Wisconsin

Velez, Private Francheska, 21, Chicago, Illinois
15th Combat Support Bn., Fort Hood,Texas

Warman, Lt. Colonel Juanita L., 55,
Havre De Grace, Maryland
1908th Medical Company, Independence, Missouri

Xiong, Specialist Kham, 23, Minneapolis, Minnesota
510th Engineer Company, 20th Engineer Battalion,
Fort Hood, Texas

Maj. Gen. William Grimsley, Fort Hood's senior commander at the time, and Ron Taylor, AUSA Central Texas-Fort Hood Chapter, unveil a new monument that rests in Memorial Park behind the III Corps headquarters on Fort Hood. Photo by Christie Vanover, Darnall Army Medical Center Public Affairs. Photo courtesy of the U.S. Army.

Trial Witnesses

Alvarado, Ssg. Juan — Witnessed gunfight between Hasan and Officer Munley

Aviles, Pvt. Lance — Sitting at Station Thirteen

Bennett, Steve — Photographer at Howze Theater who photographed Hasan

Berran, Ltc. Phillip — U.S. Army forensic pathologist

Bonfiglio, Dr. Charles — Former classmate of Hasan at Walter Reed

Brannon, Frederick the FN 5.7 — Guns Galore employee who showed Hasan

Brooks, Ronald — Attending graduation ceremony

Burgess, Ssg. Christopher — Sitting at Station Thirteen

Burnett, Spc. Logan — Shot three times

Cahill, Joleen — Surviving spouse of civilian physician assistant Michael Cahill

Campbell, Ssg. Ingar — A case manager at the SRP Center

Caraveo, Eduardo — Son of Maj. Libardo E. Caraveo

Carnahan, Tasha — Attending graduation ceremony

Carroll, Sfc. Alan — Shot five times

Carskadon, Cpt. Dorothy — Shot in hip, leg, abdomen, head

Cheadle, David — Manager of Guns Galore

Choats, John — Instructor and co-owner of Stan's Shooting Range

Clark, Ssg. Joy — Shot in arm

Cooke, Spc. Matthew — Shot five times

Coukoulis, Theodore — Civilian immunization specialist at the SRP Center

Cowling, FBI Spc. Agt. — Head of team that searched Hasan's apartment

Cox, Ssg. James — Returning from deployment with Pvt. Francesca Velez

Davis, Sgt. Michael	Shot in back
Douglass, Mark Anthony	Witnessed gunfight between Hasan and Fort Hood police
Engnehl, Pfc. Mick	Shot twice; right arm paralyzed
Foster, Spc. Joseph	Shot in hip
Gadlin, Pvt. Amber Bahr	Shot in the back
Gaffney, Christine	Surviving spouse of Capt. John Gaffney
Gilbert, William	Guns Galore customer who spoke to Hasan about the FN 5.7
Givens, Spc. Kassidy	Station Thirteen
Gorsuch, Spc. Agt. Jamey	Investigator for CID
Greene, Cristi	Surviving spouse of Spc. Frederick Greene
Guerra, Sfc. Maria	Noncommissioned officer in charge of SRP
Hairston, Shemeka	Nurse at SRP Center who called 9-1-1
Harper, Michelle	Phlebotomist at SRP Center and first to call 9-1-1
Her, Shoua	Surviving spouse of Pfc. Kham Xiong
Hewitt, Sgt. Nathan	Shot in the left leg and thigh at the reg flag area.
Holm, Tracy	FBI agent who processed Hasan's apartment
Hopewell, Maj. Clifford	Supervisor of TBI facility who identified Hasan
Howard, Ssg. Alvin	Shot in shoulder
Hunt, Gale	Mother of Spc. Jason D. Hunt
Hunt, Jennifer Nicole	Surviving spouse of Spc. Jason D. Hunt
Huseman, Kimberly R.	Head nurse at the SRP Center
Jackson, Ssg. Eric	Shot in forearm
Jameson, Spec. Agt. Kelly	Reconstructed Hasan's activities
Johnson, Elgia	Office of the Surgeon General

Johnson, Pfc. Justin	Shot in the foot at Station Thirteen.
Kosminski, Dr. Tonya	Physician who shared on-call duty with Hasan
Krueger, Geraldine	Mother of SSg. Amy Krueger
Lunsford, Ssg. Alonzo	Shot seven times by Hasan
Martin, Spec. Agt. Susan	Identified hundreds of pieces of evidence
Martin, Sgt. Paul	Shot three times
Martinez, Spc. Megan	Sitting at Station Thirteen
Marzouk, Col. Abu Pakr	U.S. Army forensic pathologist
Mason, Cpt. Brandy	Shot in thigh
Matal, Sgt. Monique A.	Supervisor of immunizations at SRP Center
Mayberry, Brenda	Civilian employee at the SRP Center
Mazuchowski, Ltc. Edw.	Pathologist who conducted autopsies of the slain
Miller, Jerry	Investigator for CID
Mills, FBI Spec. Agt. Bret	Re-created trajectories from shooting locations
Munley, Sgt. Kimberly	Officer who shot Hasan and was shot by Hasan
Nemelka, Teena	Mother of Pfc. Aaron Nemelka
Nixon, Sgt. Lamar	SRP Center staff
Nourse, Karen	Mother of Spc. Frederick Greene
Pacheco, Cpt. Veronica	OIC of case management at the SRP Center
Pearson, Sheryll	Mother of Pfc. Michael Pearson
Phillips, Ltc. Ben	Hasan's former supervisor
Reedy, Navy Cpt. Edward	Pathologist who conducted autopsies of the slain
Rivera, Angela	Widow of Maj. Libardo E. Caraveo
Royal, Cw3. Christopher	Shot in his back
Salim, Mohamed Mwaga	Congregant of the Killeen Islamic Center

Seager, Cynthia	Widow of Capt. Russell G. Seager
Sims, Pfc. Jonathan	Shot in the chest at Station Thirteen.
Sonti, Pat	Congregant of the Killeen Islamic Center
Stably, Dr. Robert	Pathologist who conducted some of the autopsies
Stratton, Pfc. George	Shot in shoulder
Suttinger, Maj. Laura	Unit commander of Hasan's unit
Sweeney, Sgt. Rene Wall	Medical records center
Tobinson, Col. Stephen	U.S. Army forensic pathologist
Todd, Sgt. Mark	Fort Hood police; shot Hasan
Tops, Maj. Terrill	Pathologist who conducted autopsies of the slain
Torina, Maj. Eric	Shot in chest
Valdiva, Sfc. Miguel	Shot in his leg, abdomen, and ear
Velez, Juan	Father of Pvt. Francesca Velez
Villa, Patricia	Hasan's neighbor at Casa Del Norte
Warman, Philip	Surviving spouse of Col. Juanita Warman
Washington, Sadaros	One of Hasan's neighbors at Casa Del Norte
Williams, Latoya	Data entry clerk at Station Thirteen
Zeigler, Ssg. Patrick	Shot in head and lost twenty per cent of his brain

Acronyms and Abbreviations

ACCA	Army Court of Criminal Appeals
ACLU	American Civil Liberties Union
ACU	Army Combat Uniform
AD	Active Duty
ADAMS	Anomaly Detection at Multiple Scales
ADSO	Active Duty Service Obligation
AIRT	Army Internal Review Team
AMEDD	Army Medical Department
ANAM	Automated Neuropsychological Assessment Metrics
AQAP	Al Qaeda in the Arabian Peninsula
AR	Army Regulation
ATO	Antiterrorism Officer
AWCP	Army Weight Control Program
BH	Behavioral Health
CF	Credentialing File
CI	Counterintelligence
CID	Criminal Investigation Division
CIO	Chief Information Officer
CIRG	Critical Incident Response Group
CMA	Court of Military Appeals
CMHC	Community Mental Health Center
CMSA	Congressional Muslim Staff Association
CO	Commanding Officer; Conscientious Objector
CRB	Crisis Response Battalion
CSG	Contract Security Guard
CT	Counter-terrorism
DA	Department of the Army
DASG	Department of the Army Security Guard
DES	Department of Emergency Services
DES	Directorate of Emergency Services
DIS	Defense Investigative Service
DoD	Department of Defense

DPSRC	Defense Personnel Security Research Center
DWS	Data Warehouse System
EC	Electronic Communications
EM	Emergency Medical
EO	Executive Order
EOC	Emergency Operations Center
ESL	English as a Second Language
FOIA	Freedom of Information
FPCON	Force Protection Condition
HIPAA	Health Insurance Portability & Accountability Act
HVE	Homegrown Violent Extremist
IC	Installation Commander
ICSR	International Center for the Study of Radicalization
IED	Improvised Explosive Device
IHV	Inmate of High Value
IIR	Intelligence Information Report (FBI)
IMCOM	Installation Management Command
INSCOM	Intelligence and Security Command
IT	International Terrorism
JTTF	Joint Terrorism Task Force
KLA	Kosovo Liberation Army
LNO	Liaison Officer
MASCAL	Mass Casualty
MEB	Medical Evaluation Board
MEDCOM	Medical Command
MOS	Military Occupational Specialty
MRE	Meals ready to eat
MRSA	Methicillin-resistant Staphylococcus aureus
NCO	Non Commissioned Officer
NSI	National Suspicious Activity Reporting Initiative
OER	Officer Evaluation Report
OIC	Officer-In-Charge
PAD	Patient Administration
PCS	Permanent Change of Station

PETN	Pentaerythritol tetranitrate
PSQ	Personal Security Questionnaire
PTSD	Post Traumatic Stress Disorder
R&R	Resilience and Restoration
RAMP	Random Antiterrorism Measures Program
RFRA	Religious Freedom Restoration Act
RTD	Returned to Duty
RVU	Relative Value Unit
SAR	Suspicious Activity Reporting
SDFO	San Diego Field Office
SRP	Soldier Readiness Processing
TA	Threat Assessment
TARP	Threat Awareness Reporting Program
TBI	Traumatic Brain Injury
TEM	Trauma Event Management
UNSC	United Nations Security Council
USUHS	Uniformed Services University of Health Sciences
WFO	Washington Field Office
WRAMC	Walter Reed Army Medical Center

Notes

Preface

1. Philip Jankowsky, "Obama at Fort Hood: 'This tragedy tears at wounds that are still raw,'" *statesman.com*, April 9, 2014. Accessed April 19, 2014.

Phillip Carter and David Barno, "How the military isolates itself—and hurts veterans," *Washington Post*, Nov. 8, 2014. Accessed April 18, 2014.

2. Richard Goldstein, "Howard Unruh, 88, Dies; Killed 13 of His Neighbors in Camden in 1949, *New York Times*, Oct. 19, 2009. Accessed March 10, 2014. http://www.nytimes.com/2009/10/20/nyregion/20unruh.html?pagewanted=all&_r=0

Ron Franscell, *Delivered from Evil: True Stories of Ordinary People Who Faced Monstrous Mass Killers and Survived* (Beverly, MA: Fair Winds Press, 2011), 12-39.

3. Neal Spelce, "Neal Spelce Collection, No. 2, UT Tower Shooting," *Texas Archive of the Moving Image*, Sound 1966, http://www.texasarchive.org/library/index.php?title=The_Neal_Spelce_Collection,_No._2_-_UT_Tower_Shooting. Accessed March 10, 2014.

1. Station Thirteen

1. Jason Whitely, "Tales of heroism, horror emerge in Fort Hood shooting hearing," *WFAA.com*, Oct. 13, 2010, http://www.wfaa.com/home/Heroism-graphic-testimony-open-Fort-Hood-shooting-hearing-104862984.html. Accessed Nov. 30, 2011.

Neill Main, "Hasan Hearing Blog," *KWTX.com* (Waco), Oct. 13, 2010, http://www.kwtx. com/news/misc/105303923.html. Accessed Nov. 29, 2011.

"Full Story: Alleged Fort Hood shooter was William Fleming graduate, son of Roanoke restaurant owners," *Roanoke Times, Associated Press, New York Times, Washington Post*, Nov. 6, 2009. Accessed Dec. 19, 2011. http://www.roanoke.com/news/breaking/wb/225326

2. Charles Schiver, "Pray for Staff Sgt. Paul Martin on Veterans Day: Adel native survives Fort Hood attack," *Adel News Tribune*, Nov. 11, 2009. Accessed Dec. 8, 2011. http://www.adelnewstribune.com/editionviewer/default.aspx?Edition=efe1384a-96f5-492f-af5d-d903e37b1f8d&Page=d867d91e-3208-45de-8acc-684300b07305

3. Wade Goodwyn, "Recalling The Chaos Of The Fort Hood Shooting," *NPR.org*, Nov. 12, 2009, http://www.npr.org/templates/story/story.php?storyId=120340098Accessed Dec. 8/20/11.

4. Schiver, "Pray."

Wade Goodwyn, "Recalling The Chaos Of The Fort Hood Shooting."

5. Schiver, "Pray."

6. Lindsey Bertomen, weapons expert, telephone interview, Feb. 11, 2012, and email correspondence.

7. Schiver, "Pray."

8. Shern-Min Chow, "Wounded Fort Hood soldier: 'I could hear him coming, shooting, getting closer,'" *KENS-5.com*, Oct. 11, 2011, http://www. kens5.com/news/Wounded-Fort-Hood-soldier-I-could-hear-him-coming-shooting-getting-closer-69745357.html. Accessed Jan. 20, 2012.

Leticia Juarez, "Fort Hood Survivor Shares Her Story," *KIAH-TV*, Nov. 12, 2009, http://www.39online.com/news/local/kiah-fort-hood-survivor. Accessed 12/06/2011.

Jackie Vega, Jarrod Wise, Angela K. Brown and Michael Graczyk, "Pregnant pvt.'s last moments remembered," *KXAN.com*, Oct. 18, 2010, http://www. kxan.com/dpp/news/crime/soldier-ft-hood-gunman-fired-randomly. Accessed 01/20/2012.

9. Lindsey J. Bertomen, "Firearms Review: FNH Five-Seven," *PoliceOne. com*, Oct. 26, 2010, http://www.policeone.com/police-products/firearms/ articles/2833266-Firearms-Review-FNH-Five-Seven/. Accessed Feb. 11, 2012.

10. Chow, "Wounded Fort Hood soldier."

"Hasan Hearing Blog," *KWTX.com*, Oct. 18, 2010, http://www.kwtx.com/ news/misc/105214429.html. Accessed Jan. 23, 2012.

11. "Woman describes horrific phone call from husband at Fort Hood," *WAVE 3 News*, Nov. 6, 2009, http://www.wave3.com/story/11456064/ woman-describes-horrific-phone-call-from-husband-at-fort-hood. Accessed Aug. 5, 2013.

12. Jason Whitely, "Fort Hood survivors recount terror of Hasan's massacre in vivid detail," *WFAA.com*, Aug. 8, 2013, updated Aug, 9, http://www. wfaa.com/news/texas-news/judge-fort-hood-hasan-can-keep-representing-himself-218839241.html. Accessed Aug. 8, 2013.

13. Ibid.

14. Patrick George and Erin Mulvaney, "Mourners grieve Cameron man shot at Fort Hood," *Austin American-Statesman*, Nov. 16, 2009. Accessed Feb. 11, 2012, http://www.statesman.com/news/content/news/stories/ local/2009/11/16/1116hoodcahill.html

15. Lee Hancock, "Court hears victim's testimony, 911 recording at probable cause hearing for accused Fort Hood shooter Nidal Hasan," *Dallas Morning News*, October 13, 2010 and updated November 26, 2010, http://www. dallasnews.com/news/state/headlines/20101013-Court-hears-victim-s-testimony-7100.ece. Accessed Aug. 3, 2013.

16. Ashley Goudeau, "Horrifying testimony at Nidal Hasan's hearing,"

KCENTV.com, Oct. 13, 2010. http://www.cbs19.tv/Global/story. asp?S=13319084. Accessed Dec. 9, 2010

17. Hancock, "Court hears victim's testimony."

18. Angela K. Brown and Michael Graczyk, "Soldier says ordered to delete Fort Hood video," *Army Times and Associated Press*, Oct. 15, 2010, Accessed Nov. 30, 2011. http://www.armytimes,com/news/2010/10/ap-fort-hood-hearing-101510/

Associated Press/USA Today, "Soldier says ordered to delete Fort Hood video," Oct. 15, 2010. Accessed 01/22/2012. http://www.usatoday.com/news/ nation/2010-10-15-fort-hood-trial_N.htm

19. "Nidal Hasan's attorneys still trying to leave case," *CNN.com*, Aug. 9, 2013, http://www.cnn.com/2013/08/09/justice/hasan-court-martial. Accessed Aug. 9, 2013.

20. Whitely, "Fort Hood survivors recount terror."

21. "Hasan Hearing Blog," *KWTX.com*, Oct. 20, 2010, http://www.kwtx. com/news/misc/105383013.html. Accessed 11/29/2011.

22. Ibid.

23. Main, "Hasan Hearing Blog."

Jeremy Swartz, "Soldiers testify about bloodbath during Fort Hood shooting," *Austin-American-Statesman*, Oct. 14, 2010. Accessed 11/28/2011. http://www. statesman.com/news/news/local/soldiers-testify-about-bloodbath-during-fort-hoo-1/nRygp/

24. Heather Graham-Ashley, "A year later, Army family finds strength in Fort Hood's darkest day," *Fort Hood Sentinel*, Nov. 11, 2010. Accessed Jan. 22, 2012.

http://www.army.mil/article/47828/One_year_later__Army_family_finds_ strength_in_Fort_Hood__039_s_darkest_day/

"Hasan Hearing Blog," *KWTX.com*, Oct. 19, 2010. http://www.kwtx.com/ news/misc/ 105303923.html. Accessed 11/29/2011.

25. Ibid.

26. Ibid.

27. Ibid.

28. Ibid.

29. Ibid.

30. A "chuck" is an absorbent pad covered with plastic on one side.

31. Jason Whitley, "Fort Hood survivors recount terror of Hasan's massacre in vivid detail," *WFAA.com*, Aug. 8, 2013, http://www.wfaa.com/news/texas-news/judge-fort-hood-hasan-can-keep-representing-himself-218839241. html. Accessed Aug. 8, 2013.

32. Ibid.

33. "Hasan Hearing Blog," *KWTX.com*, Oct. 20, 2010.

34. Moni Basu, "Screams, sirens herald Fort Hood chaos," *CNN*, Nov. 6, 2009, http://edition.cnn.com/2009/CRIME/11/06/fort.hood.shootings. scene/index.htm. Accessed Sept. 9, 2009.

35. "Hasan Hearing Blog," *KWTX.com*, Oct. 18, 2010.

36. Ibid.

37. "Hasan Hearing Blog."

38. Ibid.

39. Ibid.

40. Ibid.

41. "Hasan Hearing Blog."

42. Jarrod Wise, Pamela Cosel, Jackie Vega, "Shooting witness: 'He's one of us,'" *KXAN.com*, Oct. 20, 2010. http://www.kxan.com/dpp/news/crime/ testimony-continues-in-ft-hood-hearing. Accessed Feb. 27, 2012.

43. Captain Jay Taylor, "Eighth Army major receives medal for Fort Hood response," *Army Times*, Nov. 8, 2010. Accessed Jan. 23, 3023,http://www. army.mil/article/47784/

44. Chelsea Garrett, telephone interview, Sept. 2011, and email correspondence.

45. Tyrone Thomas, telephone interview, Sept. 2011.

46. Chelsea Garrett

47. Ibid.

48. Ibid.

49. Ibid.

50. Confidential sources.

51. *Manning, et al. v. John McHugh, et al.*, 1:12-cv-01802-CKK (2012) Confidential sources.

52. Confidential sources.

53. The "Desert Eagle" is a semi-automatic pistol that looks much like the FN Five-Seven.

54. Confidential sources.

55. Ibid.

56. Lindsay Goldwert, "Tweeting While Treating the Wounded at Fort Hood: Dentistry Specialist Rico Sanchez Tweets Details of the Shooting," *ABCNews.go.com*, Nov. 6, 2009. http://abcnews.go.com/GMA/tweeting-treating-wounded-fort-hood/story?id=9012537. Accessed Dec. 9, 2011.

57. Ibid.

58. Ibid.

2. King of the Hill

1. "Gunman Kills 12, wounds 31 at Fort Hood," *MSNBC*, Nov. 5, 2009, http://www.msnbc.msn.com/id/33678801/ns/us_news-crime_and_courts/t/gunman-kills-wounds-fort-hood/. Accessed Dec. 9, 2011.

2. Michael King, "Suspect Hospitalized in Fort Hood Shooting Rampage," *11Alive.com*, Nov. 6, 2009, http://www.11alive.com/news/national/story.aspx?storyid=137185 &catid=166. Accessed Dec. 9, 2011.

3. Ibid.

4. Edwin Chen and David Wethe, "Heartbroken Obama Goes to Fort Hood for Memorial (Update)," *Bloomberg News*, Nov. 10, 2009. Accessed Dec. 9, 2011. http://www.bloomberg.com/apps/news?pid=newsarchive&sid=aQ8WV0TG9xao&pos=9

5. George C. Werner, "Gulf, Colorado and Santa Fe Railway," *Handbook of Texas Online* (Texas Historical Association). Accessed Feb. 19, 2012. http://www.tshaonline.org/handbook/online/articles/eqg25

John Leffler, "Killeen, TX," *Handbook of Texas Online*. Accessed Dec. 12, 2011. Published by the Texas State Historical Association. http://www.tshaonline.org/handbook/online/articles/hdk01

Vivian Elizabeth Smyrl, "Temple, Tx," *Handbook of Texas Online*. Accessed March 04, 2012. Published by the Texas State Historical Association. http://www.tshaonline.org/handbook/online/articles/hdt01

6. Werner, "Gulf, Colorado and Santa Fe Railway."

7. Leffler, "Killeen, TX."

8. Ibid.

9. Ibid.

10. William P. Barrett, "The Best Little Hash House in Texas," *Forbes*, Nov. 12, 1990, 220-21.

International Directory of Company Histories, Vol. 17, *St. James Press*, 1997.

11. Jan Reid, "The Cult of Keen," *Texas Monthly*, April 1996. Accessed March 1, 2012. http://www.texasmonthly.com/1996-04-01/music.php#

12. Lori Grossman, "Luby's Cafeterias: A Texas Tradition," *Texascooking.com*, June 2007, http://www.texascooking.com/features/june2007_lubys_cafeterias.htm. Accessed Dec. 11, 2011.

Cindy Widner, "How 'King of the Hill' helped make Texas three-dimensional again," *Austin Chronicle*, Sept. 11, 2009. Accessed Dec. 11, 2011. http://www.austinchronicle.com/screens/2009-09-11/841962/

13. Kevin Sullivan, "The Madness of George Hennard," *In Cold Blog*, May 24, 2010. Accessed August 30, 2011.

"Looking Back: Shooting rampage at Killeen Luby's left 24 dead," *Houston Chronicle*, August 10, 2001. Accessed Dec. 12, 2011. http://www.chron.com/

life/article/Shooting-rampage-at-Killeen-Luby-s-left-24-dead-2037092.php#page-1

Paula Chin, "A Texas Massacre," *People Magazine*, Nov. 4, 1991. Accessed Dec. 12, 2011. http://www.people.com/people/archive/article/0,,20111193,00.html

14. Ibid.

15. Ibid.

16. Ibid.

17. Philip Jankowski, "Survivors reflect on Oct. 16, 1991, Luby's shooting," *Killeen Daily Herald*, Oct. 15, 2011, http://www.kdhnews.com/news/story.aspx?s=61624&q= George+Hennard. Accessed Feb. 20, 2012.

18. Robert L. Kelley, "EMS Revisited: Oct. 1991 Luby's Shooting," *EMSWorld*, March 31, 2010. Accessed March 19, 2012. http://www.emsworld.com/article/10319733/ems-revisited-october-1991-lubys-shooting

19. Ibid.

20. "Looking Back," *Houston Chronicle*.

21. Sullivan, "The Madness of George Hennard."

Chin, "A Texas Massacre."

22. Catherine Chriss, "Massacre in Killeen/Medical board disciplined father/Doctor reprimanded in 1989," *Houston Chronicle*, Oct. 18, 1991. Accessed March 3, 2012. http://www.chron.com/CDA/archives/archive.mpl/1991_816684/massacre-in-killeen-medical-board-disciplined-fath.html

23. "Looking Back."

24. Chin, "A Texas Massacre."

25. Katherine Ramsland, "Movies Made Me Murder: Not on the Menu," *TruTV*, http://www.trutv.com/library/crime/criminal_mind/psychology/movies_made_me_kill/6.html, Accessed Feb. 19, 2012.

26. Chin, "A Texas Massacre."

27. Ibid.

28. Ibid.

29. Ibid.

"Mass Shootings at Virginia Tech," Report of the Review Panel, Presented to Governor Kaine, Commonwealth of Virginia, (August 2007).

30. Carry laws permit the concealment of firearms on one's person

Philip Jankowski, "Survivors reflect on Oct. 16, 1991, Luby's shooting," *Killeen Daily Herald*, Oct. 15, 2011. Accessed Dec. 12, 2011. http://www.kdhnews.com/news/story.aspx?s=61624

31. Ibid.

Jankowski, "Survivors reflect."

Oliver Darcy, "This is Why Most Military Personnel Aren't Armed on Military Bases—and It's Not Clinton's Fault," *Blaze*, September 13, 2013, http://www.theblaze.com/stories/2013/09/17/this-is-why-most-military-personnel-are-disarmed-on-military-bases-and-its-not-clintons-fault/

32. John Burnett, "Hard Lessons."

33. Ibid.

3. American Dream

1. Douglas J. Hagmann, "Profile of Major Nidal Malik Hasan," *Northwest Intelligence Network*, Nov. 11, 2009, http://homelandsecurityus.com/archives/3262). Accessed Dec. 18, 2011.

Malik Hasan's 1998 obituary listed as his next of kin his wife and sons plus a sister, four brothers, thirty-three nieces and nephews, thirty-seven great-nieces and great-nephews, and dozens of other relatives. The original obituary ran in the *Roanoke Times* but is not available on line. A copy of the obituary can be found in the above citation on the Northeast Intelligence Network web site.

"Milestones: Nidal Malik Hasan," *New York Times*, Nov. 7, 2009. Accessed Dec. 21, 2011. http://www.nytimes.com/interactive/2009/11/07/us/20091107-HASAN-TIMELINE.html?ref=nidalmalikhasan

Note: This is a timeline of the "milestones" of Nidal Hasan's life up to the point of the shooting. It has been used as a general reference and has not been quoted in the text of this book.

2. Matt Chittum and Jorge Valencia, "Suspected Fort Hood shooter Maj. Nidal Malik Hasan: Social awkwardness kept with him into adulthood," *Roanoke Times*, Nov. 6, 2009. Accessed Dec. 15, 2011. http://www.roanoke.com/news/roanoke/wb/225310

Hagmann, "Profile of Major Nidal Malik Hasan."

There are numerous sources that indicate that Nidal Hasan thought of himself more as an American than as a person of Middle Eastern descent. Neither he nor his brothers spoke with a Middle Eastern accent and, as children, did not attend services at a mosque or any other religious services on a regular basis.

3. Cindy Smith and Imtiyaz Delawala, "Cousin of Fort Hood Shooter Speaks Out Against Violent Extremism," *ABCNews.go.com*, Sept. 4, 2011, http://abcnews.go.com/Politics/ft-hood-shooters-cousin-speaks-violent-extremism/story?id=14445896. Accessed Dec. 18, 2011.

4. "About City Market," http://www.downtownroanoke.org/city-market/about-city-market. Accessed Dec. 15, 2011.

5. Chittum and Valencia, "Suspected Fort Hood Shooter."

6. Ibid.

The characterizations of Malik and Nora Hasan were taken from their obituaries as reprinted by the Northeast Intelligence Network "Profile of Major Nidal Malik Hasan," as cited above. Their obituaries are not available on-line in the Roanoke Times archives but are available in the newspaper's archives on-site.

Laurence Hammack, Amanda Codispoti and Tonia Moxley, "Fort Hood shooting suspect Hasan left few impressions in schools he attended," *Roanoke Times*, Nov. 7, 2009. Accessed Dec. 16, 2011. http://www.roanoke.com/news/roanoke/wb/225422

"Full Story: Alleged Fort Hood shooter was William Fleming graduate, son of Roanoke restaurant owners," *Roanoke Times and Associated Press*, Nov. 6, 2009. Accessed Dec. 27, 2011, http://www.roanoke.com/news/breaking/wb/225326

7. Ibid.

8. "Final Report of the William H. Webster Commission on The Federal Bureau of Investigation, Counterterrorism Intelligence, and the Events at Fort Hood, Texas, Nov. 5, 2009," released July 2012, 51-52. Accessed Aug. 6, 2012.http://www.fbi.gov/news/pressrel/press-releases/final-report-of-the-william-h.-webster-commission

9. Ibid.

"Hasan graduated from William Fleming, family had Roanoke area connections," *WDBJ7.com*, Nov. 5, 2009, http://www.wdbj7.com/wdbj7-hasangraduatedfromwilliam-11454627,0,1016632,full.story. Accessed Dec. 22, 2011.

10. Ibid.

"Cousin Says Suspected Fort Hood Gunman Feared Impending War Deployment," *FOXNews.com*, Nov. 5, 2009, updated March 18, 2010, http://www.foxnews.com/story/2009/11/05/cousin-says-suspected-fort-hood-gunman-feared-impending-war-deployment/. Accessed Aug. 12, 2010.

"Full Story: Alleged Fort Hood shooter."

11. Hammack, et al., "Fort Hood Shooting Suspect."

There is little information available on Nidal Hasan's basic training at Fort Benning, GA, but an image of a certificate of completion dated Oct. 14, 1988 along with his complete application for a permit to carry a concealed weapon was obtained from the Roanoke County Circuit Court by Gawker.com. Accessed Dec. 22, 2011.

12. "Barstow Community College," http://www.irwin.army.mil/Community/AEC/Pages/ BarstowComunityCollege.aspx. Accessed Dec. 20, 2011.

Eunice Lee, "Fort Hood shooter was former Barstow college student," *Desert Dispatch*, Nov. 6, 2009. Accessed Dec. 20, 2011. http://www.desertdispatch.com/articles/hood-7250-attended-shooter.html

13. "Milestones," *New York Times*.

14. Ibid.

15. Dr. George E. Bunce, email correspondence, August 2011.

The authors contacted all of the Virginia Tech Department of Biochemistry professors listed on the VT biochemistry department web page who were teaching at VT during the time that Nidal Hasan was enrolled and received almost 100% response. Dr. Bunce was the only respondent who remembered Nidal Hasan.

16. Kathryn Simon, telephone interview, Oct. 8, 2011.

17. Ibid.

18. Dr. George E. Bunce.

19. Kathryn Simon.

20. Dr. George E. Bunce

21. Ned Potter, "Nidal Malik Hasan, Suspected Fort Hood Shooter, is Army Psychiatrist," *ABC News with Diane Sawyer*," Nov. 5, 2009, http://abcnews. go.com/WN/nadal-malik-hasan-suspected-fort-hood-shooter-psychiatrist/ Story?id=9010466&page=2). Accessed Dec. 20, 2011.

22. "Milestones," *New York Times*.

23. "Full Story."

24. Hammack, et al., "Fort Hood shooting suspect."

Smith and Delawala, "Cousin of Fort Hood Shooter Speaks Out,"

Hagmann, "Profile of Major Nidal Malik Hasan."

Philip Sherwell and Alex Spillius, "Fort Hood shooting: Texas army killer linked to September 11 terrorists," *Telegraph*, Nov. 7, 2009. Accessed Dec. 22, 2011. http://www.telegraph.co.uk/news/worldnews/northamerica/ usa/6521758/Fort-Hood-shooting-Texas-army-killer-linked-to-September-11-terrorists.html

Chittum and Valencia, "Suspected Fort Hood shooter Maj. Nidal Malik Hasan."

Smith and Delawala, "Cousin of Fort Hood Shooter."

Awlaki is sometimes spelled "Aulaqi" by government agencies and some print media.

25. "Suspected Fort Hood, Texas shooter was Vinton resident, Virginia Tech Grad," *AP and Roanoke Times*, Nov. 5, 2009, updated 12:56 a.m. Accessed Dec. 22, 2011. http://www.roanoke.com/news/breaking/wb/225202

26. Asha Beh and Jackie Bensen, "Fort Hood Shooting Suspect was 'a Calm Person,'" *NBCwashington.com*, Nov. 8, 2009, http://www.nbcwashington.com/ news/local/Ft-Hood-Shooting-Suspect-Was-a-Calm-Person--69458987. html. Accessed Dec. 27, 2011.

27. Eli Saslow, Philip Rucker, William Wan and Mary Pat Flaherty, "Unnoticed Clues Haunt Fort Hood," *NBCSanDiego.com*, Dec. 31, 2009, http://www.nbcsandiego.com/news/breaking/Unnoticed_clues_haunt_Fort_Hood-80401817.html. Accessed Dec. 27, 2011.

28. Hagmann, "Profile of Major Nidal Malik Hasan."

Chris McGreal, "Fort Hood shootings: Nidal Hasan's quiet manner hid hostility to US army," *Guardian*, Nov. 6, 2009. Accessed Dec. 22, 2011, http://www.guardian.co.uk/world/2009/nov/06/fort-hood-shootings-nidal-hasan/print

Saskow, et al, "Unnoticed Clues Haunt Fort Hood."

29. Smith and Delawala, "Cousin of Fort Hood Shooter."

30. Adrian Blomfield, "Fort Hood shooter is deeply sensitive introvert, say Palestinian relatives," *Telegraph*, Nov. 7, 2009. Accessed Dec. 23, 2011. http://www.telegraph.co.uk/news/worldnews/northamerica/usa/6521037/Fort-Hood-shooter-is-deeply-sensitive-introvert-say-Palestinian-relatives.html

31. Ibid.

32. Ibid.

33. Mary Pat Flaherty, William Wan and Christian Davenport, "Suspect, devout Muslim from Va., wanted Army discharge, aunt said," *Washington Post*, Nov. 6, 2009. Accessed Dec. 23, 2011.http://www.washingtonpost.com/wpdyn/content/article/2009/11/05/AR2009110505216.html

The psychiatry residency program is comprised of students from the Walter Reed Army Medical Center (WRAMC), the National Naval Medical Center (NNMC), the Malcolm Grow U.S. Air Force Medical Center (MGMC), and the Uniformed Services University of the Health Sciences (USUHS). First brought together in 1996, this group of residency students is called the "National Capital Consortium Psychiatry Residency Program."

34. Blomfield, "Fort Hood shooter is deeply sensitive introvert."

Joseph Rhee, Anna Schecter, and Brian Ross, "Hasan Was Worried About Results of Recent HIV Test," *ABC World News*, Nov. 19, 2009, http://abcnews.go.com/Blotter/hasan-worried-results-hiv-test/story?id=9127299. Accessed March 13, 2012.

35. James C. McKinley Jr. and James Dao, "Fort Hood Gunman Gave Signals Before His Rampage," *New York Times*, 11/09/2009. Accessed Dec. 27, 2011. http://www.nytimes.com/2009/11/09/us/09reconstruct.html?pagewanted=all

36. Maj. Kaustubh G. Joshi, "Memorandum for Defense Counsel: Full Report of Sanity Board, *US v. Maj. Nidal M. Hasan*," Jan. 13, 2011.

37. Confidential sources.

38. Ben Quinn and David Batty, "'One of our own' Nidal Malik Hasan creates carnage at Fort Hood," *Guardian*, Nov. 6, 2009. Accessed Dec. 27,

2011. http://www.guardian.co.uk/world/2009/nov/06/nidal-malik-hasan-fort-hood-shooting

Richard A. Serrano, "GI Sentenced to Death for Fatal Attack," *Los Angeles Times*, April 29, 2005. Accessed Dec. 26, 2011. http://articles.latimes.com/2005/apr/29/nation/na-akbar29

Ben Quinn and David Batty, "'One of our own' Nidal Malik Hasan creates carnage at Fort Hood," *Guardian*, Nov. 6, 2005. Accessed Dec. 27, 2011. http://www.guardian.co.uk/world/2009/nov/06/nidal-malik-hasan-fort-hood-shooting

39. Richard A. Serrano, "Hasan Akbar's Peculiar Military Career," *Los Angeles Times*, Aug. 3, 2003. Accessed Dec. 30, 2011. http://articles.latimes.com/2003/aug/03/magazine/tm-grenade31

40. Ibid.

Serrano, "GI Sentenced to Death for Fatal Attack."

41. Daniel Zwerdling and Steve Inskeep, "Hasan's Psychological Health Raised Concerns," *NPR.org*, Nov. 12, 2009, http://www.npr.org/templates/story/ story.php?storyId=120340654. Accessed Dec. 20, 2011.

42. Daniel Zwerdling and Steve Inskeep, "Former Colleagues Say Hasan Was Detached," *NPR.org*, Nov. 10, 2009, http://www.npr.org/templates/story/ story.php?storyId= 120266836. Accessed Dec. 30, 2011..

Scott Moran, M.D., "Memorandum to the National Capital Consortium Psychiatry Residency Program," May 17, 2007, regarding the performance of Nidal Hasan, http://www.npr.org/documents/2009/nov/hasanletter. pdf. Accessed Dec. 20, 2011.

43. "Residency Administrative Handbook," National Capital Consortium Psychiatry Residency Program, Effective: 01 July 2008-30 June 2009, https:// ke.army.mil/bordeninstitute/published_volumes/combat_operational/ CBM-ch42-final.pdf. Accessed Dec. 16, 2013.

44. Ibid, 103.

45. Ibid, 45-46.

46. Ibid, 4.

47. Scott Moran, M.D., "Memorandum."

48. Daniel Zwerdling, "Walter Reed Officials Asked: Was Hasan Psychotic?" *NPR.org*, Nov. 11, 2005, http://www.npr.org/templates/story/story. php?storyId=120313570. Accessed Sept. 20, 2011.

The authors contacted Nidal Hasan's professors and supervisors at USUHS and Walter Reed Army Hospital. Only three responded, Dr. Charles Engel, Dr. David Benedek, and Dr. Robert Ursano, and they declined to comment.

49. Maj. Kaustubh Joshi, "Memorandum for Defense Counsel."

50. WBVF-TV, "Troubles at Every Turn in Fort Hood Suspect's Medical

Training," *Associated Press*, Jan. 19, 2009, http://www2.wjbf.com/news/2010/jan/19/troubles_at_every_turn_in_fort_hood_shooting_suspe-ar-219253/. Accessed Jan. 1, 2012.

51. Ibid.

52. Dana Priest, "Fort Hood suspect warned of threats within the ranks," *Washington Post*, Nov. 10, 2009. Accessed Sept. 10, 2011. http://www.washingtonpost.com/wpdyn/content/article/2009/11/09/AR2009110903618.html?hpid=topnews

53. Ibid.

54. "A Ticking Time Bomb: Counterterrorism Lessons From The U.S. Government's Failure To Prevent The Fort Hood Attack," A Special Report by Joseph I. Lieberman, Chairman, Susan M. Collins, Ranking Member, U.S. Senate Committee on Homeland Security and Governmental Affairs, Feb. 2011. http://www.hsgac.senate.gov//imo/media/doc/Fort_Hood/FortHoodReport.pdf?attempt=2. Accessed May 5, 2011.

55. Ibid.

WBVF-TV, "Troubles at Every Turn."

56. Joshi, "Memorandum for Defense Counsel."

57. Imam Faizul Kahn, telephone interview, July 2011.

58. Ibid.

59. Ibid.

60. "Governor" is a term for Allah in Islam.

61. Michael Fredholm, "Islamic Extremism as a Political Force: A Comparative Study of Central Asian Extremist Movements," (Asian Cultures and Modernity, Research Report No. 12), University of Stockholm: 2006. 11-12. Accessed 01/01/2012. http://www.central-eurasia.com/uploads/files/RR12.pdf

62. Ramtanu Maitra, "Remaking Central Asia," *Asia Times*, May 27, 2005. Accessed Jan. 1, 2012. http://www.atimes.com/atimes/Central_Asia/GE27Ag01.html

63. Senate Subcommittee on Terrorism, Technology and Homeland Security of the Committee on the Judiciary, Terrorism: Growing Wahhabi Influence in the United States, 108th Cong., June 19, 2003, 2, http://www.judiciary.senate.gov/hearings/hearing.cfm?id=4f1e0899533f7680e78d03281fee07b5

64. Ibid., 2.

65. Ibid., 2.

66. Ibid., 17.

67. Ibid., 18.

68. Ibid., 18.

69. Uniformed Services University of the Health Sciences, Department of Psychiatry, Preventive/Disaster Psychiatry MPH Fellowship web site, updated 06/19/2009, http://www.usuhs.mil/psy/psyfellowship.html. Accessed 09/10/2011.

70. *CNN* televised interview with Val Finnell, M.D., by Anderson Cooper, Nov. 6, 2009, 10:00 PM EST, http://transcripts.cnn.com/TRANSCRIPTS/0911/06/acd.01.html. Accessed Nov. 8, 2011.

71. Ibid.

McKinley and Dao, "Fort Hood Gunman Gave Signals."

72. *CNN* televised interview with Val Finnell, MD.

73. Sig Christenson, "Prosecutors rest in Hasan trial," *San Antonio Express News*, August 21, 2013. Accessed Aug. 21, 2013, http://www.mysanantonio.com/news/local/article/Prosecutors-rest-in-Hasan-trial-4745574.php

74. "A Ticking Time Bomb," 35.

75. "Statement on Nidal Hasan," Press Release, Homeland Security Policy Institute, Nov. 6, 2009, http://www.prlog.org/10404022-homeland-security-policy-institute-statement-on-nidal-hasan.html. Accessed Dec. 27, 2011.

76. Annie Lowrey, "Fort Hood misinformation," *Passport, A Blog by the Editors of Foreign Policy*, Nov. 6, 2009, http://blog.foreignpolicy.com/posts/2009/11/06/ fort_hood_misinformation. Accessed Jan. 3, 2012.

77. Asra Q. Nomani, "Inside the Gunman's Mosque," *Daily Beast*, Nov. 7, 2009, http://www.thedailybeast.com/articles/2009/11/07/major-hasans-hidden-militancy.html. Accessed 01/04/2012.

78. Ibid.

79. Nidal Hasan, "Martyrdom in Islam Versus Suicide Bombing," *Scribd.com*, July 18, 2008, http://www.scribd.com/NidalHasan. Accessed Sept. 10, 2011.

80. Nick Allen, "Fort Hood gunman had told US military colleagues that infidels should have their throats cut," *Telegraph*, Nov. 8, 2009. Accessed Jan. 4, 2012. http://www.telegraph.co.uk/news/worldnews/northamerica/usa/6526030/Fort-Hood-gunman-had-told-US-military-colleagues-that-infidels-should-have-their-throats-cut.html

81. "Final Report Of The William H. Webster Commission."

Note on quoted material from "Counterterrorism Intelligence, and the Events at Fort Hood, Texas, on Nov. 5, 2009." All formatting, grammatical, and spelling errors are preserved in Hasan's emails to Awlaki and Awlaki's messages to Hasan. Computer-generated characters were removed.

82. Ibid, 41-42.

83. Ibid., 43.

84. Ibid., 44-45.

85. Ibid., 47.

86. Ibid.

87. Ibid., 47-49.

88. Ibid., 50.

89. Ibid.

90. Ibid.

91. Ibid., 51.

92. Ibid.

93. Ibid.

94. Ibid.

95. Ibid., 51-52.

96. Ibid., 52.

97. Ibid.

98. Ibid., 53.

99. Ibid.

100. Ibid., 54.

101. Ibid.

102. Ibid., 54.

103. Ibid., 54-55.

104. Dina Temple-Raston, "Mix-Up Denied Officials Info About Fort Hood Suspect," *NPR Morning Edition*, Dec. 1, 2009, http://www.npr.org/templates/story/story.php?story Id=121002448. Accessed July 3, 2011.
"A Ticking Time Bomb,"10.

105. "Army releases May officer promotions," *Army Times*, April 20, 2009. Accessed Sept. 9, 2011. http://www.armytimes.com/news/2009/04/army_officer_list_042009w/

106. "A Ticking Time Bomb,"35.

107. Ibid., 34.

4. The Great Place

1. "Religion in Early Texas," The Texas Almanac, published by the Texas State Historical Assn. Accessed Jan. 8, 2012. http://www.texasalmanac.com/topics/history/religion-early-texas

2. Mary Ann Lamanna and Jayme A. Sokolow, "McWhirter, Martha White," Handbook of Texas Online, published by the Texas State Historical Assn., http://www.tshaonline.org/handbook/online/articles/fmcax. Accessed Oct. 08, 2011.

"Religion in Early Texas," The Texas Almanac.

"Newspaper Prints Bomb Defendant's Letter," *New York Times*, April 9, 1997. Accessed Jan. 6, 2012. http://www.nytimes.com/1997/04/10/us/newspaper-prints-bomb-defendant-s-letter.html?ref=timothyjamesmcveigh

3. Robert Berg, "Camels West," *Saudi Aramco World*, Vol. 53, Number 3, (May/June, 2002): 2-7. Accessed Jan. 7, 2012. http://www.saudiaramcoworld.com/issue/200203/camels.west.htm

4. Azhar S. Rauf and Ayman Hajjaar, "Muslims," Handbook of Texas Online, published by the Texas State Historical Assn., http://www.tshaonline.org/handbook/online/ articles/irmxh. Accessed Jan. 6, 2012.

5. "Central Texas Gun Instructor Off The Hook Over Anti-Muslim Ad," *KWTX.com*, Nov. 8, 2011, http://www.kwtx.com/home/headlines/Central_Texas_Gun_Instructor_ Off_The_Hook_Over_Anti-Muslim_Ad_133435183.html. Accessed Jan. 6, 2012.

6. Brian Mockenhaupt, "Hood," *Esquire*, Feb. 23, 2010. Accessed Jan. 6, 2012. http://www.esquire.com/features/fort-hood-shooting-0310

7. USAG Fact Sheet as of Nov. 2011, http://www.hood.army.mil/facts/FortHoodFactSheet.pdf. Accessed March 13, 2012.

8. "Economic Impact of Fort Hood," Greater Killeen Chamber of Commerce, 2011, http://www.killeenchamber.com/fthood/economicimpact. Accessed Sept. 14, 2013.

9. http://www.johnbellhood.org/menu.htm. Accessed March 13, 2012.

10. "Elvis Aaron Presley - In The U.S. Army 1958-1960," Elvis Presley Music: For Elvis Fans Only, 2012, http://www.elvispresleymusic.com.au/elvis_presley_army_1958 _1960.html. Accessed March 21, 2012.

11. "Welcome to Fort Hood," Fort Hood web site, updated Jan. 16, 2012.

http://www.hood.army.mil/newcomers.hood.aspx

12. Philip Rucker, "The lonely life of 'Number Nine,'" *Washington Post*, Nov. 8, 2009. Accessed Dec. 26, 2011. http://www.washingtonpost.com/wpdyn/content/article/2009/11/07/AR2009110703449.html

13. Ibid.

Property records search of Bell County Appraisal District.

Rhee, et al, "Hasan Was Worried About Results."

14. Philip Sherwell and Nick Allen, "Fort Hood shooting: inside story of how massacre on military base happened," *Telegraph*, Nov. 7, 2009. Accessed Jan. 3, 2012. http://www.telegraph.co.uk/news/worldnews/northamerica/usa/6521578/Fort-Hood-shooting-inside-story-of-how-massacre-on-military-base-happened.html

15. Flaherty, et al, "Suspect, devout Muslim from Va."

16. Rucker, "The lonely life of 'Number Nine.'"

17. McKinley and Dao, "Fort Hood Gunman."

18. Confidential sources.

19. Ibid.

20. Ibid.

21. Ibid.

22. Ibid.

23. Ibid.

24. "2007 memo criticizes Fort Hood suspect's judgment, professionalism," *CNN*, Nov. 18, 2009, http://articles.cnn.com/2009-11-18/us/fort.hood. hasan.memo_1_nidal-hasan-memo-professionalism?_s=PM:US. Accessed Jan. 29, 2012.

25. Confidential sources.

26. Ibid.

27. Ibid.

28. Mockenhaupt, "Hood."

29. Richard Esposito, Mary-Rose Abraham, and Rhonda Swartz, "Major Hasan: Many Ties to Jihad Web Sites," *ABCNews,com*, Nov. 12, 2009, http://abcnews. go.com/Blotter/ hasan-multiple-mail-accounts-officials/story?id=9065692. Accessed Dec. 17, 2011.

Islamic-Dictionary.com, copyright 2011, http://www.islamic-dictionary.com/ index.php? word=Subhanahu+Wa+Ta%27ala. Accessed Dec. 4, 2011.

30. McKinley and Dao, "Fort Hood Gunman."

31. Frederick Brannon, telephone interview, August 19, 2011.

FNH USA, https://www.fnhusa.com/l/products/handguns/five-seven/. Accessed Sept. 2, 2013.

32. "Hydrostatic Shock," *MedLibrary.org*, http://medlibrary.org/medwiki/ Hydrostatic_shock, Accessed Sept. 14, 2013.

33. David Zucchino, "Suspect in Ft. Hood rampage sought high-tech gun, salesman says," *Los Angeles Times*, Oct. 21, 2010. Accessed Oct. 12, 2011. http://articles.latimes.com/2010/oct/21/nation/la-na-fort-hood-20101022

34. "GI Joe: The Rise of Cobra," http://www.gijoemovie.com/dvd/index. html, 2009. Accessed Sept 2, 2013.

35. "Fort Hood Killer Reportedly Chose 'Cop Killer' Handgun," Brady Campaign Press Release, Nov. 6, 2009, http://www.bradycampaign.org/ media/press/view/1194. Accessed Jan. 26, 2012.

36. Zucchino, "Suspect in Ft. Hood rampage."

Jeremy Schwartz, "Witnesses: Hasan spent weeks before Fort Hood shooting at local range," *Austin American-Statesman*, Oct. 21, 2010. Accessed Oct. 12, 2011. http://www.statesman.com/news/local/witnesses-hasan-spent-weeks-before-fort-hood-shooting-985470.html

37. Ibid.

Zucchino, "Suspect in Ft. Hood rampage," Los Angeles Times.

38. Lindsey Bertomen, telephone interview, Feb. 11, 2012.

39. Ibid.

"Hasan Hearing Blog," *KWTX.com*, Oct. 21, 2010, http://www.kwtx.com/news/ misc/105482458.html. Accessed Nov. 29, 2011.

The authors contacted John Choats, co-owner of Stan's Shooting Range, but he declined to discuss Nidal Hasan's membership. Mr. Choats stated that he was under a "gag order" imposed by the Texas Rangers. The Texas Rangers do not issue gag orders.

40. Angela Gomez (pseudonym), personal interview, Oct. 16, 2011.

41. Ibid.

42. Natasha Chen, "Hasan's neighbor jailed after vandalism over Muslim bumper sticker," *KXXVNews.com*, Nov. 13, 2009, http://www.kxxv.com/global/Story.asp?s=11502394, updated June 29, 2011. Accessed Jan. 8, 2012.

Incident/Investigation Report, Killeen Police Department, Aug. 16, 2009. Obtained through the Texas Open Records Act.

Offense Report, Killeen Police Department, signed and notarized statement of Nidal Hasan, Sept. 30, 2009.

Affidavit for Arrest, signed by Nidal Hasan, Oct. 8, 2009.

Arrest Report, John Van De Walker, Killeen Police Department, Oct. 8, 2009.

43. Angela Gomez

44. Mockenhaupt, "Hood."

45. Ibid.

46. Ibid.

47. Mark Schone, Joseph Rhee, Mary-Rose Abraham and Anna Schecter, "Major Hasan Dined with 'Jihad Hobbyist,'" *ABC News Blotter*, Nov. 17, 2009, http://abcnews.go.com/Blotter/hasans-friend-proclaimed-extremist/story?id=9100187. Accessed Jan. 30, 2012.

48. Code green refers to a combative patient who may have a weapon.

49. Confidential sources.

50. Sig Christenson, "Prosecutors rest."

51. Confidential sources.

52. Ibid.

53. *U.S. v. Maj. Nidal M. Hasan*, Trial Exhibit Four.

54. Ibid., Trial Exhibit Five.

55. Confidential sources.

56. Ibid.

57. Maj. Kaustubh Joshi, *Memorandum for Defense Counsel.*

58. "Suspected Fort Hood Shooter Was 'Calm' During Massacre, May Have Shouted 'God Is Great,'" *FOXNews*, Nov. 6, 2009, http://www.foxnews.com/story/0,2933, 572448,00.html. Accessed Feb. 27, 2012.

59. Ltc. Ben Phillips, "Officer Evaluation Report for Maj. Nidal Hasan," Nov. 3, 2009, U.S. v. Maj. Nidal M. Hasan, http://s3.documentcloud.org/documents/777750/hasan-eval.pdf. Accessed Aug. 30, 3013.

60. Ibid.

61. Confidential sources.

62. "Hasan received a glowing review three days before shooting," *MENAFN.com*, Aug. 6, 2013, http://www.menafn.com/f26f8185-a921-4c39-8256-4fe969fc4cac/Hasan-received-glowing-review-three-days-before-shooting?src=main. Accessed Aug. 6, 2013.

5. Rage Against the Machine

1. Joseph Rhee, Mary-Rose Abraham and Brian Ross, "Accused Fort Hood Shooter Was a Regular at Shooting Range, Strip Club," *ABCnews.go.com*, Nov. 16, 2009, http://abcnews.go.com/Blotter/accused-fort-hood-shooter-nidal-hasan-visited-strip/story?id=9090116. Accessed 02/24/2012.

2. "Alleged Fort Hood Shooter Frequented Local Strip Club," *FOXNews.com*, Nov. 9, 2009, http://www.foxnews.com/story/0,2933,573052,00.html. Accessed 01/15/2012.

3. Ibid.

4. "Report of the William H. Webster Commission," 69.

5. Ibid.

CAIR Houston, "Incident Report," 2006, http://cairhouston.org/incident.htm. Accessed Sept. 5, 2013.

6. Joseph Rhee, Mary-Rose Abraham and Brian Ross, "Officials: Major Hasan Sought 'War Crimes' Prosecution of U.S. Soldiers," *ABCNews.go.com*, Nov. 16, 2009, http://abcnews.go.com/Blotter/officials-major-hasan-sought-war-crimes-prosecution-us/story?id=9019904. Accessed March 11, 2012.

7. "Exclusive Video: Hasan at a convenience store," *CNN.com*, Nov. 6, 2009, http://ac360.blogs.cnn.com/2009/11/06/exclusive-video-hasan-at-a-convenience-store/. Accessed March 30, 2012.

8. "Surveillance video of Nidal Hasan," *CNN* (Anderson Cooper), Nov. 5, 2009, http://www.cnn.com/video/?/video/us/2009/11/05/ac.hasan.video.cnn. Accessed March 30, 2012.

9. Rhee, et al., "Accused Fort Hood Shooter Was a Regular."

10. Rhee, et al., "Officials: Major Hasan Sought 'War Crimes' Prosecution."

11. Bob Drogin and Faye Fiore, "Retracing steps of suspected Fort Hood shooter, Nidal Malik Hasan," *Los Angeles Times*, Nov. 7, 2009. Accessed March 11, 2012. http://articles.latimes.com/2009/nov/07/nation/na-fort-hood-hasan7

12. Sherwell and Allen, "Fort Hood shooting: inside story."

13. Eli Saslow, Philip Rucker, William Wan, Mary Pat Flaherty, "Unnoticed Clues Haunt Fort Hood," *NBC Southern California*, Dec. 31, 2009, http://www.nbclosangeles.com/news/breaking/Unnoticed_clues_haunt_Fort_Hood-80401817.html. Accessed March 11, 2012.

Sherwell and Allen, "Fort Hood shooting: inside story."

14. Ibid.

15. Ibid.

16. Jason Whitely, Nomaan Merchant, and Paul Webe, "Follow updates from Jason Whitely in Fort Hood," *KVUE.com*, August 6, 2013, http://www.kvue.com/news/state /218582451.html. Accessed August 13, 2013.

17. "Surveillance video of Nidal Hasan," *CNN*.

Saslow, et al, "Unnoticed Clues."

18. "Several hundred pray for Fort Hood victims at vigil," *Associated Press and San Antonio Express News*, Nov. 6, 2009. Accessed Feb. 27, 2012. http://www.chron.com/news/houston-texas/article/Several-hundred-pray-for-Fort-Hood-victims-at-1726649.php

19. Ibid.

20. Ibid.

21. Confidential sources.

22. Ibid.

23. "Credentials Transfer Brief," VA Form 10-0376a, OMB Number 2900-0621, July 2005.

The "Clinical Summary" portion of the form reads as follows:

"[Provider's name, ie Nidal Hasan] is known to be clinically competent to practice the full scope of privileges granted at [sending facility], to satisfactorily discharge his/her professional obligations, and to conduct himself/herself ethically, as attested to by [name and telephone number of person personally acquainted with the provider's professional and clinical performance]. [name of person giving recommendation] has/does not have additional information relating to [provider's name] competence to perform granted privileges.

Provider's credentialing file (CF) and the documents contained therein have been reviewed and verified as indicated above. The information conveyed in this letter/message reflects credentials status as of [date]. [Choose from the following sentence formats, or variations thereof, to describe the presence/absence of additional relevant information in the CF: (a) the CF contains no additional information relevant to the privileging of the provider in your medical treatment facility, (b) the CF contains additional relevant information regarding status of current license, (c) the CF contains additional relevant information that may reflect on the current competence of the provider (emphasis added). Contact this command for further information before taking appointing and privileging action.

24. Confidential sources.

25. "Hasan received a glowing review three days before shooting," Menafn. com, http://www.menafn.com/f26f8185-a921-4c39-8256-4fe969fc4cac/ Hasanreceived-glowing-review-three-days-before-shooting?src=main. Accessed August 10. 2013.

26. These facts were revealed in a debriefing of the Behavioral Health Department staff after the shooting; sources are confidential.

27. *U.S. v. MAJ Nidal Hasan*, "Sanity Board Report," Jan. 13, 2011.

28. Confidential sources.

6. A Kick in the Gut

1. Dana Hoeff, email correspondence, 2012.

2. Ibid.

Greg Jaffe and Philip Rucker, "I could hear bullets going past me," *Washington Post*, Nov. 7, 2009. Accessed Jan. 22, 2012. http://www.washingtonpost.com/wp-dyn/content/article/2009/11/07/AR2009110702657.html?nav=emailpage

3. Ibid.

4. Carlos Saucedo, "911 Calls Replayed Tuesday During Accused Fort Hood Gunman's Hearing," *KWTX*, Oct. 19, 2010, http://www.kwtx.com/news/headlines/105243288.html?site=full. Accessed Nov. 5, 2011.

5. Ibid.

6. Hasan Hearing Blog, *KWTX*, Oct. 19, 2010.

7. Ibid.

8. Ibid.

9. Ibid.

10. Ibid.

11. Ibid.

12. Ibid.

13. "Specialist Valdez Interview," YouTube, *DoDvClips*, Nov. 6, 2009, http://www.youtube.com/watch?v=Ii-bLWFy0Lo. Accessed Nov. 21, 2011.

14. Amanda Kim Stairrett, "Staff Sgt. Zackary Filip chosen as 2010 Army Times Soldier of the Year," *Killeen Daily Herald*, Oct. 18, 2012. Accessed Aug. 8, 2013. http://m.kdhnews.com/news/staff-sgt-zackary-filip-chosen-

as-army-times-soldier-of/article_6db09f9f-90b6-50b2-a9a7-78d64d7433e4. html?mode=jqm

15. Dana Hoeff, email correspondence.

16. III Corps and Fort Hood Regulation 525-6, "Military Operations Antiterrorism Program," April 27, 2006, 13-14.

17. III Corps and Fort Hood After Action Review, Nov. 17, 2009.

18. Kevin Durwa, "Alleged Fort Hood Shooter in a Coma," *KXTV* News 10, Associated Press, USA Today, Nov. 6, 2009, http://www.news10.net /news/ local/ story. aspx? storyid=69941&provider=top. Accessed Feb. 27, 2012.

19. Ibid.

20. Moni Basu, "Screams, sirens herald Fort Hood chaos," *CNN*, Nov. 6, 2009, http://articles.cnn.com/2009-11-06/justice/fort.hood.shootings.scene_1_ fort-hood-nidal-malik-hasan-soldier?_s=PM:CRIME. Accessed Sept. 6, 2011.

21. Ibid.

22. Ibid.

23. Josh Rubin and Matt Smith, "'I am the shooter,' Nidal Hasans tells Fort Hood court-martial," *CNN Justice*, Aug. 6, 2013, http://www.cnn. com/2013/08/06/justice/hasan-court-martial. Accessed Aug. 7, 2013.

Philip Jankowski, "Kim Munley on Hasan: 'We began to blindly exchange fire,'" *Killeen Daily Herald*, Aug. 16, 2013. Accessed Aug. 16, 2013.http:// kdhnews.com/military/hasan_trial/kim-munley-on-hasan-we-began-to-blindly-exchange-fire/article_c8bb168e-0682-11e3-a6b1-001a4bcf6878.html

24. Confidential sources.

25. Excludes Fort Hood.

26. Bell County 9-1-1 Center, http://www.bcc911.com. Accessed Sept. 5, 2013.

Dalton Cross, telephone, October 2012.

27. American College of Surgeons Trauma Programs, http://www.facs.org/ trauma/tsepc/ componentsmodels.html. Accessed Sept. 5, 2013.

28. "David Boyd: World Leader in Emergency Services: Medicine Focus," *McGill Publications*, Feb. 2012, Accessed March 10, 2012. http://publications. mcgill.ca/medinfocus/2012/02/10/dr-david-boyd-world-leader-in-emergency-services/

29. Texas Department of State Health Services web site, "Trauma Systems History," updated Sept. 8, 2011, http://www.dshs.state.tx.us/ emstraumasystems/Etrahist.shtm

30. American College of Surgeons Trauma Programs,http://www.facs.org/ trauma/ verifivisitoutcomes.html.

31. "How 911 Dispatchers Handled Fort Hood Shooting," *Associated Press*

video, Nov. 9, 2009, http://www.blinkx.com/watch-video/how-911-dispatchers-handled-fort-hood-shooting/S2HY3wUJg9n4HmFXy1MYhg. Accessed Feb. 27, 2012.

32. Dalton Cross.

33. In Texas, the Office of Emergency Medical Services (EMS)/Trauma Systems Coordination recommends the designation of applicant/healthcare facilities as trauma centers. Hospitals must meet the current American College of Surgeons (ACS) essential criteria for a verified trauma center at all levels, must meet the "Advanced Trauma Facility Criteria," Requirements for Trauma Facility Designation; must actively participate on the appropriate Regional Advisory Council (RAC); has appropriate services for dealing with stressful events available to emergency/trauma care providers; and submits data to the Texas EMS/Trauma Registry. Refer to Texas Administrative Code Title 25 Health Services, Part 1, Department Of State Health Services, Chapter 157 Emergency Medical Care, Subchapter G, Emergency Medical Services Trauma Systems, Rule §157.125.

The Office of EMS, under the auspices of State Health Services, also regulates rotary and fixed wing aircraft used as air ambulances. Among a myriad of other regulations, at minimum these specialized units must conform to a standard of care at the mobile intensive care level. On flights that manage emergency medical care, two Texas licensed/certified personnel on board the helicopter when in service are required (neither of these persons can perform pilot or co-pilot duties). Personnel must be Texas licensed/certified paramedics, registered nurses, or physicians. Refer to Texas Administrative Code, Title 25 Health Services, Chapter 157, Emergency Medical Care, Subchapter B, Emergency Medical Services Provider Licenses, Rule §157.12.

34. In most metropolitan areas there are also hospitals designated as cardiac, stroke, spinal cord injury, etc. centers.

35. "III Corps and Fort Hood After Action Review," Nov. 17, 2009, 16.

36. Patrice Wendling, "Fort Hood shooting: A cautionary tale for Tucson," Internal Medicine News, News and Views that Matter for Physicians, Jan.11, 2011. Accessed March 31, 2012. http://www.internalmedicinenews.com/views/blognosis-the-internal-medicine-news-blog/blogview40556/fort-hood-shooting-a-cautionary-tale-for-tucson/a4485bd86f.html

37. Ibid.

38. Patrice Wendling, "Fort Hood shooting."

39. "III Corps and Fort Hood After Action Review," 18.

40. Ibid.

41. Greg Jaffe and Philip Rucker, "I could hear bullets."

42 Ibid.

43. Wendling, "Fort Hood shooting."

44. Chelsea Garrett.

45. Texas Rangers Chief Kirby Dendy and Capt. Frank Malinak, telephone conversations.

46. Texas Ranger Chief Kirby Dendy, telephone conversation.

47. Ibid.

48. Ibid.

49. "Confirmed Shooting at Fort Hood," III Corps & Fort Hood Public Affairs Office, Press Release #20091105-01, Nov. 5, 2009.

50. "Fort Hood," The White House Blog website, http://www.whitehouse. gov/blog /2009/11/05/fort-hood, Nov. 5, 2009.

51. "Press conference about the incident on Fort Hood at Scott & White Hospital on 11/5/09," YouTube, http://www.youtube.com/watch?v=I1jc-_ DbSLQ. Accessed March 24, 3012.

Scott & White website, ©2012, http://www.sw.org/Dr-Glen-R-Couchman, and http://www.sw.org/Dr-Robert-D-Greenberg

52. Ibid.

53. Jim Garamone, "Army Sends Support Teams to Aid Hood Soldiers, Families," American Forces Press Service, Nov. 6, 2009, http://www.army. mil/article/29983/army-sends-support-teams-to-aid-fort-hood-soldiers-families. Accessed March 30, 2012.

54. Mitch Potter, "Accused Fort Hood killer 'hardworking, dedicated,'" Toronto Star, Nov. 6, 2009. Accessed Feb. 27, 2012. http://www.thestar.com/ news/world/article/722085--accused-ft-hood-killer-hardworking-dedicated

55. "Fort Hood Opens Family Hotline," III Corps & Fort Hood Public Affairs Office, Press Release #20091105-04, Nov. 5, 2009.

56. Ibid.

57. Ibid.

58. Scott Huddleston and Sig Christenson, "Military falls silent for victims of For Hood shootings," Houston Chronicle, Nov. 6, 2009. Accessed Feb. 27, 2012. http://www.chron.com/news/houston-texas/article/Military-falls-silent-for-victims-of-Fort-Hood-1609044.php

59. "U.S. Muslims Condemn Attack at Fort Hood," Council on American-Muslim Relations Press Release (Nov. 5, 2009), Council on American-Muslim Relations web site, http://www.cair.com/ArticleDetails.aspx?ArticleID=26126.

60. "Fort Hood, Texas, Shooting—Muslims Talk About It," KXAN video, Nov. 6, 2009, http://www.youtube.com/watch?v=ZeicnPcvrH8. Accessed Feb. 22, 2012.

61. "Area Muslims Shocked at Shooter's Familiar Face," The Muslim Link, Nov. 10, 2009. Accessed Feb. 27, 2012. http://muslimlinkpaper.com/index. php/community-news/community-news/1955-area-muslims-shocked-at-

shooters-familiar-face.html

62. Ibid.

63. Ibid.

64. Michael Moss, "Muslims at Fort Voice Outrage and Ask Questions," *New York Times*, Nov. 7, 2009. Accessed Feb. 27, 2012. http://www.nytimes.com/2009/11/07/us/07muslim.html?_r=0

65. "Fort Hood, Texas, shooting: Muslims talk about it," *Reuters* and *KXAN News* video, Nov. 6, 2009, http://www.youtube.com/watch?v=ZeicnPcvrH8. Accessed Feb. 27, 2012.

66. Chittum and Valencia, "Suspected Fort Hood shooter Maj. Nidal Malik Hasan."

67. "Hasan's cousin speaks," *CNN* video, Nov. 6, 2009, http://www.cnn.com/video/?/video/us/2009/11/06/hancocks.hassan.cousin.speaks.cnn. Accessed Nov. 21, 2011.

68. "*BBC* Interview from Maj. Hasan's Mosque," Nov. 9, 2009, http://www.youtube. com/watch?v=AIrmBT9FgkQ. Accessed Sept. 5, 2013.

69. Megan Chuchmach and Brian Ross, " Al Qaeda Recruiter New Focus in Fort Hood Killings Investigation," *ABC News*, Nov. 10, 2009, http://abcnews.go.com/Blotter/al-qaeda-recruiter-focus-fort-hood-killings-investigation/story?id=9045492. Accessed Feb. 27, 2009.

70. "Al-Jazeera Satellite Network Interview With Yemeni-American Cleric Shaykh Anwar al-Awlaki Regarding His Alleged Role In Radicalizing Maj. Malik Nidal Hasan," *NEFA Foundation* (released Dec. 23, 2009), http://www.nefafoundation.org/ newsite/file/NEFAal-Awlaki1209.pdf

71. Ibid.

72. Facebook posts from the group "Praying for the recovery of Dr. Nidal Malik Hasan," are no longer accessible; later posts from the new group "Praying for the Victims of Islamic Terrorist Nidal Malik Hasan," Nov. 5, 2009. http://www.facebook.com/#!/groups/170468609770/

73. Ibid.

74. Ibid.

75. "Lehigh man tries to send flowers to Ft. Hood shooter," *Lehigh Citizen*, Nov. 10, 2009. Accessed Feb. 27, 2012. http://www.lehighacrescitizen.com/page/content.detail/id/506470/Lehigh-man-tries-to-send-flowers-to-Ft--Hood-shooter.html?nav=5100

76. Ibid.

77. Ibid.

78. Huddleston and Christenson, "Military falls silent for victims of For Hood shootings."

79. Sherwell and Allen, "Fort Hood shooting: inside story."

80. "Gov. Perry Addresses Press After Fort Hood Shooting," Office of the Governor Rick Perry, transcript of Press Conference, Nov. 5, 2009, http://governor.state.tx.us/news/ speech/13905/

81. Jack Plunkett, photographer, "Slideshow: Inside Hasan's apartment," *AP and KXAN News*, updated Nov. 12, 2009, http://www.kxan.com/dpp/military/army/slideshow_inside_hasans_apartment_kxan. Accessed Feb. 27, 2012.

Alice Park and Erin Trieb, photographer, "What is Combivir, the HIV drug in Hasan's shoe box," *TIME* Photos, Nov. 12, 2009, http://www.time.com/time/nation/article/0,8599,1938870,00.html. Accessed Feb. 27, 2012.

82. "Former Fort Hood Police Officer Describes Gunfight With Hasan," *KWTX.com*, Aug. 16, 2013, http://www.kwtx.com/ourtown/communities/copperascove/headlines/Former-Fort-Hood-Police-Officer-Describes-Gunfight-With-Hasan-219959251.html. Accessed Aug. 16, 2013.

83. Lee Hancock, "The Survivors," *Texas Monthly*, June 2012.

84. Ibid.

85. "Update to Shooting at Fort Hood," III Corps & Fort Hood Public Affairs Office, Press Release #20091105-06, Nov. 6, 2009.

86. "Honoring the Victims of the Tragedy at Fort Hood, Texas," Proclamation, *The White House*, Nov. 6, 2009.

87. "Presidential Memorandum of Inventory of Files Related to Fort Hood Shooting," *The White House*, Office of the Press Secretary, Nov. 10, 2009.

88. Robert Mackey, "Updates on the Shootings at Fort Hood," The Lede blog for the *New York Times*, Nov. 6, 2009, http://thelede.blogs.nytimes.com/2009/11/06/latest-updates-on-shootings-at-fort-hood/. Accessed Feb. 27, 2012.

89. Bill Sammon, "George W. Bush Secretly Visits Fort Hood Victims," *FOX News*, Nov. 7, 2009, http://www.foxnews.com/politics/2009/11/07/george-w-bush-secretly-visits-fort-hood-victims/. Accessed Feb. 27, 2012.

90. Air Force Mortuary Affairs Operations Center, "Bodies of soldiers killed at Fort Hood transported to Dover AFB," *DoverPost.com*, Nov. 6, 2009, http://www.doverpost. com/news/x880809780/Bodies-of-soldiers-killed-at-Fort-Hood-transported-to-Dover-AFB. Accessed Feb. 27, 2012.

91. Sig Christensen and Brian Chasnoff, "Fort Hood suspect is brought to BAMC," *San Antonio Express News*, Nov. 6, 2009. Accessed Feb. 27, 2012. http://www.mysanantonio.com/news/military/article/Fort-Hood-suspect-is-brought-to-BAMC-845369.php

92. Mackey, "Updates on the Shootings."

93. Ibid.

94. "Gov. Perry Speaks After Visiting Victims of Fort Hood," Office of the Governor Rick Perry, transcript of Press Conference, Nov. 7, 2009. http://

governor.state.tx.us/news/speech/13961/

95. Christine Romo, James Hill and Stephanie Wash, "Fort Hood: How the Injured Are Coping and Recovering," *ABC News*, Nov. 9, 2009, http://abcnews.go.com/WN/fort-hood-wounded-speak-bob-woodruff-recovery/story?id=9038306. Accessed Feb. 27, 2012.

96. Philip Rucker, "For Hasan, home wasn't welcoming," *Houston Chronicle and Washington Post*, Nov. 7, 2009. Accessed Feb. 27, 2012. http://www.chron.com/news/houston-texas/article/For-Hasan-home-wasn-t-welcoming-1591263.php

97. "Update to Shooting at Fort Hood," III Corps & Fort Hood Public Affairs Office, Press Release #20091105-08, Nov. 8, 2009.

98. "A Ticking Time Bomb."

99. "Remarks by the President at Memorial Service at Fort Hood," The White House, Office of the Press Secretary, Nov. 10, 2009.

7. Judgment Day

1. "After Action Review," III Corps and Fort Hood, Nov. 12, 2009, 8,35.

2. Ibid., 9,11.

3. Ibid., 12,33.

4. Ibid., 16.

5. Ibid., 19-23.

6. Ibid., 43.

7. Ibid., 44.

Jackie Vega, "Ft. Hood suspect hearing set Tuesday," *FOX News*, updated April 12, 2012. http://www.foxtoledo.com/dpps/news/national/south/ft-hood-shooting-suspect-due-in-court_4127576. Accessed April 12, 2012.

8. "Protecting the Force: Lessons from Fort Hood," Department of Defense Independent Review, January 2010, 3.

9. Ibid., 12.

10. Ibid., 20.

11. Ibid., 36-37.

12. Ibid., D-4.

13. Ibid., Appendix C, Findings and Recommendations.

14. Angela K. Brown, "DoD releases final report on Fort Hood shootings," *AP foreign* and *The Guardian*, Aug. 20, 2010. Accessed Feb. 27, 2012. http://www.guardian.co.uk/world/feedarticle/9229497

15. "Fort Hood: Army Internal Review Team Final Report," Department of the Army, Aug. 4, 2010, 5.

16. Ibid., 8.

17. Ibid., 26-29.

18. Ibid., 8.

19. "Results of FBI Review of Fort Hood Investigation," FBI National Press Release, Jan. 15, 2010.

20. Ibid.

"Final Report Of The William H. Webster Commission," 69.

21. "A Ticking Time Bomb."

22. "Lessons learned from Fort Hood shooting: U.S. military," *Reuters*, Nov. 10, 2010. Accessed April 10, 2012. http://www.reuters.com/ article/2010/11/10/us-usa-forthood-lessons-idUSTRE6A907C20101110

23. "A Ticking Time Bomb," 7.

24. According to the report, Awlaki's name is redacted throughout the report, per the Intelligence Community [*sic*] pursuant to Executive Branch [*sic*] classification policies. Awlaki was referred to in the report as "Suspected Terrorist."

25. "A Ticking Time Bomb," 51-52.

26. Ibid., 56.

27. Ibid., 35-37.

28. Ibid., 85-89.

29. Ibid.

30. Ibid., 35-39, 51.

31. Ibid., 55.

32. Ibid., 67.

33. "Final Report Of The William H. Webster Commission," ii-iv.

34. "A Ticking Time Bomb," 71.

35. Ibid., 73-77.

36. Ibid., 73.

37. Ibid., 75.

38. Ibid., 88.

39. Ibid., 77-78.

40. Daniel Zwerdling, "Walter Reed Officials Asked: Was Hasan Psychotic?" *NPR, All Things Considered*, Nov. 11, 2009, http://www.npr.org/templates/ story/story.php? storyId=120313570. Accessed Sept. 5, 2013.

41. "Fast Facts: Conscientious Objection and Alternative Service," The Selective Service system web site, updated April 30, 2002, http://www.sss. gov/fsconsobj.htm

42. "Appointment of Commissioned and Warrant Officers in the Regular

Army," Army Regulation 601-100, 21 Nov., 2006, paragraph 1-7.

43 "A Ticking Time Bomb."

44. "Standards of Medical Fitness," Army Regulation 50-501, August 4, 2011.

Note: These standards were in effect during the time Nidal Hasan was evaluated for his recommended promotion to the rank of Major. The August 4, 2011, revision pertained to changes that resulted from "Don't Ask, Don't Tell Repeal Act of 2010."

45. Ibid.

46. Zwerdling, "Walter Reed Officials Asked: Was Hasan Psychotic?"

47. Jack Levin and James Alan Fox, *Mass Murder: America's Growing Menace* (New York: Berkley Books, 1991), 42.

48. F. Declercq and K. Audenaert, "A Case of Mass Murder: Personality Disorder, Psychopathology and Violence Mode," *Journal of Aggression and Violent Behavior* (Vol. 16, 2011), 135-143.

49. "Army Weight Control Program," Army Regulation 600-9, Nov. 27, 2006, 1.

50. Ibid., 1.

51. Ibid., 9.

52."Fast Facts: Conscientious Objection and Alternative Service," The Selective Service system web site, updated April 30, 2002, http://www.sss.gov/fsconsobj.htm.

"Appointment of Commissioned and Warrant Officers in the Regular Army," Army Regulation 601-100, Nov. 21, 2006, 1.

53. Ibid., 1.

54. "Personnel Security Program," Army Regulation 380-67, Rapid Action Revision Issue Date August, 3 2011, 2.

55. Ibid., 2-3.

56. "Protecting the Force," Department of Defense.

57. "Appointment of Commissioned and Warrant Officers in the Regular Army."

58. "Oaths of Enlistment and Oaths of Office," U.S. Army Center of Military History website, updated June 14, 2012, http://www.history.army.mil/html/faq/oaths.html. Accessed Sept. 5, 2013.

59. "Command-Directed Mental Health Evaluations," Department of the Army, Headquarters, III Corps and Fort Hood Reg. 600-10, May 1, 1996, 3.

60. "Standards of Medical Fitness," Army Regulation 50-501, August 4, 2011.

61. Confidential sources.

62. Tamar Lewin, "Few Can Avoid Deployment, Experts Say," *New*

York Times, Nov. 10, 2009. Accessed Feb 27, 2012. http://www.nytimes.com/2009/11/10/us/10army.html?_r=1&pagewanted=print

8. Ticking Time Bombs

1. "Crime in the United States, 2013," http://www.fbi.gov/about-us/cjis/ucr/crime-in-the-u.s/2013/crime-in-the-u.s.-2013/tables/1tabledatadecoverviewpdf/table_1_crime_in_the_united_states_by_volume_and_rate_per_100000_inhabitants_1994-2013.xls.

2. Grant Duwe, "Opinion: The Rise and Decline of Mass Shootings," *Huffington Post/AOL News*, March 1, 2010, http://www.aolnews.com/2010/03/01/opinion-the-rise-and-decline-of-mass-shootings/. Accessed Sept. 5, 2013.

James Alan Fox, "Mass shootings are a fact of American life," *USA Today*, Jan. 10, 2011. Accessed April 2, 2012. http://www.usatoday.com/news/opinion/forum/2011-01-11-fox11_st_N.htm

3. Mark Follman, Gavin Aronsen, and Deanna Pan, "A Guide to Mass Shootings in America," *Mother Jones*, updated Feb. 27, 2013, http://www.motherjones.com/politics/2012/07/mass-shootings-map. Accessed August, 21, 2013.

4. Kia Makarechi, "'Mad Men' & Richard Speck Murders: Season 5 Episode," April 9, 2012." *Huffington Post*, http://www.huffingtonpost.com/2012/04/09/mad-men-richard-speck-murder_n_1411587.html?view=print&comm_ref=false. Accessed April 9, 2012.

5. Gary Lavergne, *A Sniper in the Tower* (Denton: University of North Texas Press, 1997).

6. Ibid., 44, 51.

7. Ibid., 51.

8. Ibid.

9. Ibid, 70.

10. Ibid.

11. Ibid., 71.

12. Ibid., 93.

13. Ibid.

14. Ibid., 262.

15. Ibid., 8.

16. Ibid., 255.

17. Ibid.

18. Ibid., 42.

19. Pamela Colloff, "96 Minutes," *Texas Monthly*, August 2006, 108.

20. Ibid., 176.

21. Phil Bacharach, "The Prison Letters of Timothy McVeigh," *Esquire*, April 19, 2010. Accessed June 3, 2012. http://www.esquire.com/features/ ESQ0501-MAY_MCVEIGH

22. Ibid.

23. Ibid.

Levin and Fox, *Mass Murder*, 56.

24. Douglas and Olshaker, *The Anatomy of Motive*, 295.

25. Ibid., 296.

26. James Alan Fox and Jack Levin, *The Will to Kill: Making Sense of Senseless Murder*, (Boston: Allyn and Bacon, 2001), 41-42.

27. Levin and Fox, *Mass Murder*, 42, 204.

28. Lavergne, *A Sniper in the Tower*, 266.

29. "Martyrdom in Islam Versus Suicide Bombing," *Scribd.com*, July 18, 2008. Comment attributed to Nidal Hasan posted May 20, 2009, http://www.scribd. com/doc/ 3989813/Martyrdom-in-Islam-Versus-Suicide-Bombing. Accessed June 20, 2012.

30. Mark Ames, *Going Postal: Rage, Murder, and Rebellion: From Reagan's Workplaces to Clinton's Columbine and Beyond* (Berkley: Soft Skull Press, 2005), 70-71.

31. Ibid., 71.

32. Ibid., 70, 72.

33. Ibid., 183

34. "Workplace Violence: Issues in Response," *Critical Incident Response Group*, National Center for the Analysis of Violent Crime (NCAVC), FBI Academy, Quantico, Virginia, 2004.

35. Ibid., 24.

36. Ibid.

9. Playing with Fire

1. J. M. Berger, *Jihad Joe: Americans Who Go to War in the Name of Islam* (Dulles: Potomac Books, 2011),115.

2. Ibid.

Bobby Ghosh, "How Dangerous Is the Cleric Anwar al-Awlaki?" *Time*, Jan. 13, 2010, http://www.time.com/time/printout/0,8816,1953426,00.html. Accessed Jan. 22, 2012.

3. Ibid.

4. Berger, *Jihad Joe*, 116.

5. Ibid.

6. Ghosh, "How Dangerous," *Time*.

J. M. Berger, "Anwar Al-Awlaki's Links to the September 11 Hijackers," *Atlantic*, Sept. 9, 2011. Accessed April 4, 2012. http://www.theatlantic.com/international/archive/2011/09/anwar-al-awlakis-links-to-the-september-11-hijackers/244796/

"Obituary: Anwar al-Awlaki," *BBC News Middle East*, Sept. 30, 2011. Accessed Jan. 22, 2012. http://www.bbc.co.uk/news/world-middle-east-11658920

7. Citra Ragavan, "The imam's very curious story: A skirt-chasing mullah is just one more mystery for the 9/11 panel," *U. S. News & World Report*, June 13, 2004. Accessed May 20, 2012. http://www.usnews.com/usnews/news/articles/040621/21plot.htm

8. Judith Miller and Jeff Gerth, "A Nation Challenged: Al-Qaeda; Honey Trade Said to Provide Funds and Cover to bin Laden," *New York Times*, Oct. 11, 2011. Accessed May 20, 2012. http://www.nytimes.com/2001/10/11/world/nation-challenged-al-qaeda-honey-trade-said-provide-funds-cover-bin-laden.html

9. Gosh, "How Dangerous."

Berger, "Anwar Al-Awlaki's Links."

Shane and Mekhennet, "Imam's Path."

10. Ibid.

11. Jana Winter, "Some Muslims Attending Capitol Hill Prayer Group Have Terror Ties, Probe Reveals," *FoxNews.com*, Nov. 11, 2010, http://www.foxnews.com/politics/ 2010/11/11/congressional-muslim-prayer-group-terror-ties/. Accessed May 20, 2012.

Catherine Herridge, "Exclusive: Al Qaeda Leader Dined at the Pentagon Just Months After 9/11," *FoxNews.com*, Oct. 20, 2010, http://www.foxnews.com/us/2010/10/20/al-qaeda-terror-leader-dined-pentagon-months/. Accessed May 20, 2012.

12. Brian Handwerk and Zain Habboo, "Attack on America: An Islamic Scholar's Perspective," *National Geographic News*, Sept. 28, 2001. Accessed May 1, 2012. http://news.nationalgeographic.com/news/2001/09/0927_imampart1.html

13. Ghosh, "How Dangerous."

"Final Report of the William Webster Commission," 34.

14. Berger, "Anwar Al-Awlaki's Links."

15. Berger, Jihad Joe, 119.

16. Ibid.

Gosh, "How Dangerous."

17. Ragavan, "The imam's very curious story."

Eric Weiner, "The Long, Colorful History of the Mann Act," *NPR.org*, March 11, 2008, http://www.npr.org/templates/story/story.php?storyId=88104308.

Accessed May 20, 2012.

18. "9/11 Commission Report," National Commission on Terrorist Attacks Upon the United States, July 27, 2004, 517.

19. Scott Shane and Souad Mekhennet, "Imam's Path From Condemning Terror to Preaching Jihad," *New York Times*, May 6, 2010. Accessed Jan. 22, 2012. http://www.nytimes.com/2010/05/09/world/09awlaki.html?pagewanted=1&_r=1&hpw

20. Ibid.

21. Ibid.

22. "Final Report of the William Webster Commission," 65.

23. Ibid.

24. Ibid.

25. "Final Report of the William Webster Commission," 67.

26. Robert F. Worth, "The Desert War," *New York Times Magazine*, July 11, 2010, 30-47, 52-54.

Ghaith Abdul-Ahad, "Al-Qaida's wretched utopia and the battle for hearts and minds," *Guardian*, April 30, 2012. Accessed May 1, 2012. http://www.guardian.co.uk/world/2012/apr/30/alqaida-yemen-jihadis-sharia-law

27. Abdul-Ahad, "Al-Qaida's wretched utopia."

Ghaith Abdul-Ahad, "Shabwa: Blood feuds and hospitality in al-Qaida's Yemen outpost," *Guardian*, Aug. 23, 1010. Accessed May 20, 2012.http://www.guardian.co.uk/world/2010/aug/23/shabwa-al-qaida-yemen

Worth, "The Desert War."

28. Abdullah Al-Oreifij, "Suicide bomber named," *Saudi Gazette*, Sept. 1, 2009,http://www.saudigazette.com.sa/index.cfm?method=home.regcon&contentID=2009083148387. Accessed May 23, 2012.

29. "Profile: Al-Qaeda 'bomb maker' Ibrahim al-Asiri," *BBC News*, May 9, 2012, http://www.bbc.co.uk/news/world-middle-east-11662143. Accessed May 20, 2012.

30. Ibid.

Al-Oreifij, "Suicide bomber named."

31. Shaun Waterman, "Wily bomb maker fast in race with technology; informant ID'd device," *Washington Times*, May 8, 2012. Accessed May 20, 2012. http://www.washingtontimes.com/news/2012/may/8/wily-bomb-maker-fast-in-race-with-technology/

32. Al-Oreifij, "Suicide bomber named."

33. Ron Scherer, "PETN: How serious a threat is Yemen explosive to air travel?" *Christian Science Monitor*, Nov. 1, 2010. Accessed May 20, 2012.

http://www.csmonitor.com/USA/2010/1101/PETN-How-serious-a-threat-is-Yemen-explosive-to-air-travel

Ron Winslow, "A Primer in PETN," *Wall Street Journal*, Dec. 29, 2009. Accessed May 20, 2012. http://online.wsj.com/article/SB126195987401406861.html

34. Ibid.

35. "Airport Security: Why It Failed," *LiveScience*, Dec. 28, 2009, http://www.livescience.com/5973-airport-security-failed.html. Accessed May 20, 2012.

36. Lillian Hoddeson, Paul W. Henriksen, Roger A. Meade, et al, *Critical Assembly: A Technical History of Los Alamos During the Oppenheimer Years, 1943-1945* (Cambridge: Cambridge University Press, 2004), 164-165.

Cay Rademacher and Christoph Reuter, "What really happened on Flight 103?" *Guardian*, Feb. 26, 2000. Accessed May 20, 2012. http://www.guardian.co.uk/uk/2000/feb/27/lockerbie.life1

37. "Superfine PETN thin layer slurry explosive," *PatentStorm*, Patent 4132574 issued on Jan. 2, 1979, http://www.patentstorm.us/patents/4132574/description.html. Accessed May 20, 2012.

38. Dina Temple-Raston, "Grand Jury Focuses On N.C. Man Tied to Jihad Magazine," *NPR Morning Edition*, Aug. 18, 2010, http://www.npr.org/templates/story/story.php? storyId=129263809. Accessed May 20, 2012.

Matthew Chayes, Anthony M. Destefano, Robert E. Kessler, Greg Lacour, and Victor Manuel Ramos, "Samir Khan, al-Qaida figure, grew up on Long Island," *Newsday*, Oct. 7, 2011. Accessed May 20, 2012.http://homeland.house.gov/news/newsday-samir-khan-al-qaida-figure-grew-long-island

39. Ibid.

40. Ibid.

41. Michael Ganci, "Clarke Grad, High-Profile Terror Supporter Killed in Yemen," *EastMeadowPatch*, Oct. 5, 2011, http://eastmeadow.patch.com/articles/clarke-grad-high-profile-terror-supporter-killed-in-yemen. Accessed May 20, 2012.

42. Chayes, et al, "Samir Khan, al-Qaida figure."

43. Ibid.

44. Vol. 1, *Inspire, Summer 2010*. Retrieved from *publicintelligence.net* on May 15, 2012. A virus was inserted into this first issue by the British which reduced the copy to ASCII characters, but was subsequently posted by *publicintelligence.net*.

Anwar al-Awlaki, "Shakh Anwar's Message to the American People and Muslims in the West," Vol. 1, *Inspire*, Summer 2010, 56, http://info.publicintelligence.net/CompleteInspire.pdf. Accessed May 15, 2012.

45. "Sheikh Anwar Aulaqi; Suspected & Wanted Terrorist," *Yemen Post* English News Website, April 10, 2010. http://yemenpost.net/Detail123456789.aspx?ID=100&SubID=1750&MainCat=4. Accessed July 9, 2012.

46. Ibid.

47. *United States v. Umar Farouk Abdulmutallab*, 2:10-cr-20005, United States District Court, Eastern District of Michigan, Southern Division, Jury Trial Transcript No. 4, (10/11/11), 24.

48. Ibid., 24, 27-29, 99.

49. Ibid., 29, 30-33, 51.

50. Paul Egan, "Flight 253 passengers believe others involved in plot," *Detroit News*, Dec. 29, 2009. Accessed May 20, 2012. http://www.detroitnews.com/article/20091229/METRO01/912290365#nogo

51. "White House Review Summary Regarding 12/25/2009 Attempted Terrorist Attack," Office of the Press Secretary, Jan. 7, 2010.

52. *United States v. Umar Farouk Abdulmutallab*, Memorandum for the Court, 18.

53. "The Operation of Umar Al-Faruq Al-Nigiri in Response to the American Aggression on Yemen," Vol. 1, *Inspire*, Summer 2010, 5, http://publicintelligence.net/complete-inspire-al-qaeda-in-the-arabian-peninsula-aqap-magazine/. Accessed May 20, 2012.

54. "Q&A: Air freight bomb plot," *BBC News Middle East*, Nov. 2, 2010. Accessed May 20, 2012. http://www.bbc.co.uk/news/11658452

55. "The Objectives of Operation Hemorrhage," *Inspire*, Oct. 2010, 4. 2012, http://publicintelligence.net/inspire-al-qaeda-in-the-arabian-peninsula-magazine-november-2010-special-issue/. Accessed May 15,2012.

56. Mike M. Ahlers, "Security officials see renewed interest in implanted explosives," *CNN.com*, July 6, 2011, http://www.cnn.com/2011/US/07/06/bomb.implants/index.html?iref=allsearch. Accessed Aug. 15, 2013.

57. "Parcel bomb plotters 'used dry run', say US officials," *BBC News US & Canada*, Nov. 2, 2010, http://www.bbc.co.uk/news/world-us-canada-11671377. Accessed May 20, 2012.

58. "Department of State's Terrorist Designation of Ibrahim Hassan Tali Al-Asiri," U. S. Department of State Press Release, March 24, 2011.

59. Ibid.

60. "Operation Hemorrhage," *Inspire*.

61. "The Objectives of Operation Hemorrhage," *Inspire*, Oct. 2010, 4. 2012, http://publicintelligence.net/inspire-al-qaeda-in-the-arabian-peninsula-magazine november-2010-special-issue/. Accessed May 15, 2012.

62. Ahlers, "Security officials see renewed interest."

63. Kimberly Dozier, "TSA Chief: Al-Qaida altered underwear bomb formula," *denverpost.com*, July 27, 2012, http://www.denverpost.com/breakingnews/ci_21175024/tsa-chief-al-qaida-altered-underwear-bomb-formula. Accessed August 15, 2013.

"CIA Thwarts New Al-Qaida Underwear Bomb Plot," *CBSnews.com*, May 7, 2012, http://www.cbsnews.com/8301-201_16257429468/ciathwarts-new-al-qaeda-underwear-bomb-plot/. Accessed Aug. 15, 2013.

64. "Obituary: Anwar al-Awlaki," *BBC News Middle East*, Sept. 30, 2011, http://www.bbc.co.uk/news/world-middle-east-15121879. Accessed May 20, 2012.

65. Mark Mazzetti, Eric Schmitt, and Robert F. Worth, "Two-Year Manhunt Led to Killing of Awlaki in Yemen," *New York Times*, Sept. 30, 2011. Accessed Sept. 4, 2013. http://www.nytimes.com/2011/10/01/world/middleeast/anwar-al-awlaki-is-killed-in-yemen.html?pagewanted=all

66. Yahya Ibrahim, "Winning on the Ground," *Inspire*, Winter 2012, 58,http://publicintelligence.net/inspire-al-qaeda-in-the-arabian-peninsula-magazine-issues-8-and-9-may-2012/. Accessed May 15, 2012.

10. One Nation's Terrorist Is Another Nation's Freedom Fighter

1. Ben Saul, "Definition of "Terrorism" in the UN Security Council: 1985–2004," *Chinese Journal of International Law* (2005), Vol. 4, No. 1, 141–166. doi:10.1093/ chinesejil/jmi00

2. Kelly R. Buck, Andrée E. Rose, Martin F. Wiskoff, Kahlila M. Liverpool, "Screening for Potential Terrorists in the Enlisted Military Accessions Process," *DoD Accession Policy Directorate and Defense Personnel Security Research Center*, Technical Report 05-8, April 2005, vii-viii.

3. Title 22 of the U.S. Code, Section 2656f(d)

4. "Terrorism in the United States: 30 Years of Terrorism: A Retrospective Edition," *Counterterrorism Threat Assessment and Warning Unit Counterterrorism Unit* (1999), i.

5. "Terror Hits Home: The Oklahoma City Bombing," *The Federal Bureau of Investigation*, http://www.fbi.gov/about-us/history/famous-cases/oklahoma-city-bombing, accessed July 10, 2012.

6. "News Transcript," Office of the Assistant Secretary of Defense (Public Affairs), U.S. Department of Defense, April 27, 2006. Accessed July 13, 2012. http://www.defense.gov/transcripts/transcript.aspx?transcriptid=1287

7. Brian Whitaker, "The definition of terrorism," *Guardian*, May 7, 2001. Accessed July 13, 2012. http://www.guardian.co.uk/world/2001/may/07/terrorism/print

8. "Behavioral Indicators Offer Insights for Spotting Extremists Mobilizing for Violence," *National Terrorism Center*, July 22, 2011. Accessed July 13, 2012. http://info.publicintelligence.net/NCTC-SpottingHVEs.pdf

9. Ryan Hunter, M.A., and Daniel Heinke, "Perspective: Radicalization of Islamist Terrorists in the Western World," FBI *Law Enforcement Bulletin*, Sept. 2001, http://www.fbi.gov/statsservices/publications/lawenforcementbulletin/september2011/perspective. Accessed June 13, 2012.

10. "Ten-Year Anniversary of 9/11 Attacks: No Specific Threats, but a Potentially Attractive Terrorist Target," *FBI and Homeland Security Joint Intelligence Bulletin*, Aug. 10, 2001, http://publicintelligence.net/ufouo-dhs-fbi-ten-year-anniversary-of-911-attacks-warning/. Accessed July 13, 2012.

11. "Mass Shootings at Virginia Tech," Report of the Review Panel, presented to Governor Kaine, Commonwealth of Virginia, April 16, 2007, 31-34.

12. David Cho and Amy Gardner, "An Isolated Boy in a World of Strangers," *Washington Post*, April 21, 2007. Accessed June 22, 2012. http://www.washingtonpost.com/wpdyn/content/article/2007/04/20/AR2007042002366.html

13. "Mass Shootings at Virginia Tech."

14. Cho and Gardner, "An Isolated Boy."

15 "High School Classmates say gunman was bullied," *NBC, MSNBC* and news services, April 19, 2007, http://www.msnbc.msn.com/id/18169776/ns/us_newscrime_and_courts/t/high-school-classmates-say-gunman-was-bullied/. Accessed June 20, 2012.

16. "A killer's hometown reels, and reconsiders," *Associated Press and MSNBC*, April 23, 2007, http://www.msnbc.msn.com/id/18263354/ns/us_newscrime_and_courtst/killers-hometown-reels-reconsiders/. Accessed June 20, 2012.

17. "Mass Shootings at Virginia Tech," Report, 35.

18. Ibid., 36-38.

19. N. R. Kleinfield, "Before Deadly Rage, a Life Consumed by a Troubling Silence," *New York Times*, April 22, 2007. Accessed June 22, 2012.http://www.nytimes.com/2007/04/22/us/22vatech.html?_r=1&pagewanted=all

20. "Mass Shootings at Virginia Tech," Report, 40.

21. Ibid.

22. Ibid, 40-41.

23. Ibid, 42.

24. Ibid, 43.

25. "Questions linger: Why did shooter target dorm?" *Associated Press and MSNBC,* April 21, 2007, http://www.msnbc.msn.com/id/18246671/ns/us_newscrime_and_courts/t/questions-linger-why-did-shooter-target-dorm/. Accessed June 20, 2012.

26. "Mass Shootings at Virginia Tech," 45-49.

27. Ibid., 51.

28. Ibid., 52, 71, 73.

29. Ibid., 77-78.

30. Ibid., 90-92.

31. Seung Hui Cho's "Manifesto," available at http://www.schoolshooters. info/PL/Original_Documents_files/Cho%20manifesto.pdf

32. Ibid.

33. Kleinfield, "Before Deadly Rage."

34. "Talk Shows Consumed by Virginia Tech Tragedy," *PEJ Talk Show Index*, April 15-20, 2007, http://www.journalism.org/node/5197. Accessed July 13, 2012.

"Campus Rampage is 2007's Biggest Story By Far," *PEJ News Coverage Index*, April 15-20, 2007, http://www.journalism.org/node/5197. Accessed July 13, 2012.

35. Asher Price, "Suicide pilot Joe Stack had history of shutting doors on people," *American-Statesman*, March 7, 2010. Accessed July 13, 2012. http:// www.statesman.com/news/local/suicide-pilot-joe-stack-had-history-of- shutting-326300.html

36. *MiltonHershey.com*, accessed September 12, 2012, http://www.miltonhershey. com/school_chronicle.html. Accessed September 12, 2012.

37. Price, "Suicide pilot Joe Stack had history of shutting doors."

38. Ibid.

39. Ibid.

40. Price, "Suicide pilot Joe Stack."

41. "The Untold Story of Joseph Stack," *CNN transcripts*, April 18, 2012, http://transcripts.cnn.com/TRANSCRIPTS/1204/18/cnr.03.html. Accessed July 13, 2012.

42. Ibid.

43. "Raw Data," *FOX News*.

44. "Johnson S. Vernon Hunter: Joe Stack's Forgotten Victim," *New York Amsterdam News* [serial online]. Feb. 25, 2010:4. Available from: MasterFILE Premier, Ipswich, MA. Accessed July 30, 2012.

45. Ibid.

46. Eve Conant, "The Other Tax Revolt," *Newsweek*, Feb. 18, 2010. Accessed July, 5, 2012. http://www.newsweek.com/other-tax-revolt-214806?piano_ t=1

47. Edecio Martinez, "Joe Stack is a True American Hero: Facebook Groups Support Domestic Terrorist," *CBS News*, Feb. 19, 2010, http://www.cbsnews. com/8301-504083_162-6223132-504083.html. Accessed July 20, 2012.

48. "Was Joe Stack a terrorist? UT experts urge caution using the word," *KXAN* Austin, Feb. 19, 2010, updated Feb. 22, 2010, http://www.kxan. com/dpp/news/local/was-joe-stack-a-terrorist

49. Ibid.

50. Ibid.

51. "Expert offers criminal and terroristic insight on crash," *Time Warner Cable News* (Austin), Feb. 19, 2010. http://austin.twcnews.com/content/news/267401/expert-offers-criminal-and-terroristic-insight-on-crash/

52. Ibid.

53. Ibid.

54. "Should Joseph Stack Be Called a Terrorist?" *The Daily Beast*, Feb. 20, 2010, http://www.thedailybeast.com/newsweek/2010/02/20/should-josephstack-be-called-a-terrorist.html. Accessed July 5, 2012.

55. Ibid.

56. Ibid.

57. Ibid.

58. Ibid.

59. Ibid.

60. Pat Brown, telephone conversation, Feb. 23, 2012, and subsequent email correspondence.

61. Ibid.

62. Ibid.

63. A Chinese "citizen of the Internet."

64. "Why terrorist attack won't work in China: Chinese netizens' reaction to Boston Marathon Explosions," *offbeatchina.com*, http://offbeatchina.com/why-terrorist-attack-wont-work-in-china-chinese-netizens-reaction-to-boston-marathon-explosions. Accessed July 20, 2013.

65. Angie Chuang, "The Foreigner with a Gun: The Media's Depiction of Ethnic Minority Mass Shooters and Terrorists," *PRWeb* July 19, 2012, http://www.prweb.com/ releases/2012/7/prweb9716235.htm. Accessed July 20, 2013.

66. Ibid.

67. *Shawn Manning, et al. v. John McHugh, et al.,* 1:12-cv-01802-CKK (2012).

68. Angie Chuang, "When is Fort Hood Suspect's Faith Relevant in Media Coverage?" *Poynter Institute*, Nov. 9, 2009.

69. Ibid.

70. Jack Levin and James Alan Fox, *Extreme Killing: Understanding Serial and Mass Murder*, Second Edition (Thousand Oaks, CA: Sage Publications, 2012), 176.

71. Manning, et al. v. McHugh, et al.

72. Ibid., 20-21.

73. Ibid., 21-22.

74. Ibid., 25-26.

75. Ibid., 28-29.

76. Ibid., 49.

77. Ibid., 50.

78. Ibid., 50.

79. Ibid., 62.

11. Hide and Seek

1. Mark Thompson, "Fort Hood: Were Hasan's Warning Signs Ignored," Time, Nov. 18, 2009, http://www.time.com/time/nation/article/0,8599,1940011,00. html. Accessed July 22, 2013.

2. Ibid.

3. Ibid.

4. "A Ticking Time Bomb."

5. Bibb Latane and John M. Darley, "Group Inhibition of Bystander Intervention in Emergencies," *Journal of Personality and Social Psychology*, Vol. 10, No. 3 (1968): 215-221. Accessed July 22, 2013. http://psych.princeton. edu/psychology/research/darley/pdfs/Group%20Inhibition.pdf

6. Matthew Mysiak, "Sandy Hook mass murderer Adam Lanza, 20, 'deeply disturbed kid,'" *New York Daily News*, December 14, 2012. Accessed July 20, 2013. http://www.nydailynews.com/new-york/adam-lanza-20-deeply-disturbed-kid-article-1.1220752

7. "Sandy Hook shooting: What happened?" *CNN*, December 14, 2012, http://www.cnn. com/interactive/2012/12/us/sandy-hook-timeline/index. html. Accessed July 22, 2013.

8. Alaine Griffin and Josh Kovner, "Adam Lanza's Medical Records Reveal Growing Anxiety," *HartfordCourant*, Dec. 14, 2012. Accessed July 22, 2013. http://www.courant.com/news/connecticut/newtownsandyhookschoolshooting/hcadamlanzapediatricrecords20130629,0,7137229.story

9. N.R. Kleinfield, Ray Rivera and Serge F. Kovaleski, "Newtown Killer's Obsessions, in Chilling Detail, *New York Times*, March 28, 2013. Accessed July 20, 2013. http://www.nytimes.com/2013/03/29/nyregion/search-warrants-reveal-items-seized-at-adam-lanzas-home.html?pagewanted=all

10. John Paparazzo, Christine Eith, and Jennifer Tocco, "Strategic Approaches to Preventing Multiple Casualty Violence," U.S. Department of Justice, Office of Community Oriented Policing Services, Washington, D.C., 2013. Accessed July 20, 2013. http://www.fletc.gov/reference/reports/e021311546_MultiCasualtyviolence_v508_05APR13.pdf/download

11. Adrian Blomfield, "Fort Hood shooting: Nidal Malik Hasan 'was not a terrorist' Palestinian cousin says," *Telegraph*, Nov. 6, 2009. Accessed Sept. 7, 2011. http://www.telegraph.co.uk/news/worldnews/northamerica/usa/6517405/

Fort-Hood-shooting-Nidal-Malik-Hasan-was-not-a-terrorist-Palestinian-cousin-says.html

12. Bob Orr, "Newly released Jared Lee Loughner files reveal chilling details," *CBS News*, March 27, 2013, http://www.cbsnews.com/8301-18563_162-57576686/newly-released-jared-lee-loughner-files-reveal-chilling-details/. Accessed July 20, 2013.

13. Ibid.

Gillian Flaccus, How Jared Loughner Fell Through The Mental Health Cracks," *Associated Press/Huffington Post*, January 12, 2011, http://www.huffingtonpost.com/2011/01/12/jared-loughner-fell-through-mental-_n_808194.html. Accessed July 20, 2013.

Dan Gibson, "The Crazed Internet Rantings of Jared Loughner," *Tucson Weekly*, Jan. 8, 2011. Accessed July 20, 2013. http://www.tucsonweekly.com/TheRange/archives/2011/01/08/the-crazed-internet-rantings-of-jared-loughner

14. Tarasoff v. Regents of the University of California, 551 P2d 334,17 Cal. 425 (1976); California Evidence Code 1018. Accessed July 23, 2013. http://www.ohii.ca.gov/chili/node/2419

Kevin E. McCarthy, "Duty of Mental Health Professionals to Warn of Potentially Violent Conduct by Patients," Connecticut General Assembly, 2013-R-0089. http://www.cga.ct.gov/2013/rpt/2013-R-0089.htm

15. "Mental Health Professionals' Duty to Protect/Warn: Fifty State Table," *National Conference of State Legislators*, January 2013.

16. John Ingold, "Aurora theater shooting documents: Doctor reported James Holmes was threat to public," *Denver Post*, April 4, 2013, updated April 5, 2013. Accessed July 19, 2013. http://www.denverpost.com/breakingnews/ci_22955988/judge-unseals-warrants-affidavit-aurora-theater-shooting-case

17. Ibid.

Jenny Deam, "James Holmes' psychiatrist warned he may pose threat," *Los Angeles Times*, April 4, 2013. Accessed July 20, 2013. http://articles.latimes.com/2013/apr/04/nation/la-na-james-holmes-documents-20130405

18. *Chantel L. Blunk et al v. Dr. Lynne Fenton individually, Dr. Lynne Fenton as an employee of Colorado University, Colorado University, Does 1 through 5, inclusive,* 1:13-cv-00080-WYD-MJW, United States District Court for the District of Colorado, Complaint (01/14/2013), 3. Accessed July 20, 2013. http://www.docstoc.com/docs/142522312/Chantel-Blunk-vs-Lynne-Fenton---Shooter-James-Holmes-Psychiatrists-Lawsuit

19. Tom McGhee, "Theater shooting victim's wife sues Holmes' psychiatrist," *Denver Post*, Jan. 15, 2013, updated Jan. 16, 2013. Accessed July 25, 2013. http://www.denverpost.com/breakingnews/ci_22378331/theater-shooting-victims-wife-sues-holmes-psychiatrist

20. Sohom Das, "French Psychiatrist Convicted of Manslaughter Because Her Patient Killed: Is This Fair?" *HuffPost Lifestyle Great Britain*, Jan. 24, 2013. http://www.huffingtonpost.co.uk/dr-sohom-das/french-psychiatrists-convicted_b_2528092.html. Accessed July 25, 2013.

21. Angelique Chrisafis, et al, "Anger as French psychiatrist is found guilty after patient hacks man to death," *Guardian*, Dec. 19, 2012. Accessed July 25, 2013. http://www.guardian.co.uk/world/2012/dec/19/french-psychiatrists-unions-doctors-sentence

22. Ibid.

23. "If You See Something, Say Something," Department of Homeland Security, posting date not specified, http://www.dhs.gov/if-you-see-something-say-something-campaign. Accessed July 15, 2013.

24. Ibid.

25. U.S. Library of Congress, Congressional Research Service, Terrorism Information Sharing and the Nationwide Suspicious Activity Report Initiative: Background and Issues for Congress, by Jerome P. Bjelopera, CRS Report R-40901 (Washington, DC: Office of Congressional Information and Publishing), June 10, 2011, 1-2. Accessed July 20, 2013. http://fpc.state.gov/documents/organization/166837.pdf

26. Ibid., 9.

27. Ibid.

28. Ibid., 10.

29. Ibid., 11.

30. *United States v. Naser Jason Jamal Abdo*, also known as Naser Jason Abdo, Defendant-Appellant, United States Court Of Appeals For The Fifth Circuit, No. 12-50836, 1-3.

"Official: Soldier said he wanted to attack Fort Hood troops," *CNN*, July 29, 2011, http://www.cnn.com/2011/CRIME/07/28/fort.hood.arrest/, accessed May 9, 2014.

31. John Mueller, ed., Terrorism Since 9/11: The American Cases, *Ohio State University Mershon Center*, March 14, 2014, http://politicalscience.osu.edu/faculty/jmueller/45ABDO7.pdf, 1-2. Accessed May 9, 2014.

32. Ibid.

33. Ibid., 2-3.

34. Ibid.

35. Ibid., 4.

36. Ibid., 1.

"AWOL Soldier Gets Life Term for Fort Hood Plot," *Military.com/AP*, Aug. 10, 2012, http://www.military.com/daily-news/2012/08/10/awol-soldier-gets-life-term-for-fort-hood-plot.html, accessed May 5, 2014.

37. *United States v. Naser Jason Jamal Abdo.*

Jason Ryan and Lee Ferran, "Naser Jason Abdo, Fort Hood Plotter, Gets Life in Prison,"*ABC News*, August 10, 2012. Accessed May 10, 2013. http:// abcnews.go.com/Blotter/naser-jaon-abdo-ft-hood-plotter-lifeprison/ story?id=16978363

38. Angela K. Brown, "Fort Hood amps up security as murder trial nears," *AP Big Story*, July 9, 2013, http://bigstory.ap.org/article/fort-hood-amps-security-murder-trial-nears. Accessed July 9, 2013.

39. "About Gun Violence," Brady Campaign to Prevent Gun Violence, http://www.bradycampaign.org/?q=about-gun-violence. Accessed July 29, 2013.

40. Referred to as the mental health prohibitor. 18 U.S.C. 922:US Code – Section 922: Unlawful acts, 1986.

41. Ibid.

There are several other prohibitors in the statute such as persons under indictment for, or who has been convicted of, a crime punishable by imprisonment for more than one year; is a fugitive from justice; who is an unlawful user of or addicted to any controlled substance; is illegally or unlawfully in the U.S.; has been dishonorably discharged from the Armed Forces; who has renounced his citizenship; is subject to a restraining order for harassing, stalking, or threatening an "intimate partner or child of that intimate partner;" or has been convicted in any court of domestic violence.

42. PL 103-59.

43. "About Gun Violence," Brady Campaign.

44. PL 110-180.

45. "Gun Show Background Checks State Laws," Governing, Feb. 4, 2013. http://www.governing.com/gov-data/safety-justice/gun-show-firearms-bankground-checks-state-laws-map.html#. Accessed August 1, 2013.

46. "State Gun Laws," Brady Campaign.

47. Vanessa O'Connell and Gary Fields, "Many Mentally Ill Can Buy Guns," *Wall Street Journal*, Jan. 12, 2011. Accessed July 31, 2013. http://online.wsj. com/article/SB10001424052748704515904576076200491395200.html

48. "HIPAA Privacy Rule and the National Instant Criminal Background Check System (NICS)," Notice of proposed rulemaking, 78 FR 23872 (May 23, 2013), 23872-23876, https://www.federalregister.gov/ articles/2013/04/23/2013-09602/hipaa-privacy-rule-and-the-national-instant-criminal-background-check-system-nics#h-7. Accessed July 15, 2013.

49. "Now is the time to do something about gun violence," marketing brochure, 2013, http://www.whitehouse.gov/issues/preventinggunviolence#shareacc. Accessed July 25, 2013.

50. "Modifications to the HIPAA Privacy, Security, Enforcement, and Breach

Notification Rules under the Health Information Technology for Economic and "Clinical Health Act and the Genetic Information Nondiscrimination Act; Other Modifications to the HIPAA Rules," Final Rule, 45 CFR Parts 160 and 164 (March 26, 2013), https://www.federalregister.gov/articles/2013/01/25/2013-01073/modifications-to-the-hipaa-privacy-security-enforcement-and-breach-notification-rules-under-the. Accessed July 15, 2013.

51. David Eaglelman, PhD, "The Brain on Trial," *Atlantic*, July 2011. Accessed February 27, 2013. http://www.theatlantic.com/magazine/archive/2011/07/the-brain-on-trial/308520/

52. Ibid.

53. Ibid.

54. Jennifer Khan, "Trouble, Age 9," *New York Times Magazine*, May 13, 2012, 35.

55. Ibid., 57.

56. Ibid.

57. Daniel Kline, "Tierney bill urges 'smart' technology for firearms," Boston Globe, May 18, 2013. Accessed Aug. 1, 2013. http://www.bostonglobe.com/business/2013/05/17/could-smart-guns-deter-trigger-happy/sHUrBJQ4vmZYfHFKbDlHBM/story.html

58. "New Jersey Smart Gun Legislation Enacted," *Associated Press/FoxNews.com*, December 23, 2002, http://www.foxnews.com/story/2002/12/23/new-jersey-smart-gun-legislation-enacted/. Accessed Aug. 1, 2013.

59. Poll Finds Americans Skeptical of So-called Smart Guns," *NRA-ILA*, Nov. 15, 2013, http://www.nraila.org/news-issues/articles/2013/11/poll-finds-americans-skeptical-of-so-called-smart-guns.aspx. Accessed May 9, 2014.

60. Kline, "Tierney bill."

61. Mark Roberti, "James Bond's Smart Gun Misfires," *RFID Journal*, Feb, 1, 2012. Accessed Aug. 1, 2013. https://www.rfidjournal.com/purchaseaccess?type=Article&id=9150&r=%2Farticles%2Fview%3F9150

62. "Anomaly Detection at Multiple Scales (ADAMS)," http://www.darpa.mil/Our_Work/I2O/Programs/Anomaly_Detection_at_Multiple_Scales_%28ADAMS%29.aspx. Accessed August 5, 2013.

63. Joe Gould, "Army wants to monitor your computer activity," *Army Times*, May 5, 2012. Accessed August 5, 2012. http://www.armytimes.com/article/20120505/NEWS/205050306/Army-wants-monitor-your-computer-activity

12. The System

1. Confidential sources.

2. "Introducing the Man Who Will Represent Maj. Nidal Malik Hasan,"

WSJ Law Blog, Nov. 10, 2009, http://blogs.wsj.com/law/2009/11/10/ introducing-the-man-who-will-represent-maj-nidal-malik-hasan/. Accessed Aug. 9, 2013.

3. Drew Sandholm, "Hasan Permanently Paralyzed, But Out of ICU," *ABC News*, Dec. 16, 2009, http://abcnews.go.com/Blotter/FtHoodInvestigation/ nidal-hasan-fort-hood-shooter-permanently-paralyzed/story?id=9353524. Accessed Aug. 10, 2013.

4. "Fort Hood shooting suspect," *FoxNews.com*.

5. Press Release, Bell County Sheriff's Office, March 22, 2010.

6. Lauren Keeffe and Louis Ojeda, Jr., "Accused Fort Hood gunman booked into Bell County Jail early Friday morning," *KXXV.com*, April 9, 2010, http:// www.kxxv.com/ story/12282764/accused-fort-hood-gunman-booked-into-bell-county-jail-early-friday-morning. Accessed August 11, 2013.

7. Ibid.

8. Jackie Vega and Daniel Bramlette, "Ft. Hood suspect confined in Bell Co.," KXAN.com, April 9, 2010, http://www.kxan.com/dpp/news/texas/fort-hood-suspect-moved-to-jail. Accessed Aug. 12, 2013.

9. "Bell County Jail, Inmate Visitation Information, http://www.co.bell. tx.us/Sheriff/ 06visitation.htm#visit. Accessed Aug. 25, 2013.

10. Micah T. Williams and David Williams, "Accused Fort Hood Gunman Under 24-hour Watch in Local Jail," *KWTX.com*, April 4, 2010, http://www. kwtx.com/news/headlines/90338569.html?site=full. Accessed Aug. 12, 2013.

11. Ibid.

12. Texas Open Records Act, Title Five, Sec. 552.001.

13. Keeffe and Ojeda, "Accused Fort Hood gunman."

14. Jessica Chasmar, "Fort Hood shooter Nidal Hasan dishonorably discharged from Army: report," *Washington Times*, September 8, 2013. Accessed Aug. 8, 2013. http://www.washingtontimes.com/news/2013/sep/8/ford-hood-shooter-nidal-hasan-dishonorably-dischar/

15. Most media reports state that there were thirty-two injuries. Those occurred as a direct result of Hasan's shooting rampage. There were at least eleven more people injured because of other factors not directly attributable to the gunfire, but because of falls, cuts from broken glass, etc. Additionally, some of the rescuers have been diagnosed with PTSD and have never been included in any official victim count.

16. Paul Romer, "Nidal Hasan's brother frequent jail visitor," *Temple Daily Telegram*, July 19, 2011. Accessed Aug. 12, 2013. http://www.tdtnews.com/ news/the_latest/article_c936f460-ccf1-5d0e-adaf-5c66c672d12f.html

17. Ben Casselman, "Army to Delay Sanity Hearing on Hasan," *Wall Street Journal*, Jan 28, 2010. Accessed Aug. 13, 2013. http://online.wsj.com/article/

SB10001424052748704878904575031522653352104.html

18. Lack of mental responsibility in military courts-martial is similar to the civilian insanity and diminished capacity defenses.

19. Chris Lawrence, "Judge grants delay for Fort Hood shootings suspect," *CNN.com*, June 1, 2010, http://www.cnn.com/2010/CRIME/05/31/texas.fort.hood.suspect.court/. Accessed July 5, 2013.

20. Fort Hood shooting suspect," *FoxNews.com*.

21. Ibid.

22. Death Penalty Information Center, http://www.deathpenaltyinfo.org/us-military-death-penalty.

23. Fort Hood Public Affairs Office, Press Releases from Oct. 12, 2010 through November 15, 2010, http://www.forthoodpresscenter.com/go/doctype/3439/72715/.

Chie Saito, "Hearing for accused Fort Hood shooter resumes Monday," *Austin.Ynn.com*, http://austin.ynn.com/content/news/275183/hearing-for-accused-fort-hood-shooter-resumes-monday/. Accessed Aug. 16, 2013.

24. Freedom of Information Act, 5 USC (552), 1996.

25. Ibid.

26. Ibid.

Anne E. Gerhart, "Witnesses describe chaotic scene of Fort Hood," *Washington Post*, Oct. 14, 2010. Accessed Aug. 16, 2013. http://www.washingtonpost.com/wp-dyn/content/article/2010/10/13/AR201010 1302004.html

27. "Hasan Hearing Blog," *KWTX.com*, Oct. 15, 2010.

28. "MAJ Hasan Case Timeline for Judicial Process," *Fort Hood Press Center*, http://www.piersystem.com/go/doc/3439/1033923/. Accessed Aug. 7, 2013.

29. FBI Transcript.

Note: Ellipses are reproduced from the transcript.

30. Many Fernandez, "Army Major Is Arraigned in Fort Hood Killings," July 20, 2011, *New York Times*. Accessed Aug. 17, 2013. http://www.nytimes.com/2011/07/21/us/21hood.html?_r=0

31. Ibid.

32. Ibid.

33. Amanda Kim Stairett, "Galligan ends role in Hasan's defense," *Killeen Daily Herald*, July 21, 2011. Accessed Aug. 17, 2013. http://www.kxan.com/news/fort-hood-shooting-suspect-in-court

34. Fort Hood Press Center.

35. Ibid.

36. Ibid.

37. Ibid.

38. Ibid.

"Hasan Still Un-Groomed, Judge Still Unmoved, Orders Him Removed," *KWTX. com,* http://www.kwtx.com/news/local/headlines/Hasan_Still_Ungroomed_ Judge_Still_Unmoved_And_Orders_Him_Removed_159578515.html. Accessed Aug. 18, 2013.

39. Ibid.

40. "Hasan Still Un-Groomed," *KWTX.com.*

41. Fort Hood Press Center.

42. Ibid.

43. *Hasan v. United States, Army Misc. 20120877* (C.M.A. 2012), 5-6.

44. "Accused Fort Hood Gunman's Diapers Become Issue," *KWTX.com.*

45. *Hasan v. United States, Army Misc. 20120877* (C.M.A. 2012), 5-6.

46. *Hasan v. United States, Army Misc. 20120876* (A.C.C.A. 2012), 2.

47. Ibid.

48. "Are Beards obligatory for devout Muslim men?" *BBC News Africa,* June 27, 2010, http://www.bbc.co.uk/news/10369726. Accessed Aug. 20, 2012.

49. "Who are the Taliban?" *BBC News Asia,* June 18, 2013, http://www.bbc. co.uk/news/world-south-asia-11451718. Accessed Aug. 20, 2013.

50. Fort Hood Press Center.

51. *Hasan v. United States, Army Misc. 20120877* (C.M.A. 2012), 8.

52. Ibid., 9.

53. Ibid.

54. Ibid.

55. Fort Hood Press Center.

56. *Hasan v. United States, Army Misc. 20120876* (A.C.C.A. 2012).

57. Fort Hood Press Center.

58. Hasan v. United States, Army Misc. 20120876 (A.C.C.A. 2012), 2.

59. Hasan v. United States, Army Misc. 20120877 (C.M.A. 2012), 12.

60. Ibid., 14.

61. Ibid., 16.

62. Ibid., 16.

63. Ibid., 17.

64. Sig Christenson, "Fort Hood shooting suspect hospitalized," *San Antonio Express News,* Sept. 24, 2012. Accessed Aug. 21, 2013. http://www. mysanantonio.com/news/military/article/Hasan-hospitalized3889155.php

65. Ibid.

66. Angela K. Brown, "Officials: Fort Hood shooting suspect hospitalized," *Associated Press*, Sept. 24, 2012 (http://bigstory.ap.org/article/officials-fort-hood-shooting-suspect-hospitalized). Accessed Aug. 12, 2013.

67. Fort Hood Press Center.

68. *Hasan v. United States, Army Misc. 20120877* (C.M.A. 2012), 12.

69. Ibid., ii.

70. Ibid., 9-10.

71. Ibid., 10.

72. Freedom of Information Act, 5 USC (552), 1996.

73. Fort Hood Press Center.

74. Sig Christenson, "As expected, Hasan asks to act as his own lawyer," *San Antonio Express News*, May 30, 2013.

75. Ibid.

Fort Hood Press Center.

76. Due to a consolidation of military resources, BAMC became San Antonio Military Medical Center (SAMMC) in 2011.

77. Fort Hood Press Center.

78. Many Fernandez, "Lawyers Torn Over Suspect in Rampage at Fort Hood," *New York Times*, June 11, 2013.

79. Ibid.

80. Marco Bendinelli and James T. Edsall, "Defense of Others: Origins, Requirements, Limitations and Ramifications," *Regent U.L.* Rev. 153 (1995).

81. *U.S. v. MAJ Nidal Hasan*, "Sanity Board Report," Jan. 13, 2011.

82. Fernandez, "Lawyers Torn."

83. Ibid.

84. Nomaan Merchant and Paul J. Weber, "Nidal Hasan's Fort Hood trial resumes as lawyers demand removal," *Washington Times/AP*, Aug. 8, 2013. Accessed Aug. 8, 2013. http://www.washingtontimes.com/news/2013/aug/8/nidal-hasans-fort-hood-trial-resumes-lawyers-deman/

85. Ibid.

86. Fort Hood Press Center

87. Daniel Zwerdling, "Ramsey Clark for the Defense," *NPR.org*, http://www.npr.org/templates/story/story.php?storyId=5038684, Dec. 4, 2013. Accessed Aug. 23, 2013.

Don Bolding, "Former attorney general Clark may defend accused Fort Hood gunman," *Reuters*, July 2, 2013. Accessed July 5, 2013. http://www.reuters.com/article/2013/07/02/us-usa-crime-forthood-idUSBRE96116

420130702.

88. Sig Christenson, "Hasan on his own as jury selection starts," *San Antonio Express News*, July 8, 2013 (updated July 9, 2013). Accessed July 9, 2013. http://www.mysanantonio.com/news/local/military/article/Hasan-on-his-own-as-jury-selection-starts-4653286.php

89. Hesco concertainers are commonly used in combat zones for protection from explosions.

90. Angela K. Brown, "Fort Hood amps up security as murder trial nears," *Associated Press*, July 8, 2013, http://bigstory.ap.org/article/fort-hood-amps-security-murder-trial-nears. Accessed Aug. 25, 2013.

91. "Jury selection set in Fort Hood suspect's case," *KVUE.com* and *AP*, July 9, 2013, http://www.kvue.com/video?id=214728621&sec=568087&ref=articlevidmod. Accessed July 8, 2013.

Philip Jankowski, "Hasan objects to wearing military uniform; trial to start at 2:30 p.m.," *Killeen Daily Herald*, July 9, 2013. Accessed July 9, 2013. http://m.kdhnews.com/military/hasan_trial/hasan-objects-to-wearing-military-uniform-trial-to-start-at/article_1cbe39d2-e8ba-11e2-a5e7-0019bb30f31a.html?mode=jqm_com

Scott Huddleston, "Security Tight at Fort Hood," *San Antonio Express News*, July 15, 2013. Accessed Aug. 25, 2013. http://www.expressnews.com/news/local/military/article/Security-tight-at-Fort-Hood-4664915.php

92. "Jury selection set," *KVUE.com*.

93. "Fort Hood Attack: jury selection begins in trial of US officer accused of killing 13," *AP/Guardian*, July 9, 2013. Accessed Aug. 25, 2013. http://www.theguardian.com/world/2013/jul/09/fort-hood-trial-jury-selection-texas

94. Ibid.

95. "Hasan Letter," *KDHnews.com*, Aug. 18, 2013, http://kdhnews.com/military/hasan_trial/hasan-letter/pdf_b530a86a-068a-11e3-8136-001a4bcf6878.html. Accessed Aug. 23, 2013.

96. Ibid.

97. Ibid.

98. Ibid.

99. Ibid.

100. Ibid.

101. Ibid.

102. Ibid.

103. Jeremy Schwartz, "Hasan questions jury pool on Islam beliefs," *Austin Statesman,* July 10, 2013. Accessed July 10, 2013. http://www.statesman.com/news/news/hasan-questions-jury-pool-on-islam-beliefs/nYmGC/

"Fort Hood Attack," *AP/Guardian.*

104. Fort Hood Press Center

"Fort Hood trial's 1st day sees 6 in jury pool," *AP/Houston Chronicle*, July 9, 2013. Accessed July 9, 2013. http://www.houstonchronicle.com/news/article/Fort-Hood-trial-s-1st-day-sees-6-in-jury-pool-4655936.php

105. Ibid.

106. Ibid.

107. Schwartz, "Hasan questions jury pool."

Brown, "Judge reviews Fort Hood suspect's jury questions."

Fort Hood Press Center.

108. Schwartz, "Hasan questions jury pool."

Fort Hood Press Center.

109. Fort Hood Press Center

Schwartz, "Hasan questions jury pool."

110. Fort Hood Press Center.

Schwartz, "Hasan questions jury pool."

111. Fort Hood Press Center

Schwartz, "Hasan questions jury pool."

112. Schwartz, "Hasan questions jury pool."

Fort Hood Press Center

113. Fort Hood Press Center.

Molly Hennessy-Fiske, "Fort Hood shooting trial a test for military jury system," *LA Times*, Aug. 12, 2013. Accessed Aug. 12, 2013. http://articles.latimes.com/2013/aug/11/nation/la-na-fort-hood-jury-20130811

114. Catherine Herridge, Pamela Browne, "Hasan sends writings to Fox News ahead of Fort Hood shooting trial," *FoxNews.com*, Aug. 1, 2013, http://www.foxnews.com/ politics/2013/08/01/hasan-sends-writings-ahead-fort-hood-shooting-trial/. Accessed Aug. 2, 2013.

115. Ibid.

116. Ibid.

117. Ibid.

118. Ibid.

119. Josh Rubin and Matt Smith, "'I am the shooter,' Nidal Hasan tells Fort Hood court-martial," *CNN Justice*, Aug. 6, 2013, http://www.cnn.com/2013/08/06/justice/hasan-court-martial. Accessed Aug. 7, 2013.

120. Jason Whitely, Nomaan Merchant, and Paul Webe, "Staff Sgt. Wounded during Fort Hood shooting testifies," *KVUE.com*, Aug. 6, 2013, http://www.

kvue.com/news/state/218582451.html. Accessed Aug. 6, 2013.

121. Ibid.

122. Philip Jankowski, "Testimony gets underway in Hasan court-martial," *Killeen Daily Herald*, August 7, 2013. Accessed Aug. 7, 2013. http://kdhnews.com/military/hasan_trial/testimony-gets-underway-in-hasan-court-martial/article_3d97d920-ff1b-11e2-a58c-001a4bcf6878.html

123. Ken Kalthoff, "Fort Hood Mass Shooting Witnesses Fight Gag Order," *NBCDFW.com*, Aug. 15, 2013, http://www.nbcdfw.com/news/local/Fort-Hood-Mass-Shooting-Witnesses-Fight-Gag-Order-219855531.html. Accessed Aug. 30, 2013.

124. David Zucchino, "Ft. Hood shooting victim is ready for his day in court," *LA Times*, August 4, 2013. Accessed Aug. 5, 2013.

http://articles.latimes.com/2013/aug/04/nation/la-na-fort-hood-victim-20130805

125. Molly Hennessy-Fiske, "Ft. Hood shooter's documents show accolades, allege 'war crimes,' *LA Times*, Aug. 22, 2013. Accessed Aug. 23, 2013. http://www.latimes.com/nation/nationnow/la-na-nn-hasan-documents-20130822,0,1255646.story

Nidal Hasan's "Officer Evaluation Report" for the period July 1, 2009 – November 1, 2009.

Lisa Marie Garza, "Defiant Hasan tells Fort Hood trial 'I am the shooter'," *Reuters*, Aug. 6, 2013. Accessed Aug. 7, 2013. http://www.reuters.com/article/2013/08/06/us-usa-crime-forthood-idUSBRE9750BC20130806

"Lawyer: Hasan Intent On Receiving Death Sentence," *ActionNewsJax.com*, Aug. 7, 2013, http://www.actionnewsjax.com/news/national/story/Lawyer-Hasan-intent-on-getting-death-sentence/GQNjnK1e8kK7VY41gzWdPQ.cspx. Accessed Aug. 10, 2013.

126. Jeremy Swartz, "Hasan does not cross examine witness he is accused of shooting," *Austin-American Statesman*, Aug. 6, 2013. Accessed Aug. 6, 2013. http://www.statesman.com/news/news/local/opening-statements-to-begin-in-hasan-trial/nZFym/

127. Ibid.

128. Philip Jankowski, "Hasan trial recessed after attorneys request reinstatement or removal," *Killeen Daily Herald*, Aug. 7, 2013. Accessed Aug. 7, 2013. http://kdhnews.com/military/hasan_trial/hasan-trial-recessed-after-attorneys-request-reinstatement-or-removal/article_ad22ce06-ff77-11e2-9801-001a4bcf6878.html

129. Ibid.

130. "Lawyer: Hasan intent on getting death sentence," *KVUE.com*, August 7, 2013, http://www.kvue.com/news/-Lawyer-Hasan-intent-on-getting-death-sentence-218690381.html. Accessed Aug. 7, 2013.

Jankowski, "Hasan trial recessed."

131. Ibid.

132. Ibid.

133. Ibid.

134. Philip Jankowski, "Hasan trial: Witnesses testify to scene of Fort Hood shooting," *Killeen Daily Herald*, Aug. 9, 2013. Accessed Aug. 9, 2013. http://kdhnews.com/military/hasan_trial/hasan-trial-witnesses-testify-to-scene-of-fort-hood-shooting/article_a098b92e-0045-11e3-ae2d-001a4bcf6878.html

135. Ibid.

136. Sig Christenson and Scott Huddleston, "Testimony gets emotional as carnage recalled," *San Antonio Express News*, Aug. 9, 2013. Accessed Aug. 9, 2013. http://www.expressnews.com/news/local/military/article/Testimony-gets-emotional-as-carnage-recalled-4719275.php

137. Ibid.

138. Jankowski, "Hasan trial: Witnesses testify."

139. Kalthoff, "Fort Hood Mass Shooting Witnesses Fight Gag Order."

140. Jennifer Hlad, "With three words, Hasan rests his case," *Stars and Stripes*, August 27, 2013. Accessed Aug. 28, 2013. http://www.stripes.com/news/with-three-words-hasan-rests-his-case-1.237636

141. *U.S. v. MAJ Nidal Hasan*, "Sanity Board Report."

142. "Court Dispute Over Hasan's Psychiatric Evaluation," *KCENTV.com*, Aug. 14, 2013, http://www.kcentv.com/story/23136366/court-dispute-over-hasans-psychiatric-evaluation. Accessed Aug. 14, 2013.

143. Ibid.

144. Ibid.

145. Craig Kapitan, "Prosecutors told not to look at report on Hasan," *San Antonio Express News*, Aug. 14, 2013, updated Aug. 15, 2013. Accessed Aug. 16, 2013. http://www.mysanantonio.com/default/article/Prosecutors-told-not-to-look-at-report-on-Hasan-4731463.php

146. Jeremy Schwartz, "Civilian attorney: Hasan does not have a death wish," *Austin-American Statesman*, Aug. 9, 2013. Accessed Aug. 9, 2013. http://www.statesman.com/news/news/local/civilian-attorney-hasan-does-not-have-a-death-wish/nZKbg/

147. Jennifer Hlad, "Judge: Prosecutors can't use sanity-board documents leaked by Hasan," *Stars and Stripes*, Aug. 14, 2013. Accessed Aug. 14, 2013. http://www.stripes.com/news/judge-prosecutors-can-t-use-sanity-board-documents-leaked-by-hasan-1.235340

148. Fort Hood Press Center

149. Philip Jankowski, "Medical examiner: Soldier shot 12 times was charging Hasan," *Killeen Daily Herald*, Aug. 16, 2013. Accessed Aug. 16, 2013. http://kdhnews.com/military/hasan_trial/medical-examiner-soldier-shot-times-was-charging-hasan/article_ad0b61b6-05bd-11e3-9f0c-001a4bcf6878.html

150. Ibid.

151. Ibid.

152. Philip Jankowski, "Kim Munley on Hasan: 'We began to blindly exchange fire,'" *Killeen Daily Herald*, Aug. 16, 2013. Accessed Aug. 16, 2013. http://kdhnews.com/military/hasan_trial/kim-munley-on-hasan-we-began-to-blindly-exchange-fire/article_c8bb168e-0682-11e3-a6b1-001a4bcf6878.html

153. "In rare move, Fort Hood shooter cross-examines witness," *FOXnews.com*, Aug. 19, 2013, http://www.foxnews.com/us/2013/08/19/fort-hood-prosecutors-press-judge-to-allow-proof-hasan-motives-as-trial-enters/. Accessed Aug. 19, 2013.

154. Ibid.

Philip Jankowski, "Prosecution may rest case today in Hasan trial," *Killeen Daily Herald*, Aug. 20, 2013. Accessed Aug. 20, 2013. http://m.kdhnews.com/military/hasan_trial/prosecution-may-rest-case-today-in-hasan-trial/article_3deaa1e4-08e1-11e3-b23b-001a4bcf6878.html?mode=jqm

155. Ibid.

Fort Hood Press Center.

156. Philip Jankowski, "Morning Report: Aug. 20," *Killeen Daily Herald*, Aug. 20, 2013. Accessed Aug. 20, 2013. http://kdhnews.com/blogs/case_files/morning-report-aug/article_fa660050-0992-11e3-a767-001a4bcf6878.html?mode=jqm

157. Fort Hood Press Center.

158. Ibid.

159. Ibid.

160. Philip Jankowski, "Closing arguments begin in Hasan trial," *Killeen Daily Herald,* Aug. 22, 2013. Accessed Aug. 22, 2013. http://kdhnews.com/military/hasan_trial/closing-arguments-today-in-hasan-trial/article_d66c3bb8-0a6b-11e3-915e-001a4bcf6878.html

161. Philip Jankowski, "Hasan case now in hands of the jury," *Killeen Daily Herald*, Aug. 23, 2013. Accessed Aug. 23, 2013. http://kdhnews.com/military/hasan_trial/hasan-case-now-in-hands-of-the-jury/article_5bdf9e0a-0b36-11e3-a292-001a4bcf6878.html?mode=jqm_com

162. Ibid.

163. Fort Hood Press Center.

164. Scott Huddleston and Sig Christenson, "Hasan stays silent prior to his sentencing," *San Antonio Express News*, Aug. 27, 2013. Accessed Aug. 27, 2013. http://www.mysanantonio.com/default/article/Hasan-stays-silent-

prior-to-his-sentencing-4763676.php

165. Ibid.

166. Will Weissert and Paul J. Weber, "Military jury convicts soldier in Fort Hood attack," *AP Big Story*, Aug. 23, 2013, http://bigstory.ap.org/article/jury-fort-hood-rampage-resume-deliberations. Accessed Aug. 23, 2013.

167. Ibid.

168. Ibid.

169. Billy Kenber, "Nidal Malik Hasan's former lawyer says Fort Hood shooter does not have death wish," *Washington Post*, Aug. 28, 2013. Accessed Aug. 28, 2013. http://www.washingtonpost.com/world/national-security/nidal-malik-hasans-former-lawyer-says-fort-hood-shooter-does-not-have-death-wish/2013/08/28/5a92b70c-0ff1-11e3-bdf6-e4fc677d94a1_story.html

170. Ibid.

171. Philip Jankowski, "Tears from widows flood Hasan courtroom," *Killeen Daily Herald*, Aug. 27, 2013. Accessed Aug. 27, 2013. http://kdhnews.com/military/hasan_trial/tears-from-widows-flood-hasan-courtroom/article_239104dc-0e81-11e3-a137-001a4bcf6878.html

172. Ibid.

173. Sig Christenson and Scott Huddleston, "Tears flow at Fort Hood as shattered lives detailed," *San Antonio Express News*, Aug. 27, 2013. Accessed Aug. 27, 2013. http://www.expressnews.com/news/local/military/article/Tears-flow-at-Fort-Hood-as-shattered-lives-4762743.php

174. Ibid.

175. Ibid.

176. Jankowski, "Tears from widows flood Hasan courtroom."

177. Terrence Henry, "Emotional Testimony During Sentencing of Fort Hood Shooter," Aug. 27, 2013, *KUTnews.org*, http://kutnews.org/post/emotional-testimony-during-sentencing-fort-hood-shooter. Accessed Aug. 27, 2013.

178. "Paralyzed soldiers, sobbing widows testify as jury weighs death sentence for Fort Hood gunman," *AP/Washington Post*, Aug. 26, 2013. Accessed Aug. 26, 2013. http://articles.washingtonpost.com/2013-08-26/national/41446514_1_death-sentence-slain-father-fort-hood

179. Ibid.

180. Jennifer Hlad, "Prosecution rests in emotional Hasan sentencing phase," *Stripes*, Aug. 27, 2013. Accessed Aug. 27, 2013. http://www.stripes.com/news/with-three-words-hasan-rests-his-case-1.237636

181. Ibid.

182. Fort Hood Press Center.

183. Scott Huddleston, Sig Christenson, "Hasan sentenced to death," *San Antonio Express News*, Aug. 28, 2013. Accessed Aug. 28, 2013. http://www.mysanantonio.com/news/local/article/Hasan-sentenced-to-death-4767628.php

Epilogue
1. Scott Huddleston, "Killeen ready to 'move forward,'" *San Antonio Express News,* Aug 5, 2013.

2. Nomaan Merchant, "Fort Hood tears down site of 2009 massacre," *AP Big Story,* Feb. 18, 2014. Accessed March 10, 2014. http://bigstory.ap.org/article/fort-hood-tears-down-site-2009-massacre

"Lawsuit Brewing After Hasan is Shaved," *KCEN-TV*, Sept 5, 2013, updated Dec. 4, 2013, http://www.kcentv.com/story/23353463/lawsuit-brewing-after-hasan-is-shaved. Accessed March 10, 2014.

3. Scott, Neuman, "Pentagon Releases Uniform Rules To Allow Religious Headgear," *NPR,* Jan. 23, 2014, http://www.npr.org/blogs/thetwo-way/2014/01/23/265230702/pentagon-relaxes-uniform-rules-to-allow-religious-headgear. Accessed Feb. 11, 2014.

4. Lee Hancock, "The Survivors," *Texas Monthly*, June 2012.

Nawal Foundation website, http://nawalfoundation.org/beta/, accessed March 13, 2014.

5. Matthew Stolle, "For Fort Hood Victim, dinner with shooter's cousin was uplifting," *Stars and Stripes*, May 7, 2014. Accessed May 7, 2014. http://www.stripes.com/news/us/for-fort-hood-victim-dinner-with-shooter-s-cousin-was-uplifting-1.281998

6. Ibid.

7. Ibid.

8. Ibid.

9. "AUSA Dissolves 11/5 Fund," AUSA Press Release, Jan. 23, 2014.

10. Fort Hood Charity Tight-Lipped About $1 Million Collected, *CBS/DFW*, Nov. 3, 2013. Accessed Dec. 10, 2013. http://dfw.cbslocal.com/2013/11/03/fort-hood-charity-tight-lipped-about-1m-collected/

11. The Kim Munley Foundation, http://www.kimmunley.org/, accessed March 13, 2014.

Jacob Brooks, "Survivors form groups in wake of shooting," *Killeen Daily Herald*, Nov. 4, 2012. Accessed March 13, 2014. http://kdhnews.com/military/hasan_trial/survivors-form-groups-in-wake-of-shooting/article_0b9a5702-2642-11e2-8a1d-001a4bcf6878.html

12. The Truth About Fort Hood, http://truthaboutforthood.com/, accessed March 13, 2014.

13. Emily Friedman, "Accused Fort Hood Shooter Nidal Hasan Can't Find

a Bank Willing to Cash His Checks," *ABC News*, Aug. 2, 2010. Accessed September 12, 2010. http://abcnews.go.com/Business/fort-hood-suspect-nidal-hasan-find-bank/story?id=11291442

Scott Freidman, "Accused Fort Hood Shooter Paid $278,000 While Awaiting Trial," *NBC-DFW*, May 22, 2013. Accessed May 22, 2013. http://www.nbcdfw.com/investigations/Accused-Fort-Hood-Shooter-Paid-278000-While-Awaiting-Trial-208230691.html

Nomaan Merchant, "Fort Hood shooter Nidal Hasan pay likely gone: lawyers," *Washington Times/AP*, Sept 17, 2013. Accessed Sept. 18, 2013. http://www.washingtontimes.com/news/2013/sep/17/fort-hood-shooter-nidal-hasans-pay-likely-long-gon/?page=all

14. Shawn Manning telephone interview September 25, 2013.

15. Ibid.

16. Ibid.

DOD 5500.07-R, The Joint Ethics Regulation (JER), including Changes 1-7, http://ethics.iit.edu/ecodes/node/5475, accessed Sept. 26, 2014.

17. "Combat Veteran Eligibility: Enhanced Eligibility for Health Care Benefits," Department of Veterans Affairs, IB 10-438, February 2013. Accessed Sept. 28, 3013. http://www.va.gov/healthbenefits/resources/publications/IB-10-438_Combat_Veteran_Eligibility2-13.pdf

Manning interview.

18. Scott Friedman, "VIP Treatment: Accused Fort Hood Shooter Gets Daily Helicopter Rides," *NBCDFW.com*, Dec. 2, 2013, http://www.nbcdfw.com/investigations/VIP-Treatment--Accused-Fort-Hood-Shooter-Gets-Daily-Helicopter-Rides-218145071.html?akmobile=o&nms=y. Accessed Dec. 10, 2013.

19. Ibid.

20. Ibid.

21. Ibid.

22. Ibid.

23. Manny Fernandez and Alan Blinder, "Army Releases Detailed Account of Base Rampage," *New York Times*, April 7, 2014. Accessed April 7, 2014. http://www.nytimes.com/2014/04/08/us/officials-give-account-of-fort-hood-shooting.html?_r=1

24. Ibid.

Ray Sanchez and Ben Brumfield, "Fort Hood shooter was Iraq vet being treated for mental health issues," *CNN*, April 4, 2014, http://www.cnn.com/2014/04/02/us/fort-hood-shooter-profile/, accessed April 5, 2014.

25. Patrik Jonsson, "Spc. Ivan Lopez, before Fort Hood attack: 'My spiritual peace has gone away,' *Christian Science Monitor*, April 5, 2014. Accessed April

6, 2014. http://www.csmonitor.com/USA/Military/2014/0405/Spc.-Ivan-Lopez-before-Fort-Hood-attack-My-spiritual-peace-has-gone-away.

26. Ibid.

27. Molly Hennessey-Fiske, "From death row, Ft. Hood shooter requests to join Islamic State," *LA Times*, Aug. 30, 2014. Accessed Sept. 10, 2014. http://www.latimes.com/nation/nationnow/la-na-nn-fort-hood-shooter-islamic-state-20140830-story.html

28. Siobhan O'Grady, "FBI director: al-Qaeda inspired Nidal Hasan's attack," *Houston Chronicle*, May 21, 2014. Accessed Sept. 10, 2014. http://www.houstonchronicle.com/news/houston-texas/houston/article/FBI-director-al-Qaida-inspired-Hasan-s-Fort-Hood-5496546.php

29. Ibid.

30. Ashley Southall, "Purple Heart To Be Awarded To Victims At Fort Hood," *New York Times*, Feb. 7, 2015.

31. "Ft. Hood gunman tries to keep lawyer," *San Antonio Express News/AP*, Jan. 30, 2015.

Afterword
1. "Executions in the Military," Death Penalty Information Center, http://www.death penaltyinfo.org/executions-military. Accessed Sept. 1, 2013.

2. Ibid.

3. R. Chuck Mason, "Military Justice: Courts-Martial, an Overview," Congressional Research Service, Aug. 12, 2013. Accessed Sept. 1, 2013. https://www.fas.org/sgp/crs/natsec/R41739.pdf

4. Ibid.

5. Death Penalty Information Center, http://www.deathpenaltyinfo.org/us-military-death-penalty.

6. Ibid.

7. Ibid

8. Ibid.

Nancy Montgomery, "Air Force court reinstates airman's death sentence for 2004 killing," *Stars and Stripes*, July 3, 2014. Accessed Sept. 10, 2014. http://www.stripes.com/news/air-force-court-reinstates-airman-s-death-sentence-for-2004-killing-1.291833

9. Ibid.

10. Manny Fernandez, "Victims to Again Face Gunman in Fort Hood Trial," *New York Times*, Aug. 4, 2013.

11. U.S. Department of Justice, Bureau of Prisons, Notice, "Annual Determination of Average Cost of Incarceration," *Federal Register* (March 18, 2013: 78 FR 16711, https://federalregister.gov/a/2013-06139

Selected Bibliography

"A Ticking Time Bomb: Counterterrorism Lessons from the U.S. Government's Failure to Prevent the Fort Hood Attack." A Special Report by Joseph I. Lieberman, Chairman, Susan M. Collins, Ranking Member. U.S. Senate Committee on Homeland Security and Governmental Affairs, February 2011.

"After Action Review." III Corps and Fort Hood, Nov. 12, 2009."9/11 Commission Report." National Commission on Terrorist Attacks Upon the United States, July 27, 2004.

Ames, Mark. Going Postal: Rage, Murder, and Rebellion: From Reagan's Workplaces to Clinton's Columbine and Beyond. (Berkley: Soft Skull Press, 2005).

Bacharach, Phil. "The Prison Letters of Timothy McVeigh." Esquire, April 19, 2010.Barrett, William P. "The Best Little Hash House in Texas." Forbes, Nov. 12, 1990.

Berger, J. M. "Anwar Al-Awlaki's Links to the September 11 Hijackers." Atlantic, September 9, 2011.

Berger, J. M. Jihad Joe: Americans Who Go to War in the Name of Islam. Dulles: Potomac Books, 2011.

Bertomen, Lindsey. "Firearms Review: FNH Five-Seven." PoliceOne.com, Accessed February 11, 2012, http://www.policeone.com/police-products/firearms/articles/2833266-Firearms-Review-FNH-Five-Seven/

Blomfield, Adrian. "Fort Hood shooter is deeply sensitive introvert, say Palestinian relatives." Guardian, Nov. 7, 2009.

Boyd, David: World Leader in Emergency Services." Medicine Focus. McGill Publications, Feb. 2012.

Brown, Angela K. "DoD releases final report on Fort Hood shootings." AP foreign and The Guardian, Aug. 20, 2010.

Brown, Angela K. and Michael Graczyk. "Soldier says ordered to delete Fort Hood video." Army Times and Associated Press, October 15, 2010.

Bugliosi, Vincent, with Curt Gentry. Helter Skelter. New York: Bantam Books, 1975.

Chen, Edwin and David Wethe. "Heartbroken Obama Goes to Fort Hood for Memorial." Bloomberg News, Nov. 10 2009.

Chittum, Matt, and Jorge Valencia. "Suspected Fort Hood shooter Maj. Nidal Malik Hasan: Social awkwardness kept with him into adulthood" Roanoke Times, November 6, 2009.

Christensen, Sig and Brian Chasnoff. "Fort Hood suspect is brought to BAMC." San Antonio Express News, Nov. 6, 2009.

Colloff, Pamela. "96 Minutes." Texas Monthly, (August 2006).

Declercq, F. and K. Audenaert. "A Case of Mass Murder: Personality Disor der, Psychopathology and Violence Mode." *Journal of Aggression and Violent Behavior* (Vol. 16, 2011).

Douglas, John and Mark Olshaker. *The Anatomy of Motive*. New York: Pocket Books, 2000.

Douglas, John and Mark Olshaker. *Unabomber: On the Trail of America's Most Wanted Serial Killer*. New York: Pocket Books, 1996.

Drogin, Bob and Faye Fiore. "Retracing steps of suspected Fort Hood shooter, Nidal Malik Hasan." *Los Angeles Times*, Nov. 7, 2009.

"Excerpts From Unabomber's Journal," *New York Times*, April 29, 1998. Accessed May 20, 2012.

"Final Report Of The William H. Webster Commission on The Federal Bureau of Investigation, Counterterrorism Intelligence, and the Events at Fort Hood, Texas, on Nov. 5, 2009," released July 2012.

Flaherty, Mary Pat, William Wan and Christian Davenport. "Suspect, devout Muslim from Va., wanted Army discharge, aunt said." *Washington Post*, November 6, 2009.

"Fort Hood: Army Internal Review Team Final Report." Department of the Army, Aug. 4, 2010.

Fox, James Alan and Jack Levin. *The Will to Kill: Making Sense of Senseless Murder*. Boston: Allyn and Bacon, 2001.

———. *Mass Murder: America's Growing Menace*. New York: Berkley Books, 1991.

Fox, James Alan. "Mass shootings are a fact of American life." *USA Today*, January 10, 2011.

Fredholm, Michael. "Islamic Extremism as a Political Force: A Comparative Study of Central Asian Extremist Movements." *Asian Cultures and Modernity*, Research Report No. 12, University of Stockholm, (2006): 11-12.

"Full Story: Alleged Fort Hood shooter was William Fleming graduate, son of Roanoke restaurant owners." *Roanoke Times and Associated Press*, Nov. 6, 2009.

Garamone, Jim. "Army Sends Support Teams to Aid Hood Soldiers, Families." *American Forces Press Service*, Nov. 6, 2009.

George, Patrick and Erin Mulvaney. "Mourners grieve Cameron man shot at Fort Hood." *Austin-American Statesman."* November 16, 2011.

Ghosh, Bobby. "How Dangerous Is the Cleric Anwar al-Awlaki?" *Time*, January 13, 2010.

Hammack, Laurence, Amanda Codispoti and Tonia Moxley. "Fort Hood shooting suspect Hasan left few impressions in schools he attended." *Roanoke Times*, Nov. 7, 2009.

Hoddeson, Lilian and Paul W. Henriksen, Roger A. Meade, et al. *Critical Assembly: A Technical History of Los Alamos During the Oppenheimer Years, 1943-1945*. Cambridge: Cambridge University Press, 2004.

Huddleston, Scott and Sig Christenson. "Military falls silent for victims of Fort Hood shootings." *Houston Chronicle*, Nov. 6, 2009.

Jaffe, Greg and Philip Rucker. "I could hear bullets going past me." *Washington Post*, Nov. 7, 2009.

"Kaczynski Wanted Sex Change—Report Says He Became Killer in Frustration." *Seattle Times* and *Associated Press*, Sept, 12, 1998.Kaczynski, Theodore J. and David Skrbina. "Letter to M.K., Dated Oct. 4, 2003." *Technologic Slavery: The Collected Writings of Theodore J. Kaczynski, a.k.a. "The Unabomber"* (Port Townsend WA: Feral House, 2010).

Lavergne, Gary. *A Sniper in the Tower.* Denton: University of North Texas Press, 1997.

Lehigh man tries to send flowers to Ft. Hood shooter." *Lehigh Citizen*, Nov. 10, 2009.

Lessons learned from Fort Hood shooting: U.S. military." *Reuters*, Nov. 10, 2010.Levin, Jack and James Alan Fox. *Mass Murder: America's Growing Menace.* New York: Berkley Books, 1991.

Lewin, Tamar. "Few Can Avoid Deployment, Experts Say." *New York Times*, Nov. 10, 2009.Mackey, Robert. "Updates on the Shootings at Fort Hood." *The Lede* blog for the *New York Times*, Nov. 6, 2009.

McGreal, Chris. "Fort Hood shootings: "Nidal Hasan's quiet manner hid hostility to US army." *Guardian*, Nov. 6, 2009.

McKinley, Jr., James C. and James Dao. "Fort Hood Gunman Gave Signal Before His Rampage." *New York Times*, Nov. 9, 2009.

Michel, Lou and Dan Herbeck. *American Terrorist.* New York: HarperCollins, 2001.

Milestones: Nidal Malik Hasan." *New York Times*, November 7, 2009.

Miller, Judith and Jeff Gerth. "A Nation Challenged: Al-Qaeda; Honey Trade Said to Provide Funds and Cover to bin Laden." *New York Times*, October 11, 2011.

Mockenhaupt, Brian. "Hood." *Esquire*, Feb. 23, 2010.

Moran, Scott M.D. "Memorandum to the National Capital Consortium Psychiatry Residency Program." *National Capital Consortium Psychiatry Residency Program*, May 17, 2007.

Potter, Mitch. "Accused Fort Hood killer 'hardworking, dedicated.'" *Toronto Star*, Nov. 6, 2009.

Priest, Dana. "Fort Hood suspect warned of threats within the ranks." *Washington Post*, Nov. 10, 2009.

Protecting the Force: Lessons from Fort Hood." Department of Defense Independent Review, Jan. 2010.

Quinn, Ben and David Batty. "'One of our own' Nidal Malik Hasan creates carnage at Fort Hood. *Guardian*, Nov. 6, 2009.

Rademacher, Cay and Christoph Reuter. "What really happened on Flight 103?" *Guardian*. Feb. 26, 2000.

Ragavan, Citra. "The imam's very curious story: A skirt-chasing mullah is just one more mystery for the 9/11 panel." *U. S. News & World Report*, June 13, 2004.

"Remarks by the President at Memorial Service at Fort Hood." *The White House*, Office of the Press Secretary, Nov. 10, 2009.

"Residency Administrative Handbook." *National Capital Consortium Psychiatry Residency Program*. Effective 01 July 2008 – 30 June, 2009.

"Results of FBI Review of Fort Hood Investigation." *FBI National Press Release*, Jan. 15, 2010.

Rucker, Philip. "For Hasan, home wasn't welcoming." *Houston Chronicle* and *Washington Post*, Nov. 7, 2009.

Rucker, Philip. "The lonely life of 'Number Nine.'" *Washington Post*, Nov. 8, 2009.

Sageman, Marc. *Leaderless Jihad: Terror Networks in the Twenty-First Century*. Philadelphia: University of Pennsylvania Press, 2008.

Schwartz, Jeremy. "Soldiers testify about blood bath during Fort Hood shooting." *Austin-American Statesman*," October 14, 2010.

Schwartz, Jeremy. "Witnesses: Hasan spent weeks before Fort Hood shooting at local range." *Austin American-Statesman*, Oct. 21, 2010.

Several hundred pray for Fort Hood victims at vigil." *Associated Press* and *San Antonio Express News*, Nov. 6, 2009.

Shane, Scott and Souad Mekhennet. "Imam's Path From Condemning Terror to Preaching Jihad." *New York Times*, May 6, 2010

Sherwell, Philip and Alex Spillius. "Fort Hood shooting: Texas army killer linked to September 11 terrorists." *Telegraph*, Nov. 7, 2009.

Sherwell, Philip and Nick Allen. "Fort Hood shooting: Inside story of how massacre on military base happened." *Telegraph*, Nov. 7, 2009.

Taylor, Captain Jay. "Eighth Army major receives medal for Fort Hood response." *Army Times*, Nov. 8, 2010.

U.S. Congress. "Hearing before the Senate Subcommittee on Terrorism, Technology and Homeland Security. Terrorism: Growing Wahhabi Influence in the United States." 108th Congress, 2003.

Webster, Donovan. "Empty Quarter." *National Geographic*, Feb. 2005.

Wendling, Patrice. "Fort Hood shooting: A cautionary tale for Tucson," *Internal Medicine News: News and Views that Matter for Physicians*, Jan.11, 2011.

Workplace Violence: Issues in Response." *Critical Incident Response Group*. National Center for the Analysis of Violent Crime (NCAVC), FBI Academy, Quantico, Virginia, 2004.Worth, Robert F. "The Desert War." *New York Times Magazine*, July 11, 2010.

Zucchino, David. "Suspect in Ft. Hood rampage sought high-tech gun, salesman says." *Los Angeles Times*, Oct. 21, 2010.

Authors' Notes

We began working on this book in earnest in August 2011. One of our first tasks was to reach out to the Army's Office of the Chief of Public Affairs in New York to request support and assistance with contacting Army personnel who we had identified as having personal knowledge of the shooting. We spoke with Maj. Paul Island and, at first, he was very encouraging and asked for a synopsis of the book so that he could run it through the approval process. A few days later he sent us an agreement to sign in which the Army would provide the contact information for the individuals that we wanted to interview. Six days later Maj. Island faxed a letter to us abruptly withdrawing the Army's support.

In mid-September 2011, we submitted a Freedom of Information (FOIA) request to the public information officer at Fort Hood. It was not a lengthy request nor was it unreasonable. The information was not forthcoming and after many telephone calls, emails, and finally a certified letter, we filed an appeal. The FOIA officer did not acknowledge the appeal for many months, and in the meantime we contacted our senators and representatives and asked for assistance in facilitating the Army's release of the records we requested. Only one, Senator John Cornyn, agreed to help. He wrote many letters and made numerous telephone calls, all to no avail.

Without the Army's support, we tracked down and contacted individuals who were in some way connected to Nidal Hasan. In response, on October 14, 2011, the Army released "Commanding General's Policy Letter Operations Security (OPSEC)," AFZF-CBRNE, directed to Fort Hood personnel. It stated, in part,

> The threat is real! We are involved in an information war. Adversaries monitoring our activities, conversations, and communications use various tactics to gain information that can be used against us. They are surfing the internet, reading web blogs, searching our social media and even talking to us to gain access to our critical information, photographs

and structure . . . .We must maintain a constant awareness of our actions, be aware of what we post on the public domain, use secure voice phones to the maximum extent possible, and cease "shop talk" in environments where individuals without the need to know might overhear.

In mid-October 2011, we visited Nidal Hasan's haunts—Gun's Galore, Starz, Golden Corral, Casa Del Norte, and the Islamic Center of Killeen were among them. At Fort Hood we snapped photos of the memorial wall in front of the SRP Center, the Howze Theater, and the parking lot where victims were triaged. We clocked the distances between the SRP Center, Darnall Hospital, and the Fort Hood police station.

On this first of many visits to Fort Hood and Killeen, some people were reluctant to speak with us. "Fort Hood won't let me talk to any reporters," "I might get in trouble," and "I don't want to talk about it," were common responses to our queries. The entire city of Killeen seemed to be on lock-down. Thankfully, there were individuals who *did* want to talk. Several of Hasan's co-workers and individuals in the community who had contact with him seemed relieved at the opportunity to tell their stories. Some had contacted the prosecutors in the case and were told that their information was not needed. For most of these individuals, we agreed to protect their identities. Even people who were in no way connected to Fort Hood but who had information about Nidal Hasan were fearful of retribution either from the Army or from terrorists who sympathized with Hasan. We independently verified the information provided to us by confidential sources.

On another trip to Fort Hood, Killeen, and Belton, Texas, we submitted requests for documents through the Texas Open Records Act to the Bell County Commissioners Court (the county's legal authority) for copies of contracts between the Bell County Sheriff's Department and Fort Hood for housing Nidal Hasan; to the City of Killeen for police reports pertaining to the keying of Hasan's car in August 2009; for all 9-1-1 calls placed from Casa Del Norte and the Islamic Center of Killeen; and for demographic and census information.

In May 2013, we submitted another FOIA request to Fort Hood for copies of contracts that pertained to Nidal Hasan's legal proceedings such as construction, non-military security, telecommunications, road and parking lot construction, media support, food/beverage/ hospitality, expert witnesses, and transportation. We received cost information for lodging of witnesses for the first scheduled Article 32 hearing that was delayed and rescheduled (even though there was no hearing, the hotel bill had to be paid); cost of wiring the Hasan Hut for closed-circuit television; and costs of the Article 32 hearing and Hasan's court-martial. We were not provided information for the other cost data that we requested.

In an attempt to locate Nidal Hasan's teachers, we emailed faculty at Fleming High School, Barstow Community College, Virginia Tech, Uniformed Services University of the Health Sciences in Bethesda, Maryland, and Walter Reed Army Hospital in Washington, D.C. We received responses from many of them, and most indicated that they did not remember Hasan. Virginia Tech professor emeritus of biochemistry George E. Bunce replied to our email query. He remembered Hasan and generously offered his recollections, as did one of the lab instructors. Three of Hasan's professors at USUHS responded but declined to comment because of the "ongoing investigation."

We also relied heavily upon government documents, transcripts of court proceedings, scientific articles published in peer reviewed journals, stacks of books, newspaper articles, press releases, hundreds of telephone calls, and interviews. In all, we assembled thousands of pages of source materials and interview transcripts.

We wrote to Nidal Hasan and several of his family members and requested interviews but neither Hasan nor his relatives responded. The Bell County Jail returned one of our letters to Hasan because we had included a self-addressed, stamped envelope for his reply. Jail inmates are not allowed to have postage stamps. We removed the stamped envelope and mailed the letter again, but we have no way of knowing if he ever received it.

In the final analysis, we believe that this book is the most accurate account possible of the events that took place from the time of the shooting until Nidal Hasan was sentenced to death.

Index

C

G

Hasan, Nora 36, 40, 41, 147, 153
Health Insurance Portability and Accountability Act of 1996 208,
      209, 271
Hendi, Imam Yayha 60
Hennard, George 30, 31, 32, 33, 34, 144, 146, 147
Hennis, Timothy 259
Henricks, Steve 241, 245
Her, Shoua 17, 69, 186, 198, 243, 247, 267
Hewitt, Nathan 267
Hill, Anita 29, 32
HIPAA See Health Insurance Portability and Accountability Act of
      1996
Holmes, James 199, 200, 206
Holm, Tracy 267
Homeland Security Policy Institute 53, 54
Hood, John Bell 65
Hood Stadium 112
Hopewell, Clifford 267
Hot Dog Queen 36
Hough, Jibril 163
Howard, Alvin 267
Howze Theater 20, 22, 25, 28, 89, 92, 94, 103, 104, 266
Hoxworth, Bobby 250
HSPI. See Homeland Security Policy Institute
Huberty, James 32, 145, 146, 147
Hunter, Vernon 186
Hunt, Gale 267
Hunt, Jason 264
Hunt, Jennifer Nicole 267
Hupp, Suzanna Gratia 33
Huseman, Kimberly 93, 94, 267
Hussein, Saddam 232
hydrostatic shock 71

I

I.C.U. 15
IED 173, 271
Iftar 160
III Corps 65, 104, 113, 116
IIR 55, 129, 271
Inspire magazine 163, 164, 165, 169, 171, 174, 204
Intelligence Information Report. See IIR
Interlandi, Janeen 188
Internet 53, 70, 71, 75, 86, 157, 158, 162, 163, 174, 205, 215, 255

Q

Qur'an 41, 48, 53, 56, 78, 79, 86, 109, 154, 216, 227, 235, 244

R

S

Whitman, C. A. 140, 142
Whitman, Charles 140, 141, 142, 143, 144, 145, 147, 190, 199, 209
Whitman, Kathy 140, 141, 142, 188
William Fleming High School 36
William H. Webster Commission 127, 128, 192. See also FBI
Williams, Latoya 11, 90, 218, 232, 269
Witt, Andrew 259
Wong, Jiverly 190
Woodruff, Bob 41, 113
Woods, Keith 191
World Trade Center 40, 41, 155, 188, 232
World War II 28, 53, 66

X

Xiong, Kham 15, 242, 247, 265, 267

Y

Yahoo! 221
Yemen 54, 153, 154, 155, 157, 158, 159, 160, 163, 164, 166, 170, 172, 173
YouTube 65, 157, 198

Z

Zarate, Juan 61
Zeigler, Patrick 247, 250, 269.